Smith-Do. .ien:
Isandlwhana
to the Great War

Horace Smith-Dorrien

LEONAUR

Smith-Dorrien: Isandlwhana
to the Great War
by Horace Smith-Dorrien

First published under the title
Memories of Forty-Eight Years' Service

Leonaur is an imprint
of Oakpast Ltd

ISBN: 978-1-84677-680-9 (hardcover)
ISBN: 978-1-84677-679-3 (softcover)

http://www.leonaur.com

Publisher's Notes

In the interests of authenticity, the spellings, grammar and place names
used have been retained from the original editions.

The opinions of the authors represent a view of events in which he
was a participant related from his own perspective,
as such the text is relevant as an historical document.

The views expressed in this book are not necessarily
those of the publisher.

Smith-Dorrien:
Isandlwhana
to the Great War

Contents

GENERAL SIR H. SMITH-DORRIEN — G.C.B., G.C.M.G., D.S.O.

Author's Preface

When I retired from the army in September 1923 I compiled from my full diary an account of my life for the benefit of my sons. I had, then, no intention of publishing, and was only persuaded to do so by the arguments that I had been peculiarly fortunate as a soldier, having been in most campaigns since 1878, and in having served as a general officer half my time in the army. I had thus held high and interesting commands a personal account of which might throw new lights on many well-known events, and might possibly be of interest to my fellow creatures.

I submit that a perusal of these pages will justify that decision, for commencing with the Zulu War, and an account of my own escape from Isandhlwana, I am able, as an eyewitness, to give details of the saving of the colours of the 24th Regiment by Melvill and Coghill, which vary considerably from those given at the time.

My story passes thence to several campaigns in Egypt and India, and to a full, perhaps a too full, account of the Boer War. Then follow my period as adjutant-general in India under General Sir Power Palmer and Lord Kitchener, describing difficulties with the Military Department, and the lack of appreciation of the army by the Viceroy—my command at Quetta and my commander-in-chief-ships at Aldershot and Salisbury.

Through all these activities I was thrown into touch with many persons in high places and well-known public characters—amongst the latter being General Charles Gordon, the

Empress Eugénie, our principal Indian Princes, Marshals Joffre, Foch, and Lyautey, Marchand at Fashoda, and Habibullah, the late *Amir* of Afghanistan.

I have said enough to show that if my pen fails to produce an interesting book it will not be for lack of good material. My difficulty has been rather that I have had too much, and in consequence have been unable to devote as many pages to sport and the lighter side of life as I should have liked.

The end of my period at Salisbury, *i.e.* the commencement of the Great War, was to have concluded my published *Memories*, for I considered that war was too recent and too complicated to embark on without a risk of wounding feelings or unintentionally recording inaccuracies due to the limited horizon of any one person in a large arena.

My readers will naturally wonder why I have changed my mind and included my experiences in the Great War, and I give my two principal reasons.

Firstly, many generals and others who fought under me in 1914 have urged that I owe it to the Second Corps to place before the public my account, as corps commander, of their great deeds, hitherto, except in the excellent *Official History,* but scantily described.

Secondly, it has been impressed on me that a true and accurate personal story of that period is necessary for the following reasons. Shortly after the war certain misstatements were made in the Press regarding the Second Corps and its commander, and I was implored by many at the time to contradict them. This I absolutely declined to do, but felt it incumbent on me, as an officer holding a high position, to draw the attention of the War Office to these misrepresentations, and to request that an official inquiry might be held and the results made public. This request was refused.

The only other means of refuting these statements open to me was to accept one of the many offers I received to make use of the Press. This, in such a personal matter, appeared to me undignified in the extreme, and I never seriously contemplated such a course. I therefore decided to worry no more about the matters, and this required no effort; for I felt I had done my duty by recording officially that the statements in question were not supported by facts, and that the truth must see daylight when the *Official History* appeared; and this has proved correct.

The account I give in these pages of the period I spent in France in the early part of the Great War should fulfil my two avowed objects in carrying my story beyond my original intention.

It will be seen that it is a story of facts, avoiding as far as possible comment and criticism, and my hope is that what I have related will, besides enlightening the public, tend to increase their admiration of and gratitude towards the grand men who fought under me in those stirring days.

I lay great stress on the accuracy of the story, for every doubtful point has been verified, as far as is humanly possible, before appearing in print. To ensure this I have interviewed and corresponded with quite a large number of people, and take this opportunity of offering them my thanks for the willing assistance given me in this great duty to the half of "The Old Contemptibles," which I had the honour of commanding.

Especially do I owe gratitude to Brigadier-General J. E. Edmonds, the author of the *Official History*, to Major A. F. Becke, late R.F.A., and to the high officials of the War Office, who made smooth my path by placing official records at my disposal to enable me to clear up any doubtful points. I have, too, been helped greatly by the confidential military clerk who was with me at Aldershot, Salisbury, and in France, now Staff Sergeant-Major E. C. Castle, R.A.S.C, and also by the excellent maps and sketches prepared for me by Superintending Clerk and Draughtsman H. T. Torah, R.E., and to both of them I wish to tender my thanks.

Perhaps I might mention that practically all the plans of actions are improvements on those I drew myself from time to time, and embodied in my diary as the actions occurred.

Finally, I much appreciate the fact that in my story of the

Great War I have been allowed to reproduce actual maps and sketches from the *Official History*.

CHAPTER 1

The Zulu War

I wish anyone who may chance to read these pages to remember that they are written so that my sons may have some idea of how I have spent my life; and as, previous to the Great War of 1914-18, I had already passed many years on active service, it follows that the story must deal largely with happenings on campaigns.

Born in 1858, I was number eleven in a family of fifteen, six boys and nine girls. One of the boys had died in infancy; my eldest brother (for some years in the 10th Hussars, and latterly of Tresco Abbey, Isles of Scilly) died at seventy-two, and my eldest sister, Mrs. Tyrwhitt-Drake of Shardeloes, at sixty-four; of my three brothers still alive, two served in the Navy, and are referred to later, and the third, the Rev. Prebendary Walter M. Smith-Dorrien,[1] is Vicar of Crediton. He, as a young man, was a distinguished athlete, and amongst other successes won the three-mile for Oxford against Cambridge at Lillybridge. He was referred to in the *Varsity Nonsense Book of the day* as follows:

There once was a young man of Magdalen
Who could run for three miles without dawdling;
For three miles or one
No person could run
In front of this young man of Magdalen.

---

1. He and another sister, Mrs. A. G. Kirby, have died (in 1924) since this page was written.

13

My father died in 1879, a few days before I landed in England on my return from the Zulu War, and my mother at eighty-five—a wonderful woman of strong personality, full of activity to within a few days of her death, an inveterate reader of every book of interest, with a facility for remembering what she read. Her power of letter-writing was inexhaustible, and this all her sons and daughters can vouch for, though how she always found time to write to all the absent ones, and never failed, I have been quite unable to discover.

I was not a nice boy, and was always in trouble, earmarked as mischievous and wild, and credited with all minor catastrophes which happened to the family.

I went to school at seven and a half—to Egypt House, Isle of Wight, where the Rev. Arthur Watson endeavoured to mould me, and later to Harrow. I enjoyed myself at both schools, but distinguished myself at neither. My contemporaries at Harrow best known to fame were W. H. Grenfell (Lord Desborough), Walter H. Long (Viscount L.), Lords Freddy and Ernest Hamilton, the Hon. John Fortescue, Punch Hardinge (Viscount H.) and his brother C. Hardinge (Lord H. of Penshurst) and the Hon. Robert Milnes (Marquess of Crewe). The last-named has reason to remember me, for I was his fag, and only noted for inefficiency.

My father, Colonel R. A. Smith-Dorrien, had served in the 16th Lancers and 3rd Light Dragoons, then for twenty-two years with his county Militia (the Herts) as Second in Command and Commanding Officer. Nice as he always was to me, I rather doubt his having entertained hope of my ever becoming a useful member of society, and I had no idea what he intended to do with me until the autumn of 1875. He and my mother and some of my family and myself were on Lake Lucerne, and one day he asked me if I would like to go into the army. Overjoyed, and having just failed to drown myself and two sisters below the Dance of Death Bridge at Lucerne a few days before, I dashed home to a crammer, went up for the army examination in December, passed, and joined at Sandhurst on the 26th February

1876, as a 2nd Lieutenant. My name was down on H.R.H. the Duke of Cambridge's list for the Rifle Brigade, but, there being no vacancy, General Sir Alfred Horsford, who was military secretary at the time, posted me to the 95th[2] as a battalion which was very short of subalterns and likely to lead to early promotion. About eight months later a vacancy in the Rifle Brigade occurred, and I was offered it, but by then, being thoroughly happy in the 95th, with excellent prospects of rapid promotion, which could not have been possible in the Rifle Brigade, I respectfully declined.

I joined the 95th as a lieutenant in January 1877. In those days one not only joined Sandhurst as a commissioned officer, but anyone passing out with a special mention was given a year's antedate, and this I got, thus being promoted to lieutenant.

After obtaining my commission, I took an early opportunity of attending a levée, and had the honour of kissing the hand of the Great White Queen, the name by which Queen Victoria was known to the natives of South Africa.

Cork was a lively station, and the people hospitable and attractive, but I can think of only one story of sufficient interest to record. One day an individual, looking somewhat out-at-elbows, appeared in the mess and turned out to be rather a remarkable person. He had been an officer in the regiment and was well known to most of those then present. It seemed he had been very popular, but that shortage of the wherewithal to enjoy life had forced him to exchange to another regiment.

Gibraltar had become his new station, and the dangers of the bull-ring soon proved a great attraction to his Irish nature. When, therefore, the curse of shortage of cash still pursued him, he left the Army and became a matador, and a very popular one, for to this day the skill and bravery of the famous "*Matador Inglés*" O'Hara is talked of in the south of Spain. I remem-

---

2. Perhaps he regarded the new 95th as the next best thing to the old 95th for the former was formed in 1823, the old 95th of Peninsular fame having become the Rifle Brigade. The new 95th wore the Maltese cross and used the same march past, "I'm 95," as the Rifle Brigade.

ber O'Hara showing us with pride the matador pig-tail neatly plaited and curled up on the crown of his head. The next time I met him was two years later as gymnastic instructor on the Curragh. He was a man of fine physique, had enlisted in a Dragoon Regiment, and quickly been promoted sergeant. After that I lost sight of him.

From Cork we moved to Dublin, which was equally enjoyable. Oh, what fun it was, racing, dancing, and hunting, though not much of the latter until later. The Castle dances were a thing to dream of. The Duke of Marlborough was Viceroy, and the young American bride, Lady Randolph Churchill, was certainly the belle amongst many beautiful women.

From Dublin we went to Athlone in the spring of 1878—a different sort of life, but fun nevertheless, boating, shooting, and fishing up the Shannon and sailing on Lough Ree with brother-officers, especially my great friend and cousin Charlie Jenkinson.

He and I owned two boats, the one a heavy decked-in cutter which no one could sink or upset, and the other a light open boat with one enormous sprit-sail which the local fishermen called the "coffin," predicting it must be the death of someone. Imagine their "I told you so's" when one day they saw the boat, bottom up, float under the bridge at Athlone.

But they were only partly right—no one was drowned. I had been sailing with Godley (now a Brigadier-General), when a heavy gust of wind came, and he leaned forward instead of back, and over we went in the middle of the river, half a mile wide. We struggled in our thick clothes to a post marking the channel, and having seen him carefully seated on the top like an old cormorant, I swam ashore to obtain another boat.

That summer (1878) we were on the verge of a war with Russia. "Dizzy" brought Indian troops to the Mediterranean the reserves were called up, and we soldiers had a busy time, first collecting the men in England and then bringing them over to Ireland and training them. The 95th were 1,200 strong. I was acting adjutant in the absence of Sparkes (now Colonel Sparkes) away at some course, and thoroughly enjoyed drilling them. Our diplomats staved off that war, but troubles were brewing in South Africa with the Zulus.

An old 95th Commanding Officer and the full colonel of the regiment, General the Hon. F. A. Thesiger (becoming Lord Chelmsford in October this year, on the death of his father), was commanding in Natal, and, seeing war could not be avoided and wanting to get officers from his old corps, he cabled to the War Office asking for three, Captain A. Tower, Lieutenants W. Hore and H. L. Smith-Dorrien, to be sent on special service. This was wired on to the C.O. of the Battalion, and I as adjutant asked for his orders. He merely said he would allow none of us to go.

We had a few words about this, and it ended in my wiring to the Military Secretary at the War Office from myself, saying I was ready to start for the Cape at a moment's notice in any capacity in which H.R.H. the Field-Marshal commander-in-chief might think fit to employ me. It really was an unwarrantable piece of cheek, and inexcusable, but it paid, for that same afternoon orders were telegraphed to the C.O. from the War Office ordering me to proceed forthwith to Dartmouth and embark in the *Edinburgh Castle*.

So, three days later, I was on the sea with several other special service officers in a 2,000-ton boat, which was not out-of-the-way small in those days, *en route* for the Cape. We crossed the line with full ceremonies, Neptune coming on board with his staff of sea-dogs, doctor, barber, etc., and we were all initiated. Lieutenant W. F. D. Cochrane of the 32nd was the life and soul of the ship. Curiously enough, I was given his vacancy, on his time being up in the Egyptian army, twenty years later, which enabled me to take part in Lord Kitchener's overthrow of the Mahdi.

When within two days' steam of Cape Town we were met by an appalling south-eastern gale, seas mountains high, ship battened down for six days, which time it took us to get into Cape Town. The smells below, especially oil-lamps and bilge-water, cannot be forgotten; but no one complained, for such was the standard in ships in those days.

17

On[3] reaching Durban I was told off for duty with transport. This consisted of working stores up to the front at Rorke's Drift, from which place the expedition against Cetywayo, the Zulu King, was to start. It was a great experience for a boy. I found myself alone controlling the convoys, along a great stretch of road, supplying equipment, purchasing oxen, and generally keeping things going.

The skilful handling of the teams of sixteen oxen made a great impression on me. The driver who wielded the long whip was usually an Afrikander; the oxen were named and, when a pull became very heavy, were urged forward by name and pistol-like cracks of the whip. Such names as "Dootchmann," "Germann," and "Englischmann" were bestowed on them, and when a wretched animal possessed the last it seemed to me there was more emphasis in shouting it out, and more venom in the lash when applying it.

A less pleasant experience was having my young faith shaken in the uprightness of certain senior officers. I had heard of some questionable dealings in regard to military contracts in former wars, and believed such days were gone forever. I was soon to learn that we had not yet reached a plane of official integrity in such matters, but shall only relate an incident which came within my own personal experience.

There was a certain contractor who was employed in matters connected with the Commissariat. In the course of the war I found myself in temporary charge of an important centre, and one day received a telegram from the base directing me to take a lease of a local farm belonging to this contractor at a profiteering price.

Now, the occupant of the farm had just cleared all cattle off it, as it was saturated with lung-sickness. This disease was most deadly for cattle, and it was a recognised rule that no oxen should be allowed near a farm where it had appeared. I therefore wired back stating these facts, and at once got a reply directing me to carry out the transaction. I again telegraphed, respectfully

3. See general map of South Africa.

objecting to having anything to do with the deal.

The next communication was another wire saying that the lease had been signed, and I was to take over the farm. I dutifully replied that I had complied with the order, but would allow no Government cattle to graze there. I heard no more about it, and the farm was never used—facts which speak for themselves.

Whilst negotiations were going on the contractor came up from the base, and, presenting himself in my tent, suggested blandly that he should keep me supplied with champagne. He seemed immensely surprised when I rushed at him and kicked him out of my tent. He returned straight to the base, his arrival there being heralded by the wire saying the hire of the farm was *a fait accompli.*

I am bound to say that this incident gave my young mind a great shock. I have, thank goodness! had no such experience since.

My charge extended from Greytown to Helpmakaar, about a hundred miles, but the important part of it was the thorn country from Burrup's Store to Sandspruit, about fifty miles. This included the passage of the Mooi and Tugela Rivers and several dangerous "*spruits*[4]." There were certain rules which had to be observed when actually in the thorn country. (1) On no account should cattle be allowed to graze, for redwater (a fatal disease) would almost surely result. To avoid this, forage should be carried on the wagons, so that, on outspanning at a camp, bullocks could be tied to the poles and fed instead of being loosed to graze. (2) Should a wagon get stuck in a dry *spruit*, no matter how improbable rain might appear to be, it must be got out at all cost and not left there the night.

Each wagon was drawn by sixteen oxen; convoys consisted of any number, but were usually of about twenty, and were mostly in charge of an officer senior to myself, and my difficulty was to get these orders carried out. One cavalry captain scorned my instructions and broke both of the above rules, and lost three quarters of his cattle from redwater and the wagon loaded with

---

4. A *spruit* is a watercourse.

all the stores for the commander-in-chief's mess, and then called on me to help him out.

This part of the country during November and December was liable to terrific thunderstorms, the worst I have seen anywhere, and a dry *spruit* would in an hour or so become a raging torrent twelve or even twenty feet deep, and this is how Lord Chelmsford's wagon was lost. At sundown the bullocks would not pull it out of a *spruit*, and instead of getting it out somehow by fresh teams or by off-loading, my friend left it for the night, and in the morning it had disappeared, having been swept down into the main river (the Tugela) several miles below. Curiously enough, I was the person to suffer, for the commander-in-chief, becoming convinced that the officer referred to was unfit for transport work, posted him to an irregular mounted corps instead of myself, as I had been led to expect, leaving me with the Transport.

To give an instance of the terror of these thunderstorms: one day I, to avoid one, was standing inside Burrup's Canteen Store. Hail was descending as big as pigeons' eggs, the thunder was deafening, and the lightning blinding. On the road in front of the store stood a wagon with sixteen oxen. The trek-tow or rope, to which their yokes were attached, was a steel hawser. Suddenly there was a blinding flash, and when it cleared, lo and behold! sixteen oxen stretched and lying like dead, and six of them were dead.

It was in the thorn country that I first met Hallam-Parr (afterwards General Sir H. Hallam-Parr) of the 13th (Somersets), then a captain on the staff of the Lieutenant-Governor of Natal, Sir Henry Bulwer, one of the smartest and best beloved officers I have ever met, an enthusiastic Mounted Infantryman and for years adjutant-general of the Egyptian army. Alas! I attended his funeral from his own house in Somersetshire in April 1914.

By the 19th January 1879 the force, consisting of the two Battalions of the 24th, one Battery R.A., one company each of R.E. and M.T., and eight locally raised units, was ready at Rorke's Drift astride the Blood River, and, moving forward next day some ten miles, it camped that night on the east of that remarkably shaped and ill-starred hill called Isandhlwana (literally, "a little hand"), erroneously called by some "Isandula."

Some of the transport with an escort did not arrive until the morning of the 22nd. I was in charge of the transport depôt at Rorke's Drift, and had been warned before starting that I should have to return there at once from Isandhlwana with a convoy of empty wagons to bring up more stores, so I left my camp kit in a tented wagon at Rorke's Drift.

At about midnight I was sent for by General Lord Chelmsford and told to take a dispatch back to Rorke's Drift for Colonel Durnford, R.E., who was expected there with reinforcements consisting of native levies. I rode back, ten miles, arriving at Rorke's Drift just before dawn on the 22nd, and delivered my dispatch.

It ought to have been a very jumpy ride, for I was entirely alone and the country was wild and new to me, and the road little better than a track; but pride at being selected to carry an important dispatch and the valour of ignorance (for I only realised next day that the country was infested with hostile Zulus) carried me along without a thought of danger.

Colonel Durnford was just moving off with his levies towards Sandspruit (away from Isandhlwana), but on reading the dispatch, which conveyed instructions to move up to reinforce the Isandhlwana camp (as Lord Chelmsford, with the main body of the force, leaving the camp standing, was moving out some miles to the east to attack the Zulu army), he at once changed the direction of his march.

I had several arrangements to make for transport at Rorke's Drift, amongst others the erection of a gallows for making *riems*. This gallows was some fifteen feet high, and the process consisted of cutting hides of bullocks into strips about an inch wide, working in a circle; the strips then had the appearance of the peel of an apple all coiled up, and in order to be fashioned into straight straps had to be passed over the gallows and through a weighted wagon-wheel below.

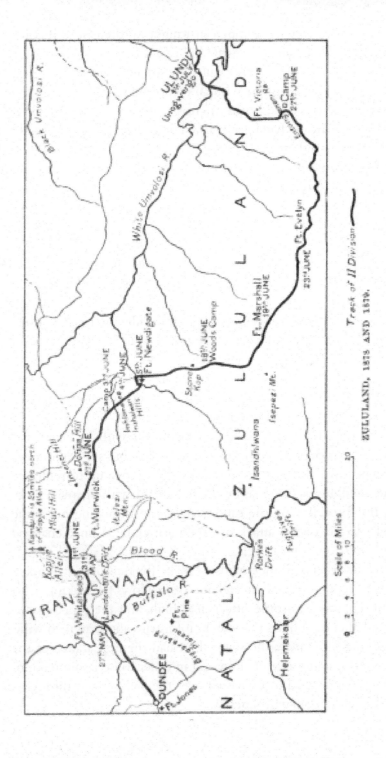

ZULULAND, 1878 AND 1879.

Scale of Miles

Track of II Division ——

These strips were then worked over the gallows and through the wheel, stretched and rubbed with fat until the curves were lost, resulting in very long, soft strips of hide, which could eventually be cut into lengths for tying to the horns of oxen as headropes. It is interesting to relate that the first use I saw the gallows put to was for hanging Zulus who were supposed to have behaved treacherously the day after the Rorke's Drift fight.

After starting the gallows, I went up to see Captain "Gonny" Bromhead,[5] in command of the company of the 24th, and I told him a big fight was expected, and that I wanted revolver ammunition. He gave me eleven rounds, and hearing heavy guns over at Isandhlwana, I rode off and got into that camp about 8 a.m., just as Colonel Durnford's force arrived. Colonel Durnford was having a discussion with Lieutenant-Colonel Pulleine of the 24th, who had been left by Lord Chelmsford in command of the camp, Lord Chelmsford and all the troops, including the 2/24th, having gone out to attack the Zulus. Lieutenant-Colonel Pulleine's force consisted of six companies of the 1/24th, two guns under Brevet-Major Smith and Lieutenant Curling, and some native levies.

As far as I could make out, the gist of Colonels Durnford and Pulleine's discussion was that the former wished to go out and attack the Zulus, whilst the latter argued that his orders were to defend the camp, and that he could not allow his infantry to move out. Colonel Durnford and his rocket battery under Russell, R.A., and his mounted Basutos under Cochrane (32nd), then rode off towards a small hill, apparently a spur of the main range, and 1½ miles from the camp (see A on sketch). Of the 24th, one company (Lieutenant Cavaye) was on picket out of sight of the camp and about a mile to the north on the main range.

We could hear heavy firing in this direction even then (8 a.m.). This company was reinforced later by two more (Mostyn's and Dyson's), and the three fell back fighting about noon and

---

5. Captain Bromhead and Captain Chard, R.E., were awarded V.C.s for their defence of Rorke's Drift.

covered the north side of the camp. The remaining three companies present (for two under Major Upcher, with Lieutenants Clements, Palmes, Heaton, and Lloyd, only reached Helpmakaar on the 22nd from the old colony) were extended round the camp in attack formation, covering especially the front and left front.

Two battalions of native levies were also in this line, but they were not to be relied on and were feebly armed, only one man in ten being allowed a rifle, lest they should desert to the enemy. In consequence of the heavy firing to the north and the appearance of large numbers of Zulus on the main range of hills, and partly, I believe, to support Colonel Durnford's movement, the line was pushed out on a curve, but to no great distance from the tents. Farther than this it never went. Our two guns were at the same time pushed out into the firing-line to the north-east of the camp (see sketch).

At about 12 a.m. the Zulus, who had apparently fallen back behind the hills, again showed in large numbers, coming down into the plain over the hills with great boldness, and our guns and rifles were pretty busy for some time, causing the Zulus again to fall back. It was difficult to see exactly what was going on, but firing was heavy. It was evident now that the Zulus were in great force, for they could be seen extending (*i.e.* throwing out their horns) away across the plain to the south-east, apparently working towards the right rear of the camp. As far as I can make out, Colonel Durnford with his force never actually left the plain, but was close under the foot of the small spur he originally went to seize.

Nothing of importance occurred, beyond the constant increase of the Zulus and the spreading out of their horns, until about 1 p.m., when they started their forward movement direct on the camp. Our troops were in the positions they had occupied hours before, our two guns busy throughout shelling the enemy. Forty-five empty wagons stood in the camp with the oxen in. It was a convoy which I was to have taken to Rorke's Drift for supplies early in the morning, but which was stopped until the enemy should be driven off.

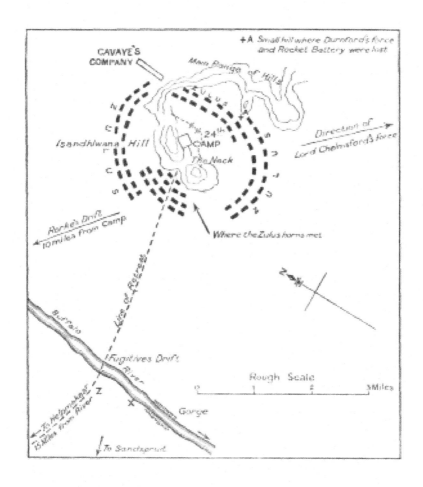

SKETCH OF ISANDHLWANA, 22ND JANUARY, 1879

These wagons might have at anytime been formed into a *laager*, but no one appeared to appreciate the gravity of the situation, so much so that no steps were taken until too late to issue extra ammunition from the large reserves we had in camp.

I will return to the advancing Zulus' line at about 1 p.m. It was a marvellous sight, line upon line of men in slightly extended order, one behind the other, firing as they came along, for a few of them had firearms, bearing all before them. The rocket battery, apparently then only a mile to our front, was firing, and suddenly it ceased, and presently we saw the remnants of Durnford's force, mostly mounted Basutos, galloping back to the right of our position. What had actually happened I don't think we ever shall know accurately. The ground was intersected with "*dongas*[6]," and in them Russell with his rocket battery was caught, and none escaped to tell the tale. I heard later[7] that Durnford, who was a gallant leader, actually reached the camp and fell there fighting.

And now the Zulu army, having swept away Durnford's force, flushed with victory, moved steadily on to where the five companies of the 24th were lying down covering the camp. They were giving vent to no loud war-cries, but to a low musical murmuring noise, which gave the impression of a gigantic swarm of bees getting nearer and nearer. Here was a more serious matter for these brave warriors, for the regiment opposed to them were no boy recruits, but war-worn, matured men, mostly with beards, and fresh from a long campaign in the old colony where they had carried everything before them. Possessed of splendid discipline and sure of success, they lay on their position making every round tell, so much so that when the Zulu army was some 400 yards off, it wavered.

After the war the Zulus, who were delightfully naive and truthful people, told us that the fire was too hot for them and

---

6. A *donga* is a deep dry watercourse.
7. Durnford's body was eventually found on the neck with many other heroes of this desperate fight; 130 dead of the 24th were counted there, and amongst them the only recognisable officers were Captain Wardell and Lieutenant Dyer.

they were on the verge of retreat, when suddenly the fire slackened and on they came again. The reader will ask why the fire slackened, and the answer is, alas! because, with thousands of rounds in the wagons 400 yards in rear, there was none in the firing line; all those had been used up.

I will mention a story which speaks for the coolness and discipline of the regiment. I, having no particular duty to perform in camp, when I saw the whole Zulu Army advancing, had collected camp stragglers, such as artillerymen in charge of spare horses, officers' servants, sick, etc., and had taken them to the ammunition-boxes, where we broke them open as fast as we could, and kept sending out the packets to the firing-line. (In those days the boxes were screwed down and it was a very difficult job to get them open, and it was owing to this battle that the construction of the ammunition-boxes was changed.)

When I had been engaged at this for some time, and the 1/24th had fallen back to where we were, with the Zulus following closely, Bloomfield, the quartermaster of the 2/24th, said to me in regard to the boxes I was then breaking open, "For heaven's sake, don't take that, man, for it belongs to our Battalion."

And I replied, "Hang it all, you don't want a requisition now, do you?"

It was about this time, too, that a Colonial named Du Bois, a wagon-conductor, said to me, "The game is up. If I had a good horse I would ride straight for Maritzburg."

I never saw him again. I then saw Surgeon-Major Shepherd, busy in a depression, treating wounded. This was also the last time I saw him.

To return to the fight. Our right flank had become enveloped by the horn of the Zulus and the levies were flying before them. All the transport drivers, panic-stricken, were jostling each other with their teams and wagons, shouting and yelling at their cattle, and striving to get over the neck (see sketch) on to the Rorke's Drift road; and the red line of the 24th, having fixed bayonets, appeared to have but one idea, and that was to defeat

27

the enemy. The Zulu charge came home, and, driven with their backs to the rock of Isandhlwana, and overpowered by about thirty to one, they sold their lives dearly. The best proof of this is the subsequent description of the Zulus themselves, who, so far from looking on it as a decisive victory, used to relate how their wagons were for days removing their dead, and how the country ran rivers of tears, almost every family bemoaning the loss of some near relative.

When this final charge took place, the transport which was in-spanned had mostly cleared the neck, and I jumped on my broken-kneed pony, which had had no rest for thirty hours, and followed it, to find on topping the neck a scene of confusion I shall never forget, for some 4,000 Zulus had come in behind and were busy with shield and *assegai*. Into this mass I rode, revolver in hand, right through the Zulus, but they completely ignored me. I heard afterwards that they had been told by their King Cetywayo that black coats were civilians and were not worth killing. I had a blue patrol jacket on, and it is noticeable that the only five officers who escaped—Essex, Cochrane, Gardner, Curling, and myself—had blue coats. The Zulus throughout my escape seemed to be set on killing natives who had sided with us, either as fighting levies or transport drivers.

After getting through the mass of Zulus busy slaying, I followed in the line of fugitives. The outer horns of the Zulu army had been directed to meet at about a mile to the south-east of the camp, and they were still some distance apart when the retreat commenced. It was this gap which fixed the line of retreat.

I could see the Zulus running in to complete their circle from both flanks, and their leading men had already reached the line of retreat long before I had got there. When I reached the point I came on the two guns, which must have been sent out of camp before the Zulus charged home. They appeared to me to be upset in a *donga* and to be surrounded by Zulus.

Again I rode through unheeded, and shortly after was passed by Lieutenant Coghill (24th), wearing a blue patrol and cord breeches and riding a red roan horse. We had just exchanged remarks about the terrible disaster, and he passed on towards Fugitives' Drift. A little farther on I caught up Lieutenant Curling, R.A., and spoke to him, pointing out to him that the Zulus were all round and urging him to push on, which he did. My own broken-kneed transport pony was done to a turn and incapable of rapid progress.

The ground was terribly bad going, all rocks and boulders, and it was about three or four miles from camp to Fugitives' Drift. When approaching this Drift, and at least half a mile behind Coghill, Lieutenant Melvill (24th), in a red coat and with a cased colour across the front of his saddle, passed me going to the Drift. I reported afterwards that the colour was broken; but as the pole was found eventually whole, I think the casing must have been half off and hanging down. It will thus be seen that Coghill (who was orderly officer to Colonel Glynn) and Melvill (who was adjutant) did not escape together with the colour. How Coghill came to be in the camp I do not know, as Colonel Glynn, whose orderly officer he was, was out with Lord Chelmsford's column.

I then came to Fugitives' Drift, the descent to which was almost a precipice. I found there a man in a red coat badly *assegaied* in the arm, unable to move. He was, I believe, a mounted infantryman of the 24th, named Macdonald, but of his name I cannot be sure. I managed to make a tourniquet with a handkerchief to stop the bleeding, and got him halfway down, when a shout from behind said, "Get on, man; the Zulus are on top of you."

I turned round and saw Major Smith, R.A., who was commanding the section of guns, as white as a sheet and bleeding profusely; and in a second we were surrounded, and *assegais* accounted for poor Smith, my wounded M.I. friend, and my horse.

With the help of my revolver and a wild jump down the rocks, I found myself in the Buffalo River, which was in flood and eighty yards broad. I was carried away, but luckily got hold of the tail of a loose horse, which towed me across to the other bank, but I was too exhausted to stick to him. Up this bank were swarming friendly natives, but I only saw one European, a Colonial and acting commissariat officer named Hamer, lying there unable to move. I managed to catch a loose horse, and put him on it, and he escaped. The Zulus were pouring in a very heavy fire from the opposite bank, and dropped several friendly natives as we climbed to the top.

No sooner had I achieved this than I saw that a lot of Zulus had crossed higher up and were running to cut me off. This drove me off to my left, but twenty of them still pursued for about three miles, and I managed to keep them off with my revolver.

I got into Helpmakaar at sundown, having done twenty miles on foot from the river, for I almost went to Sandspruit. At Helpmakaar I found Huntley of the 10th, who had been left there with a small garrison, and also Essex, Cochrane, Curling, and Gardner, from the field of Isandhlwana, all busy placing the post in a state of defence. We could see that night the watch fires of the Zulus some six miles off, and expected them to come on and attack, but we knew later they had turned off to attack Rorke's Drift.

I at once took command of one face of the *laager*, and shall never forget how pleased we weary watchers were when, shortly after midnight, Major Upcher's two companies of the 24th, with Heaton, Palmes, Clements, and Lloyd, came to reinforce. These two companies had started for Rorke's Drift that afternoon, but had been turned back to Helpmakaar by Major Spalding, a staff officer, as he said Rorke's Drift had been surrounded and captured, and that the two companies would share the same fate. Luckily, his information proved to be wrong.

Such is briefly my story of the 22nd January 1879, and I have endeavoured to avoid personal incidents as far as possible, though I should like my boys to know that on the evidence of eye-witnesses I was recommended for the V.C. for two separate acts on that day. These recommendations drew laudatory letters from the War Office, with a regret that as the proper channels for correspondence had not been observed, the Statutes of the Victoria Cross did not admit of my receiving that distinction, and having no friends at Court the matter dropped. In view of my latest experiences I am sure that decision was right, for any trivial act of good Samaritanism I may have performed that day would not have earned a M.C., much less a V.C., amidst the deeds of real heroism performed during the Great War 1914-18.

I cannot refrain from remarking that had Lord Chelmsford's orders, as laid down in his standing orders for the field force in Zululand, been carried out, the disaster would never have happened, for there it clearly directed that no force should ever camp in the enemy's country without entrenching, and yet not a sod was turned at Isandhlwana. Had our magnificent body of men been entrenched, the Zulus would have been driven off, as they were subsequently at Kambula, and even as it was, they would have repulsed the Zulus in the open had not ammunition run short.

The bodies of Lieutenants Melvill and Coghill[8] were found together with the colour, although they were so far apart in the retreat, and the explanation I would offer is as follows.

Below Fugitives' Drift the river flows into a deep gorge and the right bank is inaccessible. The river was in flood, and a lot of fugitives, men and horses, must have been swept away through this gorge, or only have succeeded in effecting a landing well below the path leading from Fugitives' Drift up the right bank. I surmise that Melvill and Coghill may both have been swept down-stream towards X (see sketch), and there have met, and in endeavouring to get back together to the path of the fugitives were killed by Zulus who had crossed higher up. As far as I can make out, their bodies were found near Z. The official account, published in 1881, is quite incorrect as to the movements of these two officers. I may say that I was never consulted.

---

8. Both these gallant officers were awarded posthumous V.C.s. Melvill's son, Brigadier-General C.W. Melvill, greatly distinguished himself in the 1914-18 War.

I had had a long enough day, having been on the move, including a stretch of twenty miles on foot, much of it at a run, for forty-two consecutive hours, and directly Lieutenant Clements (afterwards Major-General Clements of Boer War fame) told me he had relieved me, I lay down then and there on two sacks of grain and was fast asleep in a second.

The next day I rode down to Rorke's Drift, some twelve miles, to resume charge of my depot. There was the improvised little fort, built up mostly of *mealy*-sacks and biscuit-boxes and other stores which had been so gallantly defended by Chard, Bromhead, and their men, and Parson Smith, and all around lay dead Zulus, between three and four hundred; and there was my wagon, some 200 yards away, riddled and looted; and there was the *riem* gallows I had erected the previous morning. Dead animals and cattle everywhere—such a scene of devastation! To my young mind it appeared impossible that order could ever be restored, but I set to work, and next day, whilst sitting in my wagon, I saw two Zulus hanging on my gallows and was accused by the Brigade Major, Clery (afterwards General Sir Francis Clery), of having given the order. I was exonerated, however, when it was found that it was a case of lynch law performed by incensed men, who were bitter at the loss of their comrades. Other incidents of the same sort occurred in the next few days before law and order were re-established.

At that time our enemy appeared to us to be possessed of savagery beyond description, but we had no conception then of how civilisation would produce a refinement of brutality and bestiality alongside which our Zulus would be regarded as comparative angels. As a matter of fact, the Zulus were a very noble race with a high standard of morality, but they fought to kill, and undoubtedly killed the wounded and mutilated the bodies; but a predominant superstition with them was that if they did not disembowel a fallen enemy, their own stomachs would swell up when that of their dead enemy did, and that therefore they must let out the gas. It was a rule of their race that no man could marry until he had "dipped his spear"—in other words, had killed his man in battle. There had not been a war for a long time. The whole nation was military; a copy of their Army List was obtained, and it disclosed a regular territorial system. Each *kraal* (native village) or group of *kraals* provided a regiment called after the locality from which it came. Each regiment had its regular drills. The country was at the time we fought full of young men anxious to qualify for matrimony. Immorality was not tolerated; a woman falling was instantly killed, and one of the causes of the war was the fact that two such women had escaped across the border into Natal and we had refused to give them up to certain death.

They were not only a moral but a sober and honest race, and remained so until civilisation touched them. When the war was over and peace declared, so far from showing any bitterness, they were cordiality and hospitality itself, in many cases giving of their milk and food and refusing to take payment. The only spot in Zululand I know of where this high morality did not obtain was at a Christian mission station called Kamagwassa St. Paul's and over the border where the white men ruled.

They were, too, very simple and truthful, and loved to speak in metaphor. They made no attempt to minimise their own losses at Isandhlwana, and when I add that our own killed amounted to 52[9] officers, 806 white N.C.O.s and men, in addition to 200 or 300 native troops, some idea of the desperate nature of the fighting can be formed. To quote from the speech made by General Sir Reginald Hart, V.C., K.C.B., K.C.V.O., when he unveiled the 24th obelisk at Isandhlwana in March 1914:

> "The terrible disaster that overwhelmed the old 24th Regiment will always be remembered, not so much as a disaster, but as an example of heroism like that of Leonidas and the three hundred Spartans who fell at the pass of Thermopylæ."

The next few days after the battle, St. Matthew's simile, "Wheresoever the carcase is, there will the eagles be gathered

---

9. Figures taken from General Sir Reginald Hart's speech.

together," was fully illustrated, for literally the sky was darkened at times by continuous streams of *"Aasvogels"* heading from all directions to the battlefield marked by that precipitous and conspicuous crag, like a lion *couchant*, "Isandhlwana" where nearly 900 British and 2,000 or 3,000 natives, friend and foe, had breathed their last on the fatal 22nd.

Meanwhile Lord Chelmsford had withdrawn all troops from the enemy's country, had given orders that the border-line should be guarded by a series of small fortified posts, and had gone with his staff to Maritzburg to await reinforcements from home.

My fate was Helpmakaar.[10] There the commandant constructed a fort with a huge ditch, revetting the parapet with sacks full of *mealies*. The wet season came on, the grain went rotten, and the ditch filled up with putrid water, the smell of which was appalling, and out of thirty-two officers all but one were down within a couple of months with fever, mostly typhoid. I got it, and was carted in a mule-wagon *via* Dundee down to Ladysmith some seventy miles, where a general hospital had been formed in the Dutch church. Hospital comforts were conspicuous by their absence in those days. Straw on the stone floor formed our beds, and there I lay for two months, hovering between life and death. The hospital was full, as far as I recollect, almost all typhoid cases, and dead were carried out every day.

At last I was convalescent, and could get about with two sticks when I was told I was to start the following morning in a sick-convoy to Durban and thence to England.

It was the middle of May. The reinforcements had all come out, the new centre column was forming at Dundee (forty-five miles off), and it was expected would start against the enemy in a fortnight's time. I was very feeble, but the last place I wanted to go to was England until we had defeated the Zulus.

Luckily I had a splendid old soldier-servant, Private Elks of the 24th, and also three horses. I told Elks to have the horses

---

10. Helpmakaar means "Help one another." It stood high and a steep road led to it, requiring double teams of oxen. Transport drivers used to borrow each other's teams for the ascent.

ready at the corner of the churchyard at midnight, one saddled for myself to ride, one with my pack-saddle and valise strapped on, and the third bare backed. All went according to plan; Elks lifted me into the saddle and off I went. Mercifully there were no telegraphs in those days, so I was lost to all intents and purposes, and the convoy started without me. I fetched up at Dundee all right, and when I was helped off and supported into the tent of my boss, Major Essex of the Gordons and chief transport officer, he nearly had a fit, for he thought I was a walking corpse. I am full of gratitude to this day to him, for he acceded to my request that I should lie low in a tent, trusting to nature to pull me round sufficiently to do duty by the time the advance commenced. It was glorious weather, clear and bright with frost every night, and I picked up every day, and by the time the doctors traced where I had gone to I was well into Zululand.

We had crossed the Blood River at Landsman's Drift, near Kopje Allein, on the 1st June, and it was soon after this I first became acquainted with that fine old soldier, now General Sir Charles Tucker, then Major C. Tucker of the 80th, commanding the fort at Kopje Allein.

Our first day's march was productive of a tragic incident which touched the heart of every man in the force and marred the joy of being on the move again against the enemy. H.I.H. the Prince Imperial of France, previously a cadet at Woolwich, and wearing the undress uniform of the Royal Artillery, had been allowed to accompany the expedition attached to the commander-in-chief's staff. He had endeared himself to all with whom he came into touch and had been especially friendly to myself. He took deep interest in the organisation of every branch of our force, and was in my tent up to 11 p.m. the night before extracting from me a promise to write him a treatise on bullock transport.

We had moved forward a day's march, and on reaching the next camp rumours (which were soon confirmed) came in that the Prince had been killed; and next morning, when we halted for the day at Itelezi Hill camp, the body with sixteen *assegai* wounds was brought in on a stretcher formed of lances and a blanket. The brief account of this lamentable event which I am about to give is based on the stories given by those who were present, and by the story of Zulus, as told in their naive and truthful way by themselves after peace had been declared.

The prince had gone ahead of the force that morning with a small reconnaissance party consisting of a staff officer and a few (six, I think) mounted men. At about 3 p.m. they had ridden into a *kraal* and off-saddled for a short time to feed men and horses. The outlook, if kept, was indifferent, and unbeknown to them a few Zulus crept up through the crops and long grass and fired a volley at close range as the party was in the act of mounting.

No one appeared to have been hit then, but the horses were frightened and the party galloped away, doubtless thinking H.I.H. was with them. Two men were left in the *kraal*, and one of them, on mounting, was hit and knocked off his horse. Their bodies were found next day. The prince's horse, however, was exceedingly restive, and he came out of the *kraal* on foot, endeavouring to mount, but at last the horse broke loose. By this time the remainder of the party were some little way off, and the Zulus, seeing the prince alone on foot, rushed in and killed him.

The Zulus described that, being only six or eight in number, they had no intention of fighting the whole party, but seeing one man alone, took courage and attacked him. They had no idea that he was a person of the highest importance, and that the deed performed by them that day would affect very materially European politics for years.

The staff officer was tried by court-martial and sentenced to be shot, and was only saved at the request of the Prince's mother, the Empress Eugénie. The officer died a few years later of fever in India.

Lord Chelmsford's plan for our column, the one with which he was marching, was to establish food depôts along our line of advance at intervals, building forts for the purpose. The column consisted of a cavalry brigade, the King's Dragoon Guards and 17th Lancers, under Major-General Fred Marshall; the 2nd Division, under Major-General Newdigate, of two brigades, the first formed by the 2/21st R.S. Fusiliers and the 58th under Colonel Glynn, and the second by the 1/24th and the 94th under Colonel Collingwood; Batteries, R.E., etc. The first depot was at Kopje Allein, where half a battalion of the 80th were left under Major C. Tucker. The next place selected was near the River Nondweni, twenty-five miles from Kopje Allein, and was called Fort Newdigate, after the 2nd Divisional Commander.

From Fort Newdigate I accompanied Wood's Flying Column to the frontier to escort 240 empty wagons to be refilled at Landsman's Drift. It was the 17th June before we got back to Fort Newdigate again, and then with some 600 loaded wagons, having picked up some 400 extra at Landsman's Drift. Meanwhile, some of the force had been moved on, and Fort Marshall, sixteen miles farther on, was being commenced.

On arriving at the spot where Fort Newdigate was to be constructed on the 6th June, our camp was laid out as usual in the shape of a great rectangle; the wagons formed the wall, and about 200 yards outside it the new fort was commenced. By sundown the walls had begun to rise. Piquets were posted all round at some distance from the *laager*. It was a moonlight night and clouds were flitting across the moon, and a shadow from one of these was mistaken for an advancing body of Zulus.

The piquet gave the alarm and the men manned the sides of the *laager*. Unfortunately some of the piquets, in falling back, took refuge in this partially constructed fort. I was asleep in a tent outside the *laager*. The order was for all tents outside the *laager* to be lowered when the alarm sounded. My stable companion, Alexander of the 21st R.S. Fusiliers, had some difficulty in awakening me, and before I could get out of the tent[11] firing had commenced from the *laager*, so, striking the tent as best we could, we rushed into the *laager*.

11. In the hurry the tent did not fall flat, but stuck up in the moonlight, and when I came to examine it afterwards it had fifty-four bullet-holes in it, so it was as well I got out of it in time.

Undoubtedly the men's nerves were in a bad state, owing, I consider, to the fact that they were young soldiers and that the staff never misled an opportunity of instilling into their minds the fierceness of the enemy and their love of night attacks. In a few minutes every face of the *laager* was blazing away and a battery in action at one corner was firing "grape." It was a long time before the firing could be stopped, and then it was found to be a false alarm, but a disastrous one, for there were four casualties, three of them in the embryonic fort, where the walls were not high enough to give cover from fire from the *laager*.

It was found afterwards that there was no enemy within fifteen miles. Our expenditure of ammunition was heavy, 50,000 rounds it was said at the time. This place was more generally known after this as "Fort Funk." We had several more false alarms before we fought the battle of Ulundi, but these I will not describe here.

So far I have only been referring to the column to which I belonged, but there were two other forces operating, the one assembled at Eshowe, some seventy miles south-south-east of Landsman's Drift and about forty miles south of Ulundi, the 1st Division under General Hope Crealock; the other to the northwest under Colonel Evelyn Wood,V.C. Both these columns had had their share of fighting. Before General Crealock assumed command, a force under Colonel Pearson of the Buffs drove off an attack at the River Inyezane on the 22nd January, the same day as the battle of Isandhlwana, and later on had been besieged at Eshowe, but had been relieved on the 4th April by a force under the commander-in-chief by the battle of Ginginlovo, fought two days previously.

A strong naval contingent, formed from the crews of H.M. ships *Shah, Tenedos,* and *Boadicea,* took part in this battle, and with it a brother of mine, now a retired admiral. This force was destined never to reach Ulundi, for it was so long in starting, because according to an amusing but probably utterly untrue report which was circulated, the G.O.C. would not move without his full month's supply of pepper; it was still in the neighbourhood of Port Durnford when the battle of Ulundi was fought.

Evelyn Wood, however, with Buller commanding the mounted troops, was not likely to be out of it. They had had quite a lot of fighting. For months past they had been busy with bold reconnaissances twenty miles and more into Zululand. A minor disaster had befallen them on the 12th March, when a camp on the Intombie River of a company of the 80th Regiment, under Captain Moriarty, was surprised, he being killed in his pyjamas, and sixty-one others out of a total of 106 also being slain.

Wood had made his camp at Kambula[12] in February, and it was from there that the big operation on the rugged "Inhlsobana" Mountain eighteen to twenty miles distant was made, when Colonel Weatherby, Captain Ronny Campbell, Captain Barton, and nine other officers were amongst the killed, with eighty other Europeans out of a total of 400. This action was followed next day by the famous battle of Kambula, when a Zulu army attacked Wood's Camp, resulting in a loss to the Zulus of about 2,000, the British casualties only amounting to eighty-three. When the final advance into the Zulu country which I am now describing was arranged, it was planned for the three columns gradually to draw together so as to concentrate in front of Ulundi.

I have already told how the right column dropped behind, but Evelyn Wood actually camped opposite us on the bank of the Ityotyosi River on the 4th June. His force was known as Wood's flying column, always marching and camping a short distance ahead of us until we reached the Entonganeni heights on the 28th June, when we camped together. From there we could see the King's Kraal Ulundi, some fifteen miles away, and the valley of the White Umvolosi between it and ourselves.

It had taken us twenty-eight days to do about sixty-five miles, which to the ordinary mind would appear somewhat slow, but it was really a creditable performance, for the difficulties of the country were enormous—very little flat ground, no roads, deep

---

12. Kambula and the Hlobana Mountain are close to Vryheid some fifty miles from Isandhlwana.

valleys and precipitous hills—many of them covered with rocks and boulders—to climb, muddy river-beds, and we with 600 to 1,000 wagons each drawn by sixteen oxen. Occasionally we did ten miles a day, but generally far less; once, for instance, we were thirty-six hours doing one mile.

I have only mentioned the principal forts, to which should be added Fort Evelyn, constructed on the 23rd June. Other intermediate ones, at which troops had to be left, were gradually made for the safety of the lines of communication. In this way one of our infantry brigades under Colonel Collingwood, consisting of the 1/24th and the 94th, was used up and never reached Ulundi.

It must be remembered that very little of the country was really open, and much of it covered with bush, and therefore a long straggling column would have been vulnerable and difficult to guard. This accounts for slow movements, the head of the column never being very far from the tail, and long marches being only possible over open country when wagons could move twenty abreast, as we did on one or two occasions over rolling veldt covered with rich luxuriant grass, and then it was a very fine sight. Most of it was ideal country for ambushes and sharp-shooters, and I lost a great friend on the 11th or 12th June, when the adjutant of the 17th Lancers, "Frith," was killed from some rocky caves on the face of Ezunganyan Hill.

On the 30th June the order was given for the force to move from the heights down to the valley of the White Umvolosi and whilst on the move we could see across the valley some ten miles distant the Zulu army manoeuvring in mass formation. It appeared very large and imposing and to be carrying out complicated movements with the greatest accuracy. Suddenly the Staff of the 2nd Division became alarmed and ordered *laager* to be formed on the leading wagons. This—though unnecessary with the enemy ten miles off, and in view of the fact that the Flying Column, quite undismayed, was proceeding calmly on its way in front of us—was quite simple to carry out if the matter had been left to the Transport officers, who had a regular drill for "*laagering* up" on the march. Jumpy staff officers, however, were flying round issuing wild orders themselves to wagon sections with the result that they were out-spanned in the most chaotic formations, two or three wagons here, half a dozen there, and, night coming on, we had to put up with an utterly indefensible wagon fort.

To make things worse, they proceeded to post a circle of native contingent piquets right round, and when the field officer visited these piquets, an excited native shot at him, others let off their rifles, and the natives, who were friendly Swazis dressed like Zulus with shields and *assegais* and skin coverings, came running in. I, feeling sure it was one of our false alarms, remained dozing under my wagon, when I found half-naked savages crawling over me. Luckily I couldn't find my revolver. Wood's column, comfortably camped a mile away, were not in the least alarmed, for they knew too well the peculiarity of our column. Next day, however, we courageously moved forward and dumped down alongside the Flying Column.

Lord Chelmsford had heard on the 16th that Sir Garnet Wolseley was *en route* to supersede him. Sir Garnet had been induced to take Port Durnford as his place of landing, and Crealock was there to receive him; but it was a port only in exceptional weather, for heavy surf was the normal condition there. So it proved when Sir Garnet's ship, H.M.S. *Shah,* came off it, and, after wasting valuable days unable to land, he returned to Durban on the 4th July, the day of the battle of Ulundi.

An officer of the ship told me that Sir Garnet might have landed the day of reaching the coast, but the staff delayed to have breakfast, the surf increased, and the opportunity for Wolseley's getting to Ulundi in time to take command at the battle was lost. It was some satisfaction that Lord Chelmsford, who had borne the burden of the campaign, was not relieved in the hour of victory.

This day, the 2nd July, very few Zulus were to be seen. Cetywayo had been offered terms, and from reports he appeared to be wavering; but as the commander-in-chief could not wait indefinitely, he ordered Buller next day to take his irregular mounted troops, some thousand strong, composed of several small corps (named after their leaders, thus: Baker's Horse, Ferreira's Horse, Beddington's Horse, D'Arcy's Horse), across the river and make a reconnaissance. It was an interesting and picturesque operation in full view of us and supported by artillery from our side of the river. At one time part of the force nearly fell into an ambush, but the reconnaissance was successful, for it showed where the bulk of the enemy were and was able to withdraw with the loss of two or three killed and a few wounded. It was during this reconnaissance that Lord William Beresford, acting as staff officer to Buller, picked up a wounded man from the middle of the Zulus and brought him in safety away, thus earning the V.C.

King Cetywayo[13] had been called on to lay down his arms and appeared to be undecided, but to compel him to make up his mind the whole force moved across the river on Ulundi on the 4th July and, forming in a square, moved towards the Zulu army, halted and awaited attack. When this was evidently coming, the mounted troops, who till then had been covering the movement, came inside the square, and the Zulu army advanced with the greatest bravery, but thirty yards was the nearest any of them got to the square.

In twenty minutes, weary of being mown down by gun and rifle fire, they fled, pursued by the 17th Lancers. Our casualties, almost all from rifle fire, were one hundred, twelve of which were killed. It was an utter rout. Pursuit was carried out to the foot of the hills, but the fight was out of the Zulu warriors, and our troops had recrossed the river and got back to their camp of the previous night by 4 p.m. King Cetywayo became a fugitive, and after a skilful and plucky pursuit was run to ground at the end of August by Major Martyr and a squadron of the 1st Dragoon Guards.

Two days after the battle I was ordered down in charge of the transport of a convoy taking back the wounded, escorted by

13. I afterwards saw poor old Cetywayo in prison at Cape Town on my way home—a pathetic figure, his huge obese body bathed in perspiration.

the 21st R. Scots Fusiliers under Colonel Hazlerigg of the same regiment, a very fine officer.

On reaching Landsman's Drift over the Blood River, which was our destination, a somewhat serious but not unamusing breach of discipline occurred. When the force had halted at Landsman's Drift previous to its advance to Ulundi, a certain battalion had looted a barrel of rum and buried it, intending to have a "jolly" on their return. They had made great friends with another regiment and told them the secret of where this rum could be found. Consequently a night or two after our arrival several men of that other regiment were absent at evening roll-call and the orderly corporal was sent to look for them.

As he did not return, another dove in the shape of the orderly sergeant was sent out of the ark, and when he too failed to return, still another non-commissioned officer was sent. The latter came flying back to say that behind a *kopje* just outside the camp he had found an empty barrel of rum with the orderly sergeant lying alongside of it with his mouth under the bung-hole, surrounded by twenty-six others all dead to the world. Doctors were hurried out, and opinions expressed that some of these thirsty lads must die, but, by a free use of the stomach pump, luckily all lives were saved. Needless to say, a court-martial followed.

For the next two or three months I worked away passing down troops and stores from the front, and then in November got orders to return to England myself.

The difficulty was how to get down country, for it was 150 miles to Durban and no transport available. Amongst my transport was a light buggy on four spider wheels. I knew that this would soon be seized by some senior officer, so I removed and buried one of the wheels. The inspecting officer arrived, was much taken with the buggy as the very thing he wanted for himself, but agreed it was useless without a fourth wheel.

That evening, the inspector having departed, I was lucky enough to find the missing wheel, and next morning, hooking in a team of four rather wild ponies, I was tooling away for the port of embarkation.

On arriving at Madeira I heard the sad news that my father had just died—a bitter blow. He had been so interested in the war and I had been looking forward above everything else to telling him my adventures.

CHAPTER 2

Egypt, 1882

I rejoined my Regiment (the 95th) at the Curragh and had some excellent sport with hounds and gun. Next year (1880) we moved to Aldershot, where we found ourselves under an eccentric Brigadier. He had a peculiar dislike to our commander-in-chief, and one day on a ceremonial parade, when seated on his charger in front of the Brigade, on the approach of the commander-in-chief he handed his sword to his *aide-de-camp*, saying he could not trust himself with it. Another day he was to be seen charging up and down the parade-ground with a billiard-cue, imagining he was a knight-errant of old. In spite of his peculiarities he was popular, and being naturally a fine soldier and gallant fellow, beyond being amused, we thought little of his occasional outbursts.

In 1880 I was sent to our depôt at Derby, where I had some memorable sport with the Meynell, but smashed up my knee, which was to trouble me at intervals for some years. I rejoined Head-quarters at Aldershot in time to go to Gibraltar where we arrived on the 31st December 1881. I was lucky racing there, and enjoyed the gallops with the Calpe Hounds; but my stay was only three or four months, for I was away for some time on leave, from which I was recalled in July. The cause of my recall was trouble in Egypt, and the 95th had been ordered to take part in the campaign under Sir Garnet Wolseley for the restoration of Khedive Tewfik's authority, which had been rudely upset by the revolt of his War Minister, Arabi Pasha.

Affairs in Egypt had for some considerable period been watched with anxiety in Europe. The known weakness of the Khedive Mohammed Tewfik, and the widespread feeling amongst his subjects that Egypt was not being governed for the benefit of the Egyptians, made the political outlook uncertain.

The principal causes of discontent in the country were the employment of foreigners in the place of native-born Egyptians in the several Government departments and administrations, and the uneven distribution of the taxation. The foreigner dwelling in Egypt was almost exempt from taxes, whereas the peasants, or *fellaheen*, of the country were heavily burdened, and in addition to payment in kind had to give the sweat of their brows by forced labour in the much-hated *corvée*.

Towards the end of 1881 it was seen that a crisis was approaching. A zealous patriot, himself a fellah born, one Ahmed Arabi, became Minister of War, and with the army at his back threatened to undermine the authority of the lawful ruler of the country. The revolt of the army and seizure of the reins of the government by the rebels would have been a most serious affair for the 90,000 Europeans engaged in business in Egypt. The English and French Governments therefore agreed to support the Khedive Tewfik, and on the 6th January 1882 presented the famous "Dual Note," in which they informed his Highness that they considered that the only guarantee for the present and future good order and general prosperity in Egypt would be to maintain him on the throne on the terms laid down by the Sultan's *firmans*, and that they assured him of their support.

To prove that this was no idle assurance a large fleet of English and French ships took up their position off Alexandria on the 20th May 1882.

The Sultan had determined to send a high commissioner, with full powers to try to arrange matters between the Khedive and Arabi, and for this purpose Dervesh Pasha arrived in Cairo in the first week of June. Hardly had he taken up his duties when, on the 11th June, serious riots broke out in Alexandria between the Mohammedan and Christian inhabitants.

These riots caused many deaths, great wreckage of property, and drove the larger part of the European employers of labour to flee the country. This deprived numbers of Arab workmen of their means of subsistence and caused them to rove the country clamouring for bread.

Who was actually to blame for these riots has never been clearly decided, but at the trial of Arabi Pasha, subsequent to the war, although the causing of these riots was one of the charges against him, it was found impossible to prove it and the matter was allowed to drop.

The fleet now set about helping the refugees to escape from the country.

On the 23rd June a conference of six European Powers assembled at Constantinople to try to arrange some *modus operandi* for the settlement of affairs in Egypt. Not only did Turkey refuse to send a representative to this meeting, but the Sultan presented Arabi Pasha with the 1st class of the Order of the Medjidieh.

On the 24th June the English and French representatives, who, up to then, had been allowed to sit in the Egyptian Council of Ministers, received notice that they would not be allowed to do so in future. Simultaneously Arabi Pasha, as War Minister and head of the army, announced that any attempt to restore order by landing troops would be resisted, and, by way of emphasising this, earthworks were begun between Ramleh and Aboukir. Fears were now entertained for the safety of the Suez Canal, but Arabi, as it turned out, had more or less promised M. de Lesseps that it should not be interfered with, and he kept his promise.

About this time it was thought necessary to prepare an expeditionary force of two divisions and a brigade of cavalry in England; and an advance force, composed of the 1st South Staffordshire Regiment, the 3rd King's Royal Rifles, and the 17th Company R.E., was sent from Malta to Cyprus, with Sir Archibald Alison in command.

On the 11th July, owing to the refusal of the Egyptian soldiers to stop making defensive works and arming their forts, the famous bombardment of Alexandria by the British Fleet under

Admiral Sir Beauchamp Seymour took place. Six days later, owing to the disordered state of affairs in Alexandria, Alison's force was landed there from Cyprus.

The Porte having refused to send a force to restore order in Egypt, England and France had to act; but as the French Chamber refused any credit for the expedition, that country had to stand and look on whilst a British Army (for which the sum of £2,300,000 had been voted in the House of Commons on the 27th July) took the field by itself, with Sir Garnet Wolseley as commander-in-chief

The authorities, in planning the campaign, had formed a very good idea that the most suitable place for a decisive action would be near the high open desert of Tel- el-Kebir in the neighbourhood of the Egyptian barracks there, and with this object in view it had originally been planned to seize the Suez Canal at once and land at Ismailia. Events, however, had drawn our first troops to Alexandria, and as a large Egyptian army lay at Kafr ed Dauar, a few miles off, it was thought advisable to do all possible to make Arabi Pasha think that those lines were the object of attack. Consequently all troops as they arrived were landed at Alexandria, entrenchments formed at Ramleh and constant reconnaissances made against the works at Kafr ed Dauar and along the sand-hills towards Aboukir.

On the 15th August the commander-in-charge, Sir Garnet Wolseley, arrived at Alexandria and assumed command in the field. Orders were at once issued for the re-embarkation of all troops, with the exception of a small force, which was to remain under Sir Evelyn Wood to hold Alexandria and prevent the enemy from ascertaining the fact that the whole British army was not still in and about Alexandria.

When the orders reached Gibraltar for the 95th (now the 2nd Battalion Sherwood Foresters) to proceed to Egypt, it is unnecessary to remark that our joy was immense.

The first half left on the 7th August in H.M.S. *Orontes,* and the second half in the P. & O. *Verona.* I was in the latter with the Head-quarters under Colonel North Crealock. We landed at Alexandria early on the 21st, and next day two events of importance to me occurred: first, I got my promotion to the rank of captain; and, secondly, I was appointed assistant chief of police in Alexandria.

Owing to the very disturbed state of the city and to military conditions, the policing had been taken over by the services. Captain Lord Charles Beresford, R.N., noted for his handling of H.M.S. *Condor* at the bombardment of Alexandria, had just been succeeded as chief of police by Lieutenant-Colonel Wm. Cleland, Royal Dublin Fusiliers. The duties were onerous and varied. There was a permanent court-martial sitting for the trial of rioters, but the civil courts continued to function.

One of my duties was to attend at the courts-martial, and whilst not actually in the court-martial room I had opportunities of studying the methods of Egyptian civilian judges in other rooms of the same building. A matter of common occurrence was the hearing of shrieks and yells during these trials, and one day I entered the room where they were particularly loud, and learned the cause.

It appeared that when a witness was called by either side, before he was asked to give evidence a brass instrument joining his two thumbs together was fastened on. The witness then, with his hands held out across the table, stood just in front of the judge and in easy reach of him. Before commencing his interrogation, the judge stretched out and did something to the brass instrument which made the witness wince; then I recognised that the much-talked-of thumb-screws, of which I had heard, were actually being applied.

I could not understand the language, but it was apparent when the witness was not giving the sort of evidence required, because the judge would lean forward and give an extra turn to the screw and the witness would writhe with pain. At last the judge's face assumed a demoniacal expression, and he not only seized hold of the witness by the beard and tore a handful out, but screwed up the instrument so tight that the unfortunate fellow rolled over on the floor and howled for mercy.

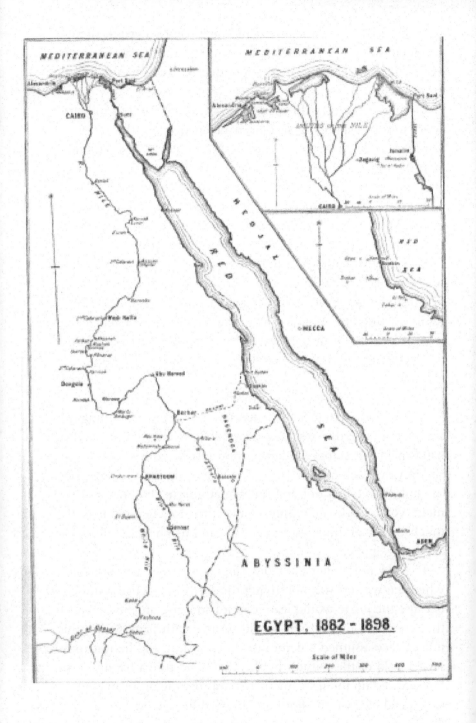

EGYPT, 1882 - 1898.

Scale of Miles

I had had enough. I daren't interfere, as we had strict orders to avoid the civil courts and I was entirely in the wrong in having entered the room, so I withdrew, disgusted and impressed by the specimen of Egyptian justice I had seen.

I can't say I enjoyed my police duties, and was heartily pleased when, early on the 3rd September, I was sent for by my General, Sir Evelyn Wood.

The main force, consisting of all but one division, under Sir Garnet Wolseley, had re-embarked at Alexandria and sailed for Ismailia a fortnight previously, and one brigade of the last division with the Divisional General, Lieutenant-General Sir Edward Hamley,[1] had departed that morning to join the c.-in-c, leaving Sir Evelyn with the other brigade in command at Alexandria without any mounted troops. It was on the latter account that I was wanted.

There was a force of 15,000 Egyptians between us and Aboukir on the coast, in addition to the 15,000 holding the lines of Kafr ed Dauar (see sketch). Sir Evelyn explained to me that the former were largely mounted troops, and that their harassing tactics about Ramleh and up to the outskirts of the city were very annoying, and he asked me if I could collect even a few mounted infantry to oppose them. He told me that I could draw on my own regiment and the 96th (the Manchester), the only two battalions in the city, for men; but he had no saddles or horses to offer me, and these he trusted to my initiative to collect. He mentioned he had heard of a few saddles in shops, and these I got hold of later.

Now, in the course of my constabulary duties I had had reason to enter the Khedive's stables, and there I had seen the horses and saddles of his body-guard, so without a word to my chief I saluted and withdrew.

Taking an *arabiyeh* (a cab), I drove to see my Colonel (Crealock), explained the situation, and asked for men. These I was given at once. Reinforced by another *arabiyeh*, I drove with some of the men and the battalion interpreter direct to the Khedive's

1. The well-known military historian.

stables. There I told an Egyptian officer that I had come to commandeer horses and saddles. He naturally remonstrated, but I said that the sound way to protect the Khedive was to keep the enemy from our gates, that I intended to take all I required, and he could explain matters to his Highness.

In half an hour I departed with both *arabiyeh* piled up with saddles, being seated in the middle of one of them myself. The men, leading the horses, two mules, and one donkey, followed.

To our barracks we went, and by the early afternoon we had fitted ourselves out with all requisites and were *en route* for Sir Evelyn's head-quarters near Ramleh. Never shall I forget his surprise when I went in and reported that the new mounted infantry was formed up outside and awaiting his orders.

Either this day or the next I was fortunate enough to meet an old friend, Captain J. H. Ewart, a retired officer of the 78th (Seaforth Highlanders), who had come out to the sound of the guns. He had recently been *aide-de-camp* to Lieutenant-General Hamilton, commanding the troops at Cork, and it was there that we had become friends. Ewart remained with me throughout the subsequent operations, and, since Sir Evelyn gave me great credit for them, I suppose they were successful, and this, I think, was largely due to Captain Ewart's help.

The following tribute to our usefulness appears in Sir Evelyn's book, *From Midshipman to Field-Marshal:*

"Within half an hour of the Divisional General embarking, Smith-Dorrien had collected fifteen men, increased in a few days to thirty. Many of them had never ridden, but before sundown a section defiled past me at Ramleh, twelve ponies, two mules, and a donkey. A somewhat motley detachment, and many of them held on to the saddle; but they proceeded five miles farther to the front, and managed to shoot an Egyptian officer that evening, and in five days killed or wounded twelve of the enemy, as they admitted. Three days later Smith-Dorrien had pushed back the Egyptian outposts, and we were not again troubled by the Bedouins looting the houses in Ramleh, as they had done the week before the other brigade of the division to which I belonged embarked."

I should mention that on our march out to Ramleh I had taken the opportunity of drilling and practising dismounted action, and found the men so keen that I got confidence.

When asked by Sir Evelyn how soon I should be able to operate, I was able to answer, "At once." I made a reconnaissance along the Mahmoudieh Canal, and had an action, resulting in the death of an Egyptian officer and the capture of two prisoners without casualties on our side, that very evening.

Next morning, the 4th September, before dawn, wanting to get some important information for Sir Evelyn, we, total seventeen, started off towards Mandara and had quite an exciting morning. We reached the enemy's outpost line at dawn, and, leaving my men dismounted in the sand-dunes, I went through the Gyppies' second line and had a good look round before I was discovered. They gave me a bad time as I galloped away, but I was able to report that the big gun (15 centimetre), which used to bombard us every afternoon, had apparently been removed and that large numbers of men were not in evidence. Beyond one man shot through the helmet, we had no casualties to report.

The first inference from this report was that large numbers had moved across to reinforce Tel-el-Kebir, but later on that inference prove to be wrong, for, curiously enough, according to the official history of the war drawn up by the late Sir Frederick Maurice, nothing was known of the move of our main force to Ismailia, and it was not until Arabi Pasha had been a prisoner a year in Ceylon that he became aware of it. Sir F. Maurice says that there were 15,000 men both at Aboukir and Kafr ed Dauar, and that they remained there until after the battle of Tel-el-Kebir. This accounts for the large numbers I frequently saw when patrolling and reconnoitring.

This small enterprise was typical of the next ten days, but there were two rather more exciting than the others which I will briefly describe.

About the 7th September I had been reinforced by a detachment from the 96th under Lieutenant Bertram, bringing my strength up to about thirty or thirty-five. The belt of country dividing the sea and Lake Aboukir between ourselves and the enemy was chiefly sand-dunes, and on them to the south-east of Ramleh and overlooking Lake Aboukir there was a very annoying Egyptian cavalry piquet post. It was in a commanding position from which most of our movements could be watched.

Ewart and I designed a little surprise packet for them. A mounted party was to make a show of advance over the rolling dunes so as to occupy their attention, but not to close with them. Away to their right a dismounted party under Ewart was to move on the flat ground bordering the bed of the lake, keeping close in to the dunes, which would hide them from the objective piquet. I was to ride on the open sands in the lake-bed farther to the right in full view of the piquet. Ewart's party was to keep level with me and to watch me. Taking out my handkerchief and wiping my face was to be the signal that Ewart's party was immediately under the piquet and was to rush up the bank and attack it.

All went according to plan, except that I had a rotten time of it, for, being in full view and only a few hundred yards off, our enemy amused themselves sniping me. Mercifully they had never been to Hythe, and the bullets merely damaged the sand. I was relieved, however, when the moment arrived for the production of my bandana. Up swarmed Ewart and his men; the surprise was complete. Two Egyptians were killed and the others fled, and they never occupied that post again.

Sir Evelyn Wood's gratitude for the change in affairs brought about by the small force of mounted infantry was tinged with fear that we might be led into an ambush, especially as one morning I reported we had been shelled from a Martello tower on the coast near Mandara, and on withdrawing had been followed up by large forces of all arms. With a view to punishing this tower and the Egyptian field works in its neighbourhood, he ordered me to accompany him and Admiral Dowell, who commanded a squadron, in H.M.S. *Condor,* on the 9th September.

There was a heavy swell on and we rolled many degrees as we went up the coast. The ship made famous by Lord Charles Beresford's handling of her in the bombardment of the 11th July was now commanded by an old friend of mine, Carter by name.

Being a particularly bad sailor, my interest in sea warfare very soon lapsed, and with the permission of the commander I lay down in his berth. Shortly afterwards Keggie Slade, R.A.,[15] *aide-de-camp* to Sir Evelyn Wood, came in and said the General wanted to see me at once, as it was believed that we were abreast of the offending Martello tower. As I did not take much notice, he shouted at me, "Both the General and Admiral require you at once"; and when I only muttered prayers for ill-health on those high officers, he realised that the power of the sea was even drowning discipline and went off to report. Back he came again with orders for me either to swear the Martello tower in range of us was the offender or to go up on deck at once.

I naturally took the line of least resistance, and two minutes later forth belched our guns. This really did stir me, and up I went into the midst of a glittering staff, to be most kindly received but to be heavily jeered at, even though I took care to explain to my General that had I understood Mounted Infantry were to be taken to sea, I should have asked him to appoint someone else to the unstable duties.

Luckily the tower was the right one, but I don't think we did it much harm. However, I did not get on shore for a long time, for we steamed back to the flagship, H.M.S. *Minotaur,* where a conference was held after an excellent lunch—enjoyed by most people I believe. After this Sir Evelyn used to send out a company or two, or even half a battalion, for the Mounted Infantry to fall back on during their morning manoeuvres.

A few days later, the 14th September, taking every man I could muster, I started before dawn, following the Damietta Railway. My chief had expressed a desire to know whether that line had

15. Afterwards Lieutenant-General F. G. Slade.

been blown up by the enemy, and where—in case he should wish to operate along it in conjunction with the armoured train. On reaching a point beyond Raben village, we estimated that we had got as near to the outposts as we dare without alarming them, so dismounting the men under Lieutenant Bertram, Ewart and I rode forward along the line. I was riding a fast Arab, and, in order to avoid any give-away noises, had nothing but a snaffle bridle and no sword.

When close enough for the outposts to be visible in the dim light, we parted, Ewart going one way and I following the railway. Just where it passed through the defensive earthworks I found an enormous hole and the railway destroyed, so I had got the information I required. As I had seen the sentries moving after I had passed them, I dared not return the same way, so I rode on right through the hostile camp.

All were asleep, and it was not until I, by circling round, passed through their lines again in a fresh place that the outposts noticed me approaching. There was nothing left but to gallop through them, and this I did under a hail of bullets, but they were such jolly bad shots that none touched me.

Ewart had retired by another route, and we met and halted behind a sand-dune some half a mile from the hostile outpost line. When fire was first opened on us, the alarm was sounded, bugles taking it up right along their lines. They sounded very clear and near in the still morning air. Then, after a short wait, out from the lines came bodies of cavalry until there appeared not less than a brigade in motion.

Towards us they came, and when quite close we galloped off, drawing them to where our dismounted men were awaiting them. We passed the latter, and the enemy suddenly found themselves under heavy infantry fire, and with a few empty saddles immediately swerved away to a respectful distance, so sobered had they become by the varied and unexpected surprises we had practised against them on the preceding days.

This, I believe, was the last skirmish which took place during the campaign, for on getting back to our camp we heard that the battle of Tel-el-Kebir had been fought the previous morning, that our cavalry had seized Cairo, and that Arabi Pasha and many of the leaders were in our hands.

The next few days were joy-rides combined with duty, for we were able to visit both the Aboukir and Kafr ed Dauar lines, and wonder at the immense power of work of the Egyptian soldier—the earthworks were huge embankments at least fifteen feet high and many miles in extent—whilst we took over their arms, horses, equipment, and all their paraphernalia of war.

On the 25th September the Khedive moved in state from Alexandria to Cairo, and very proud we M.I. were, as with a squadron of 13th Bengal Lancers, we formed up in front of Ras-el-Tin Palace and escorted his Highness to the station.

The M.I. was not finally broken up until the 2nd October, and then as a company commander I rejoined my battalion, which was in camp at Ramleh.

We spent a few pleasant days waiting for our troopship which was to take us on to India.

Sir Evelyn Wood had been summoned to Cairo, and before going I was much flattered by being sent for by him to read his dispatches. He told me his object in showing them to me was that he gathered that his Divisional General's nose had been put out of joint and that he was not inclined to support any recommendations for honours, but that there were two people who were bound to get them in spite of him, namely, myself and Lieutenant W. W. Hancock of my regiment, who had led a gallant attack on one of the forts. Sir Evelyn explained that in case none of the others were recognised, he wished me to be the means of telling them that he had done all he could to bring their good services to notice. As a matter of fact, none of us got even a mention in dispatches.

On the 14th October H.M.S. *Euphrates* arrived in the harbour and embarked two weak battalions, ourselves and the 96th, for India.

Before leaving the subject of the 1882 Egyptian Campaign I must refer to the fact that two naval brothers of mine were also busy in helping to suppress Arabi. The senior was Lieutenant H. T. Smith-Dorrien, of H.M.S. *Invincible*. Hearing the Naval C.-in-C, Admiral Sir Beauchamp Seymour (afterwards Lord Alcester), wanted information, he darkened his face and dressed himself as an Arab fisherman with a large basket under his arm. Persuading the beef contractor to give him a passage to the shore, they had to call at an American ship *en route*.

As they were shoving off again, one of the American sailors said to my brother, "You dirty-looking ruffian, you want a wash," and turned the hose on him. On reaching the shore, he went round some Egyptian forts, and then, returning to his ship, was able to report that the Egyptians had remounted the guns. This report went to Sir Beauchamp and decided him to commence the bombardment, and he eventually stated in his dispatch that he did so on Lieutenant Smith-Dorrien's reports.

Three days later he, with Lieutenant de Courcy Hamilton, of H.M.S. *Helicon,* made a daring reconnaissance, wading right across Lake Mareotis. They had heard that their chief wished to know if the water was too deep for cavalry to cross. They were discovered, but managed to lie low in the water until the alarm had subsided, when they sneaked back with the required information.

My other brother, Rear-Admiral A. H. Smith-Dorrien, was then on H.M.S. *Eclipse* and had landed with a naval brigade at Suez. He reported seeing bayonets flashing at a place called Ajud some miles up the Canal. This proved to be a force of Egyptians who had cut the Sweet-Water Canal. Ships were sent to enfilade from the Canal, whilst a force. From Suez advanced at the same time to attack the camp. After killing many and taking several prisoners, they were able to repair the Canal—an important matter.

I have already mentioned him as fighting in the Zulu War. He was to see service during the next two years in the Red Sea and later in the Boxer troubles in China.

Both these brothers were serving in H.M.S. *Shah* when that ship and H.M.S. *Amethyst* fought the would-be President of Peru in the *Huascar* and caused her to surrender in 1879.

Chapter 3

India—Nile and Suakin Expeditions, 1884–1887

After an uneventful voyage we went by rail from Bombay to Poona, and thence by march via Allahabad and Cawnpore to Lucknow, where we arrived in February 1883. We enjoyed every moment of the march up; moving in the very early morning so as to avoid the heat of the day, we were generally in our next camp by 9 or 10 a.m., and then the remainder of the day was available for sport, mainly shooting snipe, duck, partridges, and deer. Unfortunately, one day, running after a wounded peacock, I injured my knee again and had to be sent ahead by rail to Lucknow. My eldest brother's old regiment, the 10th Hussars, were there, commanded by Lieutenant-Colonel Eddy Wood. He and his wife insisted on taking me into their bungalow, where I received the greatest kindness.

The 10th Hussars had the crack polo team in those days, when two or three hundred *rupees* was quite a good price for a pony. I actually bought two myself, each under two hundred *rupees*. Whilst I was there, the 10th held a sale by auction, and I remember the excitement in India at what were then considered to be fabulous prices: two or three of the ponies fetched in the neighbourhood of 500 *rupees* each, but one, "Butcher," belonging to the colonel, actually reached the unthinkable sum of 1,000.

To illustrate how rapidly prices rose, I would instance a sale of the Queen's Bays' ponies at Umballa, ten years later —on the 13th March 1893—after a grand game in the final of the Inter-regimental Polo Tournament (at which I was umpiring), when the Queen's Bays beat the 16th Lancers. The ponies of the former were sold by auction, and twenty-nine of them fetched 30,000 *rupees*—the highest price being 2,000 paid for "Charlie Dilke." Those prices, large as they were, are small compared with the prices paid since. Before I left India, fourteen years later, 1,000 and more were common prices for likely ponies, though raw and untrained.

I was practically on my back for two months at Lucknow. The doctors could do nothing, and I was invalided home with a stiff knee, swelled as big as a football.

On arrival in London I saw some of the highest authorities, and was only just saved from losing my leg by a skilful operation, and, although on crutches for a good many months, I recovered.

And now I come to a very interesting part of my life.

At the end of 1883 I was pronounced sound enough to rejoin in India, and in January 1884 was gliding slowly along the Suez Canal in a troopship when a small post-boat proceeding the same way as ourselves passed us, and in it were seated Sir Evelyn Wood, the *Sirdar* of the Egyptian army, and the famous General Charles Gordon, and Lieutenant-Colonel Stewart, the two latter on their way to Khartoum, from which they were never to return.

How Sir Evelyn knew I was on board I have not the faintest idea, but when we were off Ismailia a telegram was brought off from him to the following effect:

Obtain a week's leave from O.C. Troops on board. Proceed to Cairo. I have an appointment to offer you. If you decline I will pay your passage by next mail steamer to India.

On arriving at Cairo I was asked to join the Egyptian army. This entailed signing a contract with the Egyptian Government.

I said I was quite ready to do so if a condition could be entered in the contract that I should be allowed to go home to read for the Staff College examination the first year there was no war. Sir Evelyn was charming, but would not agree. During the next six days I saw him frequently, lunched and dined with him, rode backwards and forwards to polo with him—I sticking to my condition, he declining to entertain it.

Then the time came when I should be off if I was to catch the next mail steamer at Suez, and I asked for my passage money. This the *Sirdar* ordered, and fifty-five golden Egyptian sovereigns were paid me. I took my ticket at Cook's and went off to Suez. Just as I was about to embark, a telegram was put into my hand from General Sir Frederick Stephenson, who was commanding the British Army of Occupation, saying that Sir Evelyn relented and that I was to return to Cairo. I did so, triumphant, and have never regretted it.

General Gordon departed for Khartoum a few days after my first journey to Cairo. I had the good fortune to meet him more than once at the *Sirdar's* house, and the last time I saw him was illustrative of how little he considered his own personal comforts. He, dressed in black (a frock coat, I think), and wearing a tall hat, was seated in a carriage about to drive to the station to catch the train which was to take him the first part of his long journey. Just as the carriage was moving off he called out that he had neither soap nor towels, and I still have a vivid recollection of Lady Wood throwing him a bundle containing the required articles from a bedroom window.

Gordon had been Governor-General of the Sudan from 1874 to 1879. Since then, a lot of fighting had taken place there, and in 1881 a certain Mohammed Ahmed, who was looked on as a prophet, had acquired power, and revolted. Several forces had been sent against him, with varying success, but resulting on the whole in an increase to Mohammed's prestige, and in 1882 he declared himself "The Mahdi." The only really successful operations conducted against him appear to have been those under Abdul Kadir Pasha, a brave man and a fine leader, but he had been superseded and was then Minister of War in Cairo. His plan, with his somewhat nervous soldiers, had been, when an attack was imminent, to form his troops into a three-deep square, the front rank lying down, the middle rank kneeling, and the rear rank standing, so that it became almost impossible to run away.

The Mahdi, by many small victories, was acquiring a large number of rifles and even guns. In September 1883 an ex-officer of the Indian army, Hicks Pasha, with a force of 8,000 men, with field-guns, Nordenfeldts, etc., proceeded against him, rendering themselves independent of a line of communication by carrying fifty days' supplies, and trusting to the country for water. The latter, however, failed them. Many died of thirst, and in October the remainder, too feeble to offer a determined resistance, were cut to pieces, and their arms, ammunition, and supplies passed over to the Mahdi.

Osman Digna, a slave-dealer in the Eastern Sudan, had also raised the standard of revolt, causing the Hadendowas, the tribe in the neighbourhood of Suakin, to join against the Government. To suppress the latter, Valentine Baker Pasha, an old 10th Hussar, the hero of the Shipka Pass and many a fight on the side of the Turks in the Russo-Turkish War of 1877, was sent against them. Baker at that time commanded the Egyptian *gendarmerie*, and his expedition was chiefly composed of that force. On the morning of the 4th February Baker, with some 3,500 men, advanced against an inferior force of Hadendowas. For some unknown reason panic set in, and his force fled, most of them being killed or wounded, the enemy appropriating some guns and 3,000 rifles. Baker himself, and staff, after trying to rally the men, charged through the enemy and got away.

Just after I had settled down to my duties with the Egyptian army, on the evening of the 4th February (1884), rumours of this disaster were in the air. I lay emphasis on this as an instance of the marvellous rate at which ill news travels. I was told that the same thing happened when Hicks Pasha's force had been cut to pieces a few months earlier. Long before it could have been possible for any authentic news to arrive, "bazaar" rumours were rife that the worst had happened, and bazaar rumours proved to be correct.

I was told about this time that why British officers were successful as company officers with native troops was because they actually went in front and led them; whereas with the Egyptians, the more senior they were, the farther behind, and when affairs were threatening, the first to depart were the seniors in rear, a process which was followed until the men, finding no seniors, officers, or non-commissioned officers behind them, followed suit.

The British Government now stepped in, deciding that the Sudanese coast of the Red Sea littoral, which includes Suakin, must be reconquered, and that a force under Major-General Sir Gerald Graham, V.C., with Colonel Herbert Stewart, commanding a Cavalry Brigade, and Sir Redvers Buller, commanding an infantry brigade, should be sent at once. Then followed Graham's victories of El Teb on the 29th February and Tamai on the 13th March. This ended that expedition.

Now to relate briefly my experiences with the Egyptian army. I was sent to Ambassieh under the Brigade Commander Sir Francis Grenfell, and a jolly, happy, though busy, life I had. There were the very best fellows[2] in the world in that army— Kitchener (just promoted captain), Wodehouse, Rundle, Hunter, Wynne, Wingate, G. E. Lloyd (afterwards killed in the Boer War), Hallam-Parr, Fraser, Teddy Barttelot (a lovable, wild, and gallant soul killed on the Congo), Surtees, Hickman, Chermside, and many others, equally good fellows but not so well known to fame later. I first went to an infantry battalion under Wynne, then to a Camel Corps.

Then in May I was ordered to raise a battalion of Turks, and this was quite an odd experience. I had to help me Surtees, as

2. Later becoming: Field-Marshals, Lord Grenfell and Lord Kitchener; Generals, Sir J. Wodehouse, Sir L. Rundle, Sir A. Hunter, Sir A. Wynne, Sir F. Wingate; Lieutenant-Generals, Sir Herbert Chermside, Sir H. F. Grant; Major-Generals, Sir H. Hallam-Parr, Sir Thomas Fraser, Sir Thomas Gallwey; Brigadier-Generals, Conyers Surtees, T. E. Hickman.

adjutant, Lysons, V.C., as quartermaster, and Besant, as musket-ry instructor and transport officer. Really good Turks were not forthcoming, so we had to recruit wherever we could, largely from the seaports, and the results were not very satisfactory, but still they made a smart-looking battalion.

That month (May 1884) matters in the Sudan were going from bad to worse. Berber had fallen to the Mahdi's troops, which were gradually drawing northwards down the Nile, Khartoum being thus cut off from the world.

Wady Haifa had to be occupied by Egyptian troops, and several units of the new Egyptian army were pushed up the Nile.

The Turkish battalion amongst others was ordered up, but when about to depart, my wretched knee gave trouble again, and I had to hand over command to Major H. F. Grant of the 4th Hussars, one of the bravest and most efficient officers in the army.

On arriving at Assiout, the rail-head, the battalion had to transfer into river-boats, when they mutinied, refused to go on board, and threatened their officers with their rifles, finally marching off in a body towards Cairo. As soon as Major Grant could get his horse, which was not for some time, as it had been already shipped, he mounted and started in pursuit alone. After going about three miles he came up with two or three hundred of the mutineers, who lined the top of some rising ground and fired at, but luckily missed, him. Undeterred he galloped up to them, when they retreated into a house. He dismounted, rushed in, and shot three of them with his revolver, when they laid down their arms. It was a very fine act, for which he was given a C.B.

The mutineers were brought to Cairo and tried by court-martial, at which I acted as judge advocate general. Two of them were shot, and about forty were sentenced to terms of penal servitude varying from life to three years.

Severe examples were necessary in view of the fact that some of the black troops had mutinied a short time before, and further, that the newly raised Egyptian Army was about to be tried in a serious campaign.

It was not until September 1884 that the Home Government decided that an expedition up the Nile above Dongola had become a necessity, and at the beginning of that month Sir Garnet Wolseley arrived and assumed command. As my bad knee kept me at the base, it is outside the scope of these personal memoirs to describe the Nile Expedition with all its difficulties: the march across the desert, the battle of Abu Klea, where General Herbert Stewart and Colonel Burnaby met their end; the battle of Kirbehan, when General Earle was killed; Sir Charles Wilson's and Lord Charles Beresford's action at Metemmeh in February 1885. It is sad to reflect that these glorious efforts were just too late, for on the 4th February 1885 Lord Wolseley had received almost certain news that Khartoum had fallen, and later that Gordon had been killed.

When I broke down I was given sedentary work in the Egyptian War Office, but as the Adjutant-General (Sir Thomas Fraser) departed up the Nile I was appointed to act for him; and later, when the Surveyor-General, Watson Pasha,[3] was appointed "Acting *Sirdar*" on the departure of Sir Evelyn Wood and Brigadier-General Grenfell up the Nile, I stepped into his shoes. This proved a responsible and deeply interesting work.

The nomenclature "Surveyor-General" is distinctly misleading, and it was not until I got into the department myself that I realised that its duties were not confined to land surveys, mapping, etc., but that it combined all supply departments under one head. It was the quartermaster-general, the master-general of the ordnance, and the director of the army service corps, all rolled into one, including factories and arsenals. I merely dropped into charge of this important office by virtue of my being the senior officer in it at the time of Watson Pasha's departure, and not through any merit of my own.

It was, however, a big job—feeding and supplying the Egyptian troops with all the requisites for carrying on war up the Nile, down at Suakin, and through the Delta—and I threw my-

---

3. Colonel Sir Charles M. Watson, R.E.

self into it, I think successfully, for later on in the spring of 1885, when I was offered command of a company of Mounted Infantry forming for a second campaign at Suakin, I was refused by the *Sirdar* on the grounds that I did two men's work and could not be spared. It was difficult for me to swallow that, but it was better than being told that the sooner I cleared out the better, so I smiled and said, "Thank you, sir." It had been a bitter disappointment that I could not get to the front myself, but I was really in a far more important position, even though kept at the base. By the middle of February we had pretty undeniable information that Gordon had been killed, and it was then that the withdrawal of Lord Wolseley's expedition was decided on.

But the power of Osman Digna in the Eastern Sudan was still unbroken, and before the railway, which it had been decided should connect Suakin with Berber, could be constructed that ex-slave-dealer had to be dealt with. The British Government accordingly determined to place Sir Gerald Graham in command of the Suakin Field Force. This force was quite a large one.[4]

The 9th Bengal Cavalry was commanded by Colonel A. P. Palmer, a popular and fine leader, whose adjutant-general I was to be seventeen years later, when he, as General Sir A. Power-Palmer, was commander-in-chief in India.

Special preparations for water had to be made before the force could move: local water was mostly unfit for humans, so condensing ships had to be provided, and the water thus obtained conveyed in trains to the force, which was mainly round Suakin,

---

4. Cavalry Brigade: two squadrons 5th Lancers, two squadrons 20th Hussars; battalion of Mounted Infantry; three batteries of artillery;
Brigade of Guards: 3rd Grenadiers, 1st Coldstreams, 2nd Scots; under Sir Lyon Fremantle (later on Governor of Malta.)
Brigade of Infantry: 2nd East Surreys, 1st Shropshire Light Infantry, 1st Berkshires, a battalion of marines; under Sir John McNeill. Major-General Sir George Greaves was chief of staff.
An Indian Mixed Brigade: 9th Bengal Cavalry, 15th Sikhs, 17th Bengal Lancers, 28th Bombay Infantry, one company Madras Sappers; under Brigadier-General J. Hudson.
One battery and one battalion from New South Wales.

and on camels to every *zeriba* and post established inland.

All was ready by the 19th March, and on that day, and the following, actions round Hashin (seven miles from Suakin) took place, and a post was established at Hashin, and held by the 2nd East Surrey Regiment. This post would guard the right flank of a force moving on Tamai, some fifteen miles from Suakin, where Osman Digna's main concentration was.

On the 22nd March Sir John McNeill was sent out to establish a post about half-way to Tamai. It was a difficult operation owing to the dense bush. The troops with him were one squadron 5th Lancers, the Berkshire (66th) Regiment and the battalion of Royal Marines, one field company Royal Engineers, and in addition the Indian Brigade. This latter was to return to Suakin, leaving British battalions to hold the *zeriba*.

When the *zeribas* were nearly completed and the troops in considerable disorder, some working, others eating their dinners, a horde of some five thousand Hadendowas rushed out of the dense bush, which was only separated from the *zeribas* by a diminutive open space. A desperate and thrilling fight ensued in which, if any could be singled out where so many did well, the Berkshires especially distinguished themselves. The fight only lasted twenty minutes, but our casualties in that short time were nearly 500, of which 150 were killed; and it was estimated that the Arabs killed were 1,500, for 1,100 were actually found and buried during the next couple of days. It is here that I come into the story. I had not been allowed to accept command of a company of Mounted Infantry, but early in March a vacancy had occurred, owing to the death of the popular Adjutant "Middy Wells." Major E. Hutton,[5] who was the staff officer in Cairo, responsible for organising and maintaining the Mounted Infantry, again applied for my services, and this time the *Sirdar* came to the conclusion that I was not indispensable— *i.e.* he had got to know me better.

I duly joined and took over the adjutancy of the Mounted Infantry, and, after the affair at McNeill's *zeriba*, was sent off with

5. The late Lieutenant-General Sir Edward Hutton.

two companies Mounted Infantry to accompany two companies of the Camel Corps, the latter under Major James, Scots Greys (the father of the subject of Millais's famous picture "Bubbles"), with orders to bury the dead Arabs lying in the bush round McNeill's *zeriba*; he, being able to carry the necessary tools, was to do the actual burying, whilst the Mounted Infantry were to form a screening force.

The bush in places was very thick, but there were open spaces. My plan was to form, on a semicircle about a quarter to half a mile beyond the burying party, a line of small groups of four men each, separated by a hundred yards. Behind them were four small local reserves under officers, and I kept a section under my own hand about the centre. If any part of the line was attacked, its own local reserve was to reinforce at once, and I would use my own discretion about employing my own reserve.

It was a deeply interesting and rather exciting day, with the object-lesson as to how large numbers could creep up unseen in that difficult country fresh in the minds of all. Beyond an occasional shot all went well until, in the early afternoon, heavy firing took place. I only had a few hundred yards to go, but although I galloped up with my reserve, as fast as the bush would let me, by the time I had got to the place where the firing had proceeded from, there was no one to be seen, neither friend nor foe, and the ground there was comparatively open.

At last I saw a solitary mounted figure riding towards me. It proved to be Sergeant Wallace, who was in charge of the group in that portion of the line. All he could tell me was the sad tale that the enemy had fired a few shots, which had been returned with interest, hence the noise, and that a sudden panic had set in and he found himself alone. So, filling up the gap with my own reserve, I spent the rest of the day, until we fell back in the evening, sharpening up my tongue for the interview with the panic-stricken men.

Beyond remarking that none of them were shot, I shall leave the matter alone. I have merely told the story as an astounding and, thank Heaven, unique experience. I tried unsuccessfully to getWallace a commission for his coolness. I have not yet told the curious part of this story. I recognised Sergeant Wallace as having been a subaltern in my own regiment when I joined it nine years previously. He was always a cheerful, good fellow, but had retired, and getting bored with civil life had enlisted, and here he was, a real good, loyal non-commissioned officer. He never presumed on the fact that he had been my senior officer, though I more than once referred to it.

Early in April General Graham moved on Tamai, but the enemy were not prepared to oppose him and retired into the hills. It being evident that Osman Digna's force had dispersed there was no object in keeping out troops in that direction in view of the difficulties of supplies, especially water, and the dangers of the daily convoys, so all, including those at McNeill's *zeriba*, were withdrawn, and the General fixed his attention on carrying out his further instructions, namely, the construction of a railway from Suakin to Berber, *via* Handoub, Otao, and Tambouk.

This involved several minor operations, during which I spent a good deal of time with Mounted Infantry at Handoub and Otao, mostly in escorting convoys, but also in two or three interesting small actions. This battalion of Mounted Infantry, for variety of corps composing it, was then, and I think still remains, unique in the annals of the British army.

It was commanded by Lieutenant-Colonel H. F. Grant of the 4th Hussars, the officer whose gallant behaviour, in the face of the mutiny of the Turkish battalion at Assiout the previous year, I have already described. Under him were officers and men of almost every branch of the service—Cavalry, Engineers, Guardsmen, Infantry, and Marines, proving that "Horse Marines" are a possibility. There were actually representatives from thirty-five different units.

The sergeant-major (Gregory) was a cavalryman. The quartermaster was a Highlander, who rose to be Governor of Koomassie and then of East Africa, where he died in 1905 as Sir Donald Stewart, K.C.M.G., generally called "Donny," a most amusing, somewhat indolent, but capable person. He was the son of the well-known General Sir Donald Stewart, who had been commander-in-chief in India and was then Governor of Chelsea Hospital. Incidentally he was godfather to my future wife, then aged four, whom I did not meet till many years later.

Since our head-quarters were always on the sea there was no difficulty about supplies, and the idea of economy never entered the mess president's head. The best of everything and hang the expense was the motto, and, being an improvised corps with little time for accounts, at the end of each month the total expenditure was divided up equally.

There was, therefore, no inducement for economy, and, being a very thirsty climate, the consumption was very large, especially of champagne, with the result that jaundice became prevalent. One after another went down, and when we embarked to return to Egypt in the middle of May, there were some very yellow faces on board, and my poor colonel was the most sorry being I have ever seen.

Before cutting myself adrift from Suakin I will say a word about the railway. What impressed one with the serious intentions of the Government and the probability of a long campaign was the daily vision of numbers of ships landing immense quantities of railway plant, and amongst the latter much rolling stock, all labelled in large letters "Berber and Suakin Railway."

Whether this was camouflage, or whether the British Government, of which Mr. Gladstone was the head, ever seriously intended to push the railway through, I am still in doubt. The making of the railway was a civil concern, although controlled by the G.O.C. Lucas & Aird were the contractors, and it was up to them to provide all plant and workmen. The latter were British navvies, thousands of them, sent out in normal corduroys as worn in England. It was a curious and sad sight to see these poor fellows working away in a tropical sun, mostly in small caps, and none with anything more sun-resisting than a billy-cock hat, each of them carrying the familiar straw basket and the tin can of beer.

Naturally the climate produced an appalling thirst, resulting in drunkenness and insubordination, to such an extent that at one time they had to be kept on board ship, watched by a gunboat. In spite of all this, the railway progressed at a commendable rate, and was completed to Otao, a distance of twenty-five miles, about the third week in April. It is sad to reflect that all this work and expense were to be thrown away on the abandonment of the railway scheme when the Suakin Field Force was withdrawn.

On arrival in Cairo I returned to my old flat, which I shared with Gerry Portal. He and Claude Macdonald were attached to Sir Evelyn Baring's Embassy, and both especial friends of mine.[6]

On the disbanding of the Mounted Infantry Battalion I resumed my duties as surveyor-general of the Egyptian army.

In consequence of orders from home in July 1885 for the evacuation of the Sudan, our horns had been drawn in, on the Red Sea littoral, to the defence of Suakin itself, and Haifa had been selected as our most advanced post up the Nile. Sir Francis Grenfell was appointed to command our Frontier Field Force. Suakin was garrisoned by Indian troops and placed under General Hudson; whilst, on the departure of Lord Wolseley, General Sir Frederick Stephenson became commander-in-chief in Egypt, which included both the above commands.

Some amusement was caused when, Sir Francis having been called on to report on the nature of the water at Assouan, was credited with the following telegraphic reply:

From G.O.C. Frontier Force to C.-in-C, Egypt. I have every reason to believe the water is excellent, but it tastes strongly of whisky towards evening.

I continued my arduous, but interesting, duties for the remainder of the year (1885), but found time for polo and racing and a good deal of enjoyment.

---

6. Portal became Sir Gerald, and died Jan. 1894 from fever caught in Abyssinia. Macdonald of the Highland Light Infantry became Colonel Sir Claude, and as an intrepid Minister Plenipotentiary became famous when our Legation in Pekin was besieged in 1900.

Sir Evelyn Wood had again taken up his duties of *Sirdar* on the breaking up of the Nile Expeditionary Force, and he agreed with me that there was every chance of my being able to get away the following spring to read for the Staff College, which I had been unable to do since I joined the Egyptian army in January 1884.

C. M. Watson Pasha, who had been acting *Sirdar* and was the real Surveyor-General, had gone to Suakin as Governor of the Red Sea littoral. In December I found it necessary to proceed up the Nile to inspect the depots on the lines of communication, and, armed with two wooden cases full of plum-puddings for my friends, I started off on the 18th, after a very delightful farewell dinner at the Club the night before.

The train could only take one to Assiout. Mules, and then river-boats, were the means of conveyance. Although slow, the journey was interesting, as it gave one an opportunity of seeing the wonders of the Nile; and they are wonders.

I reached Assouan on the 23rd December. A short railway of six miles, round the cataract, took me to Shellal, where I again had recourse to the river.

Christmas Day saw me off Korosko, and Wady Haifa, 550 miles from Cairo, was reached next day.

It may be wondered why I was in such a hurry, so I will be honest and say.

For some time the Dervishes up the Nile had become more and more aggressive; they had established themselves on both sides of the river, but their stronghold was the village of Ginniss, on the east bank of the Nile, some 110 miles south of Wady Haifa, in view of our outposts, which were entrenched at Fort Kosheh on the east bank, and Borrow's *zeriba* on the west bank. The Cameron Highlanders were garrisoning the former, and the 9th Sudanese Battalion the latter. Some 550 yards south of Kosheh was a conspicuous rock from which the Arabs used to snipe all day.

Raids had been made against this rock unsuccessfully, and in one of them Hunter,[7] who was always to the fore when there was a dangerous scrap on, had been very seriously wounded—a wound which has, unfortunately, troubled him ever since.

A little bird had whispered to me that Ginniss was to be dealt with. The commander-in-chief himself had left Cairo and gone up the Nile, and it seemed a pity that I should not personally see that the wherewithal for taking the field, which had been sent up by the Surveyor-General's Department, had really reached its destination. I had friends at all the posts along the Nile who, whilst welcoming me, hinted at "vultures flying to the carcase," and made other well-meant but pointed insinuations.

Sealing their mouths with a present of a Christmas pudding, I proceeded on my way. From Haifa, to avoid several cataracts, there was another length of railway of eighty-seven miles, ending at Akasheh, and I made the journey in the same train as the commander-in-chief, Sir F. Stephenson, and Staff. Each station was a fortified post, *i.e.* Sarras, Mohrat Wells, Ambigol Wells, Tangur—all full of interest, and from the train there were fine views of the several cataracts.

General Grenfell and his Staff were at Akasheh, and he exercised his humour pitilessly on my selecting that time for inspecting, but I thickened my skin and the shafts did not penetrate; it ended in his ordering me to drop my inspections as surveyor-general for the moment, and act as staff officer to the Egyptian Mounted Troops. So, obtaining a horse, I rode on next day to Kosheh Fort, about twenty-five miles.

The firing from the rock was heavy when I got there, and was returned from the fort, in which three casualties occurred as I arrived.

Later on I had an opportunity of visiting the rock; it was like a sheet of lead from our bullets. But what struck me most was the extraordinary bad shooting of the Arabs, for the rock looked straight into the fort, where every movement could be seen, and yet the casualties in it had only been some forty-five in the month.

It was whilst here that I had an amusing experience of the

7. Later General Sir A. Hunter.

sang-froid of Greek traders. On the banks of the river, outside the fort, some of these enterprising people had established a store, out of direct view of the enemy but not covered from their fire. I paid them a visit to obtain a few odds and ends, and amongst other things I asked for a pot of jam. Just as the man was in the act of taking the pot I had selected off the shelf a bullet smashed it, and, without turning a hair, he put it on one side, merely muttering "Damaged," and gave me another.

On the 29th December a force[8] was collected half a mile north of Kosheh, and bivouacked ready for a move against the Dervishes next day.

That night I slept under a gun of an Egyptian battery alongside an old and distinguished friend.[9] He was married, and asked me, in the event of anything happening to him next day, if I would carry out certain instructions with regard to his wife. I sleepily said, "All right, old chap," whereupon he asked me what he could for me under similar circumstances, and was much amused when I grunted out that, being the youngest son of a family of fifteen, fourteen of whom were still hale and hearty, it was unlikely that anything could happen to me, and the question was not worth discussing.

The rough sketch of the next day's fight gives a fair idea of the positions taken up and the subsequent movements. Before attacking, the General's plan was to push troops round to such a position as would enable them to cut off the enemy should they attempt to bolt up the river bank.

For this purpose the 1st Brigade, under General William Butler, and the 20th Hussars were started off at 5 a.m. At 5.20 the 2nd Brigade, under Colonel Huyshe, who had successfully commanded the Berkshires at McNeill's *zeriba* in the spring, was set in motion direct on Ginniss, whilst the Cameron Highlanders with a Sudanese battalion started at the same time from Kosheh Fort direct on Ginniss.

I, with the Egyptian cavalry, was to watch, in case the Arabs

---

8. The gunboat *Lotus,* 20th Hussars, Mounted Infantry, Egyptian Camel Corps, Egyptian Cavalry, 1st Brigade, 2nd Brigade, Camerons and Sudanese.
9. Now General Sir Joceline Wodehouse, G.C.B., etc.

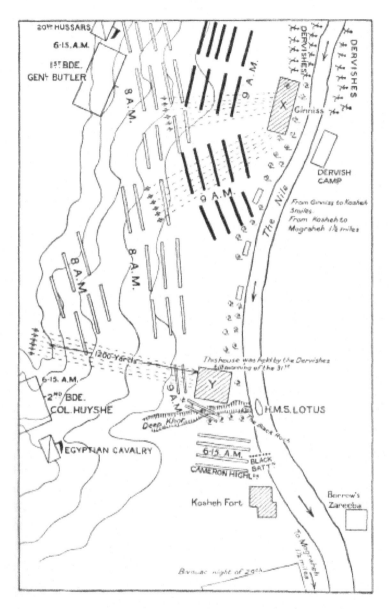

SKETCH OF GINNISS, 30TH DECEMBER, 1885

tried to escape into the desert eastwards. All this was before day-break. The batteries were placed as shown in the sketch, moving into the closer positions by 8 a.m. The ground was favourable to our movements.

"X" and "Y" show where the Dervishes were in force. The houses had been loopholed, and were manned as we advanced. I suppose my cavalry were conspicuous, for when the action commenced by the advance of the two brigades and the troops from Fort Kosheh we found ourselves under a heavy fire, and had to move over a hill.

The Camerons and Sudanese moved steadily on in extended order, clearing the small houses along the bank, but found block "Y" rather too much for them; one house in that block actually holding out until next day.

However, the main Arab body was in Ginniss itself, at "X," and at 8 a.m. both brigades were drawing in on them rapidly, pouring in volleys whilst the guns belched forth shells, which went through the mud walls like bullets through paper targets. It was about this time that the Dervishes essayed a charge, but although they got into the Egyptian Camel Corps and the 3rd Battalion of Egyptians, they could make no real headway and were soon in full flight to the south.

From the high ground where I was, one could see everything, and it was an extremely pretty sight. All the red [10]coats along the line of the hills closing in gradually on the river; our field batter-ies, Kosheh Fort, Borrow's *zeriba*, and the gunboat *Lotus* blazing away like anything; and the Dervishes skirmishing about all over the low ground on both sides of the river, and firing from the houses, with their Emirs on horseback and numbers of banner-carriers moving about amongst them; and then the finale, when the Dervishes, estimated at seven thousand, fled across the open up the river bank, and we watching eagerly for the pursuit —but none took place, and the reason I have yet to learn.

Later on, but too late, all mounted troops, including the Egyptian Camel Corps and Cavalry, were sent to Amarar, where

---

10. The last time British troops wore red in action.

we slept, and next night, New Year's Eve, we moved on to Abri, which was only ten miles from Ginniss.

That night a most unexpected order arrived for me to take command of a hundred and fifty men and go in pursuit. The force detailed was fifty of the 20th Hussars, twenty-five British Mounted Infantry, fifty Egyptian Camel Corps, and twenty-five Egyptian cavalry, and a support, under Captain Clementson, of twenty-five hussars and twenty-five mounted infantry marching one day in rear. I was fortunate in the officers actually with me—who were Legge, de Lisle, and Marriott. Legge was a very gallant officer killed in the attack on General Clements's camp at Nooitgedacht in the Boer War in 1900. De Lisle was to make a name for himself, especially in the great European War, and is now Lieutenant-General Sir H. de B. de Lisle. Marriott was a marine, a clever, refined, quiet, and most capable soldier who spoke Arabic like a native, and was my great stand-by for the next few days.

My orders were to endeavour to overtake the enemy, to co-operate with the gunboat *Lotus* in catching the large sailing *nuggers*, nine of which were known to be with the Arabs carrying their food supplies; and, finally, I was on no account to go beyond a place called Surda, some nineteen miles from Amarar.

I was given a small convoy of camels under Sergeant Sullivan fully loaded with four days' supplies. Realising that fully loaded camels would be left behind, as soon as we were clear of Abri, some six miles on our journey, I threw away half of every load. It was then 7.30 a.m. on New Year's Day, 1886, and leaving a small escort with them we proceeded on our way.

We soon began to come up with stragglers, but they were poor creatures mostly, and the last thing they wanted to do was to fight.

When off Nilwarti Island at 10.30 a.m. Lieutenant-Colonel G. E. Lloyd, the military officer working with me on the *Lotus,* signalled to me to say she had gone on a rock and would not be able to proceed before noon. At 11.45 we were abreast of Surda, having done some nineteen miles, and, posting lookouts, we halted an hour for dinners. My orders did not admit of my going beyond Surda, but as we had so far only captured one of the nine supply boats, I, regarding it as an occasion provided for in Field Service Regulations when orders should not be rigidly adhered to, decided to press on. The delight of the villagers at seeing us was very marked, especially when I bought two sheep and half an acre of *loobiyeh*[11] for the horses.

Having sent back two men to Amarar with a dispatch reporting my decision and asking for rations to be sent to Kohehmatto, we resumed our march. The two men *en route* to Amarar would meet Sergeant Sullivan in charge of the camels, and were given a note for that non-commissioned officer urging him to endeavour to reach Kohehmatto before midnight.

On reaching Eroe at 1.45 p.m. we heard that the Emir. Abdul Medjid, had marched the morning before with many men, heading for Kaibur, some sixty miles away, that forty men had left that morning for Syed Effendi, and that all *nuggers* were at that place, wind-bound.

The *Lotus* caught us up at 2.15, her bag so far being one *nugger*, and later a second fell to her, wind-bound on the far bank of the river.

On approaching Kohehmatto at 5.30 p.m., having completed some forty miles, the scouts reported that a mile and a half ahead there was a large *nugger* being towed by a number of men. I sent off de Lisle with ten mounted infantry and twelve camel corps to capture her. Quite a sharp little fight ensued, and I could just see that the *nugger* was in de Lisle's possession, for daylight was fading fast, when I decided to halt for a few hours at Kohehmatto to give men and horses a rest, and allow time for Sergeant Sullivan to catch us up.

As de Lisle did not appear I got rather anxious. From his last message I learned that he had boarded the *nugger* with some men, sent the remainder with horses and camels back to us (they had arrived), and that he was bringing the *nugger* back to where we were.

---

11. *Loobiyeh* (green fodder.)

To our delight Sergeant Sullivan appeared about 11 p.m.— a good performance, forty miles with baggage camels since 7 a.m. We filled up with rations and were just moving on again at midnight, for I could wait no longer for de Lisle, when we heard voices on the river and a *nugger* drifted in to the bank with de Lisle on board. He had had a lively experience. After he had captured the boat and pushed out into the stream, the current, instead of bringing him down, took him across to the other bank, along the top of which were the remnants of the Dervish army that had crossed over after the battle, marching south.

He could see them silhouetted against the sky, moving along in a continuous stream just above him, and was alarmed lest they should discover that the *nugger* was in the possession of British-ers. There he lay for some hours, but at last the boat drifted out into the current and, by the mercy of Providence, was carried right across to where we were.

At 7.25 a.m. on the 2nd January we reached Syed Effendi, where we captured two more *nuggers*, one laden with dates and the other with a good many rifles and revolvers. The *Lotus* was now abreast of us, and we struck across the desert for Absarat. When a mile beyond it, I heard that there was no chance of getting up with the fugitives, and, having collected all the nine *nuggers*, I decided to return to Syed Effendi and spend the night there. We had done some sixty miles in a little over twenty-four hours, and a rest was desirable.

We had not done badly in the food line, for every village had considerable stores of dried dates, and these proved to be most sustaining food for men and horses. The latter liked them im-mensely. On telling this lately to an inquiring mind, I was faced with the question:"Did the horses spit out the stones?" and had to confess that I had not noticed.

We took it easily going back, reaching Koyeh Camp on the 4th. There we found Sir William Butler, and part of his brigade, and it was not until then that I realised that we had done any-thing out of the way.

Sir William ordered me to form up the force, and addressing

us in flowery language told us that we had converted an undoubted success into a great victory. He ordered me to ride on
at once to Amarar to report myself to the commander-in-chief
and the *Sirdar*, Sir F. Grenfell. On arrival there I nearly got a bad
attack of wind in the head, for I was most warmly thanked by
Sir F. Stephenson (the most courteous and charming personality
I have ever served under), I was congratulated by Sir F. Grenfell, thanked in General Orders, and specially mentioned in dispatches; and all for the most enjoyable, dangerless, and delightful
trip I have ever made.

The fact that I had exceeded my instructions by going beyond Surda was overlooked, and only the successful results were
referred to.[12] Our casualties at Ginniss were not large; about a
hundred and fifty.

I at once started down the river, going slowly and carrying
out my inspections as surveyor-general. I had been granted the
long-deferred leave to start home at the end of February to
read for the Staff College examination which was to take place
on the 1st June and had a great deal to clear up before starting,
amongst other things to sell my horses. I sold one or two privately, and then the remaining ten by auction, for which I got
£395, nearly an average of £40 each —at that time an unprec-
edented high average.

My old friend Fenwick of the Dorsets—Fenwick Pasha as he
was known in his capacity as chief of police—came to see me
off, remarking, "I'm jolly glad to see you off, for I am tired of
riding second to you," which I took as an Irish compliment.

He was a much better horseman than I was, but it had happened that on three or four occasions I had ridden a winner
when he was on the favourite. I will mention one notable match
made between two Egyptian Pashas, lovers of horses. One of
them had a noted steeplechaser called Obeyon, and the other
matched one he had called Nadim against him—three miles

---

12. The D.S.O. was instituted about this time, and I was one of the first recipients
as a reward for the holiday trip I have described. I also got the 4th Class of the
Osmanieh.

over the steeplechase course. Fenwick rode Obeyon and I rode Nadim, and as we went out of the paddock the bookies were laying freely 11 to 1 on Obeyon. I, too, thought it was a certainty. We jumped almost side by side throughout the course, but in the run in Nadim won comfortably by two lengths.

It was the end of February when I got home, and there were barely two months to work, but I was splendidly crammed by Colonel James and Dr. Macguire, and passed tenth on the list, which was quite creditable. I had first met Colonel James as a captain of engineers the day of the battle of Ulundi.

The examination over, I returned to Egypt, arriving there on the 30th June, just at the time a new Sudanese battalion was to be raised in the Egyptian army, and I was immediately dispatched to Assouan to raise it.

The next six months were about as strenuous as any I have ever had, but in that time, helped by excellent officers, I think we managed to turn out a pretty smart battalion. They were at first raw recruits, and blacks are not very intelligent; but, by hammering away from squad drill to battalion drill and musketry, I think the results were satisfactory; so much so that by December the *Sirdar* considered the battalion efficient enough to take its place in the field, and we were moved to Wady Haifa and formed into brigade under Chermside Pasha.

On the 4th December, a Dervish force having established itself fourteen miles south of Haifa, we moved out to attack them, but the sight of us was too much for them: they fled, and we were only able to account for a few stragglers.

Shortly after this the *Sirdar*, Sir F. Grenfell, arrived and gave me permission to start on the 6th January in order that I might join the Staff College on the 1st February (1887).

I thus bade good-bye to the Egyptian army. Many of my friends said I was wrong, that my advancement in the Egyptian army was a certainty, whereas away from it, it was problematical; to which I replied that one could never become an up-to-date modern soldier in the prehistoric warfare to be met with in campaigns against the Dervishes. I am afraid this argument did not please some of my pals, especially as it was unanswerable. As a little present for a good boy, I was granted the 4th Class of the Medjidieh on departure.

CHAPTER 4

India

General E. Clive, a most considerate and delightful man, was commandant of the Staff College, and I enjoyed every minute of my two years there. I do not think we were taught as much as we might have been, but there was plenty of sport and not too much work.

I was elected Master of the Draghounds in succession to Captain Waldron (Jorrocks). I originated the Staff College coach, hiring one myself in the first instance, and horsing it with my hunters. It soon became popular, and with hired wheelers and students' hunters in the lead (of which I broke some thirty to harness myself) we attended all race meetings within hail, such as the Derby, Ascot, and Hawthorne Hill, and many social functions.

It was while I was there that we first decided to have our Staff College steeplechases under Grand National Hunt rules. This decision was forced on us, as the G.N.H. had just introduced the rule disqualifying riders as well as horses taking part in races not under their rules. Lord Wolseley honoured our meeting and dined at mess, making a pleasant speech.

When the two years' course was finished, I was anxious to get away to India as soon as possible for three reasons. (1) Because during my short stay in India I had been attracted by the life. (2) Because the standard of soldiering there was reputed high and practical. (3) Because I had spent all my ready money, and a bit more.

Accordingly, in December 1888, the examination being over, I was on the high-seas, and in January reported myself to the Head-quarters of the 95th at Jubbulpore. The commanding officer, Colonel McCleverty, sent me off to Saugor to take command of a detachment of two companies.

The nearest railway-station was seventy-five miles from Saugor, at a place called Kareli. There one hired a four-wheeled vehicle, like a menagerie cage, drawn by two camels; and, surrounded by baggage, with the servants on the roof, one moved forward, in full view of any wayfarers, at the rate of about five miles an hour. Every five miles fresh camels were hooked in. After fifteen hours, without a halt, feeling stiff and sore, and trying to believe one was not really a beast in a cage, one arrived at Saugor.

I found my cousin Charlie Jenkinson, G. E. Temple, two or three other young officers of the regiment, some sporting Gunners, the yellow-coated Bengal Cavalry (Skinner's Horse), and the 7th Bengal Infantry; the latter under Colonel Way, the father of three charming daughters, later to become Lady Bingley, Lady Willcocks, and Lady (George) Barrow.

Saugor is in the midst of jungles, and it was there that I killed my first tiger and stuck my first pig. Jenkinson, Temple, and I had a *shikari* called Moula, a real treasure. It went to his heart if his plans proved less successful than he had hoped; but he always had some unrehearsed and novel form of sport up his sleeve. He taught us how to shoot fish, as they lay basking in the clear sunlit water, with a bullet aimed about a foot below them. As the rifle went off, Moula plunged into the stream and, nine times out of ten, brought out the fish before it had time to recover from the stunning effect of the bullet striking the water.

A more exciting sport was fishing for *mugger* (the blunt-nosed alligator). A large iron, treble hook, like a boat grapple, was fastened on to a yard of telegraph wire attached to a rope. It was baited with the entrails of an animal, and suspended over a pronged stake driven into the bank, so that it hung a foot or two below the surface of a pool known to be the haunt of *mugger*.

84

At dusk the rope was made fast to a tree, the slack secured with a running knot, and next morning, if the rope was run out, it was evident that our friend the mugger had taken the bait and was sulking at the bottom of the pool. Then came the excitement of hauling him out, fighting, struggling, and lashing his tail, until settled with a bullet. The largest we ever got was not more than seven feet long, but he had a lot of curiosities inside him, including the bangle of a girl who had disappeared a short time before.

In most places the jungle was so thick that it was impossible to drive animals forward to the guns; they preferred breaking back through the line of coolies. So we invented what we called our "Monday Pop Band," after the popular concerts then being held in London at the Albert Hall. It consisted of 150 instruments, I was going to say musical instruments! but wish to avoid being misleading. There was every sort of noise-producing device—toy trombones, tambourines, trumpets, whistles—but the *pièce de résistance* (or, rather, which could not be resisted) was fifty policemen's rattles and twenty old guns for firing blank cartridges. The band was like "hell let loose." Sambur, pig, cheetah, tiger, panther, jackal, hyena, and every sort of jungle-haunting beast fled before it as though the devil was behind it.

Those were, indeed, days worth living.

One day, at a place called Piparia, a large boar had broken near a party of *grifs* (novices) who succeeded in wounding him, but in doing so broke all their spears and could not finish him off. One of them went for reinforcements, and the next party, of whom I was one, galloped back with him. The old boar was lying soothing his wounds in a pool on the edge of the jungle, and just as we came up he was attacked by some twenty-five *jungli kutta*, or wild jungle dogs. Boar and dogs disappeared into the thick scrub.

Getting up the coolies, we tried to beat them out, but only the *jungli kutta* bolted, and off we set to ride them down.

Now, the *jungli kutta* is in appearance something between a wolf and a dog, with a red-brown coat, and black tips to ears and tail; it is fast, and desperately difficult to spear, for, compared with a pig, it is small and turns and twists like a snipe. Luckily I was on the best pig-sticker I have ever owned, a white 14-2 Arab, Strathmore by name. The field got widely separated, and I found myself alone. I shall merely record results.

I finished eight or nine miles from camp, which was close to where the *jungli kutta* had been started, and got back when all had finished dinner. Davis, of the 1st Bengal Cavalry, had slain one dog, but all they got from me was a dissertation on the appalling country I had ridden over, and the waste of time in attempting to stick dogs. But my moment of triumph came two hours later, when coolies appeared carrying my bag—three *jungli kutta*! Their rich red skins with black points were the pride of my bungalow until they succumbed to moth.

The *jungli kutta* is not brave by himself, but a pack will take on any wild animal, and is the terror of the jungle. I came across many in the Central Provinces, where blank days were often traceable to the presence of a pack of these animals in the neighbourhood.

At the end of 1889 I went to Lucknow to complete my Staff College course by being attached for two months to each of the two branches of the service to which I did not belong—the cavalry and artillery. When the course was over I spent two months in the Central Provinces after tiger, with Furze[1] and Noel Fenwick. The latter killed the only tiger bagged—a fine specimen.

We had a very unpleasant experience with bees once, which was commemorated by Furze in some ribald verses, the last three of which I give:

He runs away at reckless speed,
Nor looks he where his path may lead,
Trips with his foot against a stone,
Falls headlong down and there lies prone.

Only one second there he lies—
Then up again and off he flies;

---

1. Lieutenant-General Sir William Furze, K.C.B., D.S.O.

But in that second one big bee
Has placed his sting in H. S. D.

One sting projects from out his ear;
I pull it out, and then I hear
From those mild lips of H. S. D.
Confusion take that blessed bee!

In June I rejoined my regiment at Jubbulpore. About this time I received a letter from General Sir William Galbraith, who said he had heard of me from Sir Evelyn Wood, and recommended me to go to Simla. I ran up there for ten days, and called on the military secretary, Colonel William Nicholson,[2] to ask what my chances of a staff appointment were, and whether a staff college certificate was of any value in India. The cynical reply I got was that much value was not set on the P.S.C. in India, but there was no reason why the holding of such a certificate should prevent my obtaining a staff appointment.

I had passed the higher standard in Hindustani two months previously, and was in every way qualified: I had, too, seen a good deal of active service for my age. However, I was not going to beg for a staff appointment, for I was happy with my regiment, and so returned to Jubbulpore.

I mention this to illustrate the fact that Staff College graduates were regarded with suspicion in India. None of the head-quarters staff, from the commander-in-chief downwards, had graduated, and the hostility to what was regarded at home as the magic P.S.C. was very marked. A year later, in September 1892, I attended the annual Staff College dinner at Simla. On that occasion we invited the commander-in-chief, the military member of the Viceroy's Council (Sir Henry Brackenbury), and some of the head-quarters staff who were not graduates of the college. Speeches followed, chiefly touching on the advantages of the Staff College. Lord Roberts's was kindly expressed, but far from encouraging; but that of the military member was distinctly sarcastic, and he concluded by saying that the one blot on his

---

2. Field-Marshal Lord Nicholson.

military career was that he had never obtained the staff college certificate, "but, when I look round this table, and see our noble commander-in-chief, our capable adjutant-general, our efficient quartermaster-general, and our astute military secretary, and I realise that they have risen to their present high positions without that certificate, it acts as a balm on my wounded feelings."

The effect of these speeches on the certificated hosts was like cold water down the spine. I went to bed that night confirmed in my belief that, so far, India had not grasped the necessity for specialising in staff training. At the same time I felt that the hostility came from the staff, rather than from Lord Roberts himself.

Between these two visits to Simla I acted, in November 1890, as brigade major to Colonel Waterfield, of the 45th Sikhs, at the big manoeuvres in the neighbourhood of Attock on the Indus, and Kohat; and in April 1891, as station staff officer to Colonel Colvin Birch, at Fyzabad. In October I returned to Jubbulpore until the end of the year, when I was given a temporary appointment as commandant of the chief's camp during the Cavalry Inspector-General's (Sir George Luck) cavalry manoeuvres, starting from Aligarh.

Sir George, rightly, had large ideas of the powers of cavalry, and recognised that they must be accustomed to long marches and surprise action, and during these manoeuvres immense distances were covered—as much as fifty miles in a day on one occasion. To me they were most instructive. I may mention that at that time shock action was much more likely than later on, when the necessity for efficiency in dismounted work became a principal part of the role of cavalry.

I there had my first insight into the magnificence of the commander-in-chief's camp, which reached its zenith in the final camp in Meerut, where Lady Roberts, Miss Roberts, and the remainder of his staff joined the commander-in-chief

Meanwhile the 95th were moving to Umballa, a two and a half months' march from Jubbulpore, and I was ordered to take over two companies which had been railed there in advance.

In April 1892 I was sent to Lucknow as D.A.A.G., and it was then I got to know Kitty Apthorp, of the Royal Irish, and Babington[3] of the 16th Lancers: these two were to become my life-long friends.

In April 1893 I was granted leave to England, and, as I passed through Bombay, saw the new commander-in-chief, Sir George White, and was fortunate enough to go home in the P. & O. *Rome,* which was conveying the ex-commander-in-chief, Lord Roberts, and his family to England for the last time.

I had heard of the disturbing effect the presence of a cat was supposed to exercise on Lord Roberts's nerves, and a convincing proof occurred during the voyage. One night, at dinner in a crowded saloon, he suddenly stood up and said he knew there was a cat about, and requested it might be removed. It was found at the opposite end of the saloon.

Whilst at home I saw that great horse Isinglass win the Derby, and Orme win the Eclipse Stakes, and the marriage of our present King. I also spent ten days on manoeuvres with Sir Evelyn Wood.

I was back again in Lucknow on the 15th December, and settled down in Kitty Apthorp's bungalow. Luckily this was a large one, for we did a good deal of entertaining, especially during race meetings, when, with all spare rooms filled, we might have a dozen tents pitched in the compound. Amongst our usual guests were Lord William Beresford, Jack Sherston, "Squash" Wynne, Willy Holmes, Sidney Hartwell, Colonel P. K. Beevor, and, on one occasion, the Maharajah of Cooch Behar.

Apthorp and I each had large studs, and ran many of our horses and ponies as partners—on the whole very successfully. On the 23rd February 1894, I acted as his best man, and glad as I was for him, it was a sad day for me, as it meant an end to the happy days we had lived as chums in the same bungalow.

The only experience worth recording at this time is an outbreak of cholera in the 30th (East Lancashire Regiment), in Ju-

3. Major-General Sir J. Babington, K.C.B., K.C.M.G., who distinguished himself in the Great War.

ly—the middle of the wet season, but, luckily, during a break in the rains. All the senior officers, excepting the commanding officer, were on leave, and I was the only staff officer in Lucknow.

The way to stamp cholera out of a corps is for it to go into camp, and keep moving from camp to camp. A most important person is the quartermaster, and he, in this case, was one of the first victims. However, a young officer named Mears proved equal to the occasion, and did remarkably well. I have never been so impressed with the initiative of the British subaltern—everything fell on them. By changing camps most days, including a march of five to six miles, the scourge disappeared, but not until the deaths approached one hundred.

I was always in camp shortly after daylight, starting from Lucknow at dawn and galloping out so as to report the progress of the disease to my General. The battalion moved in a circle, camping within a few miles of the cantonment. The situation was saved by the devotion of an army doctor.[4]

I left Lucknow on the 27th October, and took up the appointment of A.A.G. at Umballa. My D.A.A.G. was Major Hickman, of the Indian army, who was, I regret to say, killed in the Khyber Pass two years later. The district commander was Brigadier-General Pretyman, but he left in the spring of the following year.

My new chief was General Penn Symons, of the 24th Regiment, whom I had first met in the Zulu War: a fine rider and good shot, as hard as nails, and a remarkably skilful and up-to-date soldier—killed, alas! at Talana in the Boer War.

I had only been there five months when affairs in Chitral began to get serious. The garrison was cut off and besieged. My late chief, Sir Robert Low, was put in command of a force with orders to carry out the relief. This meant stiff fighting: first taking the Malakand Pass, held by twelve thousand tribesmen, then forcing the passage of the Swat and Panjkora Rivers. It was considered expedient to form a reserve brigade under Major-General Channer, V.C., and on the 31st March 1895 I was ordered

---

4. Now Major-General Sir H. N. Thompson, K.C.M.G.

to join him as D.A.A. and Q.M.G. at Rawal Pindi, where this brigade was forming. Colonel Ian Hamilton was military secretary at army headquarters, and I saw his friendly hand in this welcome order. Whilst at Rawal Pindi, General North Crealock, who had commanded the 95th in 1882 in Egypt, arrived to take command of the district; but he, alas! died a fortnight after his arrival from ptomaine poisoning.

On the 22nd April my General, myself, and the *aide-de-camp* went to the front in the Swat Valley, over the Malakand Pass, which had been taken after heavy fighting, and got back the next night; but otherwise we saw nothing of the campaign, which only lasted four months. We had hard work training the brigade during unpleasantly hot weather. The brigade was broken up in August, and I resumed my duties as A.A.G. at Umballa.

The great event of the year for me was the winning of the Army Cup at Lucknow by my horse Shannon on the 26th November. Hubert Gough was my jockey. He was a fine jockey then, as he was a fine general in after-life. At one meeting he rode six winners for me in two days. Shannon was one of the raw ponies I had bought on my return from England in 1893. He had won several maiden races in 1894, and ran second in the Army Cup that year. I had paid 300 *rupees* for him, and in the spring of 1894 was offered and refused 20,000 (about £1,400) for him.

It was always a maxim of mine that to be successful in the upper ranks of the service an intimate experience of regimental work was essential. So, in April 1896, I resigned the A.A.G.-ship of the Umballa District, and rejoined my regiment, of which the head-quarters and one half were at Sitapur, and the other half at Benares. It was to the latter place I went, a hot spot—*punkahs* were necessary night and day, except from the middle of November to the end of January. Enteric was bad, and we lost a lot of men.

In January 1897 we moved to Bareilly, where the whole battalion was again united under Lieutenant-Colonel Dowse.

CHAPTER 5

Tirah Campaign, 1897–1898

Bareilly was a wonderful place for sport of all sorts—pig-sticking and shooting, with local racing and facilities for attending meetings elsewhere. On the whole, I was marvellously successful on the Indian Turf from 1889 to 1898. My stud varied in size, but was always large, consisting of racing, polo, pig-sticking, harness ponies and horses—generally over twenty—and for a considerable period I was the proud possessor of thirty-two animals; and when I say that they kept themselves, as well as me and my guests, I think I have said enough to show that the number of races I won was not inconsiderable.

But the most successful event in the way of sport in which I took a leading part occurred in May 1897.

The General Officer commanding Bengal was Lieutenant-General Sir Baker Russell. He had been given permission by the Prime Minister of Nepal to shoot in lower Nepal, across the Suarda River, not far from Philibit, the very ground which had been shot over by His late Majesty King Edward VII as Prince of Wales, some twenty years before. The condition imposed was that he might shoot for a month but would be limited to six tigers; but, on Sir Baker's pointing out that he could not spare time for more than a fortnight, the Nepal Durbar relented and gave permission for an unrestricted shoot for that period. It really was a great shoot, wonderfully organised by Major Ellis, R.E.

The heat being intense, Sir Baker decided not to go himself, and the party was reduced to five guns. Our total bag was twenty-three tigers, four leopards, thirty deer, consisting of sambur, gond, parah, and cheetah, and a very large quantity of birds, such as florican, partridges (black and grey), and jungle-fowl. Truly a wonderful bag. I was myself fortunate enough to kill nine tigers.

There is an incident, however, which is interesting enough to record.

One day I was passing an extra thick bit of jungle, mounted on an elephant. An old native was walking by my side. Suddenly he shook my foot to attract attention, and pointing to the dense jungle said: "That, *Sahib*, is the thicket in which we hid the cages, which brought out the tigers for the *Shahzada Sahib* [the Prince of Wales] some twenty years ago." Little did this simple individual think that he was giving away a State secret.

On the 21st June I started home on leave, and as the train was not due until 4 a.m. I slept in the station. My astonishment can be imagined when, half-awake, I came out on to the platform to get into the train, to find not only several of my brother officers there to see me off, but also the drums (headed by the regimental ram) which played "Auld Lang Syne" as the train steamed out. It was explained to me that the band would have been there too, had they not been away in the hills. I felt very proud, though I doubt if the passengers in the train were equally pleased.

Just after arriving in England, hearing that actual operations up the Nile were about to take place, I wired offering my services to the *Sirdar* (Kitchener), but he could not find room for me, though he did the following year.

As I had been granted eight months' leave, I intended to enjoy a winter's hunting, and bought four fine hunters at the Dublin Horse Show in August. I had only just got them over to England when, on the 5th October, I saw in the evening papers that there was trouble brewing in Tirah, and that my battalion had been ordered across the frontier against the Afridis. I quickly put a war kit together and dashed up to London to secure a passage in the P. & O., but was told that every cabin was taken.

However, I left by the Indian mail train by 9 p.m. on the 8th, squeezed myself into the P. & O. express at Calais, arrived at Brindisi on the 10th and went straight on board the *Caledonia*. When out at sea I confessed to the purser that I was a stowaway, having no ticket. He was a good fellow and found me a berth, and all was well.

Before leaving England I telegraphed to my friend Kitty Apthorp at Lucknow to send me a pony and *syce* to Kohat.

Amongst the passengers was Lieutenant F. Maurice, of my regiment (now Sir Frederick Maurice), and together we journeyed to the front. The *Caledonia* reached Bombay on the 23rd October (1897), and we went off by the night mail to Rawal Pindi, arriving there on the 28th. Thence by pony and *tonga* until, on the 27th October, we reached the advanced base at Shingwari about midday, and found Leveson Gower and Hallowes of my regiment left behind with a detachment.

So far I have said nothing as to why an expedition to the wild fastnesses of Tirah had become necessary, and I confess the true reason is not easy to give.[1] For years the frontier had been in a ferment which had been increased during the past two by sundry forward movements of our troops, thus firing the natural love of the tribes there for fighting and raiding; in August the Afridis had attacked our forts in the Khyber, and shortly after our posts on the Samana range had been fiercely assailed by the Orakzais.

These aggressive acts appear to have been the final straw which decided the Indian Government to send a large force under General Sir William Lockhart against the Afridis. I draw attention to the map of Tirah, and especially to the short summary of the campaign, and will confine myself to my personal story.

Having arranged my kit I started up the pass to Chagru Kotal, seven miles—a very steep rise of 2,500 feet. There we saw Dargai, the awful place our troops had stormed on the 18th, and

---

1. For a graphic and interesting account of the cause of the campaign I recommend a little book from the Derbyshire Regiment campaign series by Captain A. K. Slessor

retaken on the 20th. Found Dobbie, 30th Punjab Infantry, on the Kotal, slept there, 28th, started at daybreak down a dangerous road, and met sundry escorts; then heard firing and saw Northamptons and 36th Sikhs taking a high hill from which Khangarbur Camp had been heavily sniped with considerable loss to us. Troops had advanced from Kharappa followed by baggage; I rode on and found the camp and Generals Nicholson, Symons, Hart, V.C., etc. I got a warm greeting, and heard my Regiment was just going to advance to reconnoitre. As a matter of fact, the commander-in-chief, Sir William Lockhart, was holding a conference, and it was into this I had blundered. From what I overheard I gathered the opinions expressed differed considerably, and that one general (not the commander-in-chief) was a good deal out of temper.

So far I was satisfied with my performance, from the Naval and Military Club to the foot of the Sampagha Pass in under nineteen days.

General Penn Symons, seeing my pony was cooked, insisted on lending me a fresh horse, and I cantered on about a mile to find the Battalion, formed up in column, ready to advance. I reported myself to Lieutenant-Colonel Dowse, who was surprised to see me and cordially greeted me, as did the other officers, and especially my old friend Harold Wylly. I was ordered to take command of half the Battalion and to seize certain ground. Off we went, crossing a deep *nullah*, for about two miles, and occupied ground from which we could see all roads and *nullahs* to the Sampagha Pass, about two miles above us; the enemy kept up steady fire and made some accurate shooting. We soon retired and the enemy followed; I was ordered to throw out four piquets and make *sangars*. The sniping was heavy; Colonel Sage (Gurkhas) was wounded, also one of our men and two or three more men of other corps.

At sundown we were relieved by the Devonshire Regiment and fell back on our Camp Gumpaki. We had a sort of meal about 8.30 p.m., bucked, and dumped down for the night.

I awoke at 3 a.m. on the 29th and was sent in advance of the army with four companies in the dark to clear hills, for an artillery position, at the point of the bayonet. The company commanders were Menzies, Wylly, Pennell, and Bowman. We made a very steady advance, and when within fifty yards of a *sangar* I saw heads showing over it, and calling men to follow led a charge. The enemy bolted. Leaving half a company to hold the hill, we swept on and occupied another ridge, 300 yards on, without opposition.

Shortly after it got light, the Devons advanced on our right and took the village of Karema. There was a good deal of firing, but not many of the enemy visible. As daylight was breaking bullets began to come in thick, when quite unconcerned our Brigade Commander Major-General Sir R. Hart, V.C., walked up. We were lying down in the position we had secured, but I had to stand up to salute him. He gave me a warm greeting, hooked his arm in mine, and insisted on walking up and down discussing the art of war, in spite of my protests that we provided the sole mark for the enemy to aim at. It was some time before I could manoeuvre him into a position of safety. Why neither of us was hit I do not know, but I came to the conclusion that a too brave general might not be a very pleasant companion. At 7.30 a.m. the guns occupied the position, but found it difficult to find any target to fire at.

The Gurkhas were advancing on our right and left. The other three brigades then passed up the *nullah* in front of us towards the pass.

About 8 a.m. General Gaselee's 2nd Brigade advanced, and the guns shelled the *sangars* on the Pass heavily, and at about 8.30 a.m. 200 of the enemy fell. Then the 2nd Brigade crossed the Pass, covered by batteries to their right rear and the batteries from in front of the Brown Hill. At noon we heard volleys and firing over the Pass; then all was quiet. We spent the rest of the day guarding the streams of transport stringing over the Sampagha Pass. At nightfall only about half of it was over, so we posted piquets and bivouacked where we were and had a cheery campfire— very necessary, as the cold was intense.

It was not until 4.30 p.m. the next day that the tail of the transport moved off and left us free to move behind it over the Pass seven miles to the Mastura Valley, which was to be the head-quarters of our brigade for some weeks. Some idea of the difficulties of supplying a large force in such a rugged country will be gained from the fact that it took our 20,000 pack animals forty hours of daylight to move seven miles. The ascent to the top of the Sampagha Pass was 3,000 feet, and single file was the broadest front possible, whilst moving after dark was too risky.

MAP OF TIRAH CAMPAIGN

Diary

31st October.—A quiet night. We were ordered to form a supporting brigade in attack on the Arhanga Pass, four miles off. Very little resistance, and we never left camp. But I was sent to raid villages towards the Bara Valley with the 2nd Derbyshire Regiment, and 2/1st Gurkhas, and a few cavalry. We only saw twenty-four of the enemy, and captured one hundred mule loads of grain, etc., and a few chickens. Got back at 8 p.m. Ice in morning.

1st November.—Getting camp straight, more raiding parties out. Pushing up transport to troops over the Arhanga. Reported that Sir William Lockhart has given out terms of peace to the Afridis. Very cold at nights, swarms of transport passing up. The main body is out five miles off just over Arhanga Pass. The enemy cut into an ammunition column, killed five men of the Queen's and looted ammunition four miles ahead. Our foraging parties fired on from two sides. I started coffee-shop for men.

2nd November.—Colonel Richardson,[1] 18th Bengal Lancers, and two squadrons joined camp. More foraging parties, escorts to road-making parties, and I had to post three companies on camp piquets. At night camp-fire, successful singing. General Hart dined. A little sniping. Ice every night.

3rd November.—Out in command of foraging party; fired at as we returned. About five hundred loads of grain got daily; vil-

---

1. Lieutenant-General Sir George Richardson, noted later as the leader of the Ulster army.

lages all full of it.

4th November.—Head-quarters and half the battalion marched to Sampagha. I went with the general officer commanding to look for place for piquet and to arrange how to raid villages to-morrow. Then went round all my companies to try to improve cover for men. Took J. Bowman's company out in afternoon to raid villages near camp; stayed too late, enemy crept up under trees and in the dark got within fifty yards of Bowman and self; luckily missed us, but shot a mule. We had to make undignified retreat, as we could not see them in the dark.

5th November.—Ordered out in command of a mixed force, about three hundred men, Gurkhas, Devons, and Derbys, to reconnoitre a fresh valley, taking six hundred animals to convey our looted forage back to camp. Very pretty day. Enemy rather truculent; a good deal of firing. We loaded and got all our mules back towards camp by 1.30. Retirement very pretty and well carried out. General Hart most complimentary about my dispositions. Being our Inkerman Day, I arranged a camp-fire and singsong at Bosanquet's piquet, with an issue of rum. Colonel Richardson and all officers 18th Bengal Lancers came.

I have an exhaustive diary, but shall only give extracts from it where incidents of sufficient interest occur:

The country was very rough and the enemy active and elusive. Sniping from a distance was their usual form of offence, except when we raided their villages for forage, as we did most days, when they were invariably most aggressive. They also were especially active in attacking convoys, and generally with casualties to ourselves. The weather was mostly bitterly cold—many degrees of frost at nights— and being without tents we were hard put to it for devices to keep ourselves warm.

We did our best to keep the men happy, and nightly singsongs round camp-fires were much in vogue—though the fires were apt to prove too attractive to wandering snipers. Our most interesting raiding party occurred on the 13th November, and we called it the battle of the Upper Mastura Valley. On this occasion I was sent in command of a foraging party to raid a village in the neighbourhood of Targhu and Kutah, some four miles away by the track up the Upper Mastura Valley.

The force consisted of two companies of the Devons, two of the Jhind Infantry, two of Gurkhas, four of my own Battalion, and a squadron of the 18th Bengal Lancers under Major G. A. Money and some five hundred mules. All went well on the way out. We piqueted all the hills and the far side of the village, and entered the village, which, excepting a few old men, women, and children, was quite empty. Not a sign of an enemy had we seen. We proceeded to load mules with forage in the village.

Then a few shots began to come in, in ever-increasing volume. Before long the hills all round, in front and on flanks, were crowded with hundreds of the tribesmen and a pitched battle commenced.

Soon it was reported that the mules were loaded, and I ordered the retirement. Immediately I saw masses of the enemy running along the crests of the hills to seize an important hilltop which absolutely commanded our road. Luckily I had the two Gurkha companies in reserve, and I sent them at top speed down a valley to seize this hill from the opposite side to that the enemy were advancing from.

It was a most exciting ten minutes. I could see both, the enemy and the Gurkhas. Which would get there first?

The latter won by a short head.

The tribesmen attacking us in front were now only some two hundred yards away. Major Money was knocked over by a Jezail bullet, and other casualties occurred. When we saw the Gurkhas had secured the hill we commenced falling back through the village, and then from position to position. The Jhind Infantry were my greatest anxiety, for being Sikhs they were full of bravery and regarded extending or falling back as derogatory to their dignity. There they remained in close order, firing hard, a grand target, refusing to budge.

At last, in despair, I sent Captain Herbert, R.A., who was act-

Mastura Valley, Scene of Action 13th November, 1897

THE PLACE WE HURLED THE MULES DOWN

ing as my staff officer for the day, to see what persuasion could do, telling him to bring the "Ginslings" (a name which stuck to them afterwards) back at all costs, and this he did successfully with considerable risk to himself.

It was at this time that Captain Bowman of the Derbyshires was severely wounded whilst standing up to hear what I was shouting to him from across a small valley; sundry other casualties also occurred. Although some of the enemy had rifles most of them had the long Jezail, not very accurate, and with a range of little over two hundred yards. And so we went on retiring over four or five miles of country, carefully guarding our flanks and disputing every yard of ground. It was nearly five hours before we got clear of the valley and the enemy gave up the chase.

As we approached our camp daylight was fast going and we were met by our gallant General. It was satisfactory to be able to report to him that we had achieved our object without any very large casualties, and further to receive his congratulations. Amongst the casualties the Jhind Infantry had had two men killed, and that night they commemorated their being "blooded" (for it was their first experience of war) by tossing their dead warriors in a blanket over a camp-fire. Money, luckily, had been struck by a bullet on his sword-belt, with a thick cummerbund underneath it, or he would have been killed. As it was, he was sufficiently recovered to dine with us, and also Herbert, Field, and Norman.

I had today a personal illustration of the hold blood feuds have over these wild tribesmen. When I entered the village a splendid old man came up to me and pointed out his own house, drawing attention to an enormous wooden stockade erected between it and the next house. Said the old man: "You, *Sahib*, are not my real enemy—my real enemy lives in that house on the far side of the stockade."

The next day we shifted our camp to escape the fleas, but found ourselves in a howling wilderness of pariahs! As someone remarked, he woke up in the morning and thought he was at the Crystal Palace dog show!

The 1st Division got orders to move on the 7th December down the Mastura Valley, whilst Head-quarters and the 2nd Division moved down the Bara Valley. On the 6th December the whole of the Bagh Valley was in flames, which indicated the farewell of the 2nd Division to that part of the country. In the evening Generals Symons and Hart attended our camp-fire sing-song.

My diary from 7th December to the 14th December, the date on which the two divisions met near Mamanai, will give an idea of our daily doings:

Diary continued

7th December.—Field Officer of the day, saw mess packed up, and joined G.O.C. at 10 a.m. as transport was leaving for new camp. The following force camped at Mishti Bazaar three miles off by 3 p.m.: 2nd Derby Regiment, No. 1 Mountain Battery Royal Artillery, 21st Madras Pioneers, one company Bengal Sappers and Miners, half a battalion Gurkhas, Malakhota Sappers. Entrenched our camp, and I put out piquets, a long round. Very cloudy, much warmer; looks like rain. Comfortable mess under large walnut-tree.

8th December.—Astir at 6 a.m., not light until 7 a.m. Alas, raining a light soft rain, but cold and raw. General Hart, with half the force, started at 7.30 a.m. over the Sangra Pass for new camp at Haidar Khel. Remainder of force, under General Symons, started at 8.15 a.m. by River Mastura. Bad road, constantly crossing river. I commanded advance guard. The roughest ground and deepest *nullahs* I have ever seen. At one place I fell down almost fifteen feet. We got to camp at 1 p.m. All transport in by 3 p.m.

Fine camping ground and splendid rich valley, highly cultivated and manured. Snow on all hills, fine trees; a sort of Scotch mist, cleared in evening, and we had a most comfortable lunch and mess under large walnut-tree with spreading roots for seats. Reconnaissance sent out at 2 p.m. to search for pass over the hills to north into Waran Valley, which they found. Orders issued for Colonel Yule to take transport under escort next day to camp

Hissar, five and a half miles. Fighting force to move over newly-found pass into Waran Valley and burn Ali Khel villages. Four companies Gurkhas, six Derbys, one Kohat Mountain Battery, No. 1 Mountain Battery R.A., six companies 21st Madras, six companies 30th P.I., Bengal Sappers and Miners. Such a glorious moonlight night. The ground all shimmering in the hoar-frost.

9th December.—Gurkhas off to seize the pass at 6 a.m. by moonlight, daylight at 7 a.m. We started at 8 p.m., other troops followed. We got to top of pass after steep climb ill. 9.30 and saw the Waran Valley below us full of villages; the people all making for the hills and driving off their cattle. Waited for guns and then moved on down a fair but rough path into valley. Gurkhas wheeled to left and went up valley to burn some villages at head. We supported and covered their right flank. The enemy soon opened fire on us; I had at first three companies, F, G, and D, the officers being Marshall,[7] Bosanquet, Mortimore, Maurice. Later Pye reinforced me with B Company.

We had great fun, firing and skirmishing. Afridis in small numbers, but wonderfully active. Gurkhas did splendid work, as did our men, and soon the valley was one huge bonfire. The 36th P.I., 21st Pioneers, and the Nabhas were burning, to our right, some very fine villages. Two batteries were in action to our rear. We covered retirement of Gurkhas, and in doing so had two men wounded. The guns were in position a mile to our rear. Firing at what? I don't know, as it was impossible to see for smoke. The force gradually fell back fighting and burning, and got on to road out of valley at 4 p.m. and into camp at 7 p.m. Luckily the moon showed us in over bad ground. Camp on River Mastura where that river is joined by the Waran.

We could see camp of 2nd Brigade at Haidar Khel as we emerged from Waran Valley. A *havildar* of the Nabha Infantry was killed, one wounded, and two other casualties. The force was well handled, but the enemy were very few. Camp in Mastura

---

7. Afterwards Lieutenant-General Sir W. Marshall, who succeeded Sir Stanley Maude in command in Mesopotamia.

riverbed. The Nabhas awfully pleased at having a *havildar* killed, their first blood. They burnt him and dried their blankets at the fire, which shows that they know how to make the best use of everything.

10th December.—Force started at 8 a.m. We marched at 9 a.m., river deep (above knees), crossed twice, men very wet; seven-mile march, threatening and dull day. Got camp settled by sundown, when it commenced to rain; drizzling night. We had arrived hours before baggage, and amused ourselves catching *chilwah* (small fish) in sacks. Others caught hill trout; some dynamited them.

11th December.—Woke early as usual; wet morning. At once started improving mess and covering it with a looted tent. Rained all day and snowed only a few feet above us. Hills all white. Parties improving Sapri Pass. The mess president (myself) had provided A1 food: pig's cheek, *pâté de foie gras*, Stilton and port; most comfortable mess in camp. Orders to cross pass tomorrow. Movement commenced two hours before daybreak. Mud awful. Pass difficult; expect to sleep by roadside.

12th December.—My expectations quite fulfilled; rain stopped at midnight, and the moon shone, and it froze. Troops commenced moving at 5 a.m. Language awful, as I lay snug under my blankets. We tried to start at 10.30 a.m., but pass was blocked, so some of us fell out and fished with ropes and bent pins—and, what is more, caught some fish, a good size, between a hill trout and a barbel. These fish are very green and easily captured. Heavy mist at top of pass, which was not very high; but road was, latterly, up a mountain torrent bed.

The hospital ponies kept breaking down, loads too heavy for them, and heavier from being wet. Densely wooded with holly, mistletoe, etc. Got to top of pass as it was getting dark. Two regiments and a half, and at least 2,500 animals, had not left camp. The descent was very rough; after two and a half miles in ever-increasing darkness we came on General Hart seated at the roadside by a roaring fire.

He ordered fires to be lit all along the road to light the transport which was to continue moving, a risky proceeding in my humble opinion in such an enemy's country, as for the next six miles the path ran along a narrow gorge through dense jungle. I was sent back to have all fires lit to top of pass—a trying job, as it was inky dark and the road crowded with transport. However, I stumbled along over stones and boulders, now wrenching one joint, now another.

At 9 p.m. I had lighted about a mile and a half, and the moon came out. All this time the transport had been halted and I ordered it forward. The moving animals looked very weird and picturesque, with the forest lit by huge bonfires and the moon throwing deep shadows. At 10 p.m. all transport on the pass had moved on, and I reported accordingly to the G.O.C., who was still sitting happily in his old place, with his orderly officer and no escort.

To tell the story of mules tumbling over rocks and down *khuds*, of *drabies*[8] lying huddled asleep around the fires, and of honking them on by telling them the enemy was coming, would take too long to relate. Luckily the officer in command on the top of the pass had ordered the tail of the convoys to halt and make themselves safe for the night. The G.O.C. was anxious about them, but had to give them up and go to camp, some four miles on at Kwaja Kidr, which I reached just before him, about 11.30.

Just before arriving some shots had been fired out of the jungle at our men, wounding one and breaking a rifle. We got a sort of dinner at 12.30 and lay down at 2 a.m. It was a cold night, frost, etc., and very damp, but huge fires kept us warm, and we slept sound till 5.30 a.m., when we commenced to stir for our next march. The camp was in a small opening in the river-bed, absolutely commanded, as was the whole length of road.

At 7.30 we started with drums playing. The morning was glorious, the scenery and the growth splendid, with snow on the hill-tops and a rapid stream down the centre of the pass. After

8. Mule-drivers.

three miles we arrived at Sapri Camp, where the valley opens out, and found the Devons, who had camped there, just moving on. As we were leaving our camp the enemy crowned the heights and poured in some shots, killing one mule. Five shots landed in the middle of a fire round which men were warming themselves. We halted for breakfast whilst the endless stream of transport pushed on.

The vegetation on the south side of the pass was much richer. Palms and maiden-hair ferns, and farther on rich cornfields. At 2 p.m. we were ordered on to Mamanai, five or six miles on, where General Symons and General Hammond with his brigade were already encamped. The 30th Punjab Infantry, following us, were fired at. We got to our new camp at sunset. The tail of the column came in at 10.30 p.m. The pass we had come down was a very lovely one, practically a mountain stream bed with high, continuous, overhanging hills on both sides, more like cliffs, densely wooded. The climate got distinctly warmer as we descended, and the valleys and lower slopes were covered with thorn jungle, amongst which we camped, within three-quarters of a mile of General Hammond's Brigade.

14th December.—Halted and watched the 2nd Division march into camp fighting a rear-guard action. The Afridis came within three-quarters of a mile of camp, and we watched them move over the hills into the Bazaar Valley. The 2nd Division had had a rough time of it, one hundred and fifty casualties in three days. Ours were only seven in the same period. Disturbed night from loose mules and wind.

In this way we reached Bara Fort on the 16th December, and on the 18th Jamrud Fort, from which Fort Maude was visible at the mouth of the Khyber Pass. We heard our next move would be up the Khyber or into the Bazaar Valley, and hoped for the latter. Our orders soon came, to the effect that Hart's Brigade was to clear the Bazaar Valley, the stronghold of the hardy Zakka Khels, and we started the 24th December in very light marching order, though I, as mess president, contrived to squeeze in beer and plum-puddings for Christmas dinners.

24th December.—Up at 6.30 a.m. Advance guard had started at same hour. Our battalion, on rear-guard, started at 9 a.m. Three miles to entrance to Khyber, level road. Got to camp at Abdurrahman Fort, seven and a quarter miles, at 3 p.m. 2nd Brigade behind us. Camp lay very prettily in Lala China Valley. Hills all round, piqueted well against snipers. Ali Masjid in full view two miles off.

25th. Christmas Day.—Got wire of greeting from our 1st Battalion just as we were starting at 9 a.m. in reply to ours sent late evening 23rd from Jamrud. Advance guard, with road-making party, had moved off at 7 a.m., three miles up the bed of the Chalanai River under Ali Masjid. Then up Sinkhar slopes to Alachi Pass, five miles; difficult track. Hills to right piqueted by Hammond's Brigade, 9th Gurkhas in bottom, 45th Sikhs engaged on heights. Descended into Alachi village after crossing pass. Found Hammond blowing up towers. I, being field officer, pushed on to Karamna.

Found advance guard engaged; 30th Punjab Infantry had one man killed and three wounded, and General Hart's horse was wounded at the same time. Karamna Valley, open, rich, and fine villages. Sniping at intervals all day. I posted piquets. A reconnaissance was ordered to the Bori Pass on the road leading to Landi Kotal under Bosanquet. Private Betts was killed, Sergeant Samworth and Corporal Bill wounded, and they did not return until midnight. As we expected, the rear-guard was left out for night. Christmas dinner; drank "Absent Friends." Expect they rather liked being absent. Sniping on and off regularly until we turned in. One man of Sussex shot in two places; this occurred before leaving Ali Masjid.

26th December.—Buried Betts early—Padre "Kirwin," a great favourite, read service—then effaced his grave and burnt straw over it. Four companies went off to Alachi Pass and brought in Gurkhas and 1st Brigade transport. Colonel H. Hart, the C.R.E. and brother of our Brigadier, and sappers and pioneers went out

111

to improve road to Burg. Great difficulties. We eventually started at 12.30 and were not all out of camp by 7.30 p.m. Withdrawing the piquets was a ticklish job; went off successfully, under me, as field officer on duty. A few of the enemy fired as we withdrew.

Only two miles to Burg Camp. Down very bad roads, all through winding and steep denies; lit fires to show the way. I came in last with General Hart at 10 p.m., delayed by Commissariat sheep and cattle; could not see camp, but very soon sniping commenced—I was too sound asleep on top of an Afridi's house to hear them. It had been a very cold day. No sun, windy and light rain, snow on hills.

27th December.—News received that 2nd Brigade was to burn China today. Half Derby and Sussex Regiments to go to Pelosi Caves to bring in Sir W. Lockhart. Ordered off to burn and blow up Karamna. I commanded advance guard. Just got there when Colonel C. Muir, 17th Bengal Lancers, caught me up and ordered all troops back. Burg is a village of fine strong houses with towers. Commanded by hills all round and good water in valley. Engineers blowing up towers and destroying villages all day. Sussex Regiment heavily engaged half a mile off covering General Gaselee's Brigade returning from China.

Three killed and five wounded. Our guns firing from camp on Afridis. An interesting fight to watch. General Lockhart's arrival counter-ordered. We, ordered to return to Karamna tomorrow. I have to start at 4.45 a.m. in command of advance guard as field officer. Three companies of Derbys, two companies 30th P.I. We are to surround all the villages in the dark and take them at point of bayonet. Expect some fun. Sniping has commenced. Beautiful echoes from bugles; a wet night.

28th December.—Wet morning; up at 3.45 a.m., started at 4.45 a.m., up river-bed in gorge, with lanterns; a very slow advance in dark. I had to post companies for piquets along whole gorge to cover subsequent advance of baggage. Only two miles to Karamna. We were all massed in dark at entrance to valley at 6.45, just as dawn was breaking. The Gurkhas, 2/Derbys and 30th P.I., each company with a party of sappers, was ordered to surround each village—all were found empty, not a man captured and only one shot fired at us, though more were fired later. The enemy, however, were following up the baggage guard. One Derby, one Sussex, four pioneers wounded, and one pioneer killed.

Two guns at Wylly's piquet helped to cover retirement, and Maurice's (D) Company got three Afridis. The firing was heavy. I was responsible for all the piquets and that they were so posted as to cover arrival of transport. I was glad to see rear-guard safely in at 2 p.m. A busy day in the wet, posting all the camp piquets which had to be changed in the middle of the day, as Colonel Hart, R.E., the 30th Punjab Infantry, two companies S. and M. and nine hundred brigade animals were ordered to Alachi, two miles off. The poor beggars on piquet had a bad time all night in the wet and cold.

An awful thing had happened during the day. All the towers and villages were being blown up by the sappers, a most interesting operation to watch. One fuse was long in action. A smart young R.E. officer, Tonge, and a *havildar* went in to put it right and were both blown to pieces. These towers, thirty to fifty feet high, were a great feature in Tirah and especially in the Bazaar Valley. They were of stone, with very solid foundations and walls several feet thick, built to stand a siege. Their destruction was no easy matter. I got G.O.C. to include in my advance guard this morning all troops for piquet so that I was able to post them at once.

29th December.—A wet morning, not too bad, but something falling, as our old butler (Mardle) used to say. Transport moving early to Alachi. I commenced to withdraw piquets at 10.30. This took a long time. Directly operation commenced the enemy occupied hills and opened fire. I had to gallop about in the plain signalling to successive piquets to retire—a most difficult operation, and, as I was alone, and in full view, the enemy concentrated their fire on me and gave me a bad time, as I had to remain exposed in the open plain until my picquets were safe.

My horse was slightly wounded at a time when I was in a

perfect storm of bullets. The piquets withdrew, one and a half companies of Gurkhas, two companies Derbys, two men of the latter wounded. All down by 11.30 a.m. Colonel Dowse commanded whole rear-guard of 2/Derby and St. John's Kohat Mountain Battery. I commanded companies actually in contact with enemy. The latter most persistent, and harassed us throughout the day.

We were safe in Alachi at 11.30. Thirteen of our regiment wounded. Colonel Dowse was distinctly cool and collected. The Maxim-gun accounted for several of enemy, getting them in the open. They fired at us from caves in the pass leading into Alachi Valley. Several narrow escapes. The only way to retire is from position to position as hard as you can lay legs to the ground, as these Afridis are marvellous skirmishers.

Enemy made it warm for us till 4.30 p.m., when we reached our new camps near Ali Masjid at 5.30 p.m. Here also more shots were fired by our undefeated enemy. Everyone thoroughly pleased with their day, which had been awfully well managed, and we were indeed lucky to have none killed. The casualties were twenty-five. The noise of the battle in the mountains was weird and loud. The echoes quite alarming. Our men did awfully well, as a Sussex man remarked who was new to the game: "The Derbys are as nippy as the Gurkhas."

One corporal (Taylor of A Company) was asked by a staff officer if everyone had returned and replied: "No, sir, there are two companies of the Derbys behind."

"Any more?" said the staff officer.

"Yes, sir," said Corporal Taylor, "there are the Zakka Khels."

That evening going round campfires I overheard a discussion on what certain men were going to do in civil life. One of them said: "I want two medals for this show, then I am going to Egypt to get two more, then to China, and then, with my chest covered with decorations I shall go home and join the volunteers, and everyone will say, 'Good old 'ero, come and 'ave a drink!'"

In falling back from Karamna Leveson Gower's company retired from a small hill and was sent to reoccupy it, and found three of the enemy's Lee-Metford cartridges on the ground, showing that a man had crept up, fired three shots, and withdrawn as our men returned. It was quite extraordinary how occasional shots took us in reverse at no great range. Before commencing to retire in the morning A company piquet shot an Afridi within fifty yards, who had sneaked up thinking they had gone.

Again within two or three minutes of the withdrawals of piquets the *sangars* vacated were occupied by the enemy. At one place I had got all troops behind me except half of Pye's B Company. I ordered them to retire into the gorge at a run; as they were descending one of the men was bowled clean over, knocking Corporal Broadhurst end over end, and the latter actually stood on his head between two rocks—a very funny sight.

The man got to the bottom all right, and when we had helped him along a hundred yards we found he had left his rifle, so back I went with Pye and some men and recovered it. The man had been badly wounded with slugs, which must have been fired within forty yards.

Another man was hit at the same time. Again, just after crossing Alachi Pass, we had hardly left it when the enemy occupied it, knocking off Sergeant Keery's helmet with a bullet, and landing another close to Pye and me directly after. We had to run for about a mile and a half, down a gorge, crossing heights on each side to cover retirement.

The whole show worked well and the enemy had no chance. If we had made a mess of it we might have shared the fate of the Northamptons at Saram Sar.[9] Once we got jammed in an awful place in a *nullah*. Most extraordinary scene. Impossible to return and twelve hospital ponies to get down a drop of seventeen feet. Manifold[10] and I took them ourselves one by one and pushed them down the rock.

We had them all down in two or three minutes, a most comical sight. Some landed on their heads, others on their sides, oth-

---

9. This was one of two disastrous rear-guard actions which had occurred to the 2nd Division.

10. Now Major-General Sir Courtenay Manifold, K.C.B., I.M.S.

ers slithered down and landed on their legs; not one walked away lame—quite marvellous. One mule driver was dragged down with his mule and the two rolled over and over to the bottom; both might have been killed, neither was hurt.

30th December.—Everyone chaffs me, as I am always selected for field officer of the day when the enemy are likely to annoy us. The duties of field officer are to post and withdraw the piquets. These latter, on withdrawal, become the rear-guard. Gurkhas and the Kohat Mountain Battery ordered to remain at Ali Masjid, whilst the remainder of the force moved to Jamrud. The 95th on rear-guard again. It took two hours to withdraw piquets. We got to Jamrud at 3.30 p.m. and camped on our old ground. The Yorkshires had kindly pitched our tents for us. Rumour has it that Sir H. Havelock Allan[11] had lost his way coming here this morning from Ali Masjid. His grooms have turned up. Strong cold wind, but line overhead and dry under foot, which was nice.

31st December.—Sir Henry Havelock Allan's horse found, shot through jaw. Heard that Sir Henry Havelock's body had been found. Saw Crocker, 9th B.L., going out with escort to bring it in. His body passed through to Peshawar about 5 p.m. Yesterday half the Oxfords going from Ali Masjid to Landi Kotal had been attacked and had three officers wounded and three men killed and ten wounded. Wind at nights awful; last night it began at 3 a.m. and blew a gale. Tents nearly blown away; dust appalling.

3rd January.—Donne, D.A.A.G. to General Hart, asked me to act for him whilst he went on ten days' leave. Making racecourse all morning. I went to Ali Masjid with the brigade on the 5th. Busy copying General Hart's dispatches. Myself extremely well mentioned as "Selected specially on two important occasions to post and withdraw piquets. Has done me most devoted service, frequently risking himself voluntarily at great personal risk. Had horse shot under him."

---

11. General Sir Henry Havelock Allan had come out to see the 18th Royal Irish, of which he was full colonel.

5th January.—Heard of General Yeatman-Bigg's death,[12] and also of Hickman's being killed up the Khyber.

The camp under Ali Masjid can hardly be called an attractive one. It is chiefly memorable to me for howling winds and bitter blizzards. Twice was our camp blown to pieces, and many rendered tentless until fresh ones arrived from Peshawar.

On the 14th January, Donne having returned, I rejoined my regiment at Jamrud. On the 27th January we again moved to Ali Masjid.

It had been decided to round up the herds of enemy cattle in the Kajupai Plain, and the plan was for our brigade to close in from the Khyber, the 2nd Brigade from Jamrud, the 3rd Brigade from Bara, and the 4th Brigade from Mamanai. Two brigades were to be the stops at the south-west end of the plain and the other two were to do the driving. I was given command of the advanced portion of our brigade, Colonel Cafe of the Sussex commanding another portion, and Colonel H. H. Hart, the C.R.E., the Reserves, with which latter the G.O.C. Brigade, General Hart, moved. Silence was of all-importance.

At 12.45 a.m. on the 29th January my force moved off, lighted by stars, crossing the Chora Pass at 4.30 a.m. and reaching Sahagari Village on the Bazaar River at 6 a.m. Posting piquets, we awaited daylight, and then, sending out reconnoitring parties under Pye and Menzies, moved silently on to the high ground and there lay down out of sight, and in full view of the plain. So far, so good, but as the light became better I saw, to my horror, about three-quarters of a mile to my left (*i.e.* south-east), at a place called Mushkimemela, a British force walking about in full view on the enemy's side of the hill, and I realised that the game was up so far as secrecy was concerned.

Walking across to this force, I found it was our reserve column, which had lost its way; I am afraid my language was not very parliamentary, although it was commanded by a senior officer. We could see herds of cattle far away in the plains, and waited hoping to see them driven towards us; but nothing hap-

12. He had been invalided from command of a division early in the campaign.

pened, and the country was too difficult to get at them, and at 1 p.m. the order came to return to the Khyber. This we did unmolested, getting back at 5 p.m., and all we had to show for the expedition were a few prisoners. Shortly after, heavy firing across the valley was heard, and this proved to be the brigade (which should have joined hands with us as stops across the plain) surprised at the Shin Kammar Pass, where the gallant Colonel Haughton of the 36th Sikhs and many others met their fate. The round-up was a miserable failure.

The next few days were filled with rumours of war. The disaster at the Shin Kammar Pass had buoyed up the enemy, and it was doubtful if they would listen to reason and make terms; in fact, a spring campaign loomed as a probability. The native opinion was that the Zakka Khels, the most truculent of the tribes, would certainly remain on the warpath, especially as the Amir of Afghanistan was said to be urging them on, though outwardly our friend, even to the extent of sending his soldiers in uniform to fight against us.

The weather was terribly rough, but we kept ourselves warm by mountain-climbing; the most interesting trip I made, in company with my Commanding Officer, Colonel Dowse, and several officers of the regiment, escorted by twenty "Catch-'em-alive ohs," was to the top of Mount Rotas, a steady climb of 3,000 feet. We were rewarded, for from the top we obtained a glorious view, seeing Jellalabad in Afghanistan, into the Mohmund country, Forts Michni, Shabkadr, and Apozai, the Cabul River, the Bonerwal Hills above Hoti Mardan, the road to Nowshera, Cherat, the Kohat Pass, the Bazaar Valley over the Chora Pass, and our old piquet hills round Karamna and on the Aspoghar heights. Truly a magnificent panorama.

Having been given a fortnight's leave, on the 5th February I started for Lucknow (taking Menzies as far as Peshawar), for the Civil Service Cup Meeting. Heard on the way that Sir William Lockhart had returned to the front from Calcutta, that an immediate advance was probable, and that I might be recalled at any moment. However, I had a splendid ten days, saw good racing, my horse Laureate win the Grand Annual Chase, and my pony Night Alarm another race; also the open Polo Tournament, in which Kitty Apthorp played brilliantly for his Regiment, the 18th Royal Irish, and left on the 15th for the front. I arrived at Ali Masjid camp at 3 p.m. on the 19th. The wind in the Khyber Pass was terrific, and had during the previous night laid the camp low and blown the tents to ribbons.

We lay in the Khyber under Ali Masjid, making short expeditions. There was always a certain amount of activity amongst the piquets, and at times the bitterest of bitter nights, raging winds down the Khyber Gorge, snow and ice, and it was all we could do to keep ourselves warm. We had some very cheerful evenings in spite of it, especially on the 1st March, when we had a swagger dinner-party in two E.P. tents lashed together, warmed by oil-stoves. We sat down twenty-three, at four tables; amongst others, Generals Symons and Hart and their Staffs, Monro,[13] and Barrett.[14] I had got flowers up from Peshawar, and we really enjoyed ourselves in spite of the Arctic weather.

One of our expeditions was to the Alachi Pass, surveying the country of our interesting retirement of the 29th December, and we were able to examine in peace the place where we had thrown the mules down. We measured it carefully, seventeen feet, and were more astonished than ever that neither mules nor men were hurt.

On the 10th March we heard that young Jones of ours had died at Nowshera. Oddly enough, his dog, left behind here, had died the same day. What with sports, *Khud* races, revolver competitions, etc., during the day, and sing-songs by camp-fires at night, we managed to keep happy and cheery. The weather really was appalling all this time; every variety, but always unpleasant.

I got leave on the 23rd March and went to the Rawal Pindi races, and rejoined my Regiment on the 2nd April at Jamrud, to which place it had moved from Ali Masjid the previous day; and, the campaign being over, we returned to our peace station

---

13. Now General Sir Charles Monro.
14. Now Field-Marshal Sir Arthur Barrett.

at Bareilly on the 9th April, and were met by Marshall and Way.

On the 21st April we heard that war had been declared between America and Spain, and next day I started off on leave in the early morning, and was much touched to find most of the Regiment at the station to see me off and to hear the drums and pipes play "*Auld Lang Syne.*"

Summary of Tirah Campaign, 1897-1898

(See Sketch Map end of Chapter 5)

General Sir W. Lockhart's plan was to move against Bagh, the recognised centre of the Afridis. With Kohat as his base, he moved outside the Southern Boundary of Tirah to Shingwari; *vide* continuous black line. Tirah was entered 17th October 1897, the heights of Dargai stormed 18th October, and later the Sampagha and Arhanga passes forced and Bagh occupied. Hart's Brigade of 1st Division was dropped to watch and round up the Mastura Valley.

A separate column under Gaselee, called the Kurram Valley Force, worked from that valley farther west. On 7th December, when Afridis refused terms, the Force moved back towards Peshawar—*vide* dotted black lines—2nd Division down the Bara Valley, and 1st Division the Mastura Valley, meeting at Mamanai on 13th December —after considerable fighting. Next the Khyber and Bazaar Valleys had to be cleared—one brigade pushing through to Landi Kotal, whilst Hart's Brigade went up bed of Chalanai River to clear up Bazaar Valley.

Egypt: Omdurman, 1898

I had always intended to try to get back to Egypt with a view to taking part in the campaign which Kitchener was conducting against the Mahdi. I landed at Suez on the 10th May 1898, and proceeded to Cairo, only to find that the *Sirdar* (Kitchener) was up the Nile with his army, which had shortly before defeated the Dervishes at the battle of the Atbara. I therefore sent him the following wire: "Am staying Shepheard's Hotel until early Sunday morning (the 15th May) when I proceed England unless you tell me to remain. Have leave to end of year. Offer my services as an old Egyptian Army Officer in any capacity without pay. Can you employ me now or later on? If now, will remain; if later on, will return when you direct. Major Smith-Dorrien."

To which a reply came next day: "No employment possible now; will not guarantee you employment later on."

Knowing Kitchener's mind pretty well, and receiving, a couple of days later, a hopeful letter from the head of his Intelligence Branch, my old friend Wingate (now General Sir Reginald Wingate), I considered this good enough, and, leaving my fighting kit in Egypt, I started for England in the P. & O. *Egypt.*

It was at this time that Mr. Chamberlain (Joe) made a great fighting speech, practically defying all Powers so long as we had one ally—suggesting an alliance with America.

On embarking at Port Said I found Walsh, son of Lord Ormathwaite, on board the P. & O. *Egypt* badly wounded at the Atbara, and, as there was no one to look after him, I took him round to London instead of carrying out my intention of going overland from Brindisi. On passing Gibraltar I received a telegram from my mother, saying I had been made a brevet-lieutenant-colonel for services in Tirah. On the 15th June the good news arrived, conveyed to me by the Adjutant-General, Sir Evelyn Wood: Kitchener had wired for me to go out! and the 30th found me on a Messageries boat steaming out of Marseilles.

I found a lot of officers at Shepheard's Hotel in Cairo, amongst them being General Leslie Rundle, and Beatty, R.N. (now the famous admiral). De Montmorency, an old friend in the 21st Lancers, had bought me two horses, Mad Moon and Mike.

I was very fortunate on my journey to the front, for Rundle was adjutant-general of the Egyptian army, and he invited me to travel with him, which meant considerable comfort. Beatty came too. The heat on the journey was very great, and when we embarked in a stern-wheeler at Shellal (just above the Assouan Cataract) at 6.30 in the evening the thermometer stood at 118 degrees.

Disembarking at Wady Haifa, we took the new desert railway across to Berber, where the army was concentrating, and arrived there at 4 a.m. on the 16th July. Whilst shaving and cleaning myself in the desert alongside the (rain, and wondering how I was to be employed, the *Sirdar* rode up, shook hands, and, laconically remarking, "You had better take command of your old battalion,[1] the 13th Sudanese," rode off. After some search I found the 13th, and announced I had come to take command, and, as no one objected, I did.

Very pleasant days, but full of hard work, followed. I found myself surrounded by old friends. Hunter (now General Sir Archibald) commanded the Division, and Maxwell (now General Sir John) commanded my brigade; others were Major Sandbach, R.E. (now Major-General), Fergusson (now General Sir Charles), Macdonald (afterwards Sir Hector), Sir Henry Rawlinson (now Lord Rawlinson), Watson (now Major-General), Jackson commanding the 11th Sudanese, Townshend (later of Kut fame) commanding the 14th Battalion, Pink, Slatin Pasha, Sloman, Eddy Stuart-Wortley, T. E. Hickman, etc., etc.; and I was

---

1. I had raised and commanded this battalion in 1886.

fortunate in finding three splendid officers in the 13th: Gamble of the Berkshires, Tommy Capper of the East Lancashires (afterwards killed in France at the head of his division), and Whigham (now Lieutenant-General Sir Robert).

On the 30th July we commenced our move south, marching by night to avoid the heat of the day.

We were on the east bank of the Nile, and were faced with the problem of crossing the river, for the enemy were at Omdurman, farther south on the west bank. Baggage animals were to cross at Dakhilla, and to continue to march, whereas troops were to be put on boats at the Atbara and proceed thence by river.

The *Sirdar* managed everything himself, and by insisting on every steamer, barge, and boat (*gyasse*) carrying three times as much as a normal person would have risked putting on them, he soon had his expedition under way. The wind and dust were appalling, and the dirt adhering to perspiring bodies indescribable. Soon the flower of the Egyptian army, the six Sudanese battalions, were steaming south. My steamer was the *Fateh,* commanded by Beatty. The Nile was very high, and rising, and getting wider as we went farther south. It was a most interesting three-days' river-trip. We tied up at nights to cut wood for the steamer. We had quite a fine gunboat fleet:

The *Zaffir, Nasr,* and *Fateh* were big stern-wheelers armed with quick-firing 3-lb. guns and Maxims, each taking two barges full of troops. The *Mellik, Sultan,* and *Sheik* were larger, newer, and more powerful screw war vessels, but little use as tugs; the *Tamai* and *El Haffir, Metemmeh* and *Abu Klea,* gunboats, and the four stern-wheeler tugs *Dal, Akasheh, Khaibur,* and *Tahra.*

General Hunter was on the *Metemmeh,* and commanded the Infantry. On the 6th August we disembarked on the east bank as near to Wady Habeshi as the flooded banks would permit. On the 11th we moved five miles to a better camp at Wad Hamad, nearer the enemy, and were joined that evening by the 32nd Field Battery from Cairo.

Before describing the further advance and decisive battle of the 2nd September it will be as well to review briefly the events of the preceding years.

Since January 1885, when our expedition under Sir Garnet Wolseley arrived too late to save General Gordon, the Mahdi had ruled the Sudan. For the next thirteen years the Egyptian troops, at times aided by British, were employed against him with varying success.

In 1897–8, the *Sirdar* of the Egyptian army, Sir Herbert Kitchener, had constructed his railway across the desert from Wady Haifa to Abu Hamed and thence to Berber; having first driven the enemy south of the Province of Dongola and captured Berber. In the spring of this year (1898) he had dealt the enemy a serious blow at the battle of the Atbara, and then prepared for his next, and what was to prove his final, blow to the Mahdi's power.

By August he was ready, and two brigades of British troops (a second having arrived from England) with four brigades of Egyptian troops, guns, Maxims, and a small force of cavalry were massed at Wad Hamad, and on the 23rd August he held a review of his army in battle array, formed in line of brigades, in mass, at deploying intervals; Maxims and field-guns were dispersed throughout the line, and one battalion in each brigade in support; one brigade in a second line as reserve, and cavalry and Camel Corps on the right flank. The force in this formation was nearly three miles long, even without the 21st Lancers, which were not all in camp until next day.

To prove the mobility of the force, it moved forward, deploying into attack formation (N.B.—"Attack formation" against the Dervishes is "Battalions in line, each with two companies in reserve"); advancing and firing, finally changing front twice—all of which was well carried out.

That night was very stormy, but we were blessed with a cool morning next day.

Our first march, made in the afternoon, was only eight miles—to Wad Bishara; the next day's march of twelve miles landing us at camp Gebel-Royan, south of the famous Shabluka

Cataract. The heat was very great, and told on the troops. For the present, the four Egyptian Brigades were marching one day ahead of the two British brigades. To give these latter a chance on their first march in this expedition, they did in four days what we had done in two.

The arrangement for transport was for a limited amount of camels to carry the immediate necessities of each battalion, and for a flotilla of sailing boats with the rest of the baggage to move up the river, parallel with the army. As the wind remained obstinately from the south and the current was running some three miles an hour, parties had to be told off to tow the boats, and their progress was necessarily very slow. The difficulties of the water transport were very great just here, and the boats did not come level with our camp at Gebel-Royan until the 29th. The banks, mostly under water, were covered with trees and scrub; hence the great difficulties of towing, as the men had often to swim to get the ropes round obstacles, and the current was tremendous.

We formed our camps in the shape of a rectangle, three faces being formed by battalions in "attack formation," with a thorn *zeriba* outside them, the east face of the rectangle (which was also one of the long faces) being the riverbank, where the gunboats and other boats tied up. The interior space of the rectangle was filled by one battalion from each brigade in reserve, by the camps of the Head-quarters, Divisional, and Brigade Staffs, and the supply department.

Just before reaching Gebel-Royan, the serious loss of the *Zaffir*, one of our gunboats, was reported. It appears that it had suddenly sunk off Metemmeh, no lives being lost, although a lot of rations and private kit went down with her. Our steam flotilla was thus reduced to nine gunboats and four other steamers. Three of the gunboats were of a new type and looked very formidable ships of war, but subsequent events proved their propelling power—the screw—to be far inferior for river purpose to the powerful stern-wheels with which all the other boats were provided.

On the 29th we were all in camp without incident at Wad Abid, eight miles from Gebel-Royan, and only twenty-seven from Omdurman. That night a daring Dervish horseman came and peeped at us over the *zeriba*. The weather continued stormy, and a gale from the south delayed all our water transport, but it abated in time to allow the *Sirdar* to issue orders for the forward move on the 30th August. From this date inclusive we moved in battle array, namely, *échelon* of brigades, right refused, left resting as near the river as swamps and thorny scrub would allow, each brigade in attack formation moving in fours, advancing from the flanks of companies—the last time probably any army will move in the presence of an enemy in the close order of the Peninsular and Crimean days.

At the same time a large mob of Jaalins and friendlies was moving up parallel with us on the east bank, under Stuart-Wortley, of the 60th Rifles. This force was unfortunate in being out of the fighting, which came off on the west bank.

Owing to information that the Khalifa intended a night attack, the *Sirdar* considered it advisable that the force should in future bivouac in a close formation, and away from the belt of jungle which fringed the riverbank. Consequently on this night we formed a huge rectangle, nearly two miles from the river. Forty yards outside was a thick thorn *zeriba*, behind which troops could fight if attacked.

Next day, the 31st August, we again moved forward in the same *échelon* formation for about eight miles, and formed camp six miles north of Kerreri and eleven from Omdurman. On this day our baggage boats, which we had last seen on the 24th, came up level with our camp, our own boat (the 18th Battalion) being head of the river.

On the morning of the 1st September we marched again in *échelon* of brigades. Each day, as we got nearer to the enemy, "Sambo," the name given to our Sudanese troops, had become more and more cheery and talkative, and as the Kerreri Ridge (which was supposed to be held by the enemy) was approached, their pace became faster and faster. It was afterwards remarked by the commander of a *Fellaheen* Brigade, that under the same circumstances the pace of his troops became visibly slower.

From the Kerreri Ridge we were able to see the top of the Mahdi's tomb, distant about seven miles, and cavalry intelligence came in to say that the Khalifa's troops were visible outside Omdurman. What caused them to leave their stronghold and come out in the open it is hard to say.

Possibly it was the new howitzer battery, firing the 50-lb. shell, which had been sent to the east bank in the morning, escorted by the gunboats *Nasr* and *Tamai,* and with these and the other gunboats had bombarded the Khalifa's stronghold known as the "Sur," and the forts. The shooting of the howitzers at 3,000 yards was most effective, breaching the great walls of the Sur, and absolutely smashing in the conical roof of the Mahdi's tomb. These breaches in the wall were to prove very useful to us on the morrow.

The force moved off Kerreri heights to a village two miles farther south, and there commenced to form camp for the night; but it had not done very much when the cavalry sent in news that the whole Dervish army, 30,000 strong, was marching to the attack. It subsequently proved to be more than double that number. It must have been a fine sight for our cavalry, as they were on some high ground, culminating in Gebel Surgham, from the foot of which extends the huge plain without any undulations, in which stands Omdurman, distant about four miles.

At about 2 p.m. this army was seen steadily moving north, and only three miles away.

A line of defence was selected in advance of our right square for the troops to fight on, should this attack be carried out, and the troops stood in attack formation on one huge curve more than two miles long with the flanks resting on the river, the point in the line farthest from the river being distant about three-quarters of a mile.

The map shows generally the situation.

The line ran to a sharp angle, the angle being held by the 13th Sudanese Battalion, an Egyptian Battery, and two Maxims.

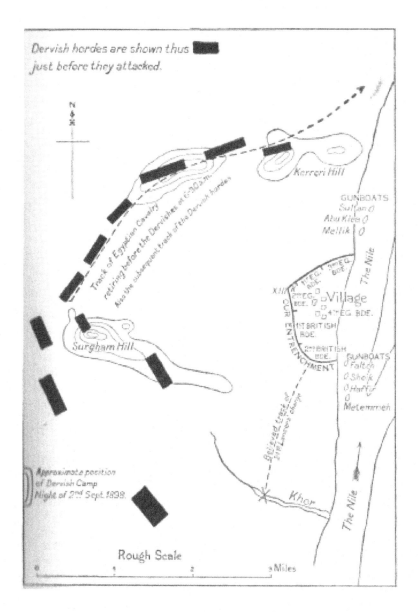

Dervish hordes are shown thus ▄▄ just before they attacked.

N

Kerreri Hill

GUNBOATS
Sultan O
Abu Klea O
Mellik O

Track of Egyptian Cavalry retiring before the Dervishes at 6.30 a.m. Also the subsequent track of the Dervish hordes

The Nile

2ND EG. BDE.
3RD EG. BDE.
XIII
2ND EG. BDE.
OVillage
4TH EG. BDE.
1ST BRITISH BDE.
2ND BRITISH BDE.

Surgham Hill

GUNBOATS
O Faltch
O Sheik
O Haffir
O Metemmeh

Belived track of 21st Lancers charge

Approximate position of Dervish Camp Night of 2nd Sept. 1898.

Khor

The Nile

Rough Scale

0 .... 1 .... 2 .... 3 Miles

MAP OF OMDURMAN, 1ST STAGE, 2ND SEPTEMBER, 1898

Orders then came to utilise our time in making defences. The British Brigades found near their part of the line some old thorn-bushes, with which they made a sort of a *zeriba*—useful against a charge but no use against bullets; and to this, and to the fact that they were the first troops which came under the Dervish fire next day, I attribute their casualties being greater in proportion to the fighting they did than the other troops which were mostly in a two-deep shelter-trench.

N.B.—British killed and wounded	171
Egyptian killed and wounded	305
Total	476

Shortly before nightfall the cavalry was seen falling back, bringing the report that the enemy had camped for the night some three miles off.

Whilst awaiting the Dervish attack that afternoon, the old Sudanese adjutant-major of our battalion, Morgan Eff Mahmoud, said to me: "*Izakan el Gaysh el Mahdi yegi hena ana isharub el shay el Khalifa bokra*," which, being interpreted, meant "If they are such fools as to attack our entrenchment I shall take tea with the Khalifa tomorrow"—a remark of which he reminded me next day.

Our troops had orders to remain where they were for the night, taking every possible precaution against a night attack. This was especially expected, as the Khalifa had expressed his intention of coming by night or in the early dawn.

It was a glorious night, with a full moon, but none of the old hands wished for a night attack, although many of the young bloods said, "Let them come on." Even with a full moon the enemy could have advanced to within 350 yards with impunity, and, from what we saw of their pluck and determination next day, we all congratulated ourselves that the night attack did not take place.

As it was, they contented themselves with firing a few shots from Surgham Hill, too far off to do us any harm, but enough to keep us on the look-out for a further development, which never came off.

Next morning the order came to continue our march in *échelon* on Omdurman, and to be on the move at 5.45 a.m. The cavalry had gone out at first streak of dawn to pick up connection with the Dervish army, and, just as we were beginning to move forward, back came the message: "The Dervishes are moving to, attack us," and we were ordered to remain in our entrenchments. We could hardly believe the news. We could not have selected a better place to be attacked in. Here was a huge open plain without an inch of cover for an attacking enemy within 2,000 yards of our position.

The English cavalry withdrew behind our left flank, and the Egyptian cavalry, Horse artillery battery, and Camel Corps retired steadily northwards, right across our front from Surgham Hill, and west of it, engaging the enemy as they did so with their guns and carbine fire. The Dervish army followed the track of the Egyptian cavalry, which moved straight on Kerreri Hill. We could see their banners and the tops of their heads, and, later on, the masses of men themselves, led by their *Emirs* on horses, as they streamed across our front. At first they were partly hidden by slightly rising ground, distant 2,000 or 3,000 yards.

It really looked as though they were marching to attack Kerreri, as it was at that place the prophets had foretold "a Turk's skull for every white stone," and that they were not aware of the fact that our main army already lay some two miles south of Kerreri. This latter they were very soon to learn, when a storm of shot and shell burst into the right of their columns, which soon wheeled towards us and moved steadily down on our entrenchments.

Our gunboats, nine in number, were disposed three of them to flank the north of our line, and four of them to perform the same duty on the south, the other two moving with the howitzer battery to shell Omdurman from the east bank.

These gunboats, with their high fighting decks, giving a command of thirty-three or thirty-five feet above the already extremely high Nile, were able to bring their quick-firing guns and Maxims to bear with deadly effect on the advancing masses. On the north side they played a most important part, as there some 10,000 Dervishes had cut off the Egyptian cavalry, Horse artillery, and Camel Corps from our position, and it was due to the gunboats that these mounted troops were able to rejoin our right.

The Egyptian cavalry and Horse artillery, in fulfilling their role of drawing the enemy on, had, for their own safety, to retire down the Nile bank some five miles north of Kerreri, leaving temporarily two guns in doing so, owing to casualties in the teams. This force must have had a very anxious time of it, but all the English officers speak in the highest terms of the steadiness and coolness of the Egyptian rank and file.

All this time column after column had been unrolling itself from behind Surgham Hill, each moving eastwards in succession to attack our line. One column also came on to the rising ground between the left of our line and Surgham Hill, right under the rifles of the two British brigades. It was a sight never to be forgotten. The endless columns of warriors, led by mounted Emirs, moving steadily on, the morning sun flashing on their white garments and long spears, with countless banners fluttering in the light breeze; but it was also a pitiable sight to see the awful effect of our fire all along the line: they were simply mown down at long ranges, and in very few parts of the line did they approach nearer than 600 yards, although in one or two instances a few men got very much closer before they were killed.

The enemy's standard-bearers were gallant beyond description, in one or two cases moving on alone with their banners until shot down. One man especially, with a white flag, came on by himself and planted it within 250 yards, and, holding it up defiantly, stood there some time before he was shot down.

As it appeared that the attack had been beaten off, at about 8.30 a.m. the *Sirdar* ordered the force to form into its usual echelon of brigades, right refused, left resting on the river, and move south direct on Omdurman. At about the same time the 21st Lancers had moved out to the south and made a most gallant charge on a body of Dervishes, behind whom unfortunately was a *khor*, or watercourse, in which was hidden a formed body of some 3,000 of the enemy: there was nothing for it but to go straight on, and on they went with their Colonel (Martin) many lengths ahead of them.

The *khor* brought several horses down. On issuing forth on the far side the regiment wheeled about, and through the Dervishes they went again. Their losses were heavy, but it is remarkable they were not heavier: one officer (Grenfell) and some thirty rank and file killed; four officers and some forty rank and file wounded. After emerging the second time and missing Grenfell, Captain Kenna and Lieutenant De Montmorency dashed back into the middle of the Dervishes, and, picking up his body, brought it away with them. It was a right gallant act, for which they were both awarded the V.C.

By 8.40 a.m. the *échelon* was in movement towards Omdurman, leaving the enemy in our rear and away to our right flank. As we moved amongst the bodies a sharp lookout had to be kept on the wounded, as from previous experience it was known that many would try to get a shot or a spear-thrust in at us as we passed over them, whereas others not wounded at all, but wishing to die, would lie prone, ready to come with a fanatical rush and kill someone before they themselves were disposed of.

The first time this happened was really rather amusing. Two or three newspaper correspondents, eager for loot, rode out amongst the wounded, when up jumped a Dervish with a huge spear and put them all to rout, pursuing them back to the nearest troops amidst a discharge of revolvers dangerous to everyone except to the Dervish, for whom the shots were intended.

The man was finally killed by Captain Smythe, of the Bays, one of General Hunter's Staff, but not before he himself got an ugly wound in the elbow.

At about 8.55 a.m. the troops were in position as shown in the map of the final stage. The 1st Egyptian Brigade (Macdonald's) was still moving out to take up its position in *échelon* when it was heavily attacked by hordes on all sides.

The enemy were also keeping up a fire from Surgham Hill. I had sent two companies of my battalion, the 13th, which was on the right of the 2nd Egyptian Brigade, under Captains (Tommy) Capper and R. Whigham, to turn them out, and right well they did it. It is a steep, stony hill, about 200 feet above the surrounding plain, and it was a very pretty sight: "The dash up the hill, occasional halts to fire, and Capper on his horse leading throughout."

On reaching the top they found, immediately underneath them on the north-west side of the hill, enormous masses of Dervishes, evidently a reserve. These latter were so taken by surprise by the sudden appearance of troops above them, and by the heavy fire and Sudanese yells of these same troops, that they bolted in confusion, leaving many dead and wounded and many banners on the ground.

It was just as they arrived on the top that the attack on Macdonald's Brigade took place, and so heavily was he assailed that the *Sirdar* ordered other brigades to go to his assistance. The 2nd Egyptian Brigade was ordered to throw back its right flank, so the remaining companies of the 13th Battalion, moving at the double, got into line to the north of and with their backs to Surgham Hill, and poured a heavy fire into masses of the enemy at about 500 yards range. Shortly afterwards the 3rd Brigade moved into the interval between the right of the 13th Battalion and Macdonald's Brigade.

The other three battalions of the 2nd Egyptian Brigade, moving west, passing Surgham Hill on their right hand, formed up to their right and formed line in the same direction as, but at some distance from, the 13th Battalion. The 2nd British Brigade, and a battery of artillery, following in the tracks of the 2nd Egyptian Brigade, after a long march westwards, formed also to its right and prolonged the line still farther to the left.

Thus the line stood interposed between the enemy and Omdurman, cutting off his line of retreat in that direction.

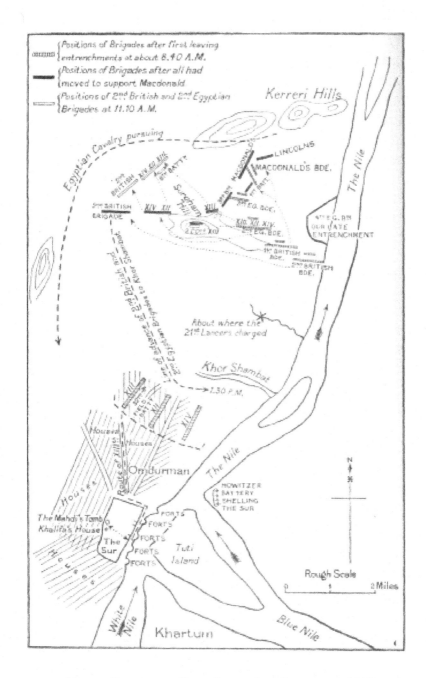

When the 3rd Brigade joined its left to the right of the 13th Battalion, there was still a considerable interval between its right and Macdonald's Brigade. To reinforce this interval the 1st British Brigade marched for all it knew, and the Lincoln Regiment, moving farther north still, went up on the right of Macdonald in time to give him material assistance in driving off the third and last attack on his brigade. This third attack was made by the horde of Dervishes under Sheik Wad Helu, flying a bright green banner; they were the men who had followed up the Egyptian cavalry in the morning, and were now on their return journey.

All this took an appreciable time, as the distances to be traversed by the supporting brigades were considerable, and there is little doubt that had the three attacks been made simultaneously, or had not Macdonald handled his brigade with the greatest skill, he would have had very considerable losses.

The individual bravery of the enemy was even greater at this phase of the battle than in the attack on our position of the morning. Dervish horsemen charged, riding to certain death. One fine charge of some eighty men—the largest formed body I saw charge at once—was a sight never to be forgotten. On they came right at the thickest of our line, saddles being emptied and horses killed every few yards. Not a man reached the line, but only two or three horses galloped riderless through.

In the angle formed by the 1st, 2nd, and 3rd Egyptian Brigades was a mass of standards, round which were heaps of bodies of men who had made no attempt to run away, but had stood by their standards until shot down. Prominent amongst them was the Khalifa's own black flag, which was soon being carried by a mounted orderly behind the *Sirdar*.

Now (10.20 a.m.) the 2nd British and Egyptian Brigades were ordered to advance and sweep all before them. This they did for about one and a half miles, firing on the fugitives as they sped westwards, gradually making a quarter left wheel as the enemy got more and more to the west. While this advance was taking place the Egyptian Cavalry, which had returned over Kerreri Hill, appeared north of the right of Macdonald's Brigade in pursuit.

At 11.15 a.m. the last shot was fired, and the *Sirdar* at once ordered the 2nd British and 2nd Egyptian Brigades to form to their left and move straight on Omdurman. As these brigades moved south the enemy was to be seen flying in thousands, many of them in a stream parallel to this movement, and some three or four miles distant. It looked as if their intention was, by a wide movement, to get back into Omdurman. It was these people that the Egyptian cavalry and Camel Corps, bringing their right shoulders up, pursued, and a very trying time they had of it. Their horses were done, having gone over thirty miles that day at a considerable pace, but, in spite of their often having to contend with formed bodies of undefeated Dervishes, they did yeoman work in the earlier part of the fight.

At 1.30 p.m. the two advanced brigades reached Khor Shambat, just north of Omdurman, and were ordered to water, the 2nd Egyptian Brigade being further ordered to be ready to move off at 2 p.m. to attack the stronghold of the Khalifa, known as the Sur.

The losses of the Dervishes had been enormous. The battlefield was a very extended one, and in all parts of it, a very large number of dead were lying about. Next day parties were sent to count them, and 10,883 bodies were counted, besides wounded. The latter at the lowest estimate must have been twice as many as the killed. This reckoning, added to the countless hordes which escaped, would make it appear that the Dervish army in the morning could not have been short of 80,000 men.

The strategical move of the *Sirdar* on Omdurman, after the attack on his entrenchment had been beaten off, was a very smart one, and one he could well risk, based on the river as he was, and with no lines of communication to defend. The enemy had all moved in the direction of his rear, and thus his force stood between them and their capital. It was this move on their capital, when their field army was away, which absolutely gave us the winning card.

At 2 p.m. the 2nd (Sudanese) Brigade, refreshed by their

drink—for it was an extremely hot day—moved off in line of columns (first of companies and later on of fours), the 14th on the left, nearest the river, the 12th in the centre, and the 13th on the right, the 32nd Field Battery accompanying the latter and the 8th Egyptian Battalion following in support. In this formation, covered by skirmishers, the Brigade moved due south through the houses and streets of Omdurman.

Two miles of houses brought them opposite to the north wall of the Sur, which was the aim and object of attack. This had a most insurmountable appearance, as nothing could be seen, except a huge dead stone wall, some twenty-five feet high. This wall was known to enclose the Khalifa's house, the Mahdi's tomb, and the quarters of the Mulasemiyeh, or picked bodyguard of the Khalifa, numbering some five or six thousand faithful blacks. It was also rumoured that the Khalifa himself had found his way back into the Sur from the battle-field; therefore some brisk work was expected.

It is difficult to describe the shape of the Sur, but its north wall was at right angles to the river, and about half a mile long. Its east wall, about a mile long, ran up the riverbank and about 100 yards from it. The other walls were less regular, but a large quadrangular space was enclosed.

Outside the eastern face of the Sur were a series of forts on the riverbank, all of which bore on the river.

Had each battalion kept its own line the 13th would have passed west of the Sur, and the other two battalions would have had the honour of attacking it; but somehow, in the intricacies of the streets, the 13th had forged slightly ahead and to their left, being directed on the Sur by an old telegraph clerk of Gordon's, who had been found in the streets and who had been a captive for fourteen years, working for the Mahdi and Khalifa the cross-river wire between Omdurman and Khartoum. Thus, when the Sur was reached the 13th were the most advanced troops, and, as there was at that point only one broad street, a judicious "Front form companies and quarter-column on the leading company" prevented them from being again passed.

Consequently, when the order came for the most advanced regiment to move eastwards along the north wall of the Sur to the river, there to turn south, attack all the forts, and assault the eastern gates of the Sur itself, the 13th was the battalion selected for the job. During this, the gunboats, which were abreast of the Sur, were keeping up a brisk fire on it, and on the forts on the riverbank. The people on board described the scene afterwards as a very pretty fight when the 13th came round the corner and through the breaches of the Sur on to the riverbank and advanced on the forts.

This move, between the east wall of the Sur and the forts on the riverbank, took all these forts in reverse. The enemy made a poor fight of it, and, firing a few shots, bolted from each fort in turn. Then a deep and forbidding-looking *khor* was reached running from under the walls of the Sur into the river, and many yards wide. It was nothing more nor less than a main drain, rendered more obnoxious by the bodies of several dead animals. However, it had to be crossed, and the fort, from which they were firing on the opposite side of it, taken. So into it we plunged, and, after a struggle with mud and water, were safely landed on the other bank, and a few minutes later were in possession of the fort. Here also was the first big gate into the Sur, which soon yielded to battering, and the troops rushed in, met by a mild discharge of rifles, the firers of which made a hasty retirement behind the houses, throwing down their arms.

After proceeding some two hundred yards into the Sur through the gate, it was ascertained that the main gate leading to the Khalifa's house was some five hundred yards farther on, so back came the leading companies of the 13th outside the Sur, and, again moving south, came opposite the main gate. Much the same thing happened here as at the first gate, and soon the regiment was moving in column of half companies straight up the main street on the Mahdi's tomb. Some of the Mulasemiyeh fired a few shots, but most of them suddenly threw down their arms. Amongst them were a lot of wounded men who had escaped from the battle, and both inside and outside the Sur were a good many killed and wounded lying about, especially round the Mahdi's tomb; evidently these latter were the result of the shelling in the morning and on the previous day.

All reports said that the Khalifa was still in his house, so, breaking open the door of the outer courtyard, I, with six men of my battalion, rushed through the latter to see, in the open mosque square beyond (where the followers of the Khalifa used daily to assemble for prayer), Baggara horsemen, evidently the Khalifa's bodyguard, covering his retreat—and right nobly they did it, two of them charging in with their huge spears, killing a corporal and wounding two of my men before we could dispatch them, and gaining thereby time for the rest of the bodyguard to get lost in the intricacies of the streets and houses beyond.

Unfortunately, at this moment we found ourselves under heavy shrapnel fire, two of our guns having selected this moment to shell the Mahdi's house. Retreating through the house, we found in the back yard an Englishman lying stretched. It was an unfortunate correspondent, the Hon. H. Howard, breathing his last with what could only have been a shrapnel bullet through his head. We got stretchers up and conveyed his body and our own casualties away. The rest of the battalion had now come up, and when I met my adjutant-major he reminded me of the remark he had made on the previous day by saying, "Didn't I tell you that we should take tea with the Khalifa today if he attacked our entrenchments?"

There were now signs of night coming on, and the *Sirdar* ordered the troops to fall back the way they came, he himself going off to open the prison with his escort of two companies of the 14th Battalion. He released, amongst others, Neufelt, who had been a prisoner since 1886.

It was now getting dark, and we had a long and wearisome business getting clear of the Sur. A very interesting incident happened as the 13th marched out of the Sur. Suddenly some thirty Dervishes with brass instruments and drums, possibly the Khalifa's own band, placed themselves at the head of the regiment, and, playing most excellent Sudanese marches, insisted on leading them, until they were voted a nuisance as they drowned words of command, when, they were suppressed.

Whilst the 13th had been taking the Sur the remainder of the brigades, with transport, had gradually moved up into the streets of Omdurman. It was quite dark. Frequent firing was going on by small bodies of Dervishes and marauders, and the work of getting each brigade to the bivouac selected for it looked quite hopeless. However, by 10 p.m. the 2nd Egyptian Brigade was camped in the desert west of the town, and they were fortunate enough to get their transport by 10 p.m., and by midnight the officers of the 13th had the satisfaction of finding General Hunter and Staff near them, having lost their baggage, and they were able to provide them with dinner and to join with them in emptying a few bottles of sparkling wine which had been nursed for the purpose of commemorating the fall of Omdurman.

One of my men looted a very fine tame Crowned Crane of Africa from the Mahdi's house. I later took it with me to Malta. Thence Captain (afterwards Admiral Sir Percy) Scott kindly took it home in H.M.S. *Dido* for my brother in the Scilly Isles, and there it lived for six years, and can still be seen stuffed in a case, in perfect plumage.

I have not attempted to describe the filth of the town and the Sur. The smells beggared all description. There had evidently never been any regard for sanitation, added to which dead bodies of men and animals, some of them killed in the bombardment of the day before, helped to make the whole air putrid.

The fall of Omdurman meant that Khartoum, across the river, was again in our hands.

For the next few days the cavalry and many bands of friendly Arabs scoured the country for the Khalifa without success, whilst the troops were employed re-establishing law and order in Omdurman and disarming the inhabitants.

For many days, however, looting and indiscriminate shooting, chiefly by *quondam* Dervishes, went on before matters really quieted down.

Two of Gordon's old steamers, the *Bordein* and *Tufekiyeh,* were captured, the first on the day of the action, and the latter, returning from a raid south and quite unaware of the defeat of the Dervishes, ran straight into our hands the next day.

There still remained one more steamer to be accounted for, the *Saffiyeh*. She was at a Dervish post 270 miles up the river, and fell into our hands up the White Nile on the 15th September, as I describe later.

Then followed a busy time, disarming inhabitants, searching houses, cleaning up indescribable filth, cutting and collecting wood.

On the 4th the wonderfully impressive service in memory of poor Gordon took place across the river at Khartoum. My hands were too full to go, and I have regretted it ever since.

On the 5th John Maxwell was appointed Governor of Omdurman. A more suitable choice could not have been made, and I temporarily commanded the 2nd Sudanese Brigade. There was daily a good deal of shooting going on, mostly by camp followers, and masses of prisoners and wounded Dervishes had to be arranged for. The smells of Omdurman have only once been surpassed in my experience, and that was on visiting the Whaling Station opposite Gibraltar many years later.

It was no climate to keep British troops in a moment longer than necessary, and on the 9th September they headed for England. Next day I was appointed to command the troops detailed to move with the chief to Fashoda, but found time to gallop with Tommy Capper over the battle-field of the 2nd and saw enough horrors to last me a lifetime.

The Fashoda episode has, I think, never been told in detail, and, being of historical interest, I shall describe it rather fully.

CHAPTER 7

Fashoda

The force consisted of one strong company of British troops (Cameron Highlanders), two Sudanese Battalions, the 11th and 13th, each six hundred strong, and one Mountain Battery, and was conveyed in four steamers. The *Sirdar*, with Wingate, Watson, Freddy Roberts, Lord Roberts's only son killed in the Boer War), Lord Edward Cecil, and the artillery under Peake, were in the *Dal;* Jackson, Stanton, Smith, and the 11th Sudanese Battalion in the *Nasr;* Keppel and Cowan[1] in the *Sultan;* myself in my old friend Beatty's boat, the *Fateh*, with Gamble and Capper, my own battalion, and a company of Cameron Highlanders, Andrew Murray, Neville Cameron, Horn, Adlercron, and Surgeon-Captain Luther—a very happy party, and we enjoyed ourselves thoroughly.

Our fleet sailed on the 10th September, Fashoda, some five hundred miles above Khartoum, being our objective. The river was very full, like an inland sea, and, just above Khartoum, at least five miles wide, but narrowed as we got farther south. Each steamer, except the *Sultan,* had barges lashed alongside for the troops. Each night we tied up to the bank and cut wood for the furnaces. Hot and trying work, generally in the jungle, and two or three times attacked by bees, but always worried by mosquitoes and soucat flies. The wind, too, was troublesome, and interfered with progress: occasional heavy rain did not increase our comfort. Sometimes for hours together we could not land

---

1. Now Admirals—Sir Colin Keppel and Sir Walter Cowan.

owing to heavy sedge.

None of us knew the object of our mission, and it was only at one of our halts, on the 12th, that I gleaned from a private talk with Wingate that our chief's aim was to go to Fashoda, in order to try to have a discussion with a French force reported to be there, then to move fifty miles farther south to the Sobat River, to see what a force reported as being there consisted of. Possibly we might leave the steamers there and march east, or meet the Belgians at Bohr.

We saw plenty of hippos—five at a time once—and some crocodiles. On the 14th the gunboat *Abu Klea* caught us up with more supplies, thus bringing our fleet to five. We were now in the country of the Dinkhas and Shilluks, and got information that the "*Fransowi*"[2] force at Fashoda had driven back the Dervishes and made an alliance with the chiefs of these two tribes. These two chiefs found themselves in a quandary on seeing us, and announced that they did not know there were two kinds of Turks (to them a Turk and white man are synonymous) but were quite ready to swear allegiance to us.

We heard that a Dervish force was a few miles above us, in *zeriba*, actually on the edge of the east bank of the river, and orders were given that we should move prepared to attack next morning. Then, as we moved forward in line of battleships, with our best fighting ship, the *Sultan*, leading, we saw large herds of hartebeest on the east bank. These were soon startled by the guns of the *Sultan*. This was about 7 a.m., and we could see the last remaining Dervish steamer, the *Saffiyeh*, tied up off a large encampment, with white tents studded about with Dervish banners. The fire was returned by a gun on shore, but the shot from the enemy's antiquated brass gun fell short every time, except one, which burst over the *Sultan's* funnel. Soon we saw the *Saffiyeh*[3] in a cloud of smoke, apparently on fire, and the Dervishes

2. "*Fransowi*" was a general term used by natives for a white force
3. The steamer *Saffiyeh* had a history. After the battle of Abu Klea, Gubat, on the Nile, 100 miles below Khartoum, was reached on the 22nd January 1885, and two days later, there being hope that Khartoum was still holding out, Colonel Sir Charles Wilson started off with two steamers..(Continued next page.)

Streaming out of the *zeriba* into the open country. Our Maxims and quick-firers were all in action. We soon steamed in close, and I landed with troops. Some twenty-five bodies were found in the *zeriba*, and the *Saffiyeh* was riddled. A naval officer told me that Kitchener chaffed him about it, and said, "You d—d sailors can never see anything afloat without wishing to destroy it." The *Emir* of this band of some four hundred Dervishes, "Said" by name, was wounded and captured and was quite ignorant of the defeat of his main army at Omdurman.

After destroying the huts and loading up the wood for our steamers and dividing the looted cattle—some eighty sheep, goats, and calves—we started off again at midday. It really was a very picturesque little action, without any danger to ourselves. The actual place was not far from two prominent hills called El Duem, and was called by the natives *Dem-el-Zekhi*, from its being an old slave camp. At 2 p.m. on the 17th we reached the big Shilluk village of Kaka, and the chiefs were received by the *Sirdar*, and tribal war-dances took place to the Shilluk tunes played by our bands.

From this village the *Sirdar* sent a native runner to Fashoda, some fifty miles, with a letter to the commander of the force there to warn him of our coming. The weather for days had been cloudy, heavy, and muggy with a good deal of rain, at times tropical, which made landing and cutting wood for steamers anything but a pleasant operation, especially as more frequently than not it had to be carried out in the dark by the light of flickering candles.

Sunday, the 18th September, was a day of wondering. Our information about the French, their numbers and intentions,

He arrived off Khartoum on the 28th to find that town in the hands of the enemy, and to get news that Gordon had been killed two days before. Too late, and only by two days! So, being under a heavy fire from both sides, there was nothing left but to turn round and run down-stream. Both steamers on their way down ran aground and Wilson established himself on Mermat Island, forty miles from Gubat, to which place he sent Stuart-Wortley in a small boat for assistance. The *Saffiyeh* was the steamer sent, and made a name for itself in the capable hands of Lord Charles Beresford, for it had to run a gauntlet of fire to Mermat Island to relieve Wilson and back again.

was very vague. "Were they likely to be pugnacious or were they not?" were the chief thoughts which occurred to most of us.

After a very damp night we were steaming slowly south by 6 a.m. After proceeding for two hours we saw crowds of Dinkhas on the east bank moving south with shields and spears, the first time we had seen any large number of natives since leaving Omdurman. The country appeared rich in grass with many herds of cattle.

At 11.30 a.m., conforming to the steamers ahead of us, we moved to the bank and cut wood, but were on the move again at 1.30, coming abreast of several large Shilluk villages on the west bank, and from them we gathered that the Dinkhas we had seen on the other bank were moving to avoid a raid by a party of Dervishes who had been absent from the *zeriba* when we attacked three days previously.

Here we remained until 7.30 a.m. on the 19th, the *Sirdar* being anxious to allow plenty of time for the French commander at Fashoda to receive and digest his note dispatched by runner on the 17th. Half an hour previously I had been sent for to the *Dal* for what proved to be a most interesting interview with the *Sirdar*. Sir Herbert told me he had no definite news of the situation at Fashoda, but believed the force there was French, and that the commandant's name was Marchand, that he had a few other Frenchmen with him, but that the actual troops consisted of only a hundred and twenty Senegalese.

He could give no definite orders until he knew what line the French would take. If they fired at us I was to land the battery, supported by infantry, and pound them, but he hoped reason would prevail and that an amiable "confab" might take place. If this took place we were all to adopt a very official and stand-off attitude, until the results of the "confab" warranted our becoming genial and hospitable, which was our inclination, having nothing but friendly feelings towards the French.

Kitchener, in his capacity of governor-general of the Sudan, would insist on Marchand recognising the Egyptian flag.

If Marchand should prove to be amenable and agree to withdraw, I was to land all troops, salute the French flag, and play the "Marseillaise." In this case the *Sirdar* would offer to transport the whole French expedition to Cairo. If, however, Marchand was argumentative I would receive a signal "Hoist flag," and was to land all troops at once, sufficiently far from the French position to avoid bringing on an action, form them in line (battery on the right in action, then the company of the Camerons, the 11th and 13th Sudanese Battalions), and erect a flagstaff. When all should be ready I was to send to inform the *Sirdar*, who would come at once, when the ceremony of hoisting the Egyptian flag, under a salute from the guns, would take place.

I was then to leave a force under Jackson consisting of four guns and his own battalion, the 11th, to watch the French, re-embark two guns and the 13th, and accompany the *Sirdar* to the mouth of the Sobat River, some fifty miles farther up the Nile.

Jackson would remain as a blockading force, isolating the French until orders could be obtained from Cairo as to action regarding them. If there were no actual hostilities, the *Sirdar*, directly Marchand had gone back to his fort, would return his visit and would keep Marchand occupied so that he would not be aware I was landing troops and erecting a flagstaff farther up the river; directly a message should reach him saying all was ready he would at once proceed to the flagstaff. He explained that he wished to avoid remonstrances from Marchand, and that the latter should know nothing of it until it was a *fait accompli.*

I have given at length the verbal instructions from my remarkable chief. He had prepared for all the eventualities which might occur, and had told me how he wished me to act. He was most emphatic in impressing on me that I would get no further instructions, but must myself watch, form my own conclusions, and act.

Now for the story of this interesting day, the 19th September, which will show how clearly the *Sirdar* had foreseen and prepared.

At 9.15 a.m. a small boat was reported as coming down the Nile, flying the French flag. We could certainly see a large flag, which appeared to be standing upright in the water, and it wasn't until we got nearer to it that we saw it was attached to a small boat with red[4] figures in it bending to the oars. Our flotilla stopped engines, the French boat went alongside the *Dal,* and an officer in spotless white went on board, and our engines were set in motion again.

We could see Fashoda Fort, some five miles off, flying a huge French flag. At last we drew opposite the fort, which was a puny little thing. Were we to be compelled to knock it to pieces? Not being on the *Sirdar's* boat, I had no idea of the gist of his conversation with the French officer. I had got my orders and must use my own gumption! So, standing on the roof of my sternwheeler with my field-glasses glued to my eyes, I waited and watched. Two French officers were coming from the fort to the riverbank, also in spotless white clothes, and the *Dal* had moved into the bank. Beatty's boat, the *Fateh,* on the roof of which I was perched, was some two hundred yards away. The *Sirdar* and Wingate were alone on the upper deck. (N.B.—in these riverboats the two decks were open to view.) The two French officers went on board and were taken by the *aide-de-camp,* Lord E. Cecil, up the ladder into the presence of the *Sirdar.*

After much bowing and scraping and saluting, what I supposed to be a map was spread on the table, then followed much gesticulation and apparently angry conversation. Distinct signs of hostility on both sides. I was beginning to think there could be only one ending to such forcible discussion, and that I should see negotiations broken off, when up the ladder moved a native, bearing a tray of bottles and glasses, and these, full of golden liquid, were soon being clinked together by the two central figures, who until that moment I had believed engaged in a deadly dispute.

It was an entertaining dumb-crambo show to watch, and the gesticulating figures are as clear to me now, writing twenty-four years after, as they were then.

I cannot remember that the actual signal "Hoist flag" was

---

4. The Senegalese were all clothed in bright red jerseys.

ever made, but I at once gave the order for the boats with the troops on board to proceed up the river. The *Dal,* having landed the *Sirdar* for his return visit, followed with the battery. Then everything proceeded according to programme.

The Egyptian flag was hoisted. When the *Sirdar,* having been sent for, arrived, twenty-one guns were fired, three cheers were given for the Khedive in the Egyptian tongue—"*Effendines Choke Yassa*"—and the 13th Battalion was re-embarked.

The *Sirdar* had, meanwhile, returned for a farewell conversation with Marchand, leaving word I was to notify him directly I was ready to proceed south. An interesting sidelight is thrown on the working of Kitchener's mind by an account which was current at the time of his farewell to the enterprising Frenchman. The story ran that he had so far avoided discussing his intentions regarding Marchand's force, and on rising to depart turned to Cecil, as though a matter of no importance had suddenly struck him, and said: "By the way, Cecil, haven't you a letter for Monsieur Marchand?"

Cecil, who had been well drilled, muttered he believed he had one somewhere, and, after fumbling in all his pockets, produced an envelope which was handed to M. Marchand just as Kitchener and his staff re-embarked. That letter was an ultimatum from the Governor-General of the Sudan laying down the conditions which the French were to observe, to the following effect: No man was to carry arms outside the fort. No communication with the natives was to take place. No one might embark on the river, etc., etc., concluding with the information that a *force majeure* was being left to see that these conditions were carried out.

We had great sympathy with the enterprise and sporting spirit shown by this French Expedition. It was a great performance. They had marched right across Africa, and thence from the Congo to the Nile, carrying their provisions and steel boats in sections—it was one of these which brought their emissary to the *Sirdar* on the 19th. They were charmingly courteous and civil, but perhaps what appealed to us most was the weakness of their force—seven Europeans[5] and 120 blacks—the immaculate turn-out of everyone, officers in white which might just have emerged from the best French laundry, men in smart red jerseys which appeared to be new, and finally the fact that they were able to regale their visitors on what the *Sirdar*'s Staff described as excellent red wine, and plenty of it.

It appears that M. Marchand told the *Sirdar* that, in accepting the situation, he was only yielding to *force majeure*.[6] He admitted that previous to our arrival they had been in considerable anxiety, for they had heard that the Dervishes were on their way in five steamers to attack them, and it was a distinct relief to find we had no hostile intentions. They had been living in their trenches for the three previous nights. Undoubtedly it was due to the fact of our advance to Omdurman that they were able to get as far as they did, without being overwhelmed by a force of the Khalifa's followers.

Leaving the *Nasr* as a guard on the river to help Jackson, the other four boats started south at 4.30 p.m., and, tying up for the early part of the night, reached the Sobat River about 3 p.m. on the 20th, ascended it for half an hour, and tied up to the bank. It had been reported that we might find a French or Abyssinian force here, but, as there was neither, the *Sirdar* ordered me to leave two guns, two Maxims, and three companies, with Gamble and Capper, and a month's rations, and as soon as they were settled I was to follow him down to Khartoum, picking up the riddled *Saffiyeh* on the way; but on no account was I to hold any communication with Marchand, as he wished the French and British Governments to consider his own reports, which he had sent, before any representation from Marchand could reach them; and off he steamed.

It was a poisonous spot, this mouth of the Sobat: heavy, rank vegetation, and the largest mosquitoes I have ever seen, so much so that curtains had to be sent up even for the black soldiers. I

---

5. One of these was to become very famous in the Great War as General Mangin.
6. Consideration for the French was shown, and their flag was allowed to remain over their fort until they evacuated Fashoda two months later.

was sorry for Gamble and Capper.

Next morning, the 21st September, I started north early, and was off Fashoda about 4 p.m. Thither the *Sultan* had preceded us, having been dropped by the *Sirdar*, as he passed, to guard the river jointly with the *Nasr*. Beatty had arranged to get some coal from the *Sultan*, and in order to avoid the French he decided to stop on the east or opposite bank to Fashoda, one mile below it, and he signalled to the *Sultan* to bring him his coal there. All proceeded according to plan, but, shortly after tying up, Walter Cowan was seen coming on board the *Fatteh* with a letter[7] in his hand. Beatty having refused to take this letter, Cowan came to me, explaining that it was a letter which Marchand wished to send down river, saying I must take it as it was impossible for him to make a suitable excuse to Marchand for my not doing so.

I replied that I would take no letter for Marchand, and suggested he might give as an excuse that I was not going straight to Khartoum, as I might be delayed some days, whilst Beatty patched up the *Saffiyeh,* which I had orders should go down with us. I thought it advisable to remain silent about this episode when I met the *Sirdar* on reaching Khartoum. It was not until three years later that I told him the story, and I have never seen him so genuinely pleased. He explained that he had officially stated that Marchand had not sent any letter for his Government, a statement he could not have adhered to had he known the episode related here.

Next day we reached the scene of our fight of the 15th, the "Dem-el-Zekhi." Beatty managed to patch up the old *Saffiyeh* in twenty-four hours, and we, towing her down, eventually reached Omdurman on the 25th.

---

7. Sir Walter Cowan tells me that he is doubtful if the story (as heard and related by me) about Cecil's handing a letter to Marchand is correct, for it appears that the *Sirdar* gave him (Cowan) a letter with orders not to deliver it to Marchand until he (the *Sirdar*) had gone north. Sir Walter believes it was Marchand's answer to this letter which I declined to take down. He says Marchand was upset by my refusal and in a letter to Jackson complained of unnecessary delay in sending him feeble excuses.

There we heard that our chief, Sir Herbert Kitchener, had been made a Peer, that the Empress of Austria had been assassinated, that affairs in Crete had become serious, Haldane and twenty men of the 71st (H.L.I.) being killed, that five British battalions were being sent there, and finally that the French Government regarded Marchand's small force at Fashoda merely as an exploring party. I was delighted to find that General Sir Francis Grenfell, commanding the British army in Egypt, had arrived at Omdurman. Kitchener had succeeded him as *Sirdar*, and was his junior, and it was refreshing to see how genuinely delighted he was at Kitchener's success, to which his own unselfish and hearty assistance so largely contributed.

There were still outlying bodies of the Dervishes to be dealt with. Parsons (General Sir Charles) was doing excellent work on the Suakin side, and had utterly defeated the enemy and captured Gudaref on the 22nd September. Later he was hard pressed there, and a force was placed under General Rundle, up the Blue Nile, to operate towards him, a force to which I was sent with my battalion, leaving Omdurman on the 7th October.

This expedition was full of interest, and it was pleasant serving under my friend of many years, Rundle. Quite a lot of troops were employed, and a great deal of arduous work performed under trying conditions of weather, but there was nothing sufficiently marked in my own experiences to call for more than a few words here. I became a sort of base commandant at Abu Haraz, but also had charge of what was called the Blue Nile District, covering from 400 to 500 miles of river, which involved a good deal of movement on my part. It was campaigning under most unpleasant conditions of weather, and the percentage of sick was very heavy. Many officers were down, and on the 18th October young Cottingham, of the 10th Sudanese Battalion, died, and I read the funeral service, or rather an improvised one (for there was not a prayer book available), over him next day, the firing-party of 300 being under Walter, of the Lanc's Fusiliers.

We were amused, at this time, to see in the papers that

"The Guards had arrived in London, worn and weary,

with the light of battle in their eyes."

They would be the last to welcome such a description, having been in the field only for a few weeks.

The birds and beasts were an ever-present source of enjoyment, and I think the masses of cranes on the riverbed, especially the graceful "*Demoiselle*," interested me more than anything else. They are quite good to eat, too, and I shot a few, as also guinea-fowl and pigeons, from time to time.

The devastation caused by the Mahdi's rule was everywhere apparent. For instance, Rufaa was one of the largest and wealthiest towns on the Blue Nile, but was then partly deserted and in a miserable state of poverty and squalor. Just after the battle of Omdurman the Emir, Ahmed Fedeel, fleeing there, gutted the place of money and food. Not a single chicken was left, and there were still over 2,000 inhabitants. Judging by the large enclosing walls, it must have been a fine town once.

On the 27th November I got back to Omdurman, and found orders for half of the 13th to proceed up the White Nile again under Maxse.[8] It was with a sad heart that I saw this detachment of my Sudanese Battalion off on the 29th November to the feverish and unpleasant Sobat River again, but was proud of their bearing and of the uncomplaining spirit they showed.

It was on this day, too, that I saw the gallant Marchand and Baratier leave Omdurman, to the strains of the "Marseillaise" played by our battalion band.

I had heard recently that I had been promoted brevet-colonel for this campaign, and that I was to proceed to Malta in time to take over command of the 1st Battalion of my British regiment, the Sherwood Foresters, on the 1st January. So for the next few days I was busy winding up battalion affairs, saying farewell to all my friends, playing a few games of polo, and selling superfluous articles at a loss —such as three camels for £16 which had cost me £41—and finally started north on the 10th December with three ponies and two donkeys. The former I took to Malta,

---

8. Now Lieutenant-General Sir Ivor Maxse

153

with two others, which I bought from Mahon[9] at Wad Hamad on my way down.

Again I had the luck to find Rundle travelling in the same direction as myself, and he gave me a passage from Haifa to Shellal in the *Sirdar's* own boat, the *Water Lily*. Major Pedley, the commandant at Assouan, who has since become one of my greatest friends, met us, and I have recorded in my diary that he entertained us royally at lunch with turkey and champagne. Twenty years later I had the good fortune to have Pedley as my military secretary at Gibraltar.

I found many old friends in Cairo, where I spent five delightful days receiving much kindness—amongst others from the *Sirdar* (Sir F. Grenfell), Lady Grenfell, and General Sir Ronald Lane—and got to Alexandria on the 24th, and shipped my five ponies, and myself, expecting to sail at once; but it blew such a gale that we could not put to sea until the 26th, though we moved to the outer harbour to safeguard the crew from getting drunk early on the 25th. That Christmas Day was one of the most miserable I have ever spent, for it was bitterly cold and I was racked with fever and rheumatism.

However, I reached Malta on the 30th and took over command from Colonel Hume of the 1st Battalion Sherwood Foresters, the old 45th, the next day.

9. Now Lieutenant-General Sir Brian Mahon

CHAPTER 8

Malta

New Year's Day, 1899, saw the departure of the outgoing Governor, Sir Lyon Fremantle, and, as he had refused me leave to go to England for three weeks to get uniform (I had nothing but service kit, and that Egyptian), I did not regret his departure. Major-General Lord Congleton became temporary Governor, and he, too, would not take the responsibility of letting me go, so I had to wait the arrival of the new Governor, Sir Francis Grenfell, of whose decision I had no doubt. He and Lady Grenfell arrived on the 6th January, and the next day saw me tossing about in the 1,000-ton *Carola en route* for Syracuse.

I got home on the 11th, came in for a dance at Haresfoot (my home in Herts); was given a public dinner of welcome by the people of Berkhampsted, which pleased me very much; had some excellent days' shooting, and left England again on the 9th February for Marseilles, whence I reached Malta on the 13th.

I quickly settled down to work, finding many delightful and capable people: I have particularly in mind the C.R.A., Colonel O'Callaghan[1], and Colonel Spence, the chief staff officer.

Owing to reported trouble with the Khalifa, who was still at large in the Sudan, a company of the battalion was sent to Cyprus with Radford, Anley, and Percival; two companies, under F. Shaw,[2] were already in Crete, where I paid them an interesting visit.

---

1. Lieutenant-General Sir Desmond O'Callaghan.
2. Lieutenant-General the Rt. Hon. Sir F. Shaw, K.C.B.

In April we had most instructive manoeuvres. Lord Congleton commanded the defending forces, which occupied the Victoria lines; I commanded the invading forces, which assembled beyond Melleiha Bay, to the west of the island. My force was a brigade of infantry, and a Naval brigade, backed by a Fleet, from which we were supposed to have landed, under Sir Richard Poore, Bt. We had three quite exciting days, ending in our having to retire, and actually re-embark and put to sea in the face of our enemy. This was judged to have been done successfully—the enemy having been misled as to our place of embarkation, and having been kept at a distance by rear-guards, disputing every inch of the way in the manner learned in the Tirah Campaign, and by the guns of Sir R. Poore's Fleet.

The great advantage of Malta was the close touch it brought us into with the officers of the Royal Navy, in which I made many friends. The two Services were always meeting and engaging in friendly competitions at racquets, polo, and on the race-course. My great triumph there was winning the Gibraltar Jockey Club Challenge Cup on my pony Mad Moon, by a short head from my friend Godfrey Faussett (now the King's Naval Equerry), who rode Victor Stanley's pony (Vice-Admiral the Hon. Victor Stanley).

Rumours were abroad of trouble in the Transvaal, and I cabled privately to the Adjutant-General, Sir Evelyn Wood, to impress on him the fitness of the 1st Battalion Sherwood Foresters.

On the 2nd August I received a letter from the adjutant-general, and a cable from Kitchener in Egypt, offering me the Governorship of the province of Omdurman, which I refused with thanks. I heard afterwards that the main object was to get me out there, so that I might succeed Kitchener as *Sirdar* of the Egyptian army. If that was true it was lucky I did not go, for I could never have risen to the high standard of Governorship of the Sudan attained by Sir Reginald Wingate.

At this time Maurice (now Major-General Sir F. Maurice) of the regiment was at home and engaged in ascertaining, should war with the Boers become a *fait accompli,* what chance we had of going: if he heard the Battalion was to mobilise, he was to send me the one word "Nottingham." This duly arrived on the 8th October, to the great satisfaction of everybody. The A.A.G., Colonel J. Spence, was particularly triumphant, as he had always been a good friend to me and the regiment, and whenever I grumbled to him, on hearing of other units being ordered out, he always told me I needn't worry, for before the Boers could be beaten we should see half the British army in South Africa. Events proved him to be under the mark, for over 400,000 were mobilised in the next three years.

Alas! on the 12th October Maurice cabled again, cancelling his former good news, and down fell our mental barometers. This news was especially depressing, as we knew then that the Boers had practically declared war from the previous day, the 11th. Our impatience was not lessened when we heard of the fights of Talana on the 20th October, where my late General, Penn Symons, Jack Sherston, and my cousin Jack Pechel were killed, followed next day by Elandslaagte and, eight days later, by the disastrous affair at Nicholson's Nek which resulted in the investment of the force under Sir George White in Ladysmith.

On the 25th October our 2nd Battalion, the old 95th, in which I had spent all my service, arrived, under Lieutenant-Colonel Bulpett, from Aden, and was landed.

The long-hoped-for order to proceed with the Battalion to the Cape came on the 31st October, but it was not until after many games of polo and racquets, and a series of farewell dinners with the Governor, Admiral, and Fleet that we embarked on the transport *Dunera* on the 21st November, and steamed out of the Grand Harbour.

As far as Malta was concerned, I cannot honestly say I fell a slave to its charms; especially as I had, throughout my stay there, suffered from attacks of fever and neuralgia, doubtless the result of much campaigning and roughing it in extremes of climate. It was unfortunate, too, for it took many years to shake them off, and I was to have many *mauvais quarts d'heure* during the coming campaign, though I was never prevented from carrying out my duties.

Before leaving the subject of Malta, I must refer to the many distinguished friends I made there. The best known perhaps was Admiral Sir John Fisher (afterwards Lord Fisher). His arrival as commander-in-chief of the Fleet was viewed with some anxiety, as his powers of handling a fleet at full speed had yet to be proved, but that anxiety was soon allayed. I have seen few men more alive or more bristling with energy, which did not lessen in a ball-room.

Then there were Admiral Sir Gerald Noel, Madden (becoming Admiral Sir Charles), Chatfield (becoming Rear-Admiral Sir A.); also Kirkpatrick (becoming Lieutenant-General Sir G. M.), who, then a junior officer, was my most efficient C.R.E. at manoeuvres. Another very distinguished officer I met there was Tyrwhitt (now Vice-Admiral Sir Reginald). We played much polo together. On one occasion, he, with Erskine, Victor Stanley, and Lord Kelburn (now Lord Glasgow), played my regiment, represented by Weldon, Leveson Gower, Burnett-Hitchcock, and myself, and we beat them by one goal.

There was our excellent *padre* there, too, the Rev. A. G. Pentreath, who assisted me in organising a club for sailors and soldiers, which consisted of two houses and beds for forty men. A salient rule of the club was that questions of religion and the men's souls could only be discussed in the top room of one of the houses.

When the battalion sailed from Malta on the 21st November we were given a thrilling send-off. We steamed out of the Grand Harbour, through the Fleet, which was manned, and a double line of boats amidst deafening cheers, the Governor and Admiral accompanying us in their barges to the mouth of the harbour.

Our reservists who had joined us from England were a fine body of men. The battalion was 1,100 strong. The officers on board, besides myself, were: Majors Gosset, Godley (Brigadier-General Godley), Shaw (Lieutenant-General Sir F.); Captains England, Weldon, Rigby, Leveson Gower (Brigadier-General Leveson Gower), Radford; Lieutenants Sadler, Keller, Morley, Anley, Burnett-Hitchcock (Major-General Burnett-Hitchcock),

Murray, Watson, De Pledge, Percival, Wybergh, Frend, Rhodes, Gibson; 2nd Lieutenants Wilkin, Manby, Popham, Webb; also Lieutenant Casswell (Adjutant), Lieutenant and Quartermaster Tylor, and Major Duncan, the medical officer.

We called at Cyprus to pick up our detached company, which brought us up to 1,200, Shaw's two companies having returned from Crete some time previously.

CHAPTER 9

South African War: Paardeberg

We touched at Aden and landed for a route march at Zanzibar, where the whole battalion were treated with royal hospitality by the Prime Minister, General Mathews, and our consul, Mr. B. S. Cave (now Consul-General at Algiers). As we entered Durban Harbour late on the 13th December the excitement of everyone to get news can be imagined. The days of wireless had not then been reached. The last certain news we had had was that following the successful actions at Talana on the 20th and Elandslaagte on the 21st October, Sir G. White had taken the offensive on the 30th October, which had resulted in the disaster of Nicholson's Nek and the investment of the British force in Ladysmith.

We knew, too, that a complete Army Corps under Sir Redvers Buller had landed in South Africa, and that the bulk of them had marched to the relief of Ladysmith. We expected orders to land at once, although it was 10 p.m.; but not a soul came near us, so we took to signalling, asking such questions as: "Has Ladysmith been relieved?" "Are we still in time to reach Buller before he fights his way into Ladysmith?" "Cannot we land at once?" But all we could glean in reply was that they knew nothing, except that we should have to lie out at anchor till next morning.

Durban Harbour is one of the most beautiful I know, and with the lights of the many transports and ships, and those on shore, the scene was a very impressive one, but didn't satisfy our craving for news; so, trying to possess our souls in patience, we turned in and rolled to sleep, for there was a heavy swell.

The next day, the 14th, is best described *verbatim* from my diary:

"Up at 5 a.m. Cold, fresh morning; Durban looked lovely. At 6.30 a.m. tug came off ordering us to East London at once. Got local newspaper. Our force moving In within three miles of Colenso. Metcalfe had made sortie from La-dysmith. Mafeking and Kimberley still besieged. Methuen apparently still fighting at Modder River. Gatacre had had bad reverse at Stormberg. Evidently we are to join him. Started at 8 a.m. on our 252 miles to East London."

We disembarked under difficulties from the open roads. The enthusiasm of the Colonists was very pleasing, and they were most hospitable; but many of our men were foolish enough to fall to the attractions of young women and parted with their badges and buttons as souvenirs, which was very annoying.

Eventually we got off in three trains and reached Sterkstroom, General Gatacre's head-quarters, on the afternoon of the 17th December, and, by virtue of my being the senior infantry officer present, I assumed command of the infantry brigade consisting of the 2nd Royal Irish Rifles, half the 1st Royal Scots, the 2nd Northumberland Fusiliers, and half the Berkshires, in addition to the 1st Battalion Sherwood Foresters; Lieutenant Burnett-Hitchcock acted as Brigade Major, and a very capable one too.

It was only now that we got authentic news of what had hap-pened. We had had three reverses in less than a week, dulled since "the Black Week." Gatacre had been badly mauled at Stormberg on the 9th December. Methuen, after two successful fights at Belmont and Graspan, on the 22nd and the 25th of November, had been driven back at Magersfontein on the 11th December, and Buller had failed in a frontal attack on Colenso for the relief of Ladysmith.

In order to make it easy to follow my story, I will briefly describe the cause of the war and the situation of the several forces.

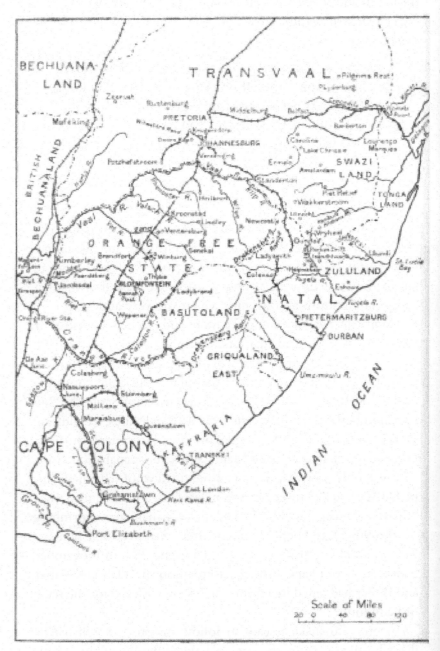

GENERAL MAP OF SOUTH AFRICA

The Boers, under President Kruger, had for a long time shown their disregard of requests made by England. The Transvaal was rich in mines, and large numbers of Englishmen had settled there, developed the mines, and brought great wealth to the Boer Government, which, in spite of representations from England, definitely refused to grant them the rights of Burghership. This meant that, although they had large; interests in the country, they saw measures and legislation hostile to themselves introduced without any right of vote. The irritation caused by the fruitless Jameson Raid in 1896 had not tended to conciliation. The British Government demanded that the rights of Burghership be granted to these settlers, but it was refused.

In August 1899 reinforcements were sent to the weak garrison of British troops in South Africa. The two Boer States, the Transvaal and Orange Free State, imagining that matters could not be settled without a fight, and thinking it was a case of "now or never," issued an ultimatum to the effect that the British troops on their frontier must be withdrawn by the 11th October, and further, that other reinforcements which they heard were on the high seas approaching South Africa must never land. At this time Major-General Sir W. P. Symons was commanding in Natal, fresh troops were being sent from India, and on the 7th October Sir George White landed and assumed command, having under him 15,000 troops, which he concentrated at Ladysmith, except a detachment under General Symons and a force just north of Ladysmith.

The Boers had 50,000 men ready to take the field, and on the 11th October began to move 18,000 under Joubert into Natal, 8,000 to invest Mafeking and Kimberley, and to assemble 4,000 in the Orange River Free State. On the 20th October they attacked General Symons at Talana, a hill just north of Dundee, and got beaten, though our general was killed, and next day they were again beaten at Elandslaagte; but on the 31st October came the disaster at Nicholson' Nek, after which they invested the British forces, which had retired on Ladysmith. The Home Government then sent out a fresh army corps under Sir Redvers Buller; he, considering matters serious towards Kimberley, towards Queenstown, and thirdly towards Ladysmith, split up his forces, so that the end of November saw 15,000 under Clery[1] in Natal to relieve Ladysmith, 4,900 under French[2] at Naauwpoort, to move on Colesberg, 4,300 under Gatacre[3] at Queenstown, and 9,400 under Methuen[4] at De Aar, to relieve Kimberley.

I have already described how three of these four columns suffered defeat about the time the 1st Battalion Sherwood Foresters landed at East London. The 6th Division under General Kelly-Kenny was in course of arriving, and the 7th Division was being formed at home under General Tucker.

Now I will continue my own experiences.

The matter of first local importance was to guard against surprise by an elaborate system of piquets and entrenched posts, and the next matter was to train for all we were worth for the class of warfare before us, and this we did, both by battalion and brigade. I was very cross because I was forced to observe Christmas Day as a holiday, and am afraid I made some pointed remarks to the effect that we were not out there to observe Christmas Day. Next day I was cheered by the arrival, to join our battalion, of an excellent officer with great active service experience, Lieutenant-Colonel Cunningham. He, later, successfully commanded a brigade.

Our general, Gatacre, who was always full of fight, chafed at our enforced inaction, and made sundry plans for expeditions, but desisted from carrying them out in view of explicit orders issued by the commander-in-chief However, the Boers forced his hand once or twice up the railway at Molteno, and I was sent out with a mixed force, including an armoured train, on two occasions, with Jeffreys (Major-General P. D. Jeffreys) as C.R.A., and we had some quite interesting but almost bloodless operations. It was on one of these that we found ourselves being

1. Lieutenant-General Sir Francis Clery.
2. Field-Marshal the Earl of Ypres.
3. Lieutenant-General Sir William Gatacre.
4. Field-Marshal Lord Methuen.

shelled at a range of 7,000 yards from two Boer guns in action from the top of the Loopersberg. None of the shells burst, and on examining them we found they were English 15-lb. shells, fired from guns captured from us in Natal. By depressing the trails and firing from a height this range, so far beyond what the guns were designed for, had been obtained; but their effect was nil, as they had no velocity and no suitable fuses.

On the 9th January (1900) we got news that French was having active fighting, and that the Suffolks had been roughly handled at Colesberg; and the next day we heard of the heavy fighting at Wagon Hill, Ladysmith, and that Johnnie Hamilton (General Sir Ian Hamilton) had distinguished himself there.

On the 19th January I was sent to take command of a mixed force of 2,492 men at Bushman's Hoek, ten miles south of Molteno. Major Maxwell, R.E., was my staff officer and Jeffreys again C.R.A. This was very interesting. The high Loopersberg was the main feature, and in the next few days we prepared and entrenched a considerable position, covering twelve miles of front, including works on the Loopersberg itself. It was whilst there that General Gatacre's *aide-de-camp*, Angus McNeill, procured for me a really good horse, Beggar-man, which had won several races. One spent long hours in the saddle, and good horses were worth their weight in gold.

The new commander-in-chief, Field-Marshal Lord Roberts, with Major-General Lord Kitchener as his chief of staff, arrived at Cape Town on the 10th January, and we saw early signs of developments; one which affected the Battalion was a decision on the part of the chief to increase very materially the number of mounted troops, realising that, as the bulk of the Boers were mounted, they must be opposed by their own arm. Accordingly every infantry battalion was ordered to hand over a company for conversion into Mounted Infantry, We thus lost the strength of a company under Major Godley. Lord Roberts's view was that, to relieve Ladysmith and Kimberley, the most expeditious plan would be to take the offensive on a large scale and aim at Bloemfontein, the capital of the Orange Free State.

There were three lines of advance, and he chose the longest, because he realised that it would be safer and less liable to interference than the other two. This was the line of the railway from the old Colony *via* De Aar Junction to the Modder River, where Methuen's force was facing the Boers covering Kimberley, the men who had repulsed him at Magersfontein.

The two fresh Divisions, the 6th and 7th, had just arrived from England, and were being collected at Graspan and Modder River under cover of Methuen's force. A cavalry division under French, who had done so well at Colesberg, and was about to be withdrawn after handing over to General Clements, was also forming.

There were also 2,000 Mounted Infantry under Colonel Hannay, a similar number under Colonel Alderson,[5] and a third division, to be called the 9th, was also being formed there from Methuen's Highland Brigade, together with a brigade composed of battalions hitherto employed upon the lines of communication. This latter is the brigade in which I take especial interest.

I remained commanding Gatacre's advanced position until the 2nd February, and getting back to my camp at Philip's Farm that evening, after a long day, the fatigue was knocked bang out of me by a wire from Lord Roberts, offering me a brigade. There was no time wasted in sending off a reply, and also a request that Lieutenant Hood of the R.M.L.I. might be sent from Malta as my *aide-de-camp* I would have preferred taking a Sherwood Forester, but the boy was very keen to come, and before leaving Malta had extracted a promise from me that if I were given a brigade I would ask for him.

At the time, never dreaming that I should get such a command, I said "Yes," and of course my promise had to be kept, and glad I was, for he proved most useful and a really pleasant and cheerful addition to my staff.

Now the brigade, numbered the 19th, which was given to me was the one composed of line of communication units:

---

5. Lieutenant-General Sir E. Alderson.

2nd Batt. Duke of Cornwall's Light Infantry (Aldworth),
1st Batt. The Gordon Highlanders (Macbean),
2nd Batt. The K. Shropshire Light Infantry (Spens),
The Royal Canadian Regiment (Otter),

And my orders were to proceed with all dispatch to assume command of it at Orange River. This involved riding some eighty-seven miles through a country where it was undesirable to travel alone, and as some Mounted Infantry, under Dewar and Amphlett, were to start in thirty-six hours I made arrangements to go with them. Joyful as the news was, there was a sad side to it, for I had to say farewell to my dear old Sherwood Foresters, and never have I hated a parade more.

The Mounted Infantry started at 7 a.m. on the 3rd February, but, as I had to await a telegram from the chief of the staff, I did not get off until the afternoon, when I galloped after them some fifteen miles across the *veldt*, *via* Karn Nek, and joined them in their camp at Pretoria's Farm.

It was an experience I do not wish to repeat, for the whole country was inches deep in locusts, and as one's horse kicked them up they flew in one's face with stinging force. The countryside was soon converted from a rich expanse of green luxuriant grass into a bare waste almost without a blade. No one who has not seen what I saw that day can picture the devastating effect of a gigantic swarm of locusts.

Five days' march took us to Thebus Station, a distance of eighty-seven miles, whence we were to start on our 250-miles railway journey to the rendezvous north of the Orange River where the army was assembling.

The only important town passed through was Maraisburg. We found the Colonists, with one or two exceptions, most cordial and hospitable. After trekking seven miles from Maraisburg I was able to entrain at once (4.30 p.m. on the 7th February) and reached De Aar Junction in the small hours next morning, to find the commander-in-chief and his chief of staff (Lords Roberts and Kitchener) had left the station for the front an hour previously. I will not attempt to describe the crowded train or the masses of troops, horses, and transport, and the bustling activity I found at Orange River Station on detraining there on the afternoon of the 8th February. We heard that Major-General Macdonald, with some eight battalions, and General Babington's Cavalry Brigade had had a smart fight on the 6th February at Koedoesberg, the object being to distract the enemy's attention from the move the commander-in-chief was preparing towards Bloemfontein, and also to drive them from a strong position on the Modder River west of the railway, where their presence prevented a direct advance to relieve Kimberley. They had not been successful in the latter object.

The important news was that all mounted troops were then being pushed out to the front. I met a heap of old friends—Aldworth, Spens, Ridley, Kirkpatrick, R.E. (so recently with me at Malta), and a most important person in the form of my Brigade Major, Major F. S. Inglefield, with whom I was to spend some eighteen months, a very agreeable association. I was also joined this day by my nephew, Eddy Dorrien-Smith of the K.S.L.I., as temporary *aide-de-camp* The next three days were spent visiting the scattered portions of my new Brigade, getting personally acquainted with commanding officers, and collecting the battalions, transport, field hospital, etc. at Graspan; but by the night of the 12th February all were ready.

I was, of course, a stranger to the men, and was usually called General Smith. I heard of one man who had been told that, as I was brother to a king, he must address me as "your Royal Highness"; luckily, he did not act on it, for my only claim to such an honour was founded on my being a brother of "the King of the Scillies," as my eldest brother was chaffingly styled.

I had that day met my Divisional General, Sir H. Colvile, and heard from him the plan of campaign; up till then I had not the faintest idea when and where, and with what object in view, we were going to move. Secrecy, in Lord Roberts's opinion, was of the utmost importance. I have already said that the force consisted of a Cavalry Division and three Infantry Divisions. The cavalry had moved on the 12th, followed by the 7th and 6th

Infantry Divisions in that order on the same day. Our Division, the 9th, was to bring up the rear a day behind.

Before dawn on the 13th[6] we were on the move east to the Riet River. The heat was intense, water scarce, and the men found the march trying. Many men and animals died from the heat and lack of water. The 15th Brigade alone had lost twenty-one men on this very march the day before; but they had come from on board ship and a long railway journey.

It was not until 1 p.m. next day, the 14th February, that we reached Waterval Drift over the Riet River, about eighteen miles from Graspan. Crossing the drift was a lengthy business, and it was dark when we were all over. It was then that the commander-in-chief sent for me. I found him more charming than ever, and apparently without a care in the world. (He was then sixty-eight.) I also saw Prince Adolphus of Teck, Neville Chamberlain, Charlie Gough, and Sir William Nicholson. It had been a desperately hot march, with dust-storms and no water, and the men were very beat.

On the 15th February the 19th Brigade was on divisional rear-guard with the following mounted troops (not directly under me): Kitchener's Horse, the Grahamstown M.I., and Cholmondeley's C.I.V. Mounted Infantry. As we were moving off I saw a large ox-wagon convoy across the drift. I had no knowledge of its existence before, and found it had its own escort of 250 M.I. under Ridley; but I left Kitchener's Horse and one company of Gordon Highlanders to help the wagons through the drift.

We reached Wegdraai Drift, eight miles off, about 10 a.m., to hear that Boers were attacking the convoy. Lord Roberts at once sent back one battalion (the 25th K.O.S.B.s) and 400 M.I. Heavy firing was soon heard.

General Wavell's Brigade, of the 7th Division, was at the same time attacking Jacobsdal, five miles ahead of us, so we had fighting in front and behind. The fight at the drift proved serious, for the same body of Boers, under de Wet, which had opposed

6. For the movements of the following days see the map of action at Poplar Grove.

French's cavalry crossing the Riet River two days previously, had reoccupied the positions covering the drift, and it proved impossible for the escort to give adequate protection for so lengthy a convoy. The bullocks were shot down, and that night Lord Roberts decided, rather than delay his operation and send back more troops, to put up with the loss of the convoy. Thus 200 wagons, with 280,000 rations for men and 38,000 for horses, fell into the hands of the enemy (being eight days' rations for the whole army), and although, by utilising the transport of Methuen's force still on the railway, 100 fresh wagon loads were brought up at once, the army had to be content with half-rations until we reached Bloemfontein.

Many commanders would have allowed their plans to be interfered with by such a serious loss; not so the determined "Bobs," and although we suffered in efficiency, especially our horses and cattle, owing to this shortage of food, the commander-in-chief's plans for the relief of Kimberley and the seizure of the capital of the Orange Free State were carried through.

To make the story intelligible I had better describe the movements of the cavalry sent to relieve Kimberley.

Skilfully forcing the Riet River on the 12th February, and the Modder River on the 14th, they were about Klip Drift when, in the early morning of the 15th, they were joined by Lord Kitchener and the 6th Division. It appears that during the night of the 14th-15th the Boers had abandoned the investment of Kimberley on the south side, but this was not known to the cavalry. Nine hundred Boers were, however, holding a line of *kopjes* about three and a half miles north of Klip Drift and between it and Kimberley, and they had to be dealt with in order to open the road.

Thus came the famous charge of the Cavalry Division through the middle of the Boers' position, covered by their own artillery and the guns and infantry of the 6th Division. It must have been a magnificent sight: six thousand horsemen riding straight into what appeared to the spectators the jaws of death, for a withering rifle fire was being poured into them. The dust raised by the galloping horses hid everything from friend and foe, and when it cleared General French and his gallant men were seen rallying a mile beyond the Boer position; their casualties were only sixteen killed and wounded and some twenty horses.

Truly it was a bold conception, splendidly carried out, and rightly raised the reputation of the general commanding the Cavalry Division. The road was now open, and French reached Kimberley the same evening, to find that the investing Boers had withdrawn.

The German official account states that throughout these operations, patrolling and reconnoitring, either by the cavalry or mounted troops with divisions, was conspicuous by its absence, and to that they ascribe the unexpected seizure of the convoy by de Wet on the Riet River, our ignorance of the Boers having given up the siege of Kimberley, and of Cronje's leaving Magersfontein on the night of the 15th. This march of Cronje right across the front of the 6th Division and only two miles from it, was only discovered by the dust he raised on the morning of the 16th February. What had actually happened was this:

Cronje, who was commanding the 4,000 to 5,000 Boers facing Lord Methuen at Magersfontein, finding his position being turned by Lord Roberts's army, had decided to try to reach Bloemfontein, and had started off on the night of the 15th, with many women and children and a large train of ox-wagons laden with quantities of baggage, intending to cross the Modder River at Koedoesrand Drift. It was a wild plan, for it was almost sure to take him right into the lion's jaws.

As soon as this move was discovered by Lord Kitchener on the morning of the 16th, he started off east on the south bank of the river to try to intercept him.

Jacobsdal had fallen to the 7th Division, and the chief had established his head-quarters there. Our division marched in there early on the 16th, and as the commander-in-chief did not believe Cronje's force constituted the whole of the Boers covering Kimberley, he personally ordered me to march with the 19th Brigade direct on Kimberley, a distance of thirty-two miles, so as to reach that place on the 18th. This order was changed later into one for the whole 9th Division to follow the 6th, which was having a merry time of it engaged with Cronje's rear-guards, the Boer leader having nearly evaded them in his march on Koedoesrand Drift.

Starting at 9.30 p.m., in moonlight, the 19th Brigade reached Klip Drift (twelve miles) at 4 a.m. next day, to find Kitchener still there, but on the point of following the 6th Division, which had moved farther east. That afternoon we again started off, and caught up Macdonald's Highland Brigade, the leading brigade of our division, which was moving off after a halt and which we followed, arriving at Paardeberg Drift, fourteen miles farther on, in the small hours of the 18th February.

We had done sixty-six miles in five days, mostly at night, and my *aide-de-camp* became an expert at sleeping on horseback; his powers of balancing seemed supernatural.

Just after daylight heavy firing was to be heard farther up-stream (*i.e.* east of us) and I received orders to fall in and follow Macdonald's Brigade, which was already moving east. When the order arrived I was chatting to an old friend (Brigadier-General C. P. Ridley, C.B.) commanding a battalion of Mounted Infantry, who was filling his pipe from my pouch, which, in the confusion, he put into his own pocket instead of into mine, leaving me baccyless.

It will be as well, before proceeding further, to bring the cavalry into the narrative again.

French, after reaching Kimberley, had pursued the Boers to the north of that place, but early on the 17th, hearing of Cronje's move east, and that the chief of the staff wanted him to try to head the Boers off at Koedoesrand Drift, he started off Broadwood's Brigade, the only one which was not too exhausted to move, with Q and R Batteries R.A., and accompanying it himself, reached Kameelfontein, four miles north of Wolves' Kraal Drift, at 11 a.m.: a great performance, considering the exhaustion of the horses and men, and the absence of water on the long march of twenty-five to thirty miles.

I will now describe the effect of this move on Cronje. The latter had halted at Wolves' Kraal Drift on the morning of the 17th, believing he was far enough ahead of his pursuers to be able to take a short rest, but on moving off again, about noon, towards the drift, his force was thrown into utter confusion by a bouquet of shells from an utterly unexpected quarter. Our cavalry was very weak, but luckily the Boers did not know how weak, or they might still have broken through.

Although heavily attacked by far superior numbers, our cavalry, distributed in small bodies, held their own and showed a grand example of how cavalry can hold up a force encumbered with transport long enough for supporting infantry to arrive. The rounding up of Cronje was undoubtedly due to the energy and pluck of General French and his cavalry.

During the nights of the 17th and 18th the 6th Division, under Kelly-Kenny, were marching for all they were worth to the sound of French's guns, and on the morning of the 18th were rewarded by finding themselves abreast of Cronje's *laager*, distant under a mile, but with the Modder River flowing between them.

It was during the night of the 17th and 18th that Cronje came to the conclusion that his escape with his wagons across Koedoesrand and Wolves' Kraal Drifts was no longer possible, and that he must entrench where he was; and he did so on both banks.

Now to return to the 19th Brigade.

The firing we heard early on the 18th was between the 6th Division and Cronje's men. Macdonald's Brigade was moving east to get into touch with the 6th Division, and the 19th Brigade had orders to fall in and move a short distance to where some of the guns were in action. We knew nothing of what was happening, but we heard our guns firing and heavy musketry fire.

On arriving near our guns it was soon evident that the Boers were lining the whole length of the opposite side of the river. After halting for a few minutes one of Lord Kitchener's Staff,

Major Hubert Hamilton,[7] rode up, and ordered me to cross the river with (Major Pratt's) 82nd Field Battery and establish myself on the other side of it. I asked him where I could cross, to which he replied: "The river is in flood, and as far as I have heard, Paardeberg Drift, the only one available, is unfordable; but Lord Kitchener, knowing your resourcefulness, feels sure you will get across somehow."

To which I jeeringly replied, as he turned to ride off, that such a message was more fitting to a courtier than a staff officer.

Ordering the brigade to follow me, I galloped off to the river, and plunging in found myself being swept away, and only regained the bank with difficulty. This was somewhat above the drift, and moving to the drift itself, I found that my horse could just get across without swimming, but the current was very strong. The river must have been at least fifty yards wide. The engineers then got a rope across, which they made fast on both sides, and, supported by this, for the water was up to the men's armpits, we got the whole brigade across, including the battery, though the water swept over the guns.

By 10.15 a.m. we were all across except the Cornwalls, left to guard the transport, and two companies of the Shropshires. We had two to three miles to reach the small *kopje* subsequently known as Gun Hill, which was my objective and proved to be under severe fire. I have reproduced an eye-sketch which I made at the time, on which the subsequent movements can be followed.

In order to avoid the fire from the Boer trenches on the riverbank, the brigade, covered by the Shropshires widely extended, swept away from the river. At 11 a.m. this high ground was secured by the Shropshires, and the Gordons were swung round to the north-east of the *kopje*, to prolong the line, to the left of the Shropshires, whilst the Canadians were directed to work up the riverbank with a view to continuing the line from

---

7. Major-General Hubert Hamilton, killed at the head of the 3rd Division in October 1914.

the river to the right of the Shropshires. At the same time the battery was told to come into action in a position about a mile north-east of the drift.

The enemy appeared to be strongest at a re-entrant of the river about 1,000 yards south of Gun Hill, marked "A" in sketch. The movement brought the Brigade within admirable range of "A," troops on Gun Hill commanding that position and enfilading it at a range of 900 yards. A machine-gun of the Royal Canadians, under Captain Bell, was on Gun Hill throughout the day, and did yeoman service. Gun Hill was u dominating position, which I made my head-quarters.

From there we looked straight into the Boers' trenches at "A," and could see the whole line of the river, Cronje's *laager* in full view across a flat open plain a mile and a half distant, and, across the river, the Highland Brigade opposite us with the 6th Division farther east of them. We could hear French's guns towards Kameelfontein and could see shells bursting on the Boer *laager* from every direction. It was really a thrilling sight, and it was evident that Cronje was cornered. We were hot, dirty, unshaven and hungry, for no food could be brought to us until the river subsided.

It was then, in conversation with the commanding officer of the Gordons, Lieutenant-Colonel Macbean,[8] that I took an oath, which became known to the Brigade, that I would not shave again until we had taken the *laager*.

At 3.30 p.m., seeing the Canadians had got rather closer to "A" than necessary, *i.e.* 500 to 800 yards, and were under a heavy fire, I moved the battery (See Map, Battle of Paardeberg) to a position where they could bring a traversing fire on "A." Previous to this we had heard a terrific burst of fire from the *laager*, and could see that something active was taking place at the other side of it. Later we heard that this was a desperate charge of a handful of Mounted Infantry under Colonel Hannay, in which he and many men were killed—the charge having been ordered by Head-quarters in spite of his protest.

---

8. Major-General Forbes Macbean.

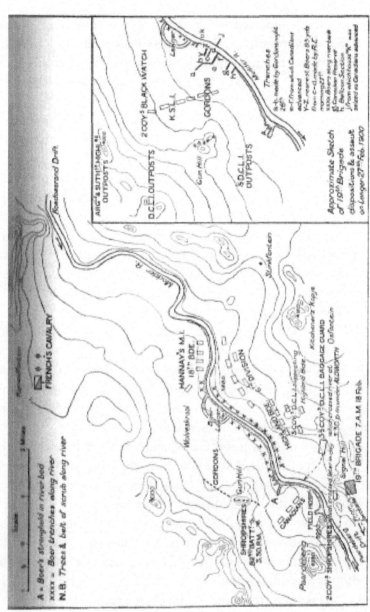

BATTLE OF PAARDEBERG

I was in a complete fog as to what was happening, and knew nothing of the situation, either of our own troops or of the Boers, beyond what I could see and infer myself.

It was not until next day that I learnt that the guns about Kameelfontein belonged to our cavalry. The only order I had received was the one to establish my brigade on the north side of the river, and I could get neither instructions nor information from anyone.

At about 4 p.m., seeing the Highland Brigade were out in the open under a warm fire from the opposite bank, I directed, with the idea of drawing some of the fire from the Canadians and Highlanders, a gradual advance from Gun Hill, which was skilfully carried out by the Shropshires, not, however, without casualties.

At 5.15 p.m. I was horrified at seeing our troops on the right of my line rise and charge forward with a ringing cheer. I, at that time, believed that only Canadians were there; but it appeared that Lieutenant-Colonel Aldworth, D.S.O., with three and a half companies of my baggage guard, the Cornwalls, and some Seaforth Highlanders, on the far side of the river, had been sent over by a higher authority to charge the Boer position, and that the Canadians, who would not be left behind, had joined in. Of course it was quite irregular that my troops should have been ordered to execute such an important movement, except through me, as any possibility of my supporting the charge with the rest of the Brigade was effectually prevented, for by the time I realised what was happening, the attack was over, since it only occupied a minute or two.

It was a gallant charge, gallantly led, but the fact that not one of them got within 300 yards of the enemy is sufficient proof of its futility. No further movement occurred, but the battle of shell and shot continued until dark, when we were able to withdraw and take up outpost positions. I then, in response to an order, rode to the Divisional Headquarters on the far side of the river, a ride of some fourteen miles there and back. Luckily the river had fallen considerably, or crossing the drift in the dark would

177

have been distinctly dangerous. All that my divisional general wanted was a report of the day's proceedings, information he could have obtained by sending a staff officer to get it. It was past midnight when my Staff and I, our saddles for pillows, lay down amongst the rocks on Gun Hill. Our casualties during the day had been 228, the gallant Aldworth being amongst the killed.

Next morning (the 19th February) I moved the Gordons and Canadians, who had fallen back to rest, forward again, and taking two companies of the Shropshires with me, advanced in the grey dawn to reconnoitre "A" and the riverbank. We found "A" empty, and that the Boers had fallen back some 1,500 yards; so, leaving troops to entrench themselves 700 yards from them, I returned to see to the burying of our dead. Poor Aldworth's body was the one nearest the Boer position at "A."

About 3 p.m. a signal from Head-quarters told me that Cronje had surrendered, and I was to cease fire; but it was quickly followed by a signal to open fire again.

As I realised that my troops were the only ones so placed as to be able to prevent the Boers from breaking out on the north-west, I had to extend the brigade so as to form an investing line in a semicircle three miles long, right resting on the river. The line was about 2,600 yards from the *laager*. Night outposts had to be very carefully posted, and it was 11 p.m. before I got back to my bivouac to eat the first meal I had had for over two days, except for a mouthful at dawn on I lie 17th, and a biscuit at midday this day. The troops, also, had got their rations, which were very welcome as they had been without food for thirty-six hours. The emergency ration was only introduced later.

Lord Roberts had arrived that morning and taken over the conduct of the battle. The artillery and the 14th Brigade of the 7th Division reinforced the troops on the south bank from Jacobsdal on this day (the 19th).

Having received orders to close my line in nearer to the *laager* before dawn (the 20th), the whole outpost moved forward along the river—our right gaining half a mile, for the Boers had fallen back on their main trenches covering the *laager*. This necessitated the whole line, excepting that part in the trees on the riverbank, lying in the flat open plain under a constant fire, which, however, only caused eight casualties.

During this morning I was sent for by Lord Roberts and asked, in the presence of Lord Kitchener, Generals French and Colvile, whether I thought I could at once carry the *laager* by direct assault. Kitchener and Colvile seemed to be in favour of such action, but I deprecated it most strongly, saying that the losses would be great and our chances of success small. I urged a bombardment for a few days with our fine force of artillery, and constant harassing on all sides, whilst I pushed my trenches nearer every night, until I was satisfied that an assault must succeed. My views were accepted, and, as I mounted to ride back, Lord Kitchener came up to me, saying that if I would attack them at once, I should be a made man.

To which I, with a smile, replied: "You heard my views, and I shall only attack now if ordered to." It was then decided that the investment, so far as the open ground was concerned, could be carried out as well from a distance, and after dark the exposed part of the line was withdrawn again to the high ground, where it remained during the night. It must be remembered that the light entrenching tools had not then been invented, and that very few heavy entrenching tools were available.

Four Boers surrendered this day, and I sent one of them back to tell his friends how hopeless the situation was for them.

It had been a very exhausting time for the Gordons, Canadians, and Shropshires lying all day in the burning sun far away from water and under a continuous rifle-fire. The withdrawal after dark was carried out under fire of one field and three howitzer batteries, and two naval guns, from about Gun Hill, and two field batteries from across the river.[9]

In order to rest the infantry, I sent one battalion each day back to the Drift for twenty-four hours' rest.

The morning of the 21st February broke with a tremen-

---

9. Three howitzer batteries, the 76th, 81st, and 65th, and two naval 4.7 guns had crossed from the south bank, and joined the 82nd Field Battery during the day.

dous fusillade, brought on, I thought, by the movements of the Shropshires on the riverbank. They, in the small hours, had made a splendid advance, and had dug themselves in within 500 yards of the line of hostile trenches facing them; but it appeared later that a Boer commando from the south had made an attempt to relieve Cronje, and had been roughly handled by General French, who gained an important height known to us as Kitchener's Kop.

That afternoon, seeing white flags over the Boer trenches, I called for my white pony, which seemed a suitable colour, and arming myself with a towel tied to a stick galloped alone to within 200 yards of the enemy's trenches, where I was met by a Boer Field Cornet. He told me the white flags were in consequence of a message from Lord Roberts to General Cronje, so, handing him a packet of proclamations, which I had been told to get into the hostile lines on the first opportunity, and having a good look round their position and trenches, I bowed and retired, and war commenced again.

I had gained important knowledge, confirmed next day by a sketch made from a reconnoitring captive balloon, which convinced me that trenches were necessary on the opposite side of the river as well. I had already asked and been promised that they should be made by a brigade on that side; but, as nothing had been done, I got fifty Shropshires across the river after dark, in a punt, and having got permission from the chief of the staff to employ artillery to cover the movement, soon had a line of trenches forward on the far bank. Our night was somewhat disturbed, as a cow stampeded the horses of the 82nd Battery, which went with limbers straight for the enemy. We recovered the limbers, but not all the horses.

A commando of Boers appeared from the north, but, opposed by De Lisle's Mounted Infantry, Broadwood's Cavalry Brigade, and the Canadians and Cornwalls, were driven off. Very heavy rain drenched us all, and made work in the trenches very difficult; but extensions were gradually going on, and a few Royal Engineers were sent agreeably to my request for help.

Lord Kitchener went this day (22nd February) to Naauw-poort to urge forward troops from Gatacre and Clements to Orange River, and to organise the lines of communication.

During the next two days there was a good deal of fighting with outside commandos to the south, resulting in the capture of ninety, and the surrendering of sixty prisoners. As usual, I spent part of the night in the trenches. Torrents of rain again.

Gradually the 19th Brigade had had to extend farther and farther, and now its outpost line was four miles long. As its numbers were insufficient to watch a large front, and get on with the trenches at the same time, I borrowed the Argyll and Sutherland Highlanders, and a great help they were. I have never understood why more troops could not be spared, for the date when the *laager* could be rushed largely depended on the operations on the north side of the river. It was not until two days later, after many requests, that a company of engineers under Kincaid came over the river.

The torrents of rain, mostly at night, had raised the height of the river very considerably, rendering it impassable, and hundreds of dead animals from Cronje's *laager* floated down. The ground on our side of the river was already studded with rotting corpses of cattle killed whilst grazing on the first day of battle. It was then that we suggested the name of "Stinkfontein," a farm as close to the Boer *laager* as Paardeberg *(vide* map), as more suitable than "Paardeberg" to remember the battle by.

Curiously enough there were no vultures, so different from my experiences in the Zulu War. Report said that the vultures had all died from feeding on animals the victims of *rinderpest.*

The state of the river completely isolated us, and we could only get rations over with great difficulty by boats. A fine night enabled the D.C.L.I, to throw out an excellent trench towards the Boers, and bend it back, so as not to be enfiladed. This trench was 460 yards long, and within 200 yards of the enemy's line. The shape of the trench can be seen on the sketch. From this forward trench I heard the Boers singing hymns.

Considering on the 26th February that we were in a position

to assault, I crossed to Head-quarters and got permission to do so at dawn next day. I asked for special artillery support, and that demonstrations might be made from all sides. This was agreed to, and two batteries under an old friend of Staff College days, Lieutenant-Colonel Barker, [10]came across and joined those already on our side. It was the turn of the Canadians to be in the trenches, and they had already relieved the Cornwalls.

In constructing the trenches the following points had been considered. The only cover and broken ground was a belt under 300 yards wide on the riverbank; beyond that was open flat ground over which an advance would be costly; therefore the actual assault should take place close to the river, whilst flank fire at a short range to cover the assault was desirable.

The result was the trenches 'a–b–e–f.' My plans, to be carried out after nightfall, were as follows:

Two hundred Gordons to complete and hold the flank trench 'a–b' and partly to occupy 'b–e.'

Four hundred and eighty Canadians in two ranks to occupy 'e–f,' the front rank to be in front of the trench as a covering party, the rear rank in the trench itself with rifles slung and entrenching tools. On their immediate right, actually next to the river, thirty sappers under Lieutenant-Colonel W. F. H. Kincaid with Lieutenants F. R. F. Boileau and Wilson of the Royal Engineers. Fifty Canadians in the trenches on the south bank, remainder in support in trench 'g.' The balloon section and bearer company in 'h.'

Besides the Argyll and Sutherland Highlanders I had been lent two companies of the Black Watch. The former and the Cornwalls were on outpost on a large semicircle over two miles from the *laager*, on high ground facing north and north-west, to prevent interference from outside; the Black Watch and Shropshires were to close in to within 1,000 yards from the *laager* after dark, and the Gordons to within 500 to 400 yards. The two first-named units were to open on the Boers with heavy fire directly

---

10. Major-General J. S. S. Barker.

they heard firing in their trenches, whilst the Gordons were to be ready to support the attack.

Then, seeing all in position after dark, stretcher parties and other arrangements complete, I with the Brigade Major, Inglefield, and *aide-de-camp*, went at 10.30 p.m. and dossed down in the trench with the Canadians. Very heavy dew, wetting everything, but mercifully no fog, from which we had suffered on two nights lately.

The 27th February (Shrove Tuesday): 1.45 a.m. All awake and at 2.15 a.m. the Canadians and Royal Engineers advanced slowly and silently.[11] Owing to the bushes it was difficult to maintain the line, though they were moving shoulder to shoulder, and keeping touch by the right. We knew it was only about 500 yards to the Boer trenches, and that only twenty yards a minute would bring us there in twenty-five minutes; but, although I did not realise it at the moment, we were going slower than that even, and thinking it over afterwards, I was not surprised, for it was a stealthy step-by-step advance in perfect silence, except for the occasional breaking of a twig or kicking of a stone—a movement most creditable to the troops.

Not realising this at the moment, on coming across no enemy at 2.45 a.m. I began to get anxious and sent back my *aide-de-camp* to call up the supports. Five minutes later a terrific fire opened, mercifully too high, within sixty yards of our front line. This latter recoiled slightly, but threw itself on the ground and returned the fire—chiefly by volleys. The Royal Engineers on the bank set to work with a will to dig, and luckily a fold in the ground protected them. The rear-rank of the Canadians also dug.

The right of the Canadians under Captains Macdonell and Stairs had only fallen back some twenty yards, whilst the left which was in more open ground had fallen back rather farther. For the next hour and a half the digging continued, and also the volleys from the covering party, and the other troops round the

---

11. Lieutenant-Colonels W. D. Otter (commanding) and L. Buchan and O. C. C. Pelletier were the senior officers with the Canadians—Pelletier was wounded.

laager. The artillery being uncertain in the dark of our proximity to the *laager* could not assist.

By dawn a good trench had been dug in the open, to the left of 'y,' and an admirable work constructed by Colonel Kincaid and his men, 'y-z.' This latter not only gave cover from fire in all threatened directions, but was so well traversed with earth-banks and sandbags, and so well loopholed, that not a casualty occurred in it after it was occupied. It proved to be only 93 yards from the Boer trenches, and being on higher ground, looked straight into them, for the Boers had deep trenches without any parapets, so that a man in them could only see out to fire by standing (in the very deep trenches putting something to stand on) with his head in full view.

Incidentally another peculiarity of their trenches was that they were, except some near the *laager,* all in short lengths, traced to suit the ground and seldom connected—much as they appear in the sketch. Some of them were nine feet deep, and cut under to give shelter. Some of them were only large enough for two men and seldom for more than three or four; often there were considerable gaps between, so any question of fire discipline was non-existent.

At daylight, seeing danger of having the new trench enfiladed from the opposite bank, I signalled to a support at 'j' to move up and occupy a small house 'k,' which they did. I then, from Kincaid's work, called to the Boers to surrender; not a man was showing. It can be seen from the sketch that the Boer *laager* was 400 or 500 yards behind their trenches, close to us; and, further, that we were looking straight along all their trenches on the riverbank. After calling a few times a white flag handkerchief appeared from the nearest trench, and at last, on my promise not to shoot, a head appeared, then another and another, and this ran along all the trenches until there were heads and white flags up to the *laager.* I remarked at the time: "It's just like the resurrection."

They seemed glad that it was over, and told us they had no orders to surrender from Cronje, who had settled to do so on the morrow, but had been forced to surrender by our attack. It was pleasing to the 19th Brigade to have saved them a day, and gratifying to all that we should have made a "grand slam" on the anniversary of Majuba. Our total casualties on this day's attack were only forty-five, of which twelve were killed.

My next move was to gallop a mile and a half back to my bivouac on Gun Hill, shout for a razor, and carry out my oath taken nine days before—much to the amusement of Macbean, of the Gordons, who happened to come up at the moment.

I have merely been telling the story of the 19th Brigade, and have not attempted to describe the daily fighting on other parts of the field; for instance, the 14th Brigade of the 7th Division under General Chermside were also on our side of the river, but on the east or far side of the *laager*, and also trenching up towards it. Just as I had finished shaving, and had had a bite of food, I got a message from Lord Roberts congratulating me and saying that, since to our brigade belonged the honours of the day, he wished me to move at once, with the whole brigade, to occupy the *laager*, which we did, sweeping in extended order right across the plain.

The scene of confusion and devastation there impressed us all, but, viewed in the light of experiences in the Great War of 1914-18, the damage done is hardly worth describing, whilst my vocabulary is too limited to convey a true idea of the insanitary conditions and the appalling smells, mostly from dead beasts.

The Boer trenches close round the *laager* were extremely strong, well traced and well constructed, and were evidence that a frontal attack by day, a week previously, would only have succeeded with heavy casualties. We learned, too, why their losses had not been heavier, for they had only had some seventy killed and under two hundred wounded, when we saw that they had lived underground, and in very deep narrow trenches nine and ten feet deep, where nothing could touch them, unless a shell fell plumb in.

They appeared to have an immense supply of ammunition. Our total captures were 4,200 prisoners, Cronje, Wolmarans,

Jourdain, Aldbrecht, several women, and 5,000 rifles. That evening Cronje, with his wife, in a cart with six horses, left for Capetown under escort, also all the other prisoners. After placing a cordon of men to prevent looting, we settled down in camp. The bodies of Colonel Hannay and others of the Mounted Infantry, shot in their wild charge on the *laager* on the 18th February, were found not far from the *laager*.

The immediate result of Lord Roberts's strategy was the withdrawal of the Boer forces investing Ladysmith, enabling Buller to relieve that town on the 1st March.

CHAPTER 10

Bloemfontein, March 1900

Although the Boer *laager* at Paardeberg might be regarded as the post of honour, it was hardly an agreeable spot for a bivouac, and we were glad to get permission to move on the morrow to a clean camp, clear of the sickening smell of dead animals, from which we had suffered with varying intensity for the past ten days. It was shortly after settling down in this haven of rest amongst shady bushes, where the peaceful partridges rejoiced our sporting spirits, that we beard definitely of the move of the Boers from the neighbourhood of Ladysmith to oppose us, and that Sir Redvers Buller, after the battle of Pieter's Hill, on the 27th February, had joined hands with Sir George White in that, till then, beleaguered township.

On this day—the 1st March—Lord Roberts went to Kimberley to discuss with Lord Kitchener plans for further moves, and it was decided, in view of the precarious lines of communication, the need of rest for the horses and the necessity for improving the supply system, that no further move could be made for a week. A reorganisation of the force, too, was necessary, which involved bringing up the 15th and Guards Brigades and some artillery left at Jacobsdal and elsewhere, and the formation of the Mounted Infantry into four Brigades. The actual combatant strength of the reinforced army stood at about 30,000 men and 116 guns.

The next few days, although our bivouacs were constantly soaked by heavy rainstorms, gave us a welcome rest; most of my time, however, was spent in preparing the Brigade for the coming move on Bloemfontein, the first step towards which was taken on the 6th March, when our Division moved some live to six miles east, to the neighbourhood of Makauw's Drift.

The heavy rains had converted our camps into seas of mud; wagons in some cases had sunk up to their axles; and it took us some four hours to carry out this short march. That afternoon all generals were summoned to the commander-in-chief's camp at Osfontein, and I rode there with General French. I was gratified by a cordial reception from Lord Downe, who said he had heard that my Brigade was chiefly responsible for the surrender of Cronje.

It was a most interesting assembly, and I was much impressed by the charming and yet firm manner in which Lord "Bobs" gave out his instructions—based on reconnaissances made by himself and the cavalry during the previous days.

A glance at the sketch map will show that the Boers had not gone far, but were occupying a chain of hills astride the river, some twelve miles in length, the nearest part of which was only about five and a half miles from our chief's head-quarters at Osfontein; that their right flank was on Leeuwkop,[1] north of the river; their centre on the high *Tafelberg*, or Table Mountain; and their left on the lower range known as the Seven Kopjes, or Seven Sisters.

The ground in front of the latter, in fact generally on the south side of the Modder River, was flat and open, whilst on the north side it was more undulating. The position appeared to be strongly held, on the flanks, and in the centre on the Tafelberg, and at those points guns had been located.

The strength of the enemy was supposed to be 14,000 and twenty guns, and it was reported that they were immediately covering the Poplar Grove Drift over the Modder, and that trenches had been located along the foothills on the south bank, which would make a direct advance on the Seven Sisters a matter of some difficulty.

---

1. It proved actually to be on the Blaauberg, three miles farther north.

ACTION OF POPLAR GROVE

The object of the enemy appeared to be to stop our advance on Bloemfontein, and as this was the only position of any strength between us and that town, it seemed likely that the fight might be an obstinate one.

Such was roughly the information that the commander-in-chief gave us, and his instructions for the morrow were to the following effect:

The cavalry with two brigades of Mounted Infantry (Alderson's and Ridley's) and seven batteries Royal Horse Artillery was to threaten the enemy's line of retreat, by making a long turning movement round their left flank resting on Seven Sisters—a march of some seventeen miles—aiming at the Modder River, two and a half miles above Poplar Grove, but, if opportunity offered, they were to attack before reaching the river. The 6th Division was to follow the cavalry until south of the Boer left on Seven Sisters, when it was to attack those hills and later the Tafelberg, which Lord Roberts regarded as the key of the position.

The 7th Division was to advance between the 6th Division and the river; whilst the 9th Division, which was on the north bank, was to attack the enemy's right wing, accompanied by two naval guns and two regiments of Mounted Infantry under Henry and de Lisle. The chief laid stress on the importance of dealing with the Boer gun or guns posted on the commanding Leeuwkop, but he did not expect the division would bear an important part in the fight, though if we saw the enemy retiring we were to develop our own initiative for cutting them off.

The day proved to be a most disappointing one. The cavalry, starting at 2 a.m., were expected to be in rear of the Boers at daybreak; but it was now that the effect of de Wet's capture of our large convoy on the Riet River, some three weeks previously, was to be felt, for shortage of food and endless work had told on the horses to such an extent, that not only was it difficult to raise a trot, but frequent halts of considerable duration were essential.

Thus the whole operation was delayed, as the movements of

the infantry divisions were to a great extent dependent on the cavalry getting in rear of the Boers.

It has been suggested that with horses in that tired state it was asking too much to expect them to do the whole turning movement in one march; that if they had done the first half after sundown on the 6th, there would have been no difficulty about their reaching the Modder River soon after dawn: and then an overwhelming disaster must have resulted to the Boers, which in their dispirited state might have ended the war.

The enemy were undoubtedly depressed by the result of the battle of Paardeberg, but were quite ready to put up a good fight against a frontal attack, which they fully expected the British would make. When, however, they found their flank being turned, their will to resist disappeared, and they were soon in full retreat; according to their commander (Christian de Wet) nothing could stop them, in spite of the fact that President Kruger, who had come up from Bloemfontein, was in the field and, with him, had urged the Burghers to turn and fight.

It may be wondered, since the day was so unproductive of results, why I have thought it necessary to describe it at such length, and deemed it worthy of a sketch plan. My answer is that the situation before the action, with the possibility of bringing off a success so complete as to end the war in one fell swoop, together with the reason why the results were practically nil, form a deeply interesting study for any military student. I would liken the day to a grouse drive, where the game was disturbed and alarmed before the guns had taken up their positions in the butts.

I will now briefly describe the part borne in this none too glorious action by the 19th Brigade.

At 4.30 a.m. the 9th Division was moving from its camp north-west of Makauw's Drift; the Highland Brigade on the right, its right resting on the riverbank; the 19th Brigade on the left. The only artillery was two naval guns—the whole of the guns belonging to our Division having been taken for action on the south bank. The advance was slow, and it was 7 a.m. before we established ourselves on the small hill east of our camp on map; our baggage, under two companies of the R. Canadians, was parked near the river.

Shortly after reaching the hill I received two bits of important information: the first came from hearing heavy Bring to the south-east of Seven Kopjes, when I remarked to my staff, "The game is up so far as achieving a great success today is concerned, for our cavalry have evidently been drawn into a fight, and can now never reach the river and stop a retreat"; and the second came from the Mounted Troops to the north of me, to the effect that the Blue Mountain (Blaauberg), as well as the Leeuwkop, was strongly held by the enemy.

The second piece of information made me realise that if those two hills were really strongly held it would be risky to move the Brigade between them until the situation cleared a little. Sometime later, however, I could see the Boer wagons trekking off from behind their position on the south of the river, but it was not until 11.30 a.m. that I noticed the enemy leaving their trenches, and then I saw a rush back from trench C-D on map, the only one I had a good view of, the men disappearing down the reverse slope and reappearing mounted and galloping away. Meanwhile the Boer gun on the Leeuwkop was steadily engaged with our two naval guns. From the Leeuwkop to the riverbank what looked like a continuous trench, strongly held by the enemy, was apparent, and this was faced by the Highland Brigade lying down in extended order.

My divisional general being a secretive person, I was not aware what orders had been given to him, but his orders to me were not to move farther without his permission, and it was distinctly trying to have to sit and watch our opportunities fleeting away, and have my signals to be allowed to move answered in the negative.

At last permission was accorded. I had already decided, when my leash was let go, to try to turn the Leeuwkop by the north, so, giving orders to the Shropshires to lead, I impressed on them, before they started, that, on getting past that hill, they should detach a body to swing to their right, and climb the hill, which was very steep, and seize the gun. I hoped in this way to secure the Leeuwkop without coming under fire from the Blue Mountain, and then to push on and threaten its rear. I had heard from Colonel Henry, away to the north with his own Mounted Infantry and Roberts's Horse, that he was held up by the Blue Mountain, so I dispatched a note to tell him what I was doing, and that I believed he would soon be able to advance—a surmise which turned out to be justified.

When the brigade was in motion an order reached me from my divisional general, who was with the Highland Brigade near the riverbank, telling me he was going to make a frontal attack on the trenches connecting the Leeuwkop with the riverbank, and expressing a wish that the 19th Brigade should be brought south to act as a support, but adding that if I considered it inadvisable to withdraw the whole brigade I was at any rate to send one battalion. Accordingly I sent the Royal Canadians, explaining that I was already committed to a movement which would do far more to support the Highland Brigade's attack than if I brought my whole brigade across to join hands with them.

All subsequent movements can be followed on the sketch. The Shropshires were splendidly handled by Lieutenant-Colonel Spens. They moved in very extended order so as to avoid losses, and as they threatened the rear of successive heights, these were immediately evacuated by the enemy, and so suddenly did the party allotted to the Leeuwkop swing on to it and crown its height, that the gun which had annoyed us till then had to be abandoned, when it became the property of the Shropshires.

At first Colonel Spens, to avoid fire from the Leeuwkop, had left-wheeled away from it, and later had swung to the right again to avoid the Blue Mountain, and then swept straight on to the Poplar Tree Farm and the *kopjes* in its neighbourhood, all of which he cleared of the enemy. So successful was the movement that eventually, when the Highland Brigade moved against the trenches, not a shot was fired at them, and when they crossed the trenches and passed to the south-east of the Leeuwkop they saw the reason, for the 19th Brigade was to be seen far in advance of their left front pushing large numbers of retreating Boers before them.

By 2 p.m. the Leeuwkop had been crowned, the gun captured, and a signal-station established. The sketch is to scale, and the story of this most successful flank move of the 19th Brigade can be read from it. It shows how for some hours many mounted Boers kept on our flanks, 2,000 to 3,000 yards away, dismounting and firing at extreme range. Our infantry kept steadily pursuing; but what could they do? We had no guns and no mounted troops. The only mounted troops north of the river were not under my orders.

Looking back at the end of the war, I was convinced that on no other occasion had I seen so many Boers at one time. There appeared to be an endless stream of them going leisurely away. They knew we had no guns, and hardly appeared to hurry. A large number of them were on foot, retiring along the riverbank; again from 2.30 to 5 p.m. numbers of the enemy were moving away north-east, across the front of the Gordons, at a range of about 3,000 yards, covered by their own guns on Hill H.

It had been a hard day marching in a waterless country, and the men were tired and footsore when they settled down in bivouac close to the Poplar Grove Drift. The Shropshires had marched over twenty miles—the remainder rather less —and often at a great pace. We certainly had had a most instructive day of manoeuvre, but, owing to the demoralised state of our enemy, hardly a dangerous one, for we only had one man wounded in the brigade. As a matter of fact, our casualties in the whole army only amounted to about fifty, and they were almost all in the cavalry—amongst those, however, was an especially gallant and valuable officer, de Montmorency, V.C., of the 21st Lancers, who had distinguished himself on many occasions. Our transport did us very badly, and it was two hours after midnight before it came up and the men got a square meal and their blankets.

To complete the story of the action, I will refer briefly to the operations on the south of the river. The cavalry, with their horses stone cold, had been led into an action three miles south-east of the Seven Kopjes—seven or eight miles from their objective on the river—and from there had endured the agony of seeing the enemy withdrawing unmolested through the door they had been unable to close. Eventually they followed slowly, without being able to interfere with the retreating Boers, and settled down for the night about Slaag Laagte Drift, two miles east of Poplar Grove Drift.

The 6th Division had made no attempt to close with the enemy, but had advanced very slowly and stickily, until they were sure the positions in front of them had been vacated: and the 7th Division had conformed to their movements, and did not reach their bivouac in the neighbourhood of Poplar Grove until two hours after the 9th Division had settled down: the 6th Division were an hour later still—it being 6 p.m. before they reached their place of halt for the night.

Perhaps I may be forgiven for quoting from page 207, Volume 2, of the official *History of the War*.

"Smith-Dorrien alone seems to have as yet realised that the Boers had been morally shattered by the very struggles which had impressed the need of caution on the victors."

The next two days, beyond crossing to the south bank of the river, we did nothing, but we heard that President Steyn, of the Orange Free State, as well as Kruger, had been in the field on the 7th, and further, that our troops from the old colony were moving forward and had occupied Norval's Pont only to find the big railway bridge across the river destroyed.

On the 10th March we were on the move again. The commander-in-chief accompanied our column, also the Guards Brigade under General Pole-Carew. Halting at Grasveldt, after eight miles, we moved on again, reaching Driefontein Farm at 5 p.m., a hot march totalling eighteen miles. The last part of the march was to the sound of the guns of the 6th Division which, with some of French's cavalry, were in advance and hotly engaged.

I should mention here that the force had been divided into

three columns—each consisting of a cavalry and Mounted Infantry Brigade and an infantry division, except the centre column which had, in addition, the Guards Brigade, an extra Mounted Infantry Brigade, army troops, and the supply columns. The left column, under General French, was given a road just south of the Modder. The centre column, under Lord Roberts himself, was to move some five miles farther south, and the right division, under General Tucker, still farther south *via* Petrusberg.

The chief had had information that the Boers had taken up a position about Abraham's Kraal and Driefontein, east of Poplar Grove. It seemed as if our left column was engaged with those Boers, and so it turned out. The Boers had fought in their very best style, and so had the 6th Division under General Kelly-Kenny. It had been almost entirely an infantry fight supported by artillery, for the cavalry appear to have given very little assistance. The results were decisive, the Boers flying from the field, though unpursued; but our losses, considering the small numbers engaged, were severe—over 400 casualties, of which six officers and fifty-two men were killed.

As the 19th Brigade was not engaged, beyond the bringing in of wounded from the field throughout the night by our Bearer Company, I shall not describe the battle of Driefontein in detail; but I am satisfied that General Kelly-Kenny's determined action showed the Boers, in a manner which they had not learned before, except perhaps at Elandslaagte, what a resolute attack by British troops was like, and that it had a very big effect on the moral of the enemy for the rest of the campaign.

Next day we moved to Aasvogel Kop, across the 6th Division battle-field of the previous day, where 103 Boers were being buried.

Sixteen more miles, on the 12th March, brought us to Venters Vlei, where the final opposition before reaching the capital of the Free State was expected, but nothing happened; and the next day we camped round Bloemfontein, which the Boers had just vacated.

My head-quarters were some eight miles from the town, at

the farm of a Mr. Steyn, brother of the president. The account he gave of the anxieties, hopes, and disappointments he had undergone during the past three weeks amused us more than himself. We heard that before the Boers evacuated Bloemfontein, considerable difference of opinion had been shown and illustrated by the "peace" and "continue the war" advocates firing on each other.

We managed to replenish our larder from our involuntary host's farm, buying turkeys for fifteen shillings and Aylesbury ducks at three shillings apiece.

We liked our quarters far from "Brass Hats," and were not at all pleased when we were ordered to move, on the 15th, to a camp just outside the north-west of Bloemfontein. Getting so close to civilisation, we thought we should like to get a share of it, so Eddy Dorrien-Smith, in order to procure a house, used his persuasive powers successfully on Mr. Fraser, who had been first favourite for the presidency in 1896 when the Jameson Raid had upset his chances. Our garden, in which we lived entirely, except when it rained, was next to the presidency, which was occupied by Lord Roberts.

Bloemfontein struck me as a pleasant and picturesque town, with a good many trees, and I had time to become confirmed in this impression, for it was some six weeks before the necessary preparations could be made for finally leaving it on our way to Pretoria.

It was a very welcome rest, though we were by no means idle all the time, as my story will show. We had a valuable addition to our mess on the 19th March, when the Rev. H. K. Southwell (now Bishop of Lewes) joined us and took charge of it. He proved not only a most earnest, efficient, and popular padre, but a most capable caterer, and we sometimes wondered if his skill at procuring supplies of milk, poultry, and vegetables was entirely due to his calling.

The weather was very trying—a great deal of rain, which had a bad effect on the health of the men who had undergone such a heavy strain on short rations; this resulted in an epidemic of enteric fever which cost us many a good man. Enteric was to prove our greatest scourge, and far more deadly than the bullet of the enemy, especially as it could not be eradicated, but was prevalent throughout the campaign. (See table following.)

The long halt at Bloemfontein, and the reports of our still being unready to take the field, had put fresh heart into the Boers, and considerable forces of them, under Christian de Wet and de la Rey, were becoming active to the north-west of Blo-emfontein between Brandfort and Thabanchu, which latter is about forty-five miles due west from the capital. On the 31st March news came in that de Wet had succeeded in surprising and defeating with much loss General Broadwood's Mounted Force at Thabanchu, where it had been sent to protect the very important waterworks at Sannah's Post on the Modder River.

That evening General Colvile received orders to move to its relief. For some unknown reason the march was delayed until the following morning, and this was too late to save an even graver defeat.

Inoculation for enteric was not practised at this time, and the following table comparing relative results in this and the Great War, when inoculation was almost universal, is deeply significant. I am indebted to Colonel D. Harvey, C.M.G., C.B.E., M.D., R.A.M.C., for this table :

	Total Cases.	Total Deaths.	Mean Annual Strength.	Annual Incidence per 1,000 of Strength.	Annual Death-rate per 1,000 of Strength.
S. African War, 1899–1902	57,684	8,022	208,226	105·00	14·8
The Great War, 1914–18	20,139	1,191	2,000,000	2·35	0·139

CHAPTER 11

Sannah's Post, 31st March 1900

On the 31st March the 9th Division marched from Bloemfontein at 5.30 a.m., the Highland Brigade leading. When we were approaching Springfield (eight miles out) at 8 a.m. we heard heavy and rapid gun-fire towards the Waterworks. Colonel Martyr's Mounted Infantry had preceded the division.

It was getting on for noon when the head of the infantry reached Boesman's Kop (fourteen miles from Bloemfontein). General Colvile, who had preceded the division to see Colonel Martyr, already there with his Mounted Infantry, sent for General Macdonald and myself to join him on the top of the Kop. On arriving there we could see the tall waterworks' chimney, about seven miles away, and also a lot of mounted troops in the same direction and about two miles from us. These latter, General Colvile said, were Broadwood's troops, and that he had sent for "that officer."

I tried to ascertain from General Colvile what the situation was, and where the disaster to the guns, of which we had only heard a rumour, had taken place; but could get very little information, and was left with the impression that it was at Waterval Drift, six miles north-east of us. Both Macdonald and I urged General Colvile to go and see Broadwood, instead of waiting for him, so as to learn the exact situation; but he assured us that in any case he would get nothing out of Broadwood, as he believed he was in a state of collapse, and, after waiting for some twenty minutes, he ordered the division to march on Waterval Drift; so we resumed our march. Martyr's Mounted Infantry had moved off to that very drift.

It turned out that the enemy were in considerable strength at Waterval Drift, and we had quite a pretty action before we cleared them from the riverbank. Great delay was caused by the fact that, although the lieutenant-general sent off the two infantry brigades post haste, he remained a long way behind himself, keeping all the guns with him—it was 5 p.m. before any artillery appeared, and then only in time to fire a few long-range shells at retiring Boers.

It was whilst this was going on that Broadwood rode up to me and asked where General Colvile was, as he had orders to report himself to him, and I was surprised to see him looking particularly active and well, after what Colvile had told us about him at Boesman's Kop. It appears that Colvile had been entirely misinformed about him. I then learned for the first time that the disaster to the guns had not taken place at Waterval Drift, but some four or five miles south-east of that drift—namely, on Korn Spruit; *vide* X on sketch.

Waterval Drift was a very steep one, and difficult to cross, and it was midnight before all our wagons were over, and we were bivouacked, after an arduous march of over twenty miles, on the northern bank of the Modder River, in a most unpleasant tactical position. Our orders were to be ready to move at daylight the next morning, but from then to 10 a.m. we watched a large force of Boers moving about on the higher ground some six or seven miles on our line of advance.

At that hour General French arrived, and shortly after Colvile gave orders to recross the river, directing me with my brigade, the Royal Engineers Company, and the Brigade Division of Artillery, to prepare to march on the Waterworks, which he had every reason to believe was clear of the enemy.

At 2 p.m. we had crossed the drift, and were formed up about a mile east of it, when the G.O.C. Division arrived, and Ordered me to move on, saying he had information that the Boers had vacated the Waterworks.

SANNAH'S POST, 31st MARCH 1900.

(This name given to the action is taken from a hill four miles south of the Waterworks.)

A = Position of Broadwood's troops as seen from Boesman's Kop noon of 31st March.
B = Position of Porter's force on 1st April when 19th Brigade joined him.
C = Iron houses where wounded were.
D = Waterval Drift.
X = Scene of Korn Spruit disaster, 31st March 1900.

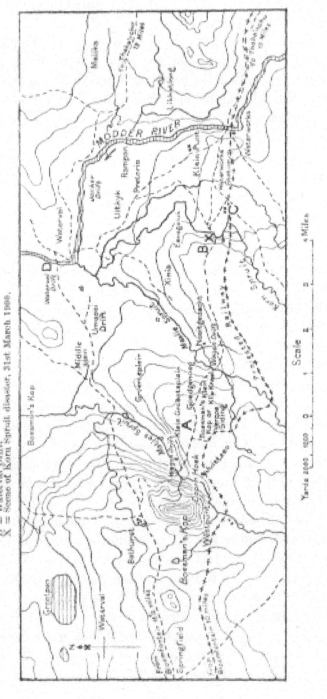

Scale

Yards 500 500 0   1   2   3 Miles

We moved on, covered by the Shropshires, behind whom came Colonel Flint's three batteries, escorted by three companies of the Duke of Cornwall's Light Infantry, with the Gordons on the left or the dangerous flank, and the remainder of the Duke of Cornwall's Light Infantry bringing up the rear with the ammunition column.

At about 3.30 p.m. we were approaching the scene of the disaster two miles short of or west of the Waterworks, when I received an order from the G.O.C. that, as that place was held by the enemy after all, he wished all troops to retire on Boesman's Kop. I issued the necessary orders and drew the Shropshires to a commanding position by a white farmhouse, 300 yards west of the drift, across the deep donga where the Boers had ambushed and captured the guns the day before. Brigadier-General T. C. Porter, with Colonel Davidson, R.H.A., four guns R.H.A., and about eighty cavalry, were on this position when we arrived.

At 3.45 p.m. Porter told me that some eighty-seven of our wounded were in some corrugated iron houses at the projected Waterworks Station about 1,400 yards to our front, and between us and a largish force of Boers with whose guns our guns were engaged at a range of 4,000 yards. The Boers were also firing with some long-range guns still farther off, on the far side of the Modder. I at once sent back both my *aide-de-camps*—Lieutenants Hood and Dorrien-Smith—to Macdonald's Brigade to ask for all available ambulances and empty carts. Just before the *aide-de-camps* started I saw the G.O.C. Division, who said the wounded belonged to the mounted troops, and they must get their own wounded away, as they were no concern of ours. However, I didn't think he could mean this seriously, so I sent the *aide-de-camps* off.

Shortly after Lieutenant-Colonel Ewart,[1] A.A.G., 9th Division, rode up to me and gave me a written order to withdraw immediately all troops of the 9th Division and to camp at Boesman's Kop. At this time the Boers were very active, and attempt-

---

1. Lieutenant-General Sir Spencer Ewart, G.C.B., etc., afterwards adjutant general of the Forces.

ing to get down to the iron houses, and I saw that if our force went away, the small party of cavalry and guns couldn't possibly prevent the wounded from falling into their hands.

I remonstrated with Ewart, but he replied that the G.O.C. Division had already gone to Boesman's Kop, and had sent all three batteries away there, and that he had no authority to change the orders. I shall never forget the indignation of General Porter and his men when they heard of this inhuman order. So, leaving the Shropshires as a support just behind the position, and remaining myself, I sent the oilier battalions back by slow stages to camp.

By dark, thanks to the fire of the R.H.A. guns, and the splendid work of Lieutenant-Colonel Dorman, Majors Nichol and Bond, all of the Royal Army Medical Corps, we were able to load up and bring away all our wounded, marvellous to say, without any casualties, in spite of the heavy fire of the Boer guns at our carts, ambulances, and stretcher parties. Remembrance of the gratitude of General Porter, the cavalry and the R.H.A. with him, for not having left them in the lurch still gives me the most intense satisfaction.

Broadwood's losses at Thabanchu had been heavy, and the surprise at Korn Spruit had amounted to a disaster, for the casualties in this last action alone amounted to 570 men and seven guns. These latter had not all been removed when we reached Boesman's Kop, and I still wonder why our divisional general refused to march straight to the scene of the disaster, which was bang in front of us, instead of going on a wild-goose chase to Waterval Drift. We must have saved men and possibly some guns.

Colvile appears to have been dominated by a wish expressed by the commander-in-chief, that he should avoid losses as far as possible.

The story of Korn Spruit, with the heroism shown, is worth reading in the official history, but it is outside my personal knowledge, and therefore I do not record it.

The Shropshire Regiment escorted the wounded back to camp, which we reached about 9.30 p.m. I went to report my return, but was told the divisional general was snugly asleep in a farmhouse, and that the orders were not to disturb him; and perhaps it was just as well, for I was boiling with indignation, and might have said more than was discreet.

Next morning, the 2nd April, the Boers were still in position west of the Waterworks, and I expected to be ordered to attack them, but instead was directed to return to Bloemfontein, which we did in two days' march. Riding along I was amused by the divisional general remarking to me: "I hear you got away those wounded fellows last night, and think it was a good thing to have done."

The day of our arrival at Bloemfontein the Boers from the Waterworks attacked Boesman's Kop, but found it strongly held by our cavalry. News came in too that a battalion of the Irish Rifles was in difficulties at Reddersberg, and further that the township of Wepener was being threatened. Troops were hastily collected and sent off to deal with these situations, but too late for Reddersberg, for on the 4th April the Irish Rifles, surrounded by the enterprising de Wet, had been forced to surrender.

This same day the commander-in-chief got news of an intended conference of Boer leaders on the Leeuwkop on the Wepener Road, some twenty miles south-east of Bloemfontein, and the 9th Division, and what was left of Porter's Cavalry Brigade (which was only four R.H.A. guns and 130 men), were started off to try to surround them, and reached the vicinity aimed at next morning, only to find either that the report was a myth, or else our approach had been noticed and objections raised to our attending their conference, for beyond shelling a party of some 200 Boers, nothing happened.

We got back to Bloemfontein on the 6th, having had a forty-mile trek for nothing—not that such is an unusual and avoidable incident in war.

This day we heard of Lord Methuen's success at Boshof up Kimberley way, where we had captured several Boers, and killed their leader Villebois, who from all accounts was a fine soldier and good fellow.

These days in Bloemfontein, though irksome to the fighting spirits, had many compensations, for old friends, separated for long periods, met again, and many a long and pleasant chat resulted. We had guests to dinner or lunch most days, and amongst them I find the names of Prince Adolphus of Teck, Colonels Otter, Buchan and Ashby, "Nunky" Dawson (9th Bengal Lancers), Clowes (Gordons), Clement Wood (Cameronians), and the following—18th Royal Irish—Guinness, Doran, Kitty Apthorp and Daniell,[2] Sir Kendal Franks, Charlie Gough, Spens, Peter Buston, R.E., Neville Chamberlain, Watty Ross, Macbean, H. H. Burney, Towse, Ogilvie, Bannatyne Allason, Jimmy Grierson.

Fighting departments for requisites for my men, and visiting outposts and inspections gave me enough to do to prevent time hanging on my hands; and through it all there was sufficient rain to prevent the camps from ever being really dry, and to ensure a fine supply of mud— not only round the tents, but in all the paths and roads trodden by the feet of men or beasts, and furrowed by the wheels of the heavy transport wagons.

Is it surprising, under such adverse circumstances, and the possession of our only pure water supply at Sannah's Post by the enemy, that enteric fever gained the upper hand, filling our hospitals and also many a grave?

Our minds, however, were kept constantly alive by the activities of the enemy and by the shaves and reports which are inherent to any force on active service, many of them grossly exaggerated, many totally untrue, but a large number of them founded on fact, and all of them interesting.

The unretrieved disasters of Reddersberg and Wepener and the fact that Thabanchu and the Waterworks were still held by the enemy confirmed the commander-in-chief's opinion that to move the army north, without detaching a considerable force to clear up the country to the east and to guard his lines of communication, would be taking too serious a risk, and for these purposes he detached Rundle's newly arrived 8th Division, and

---

2. Killed under me in France in October 1914—a very fine officer.

added Hart's Brigade of the 10th Division, brought round from Natal to the Colonial Force under General Brabant.

Again, before actually moving on Pretoria, Wepener had to be relieved, and to do this, General French was sent with mounted troops, and the 11th Division under General Pole-Carew. This latter had been formed from the Guards Brigade and the 18th (Stephenson's) Brigade, taken from the 6th Division, which was in process of allotment to the defence of Bloemfontein. The 3rd Division, the command of which Gatacre had recently given up, had been reconstructed to include certain militia battalions, and placed under the command of Chermside[3]; this division was also put at French's disposal.

Lastly, the Waterworks had to be wrested again from the Boers, and to carry this out Ian Hamilton was detailed, and the force under him was to consist of his own Mounted Infantry Division and the 19th Brigade.

The first I knew of these moves was an order late on the 20th April to move at dawn next day to Springfield, *en route* for Sannah's Post; but as we were on the point of starting Lord Roberts sent for Pole-Carew and me. It was then that the latter got orders to act under French, and to move with his division to reinforce Rundle, who was having rather a merry time of it. I was still to move to Springfield, but the chief explained that my first object was merely to relieve the 18th Brigade already there, so that Stephenson might join Pole-Carew, to whose division he belonged.

Stephenson moved early (the 22nd April) south-east, and we soon heard heavy firing. I had no guns with me, but was glad when, at my request, "P" Battery, R.H.A. (Major Sir Godfrey Thomas), arrived. Heavy firing continued all day towards Leeuwkop, and we heard after that the Warwicks, one of Stephenson's battalions, had suffered severely.

Late at night, Ian Hamilton, with the Mounted Infantry Division, camped two miles away, and I came under his orders. From now on I enjoyed every moment of the campaign. He

_____
3. Lieutenant-General Sir Herbert Chermside, R.E.

was a delightful leader to follow, always definite and clear in his instructions, always ready to listen and willing to adopt suggestions, and, what is more important, always ready to go for the enemy and extremely quick at seizing a tactical advantage, and, with it all, always in a good temper.

Hamilton told me his instructions were to strike towards Thabanchu, which included the recapture of the Waterworks; so, leaving the Duke of Cornwall's Light Infantry to hold Springfield, I followed the Mounted Infantry *via* Boesman's Kop with three battalions. The Boers were still covering the Waterworks sufficiently strongly to prevent our force from retaking them for a few hours. The Mounted Infantry had a good deal of ground to cover, for Waterval Drift had to lie secured as well, and, although the Waterworks were recovered, darkness decided Hamilton to content himself with remaining west of the Modder River for the night; so, placing outposts, we bivouacked about Klip Kraal. Boesman's Kop, always a source of danger in the hands of an enemy, was held this night by two companies sent out from Springfield.

The Brigade advanced at 6 a.m. (the 24th April) to cross the river at the Waterworks, whilst the whole of the Mounted Infantry (1,700 strong) made a long turning movement *via* Waterval Drift—an interesting and successful day, after which we camped east of the Modder River, to await supplies. That evening, General Colvile camped at Klip Kraal with two 4.7 guns and the Highland Brigade, having sent on the Duke of Cornwall's Light Infantry from Springfield to join me. Colvile's orders were to guard our lines of communication.

During the afternoon news reached us that the Boers were retiring north, in front of Rundle and Pole-Carew from Dewetsdorp, and that French was in pursuit.

This, as a glance at the map will show, indicated finding the Boers in strength at Thabanchu, and I was not surprised to get a message from Hamilton, who was in advance with his Mounted Infantry, urging me to support him as soon as our supplies arrived.

CHAPTER 12

Thabanchu, Thoba

Supplies having arrived, the Brigade started at 9 a.m. on the 25th April to support Ian Hamilton's Mounted Infantry Division moving east. Soon it was reported by the Mounted Infantry that the Boers were in strength astride our road at Israel's Poort, some seven miles from the Waterworks—*vide* sketch.

Major Shee's No. 2 Field Battery having been placed at my disposal, I sent back to hurry it up.

The Mounted Infantry were reconnoitring the whole of a very long and strong position, and it was not till noon that the Boers opened fire from a gun on hill north-west of A.

Shortly after, the R.H.A. guns came into action, and the 19th Brigade with No. 2 Field Battery (which arrived at 1.30 p.m.) were lying down east of *spruit* K.

The position had both flanks secured, and it would have been a difficult nut to crack if held in strength, unless a long turning movement was possible by the left or north.

Ridge A was being threatened at its western extremity by Mounted Infantry, and Hamilton had sent a force of Mounted Infantry to threaten the enemy's rear by a wider encircling movement to the north-west.

The Mounted Infantry patrols and R.H.A. guns were engaging *kopjes* G, H, and L, and trying to make the enemy show his strength. This drew a heavy fire from these *kopjes*. Some of the patrols, especially Marshall's Horse, caught it rather badly. At 2 p.m. the Royal Canadians, their left directed on *Kopje* F, their right on *Kopje* L, moved forward, covering nearly 2,000 yards of front on an extension of 15 to 20 yards between men.

Their orders were to move forward until the fire became really heavy, then to lie down and hold the enemy with fire. They got to within 800 yards, when the fire was too hot for further advance. Whilst this was happening, the Cornwalls, followed by the Shropshires and half the Gordons (the other half was guarding the baggage), moved to seize the rugged *kopjes* at B.

At 2.30 the Cornwalls occupied B, and at 2.45 No. 2 Battery R.F.A. came into action from the same *kopjes*, the Cornwalls pressing on and seizing D under a heavy flank fire from line of hills A2, distant 2,000 yards. The Shropshires, rather to the left of the Cornwalls, came under a heavy lire from the same hills and left three companies to engage them; two guns also turned their attention to the same heights.

At 3.30, seeing the Cornwalls held at D, I moved half the Shropshires, supported by the Gordons, along low ground and took first C and then E; I had seen, about 3.15, a few mounted Boers and a mule wagon going off towards Thabanchu from H and L.

By 4.40 we were penetrating the position everywhere; the Canadians were charging forward on G, H, and L, and I ordered up the guns to the plain east of E and F, and signalled back for our baggage. Our brigade casualties, considering the very heavy fire, were extremely small.

We should not have succeeded so easily without the help of Major Shee and his battery, or the Mounted Infantry turning movement. Colonel Otter, as usual, handled his battalion perfectly, and I much regretted he was wounded.

On the 26th April Ridley's Mounted Infantry started before dawn to seize the Poort, or gap in the hills, through which the road from Dewetsdorp passes to Thabanchu. Dawson's mounted command and Bainbridge's Mounted Infantry pushed on through Thabanchu, and reconnoitred the Poort seven miles east of it: they reported it and Eden Hill strongly held. The 19th Brigade moved in support, starting at dawn, and eventually camped just north-east of Thabanchu.

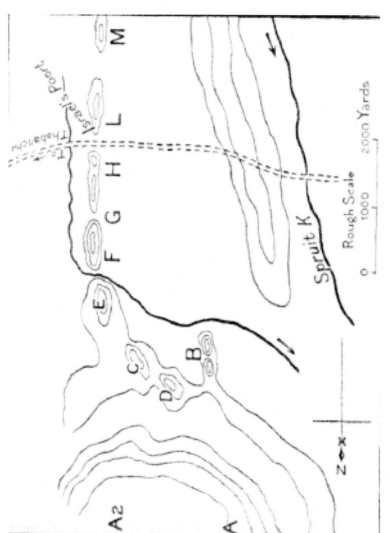

ISRAEL'S POORT

We found very welcome additions to our rations in the form of poultry, fresh butter, and milk.

The Canadians were detailed to hold the Poort, on the Dewetsdorp Road, three miles out, whilst a hundred Gordons and seventy Mounted Infantry, under Captain Meyrick,[1] held Israel's Poort. We had just missed a good chance, for 3,000 Boers with 200 wagons, retiring before French, had passed through that morning to Ladybrand, and de Lisle reported seeing them in the distance, too far off to follow. The operation of the past three days proved to be typical of the skill of the Boers in delaying us long enough to get their wagons away. On the 27th April the Boers, evident all along positions on hills east and north-east from Thabanchu, sniped the Mounted Infantry who were reconnoitring towards *Kopje* A. More Mounted Infantry worked south and east round Thabanchu.

I sent two guns to Shropshire Hill, which fired on Boer Infantry until Boer guns (see sketch) opened in the afternoon. Our guns fired at 4,000 to 5,000 yards.

At 1 p.m. Lieutenant-Colonel Spens, K.S.L.I., and two guns, went towards *Kopje* A (Schutts Kop) to support Mounted Infantry, whilst the Gordons occupied Shropshire Ridge.

At 3.45 p.m. Lieutenant-Colonel Spens' force came under fire of Boer guns. His orders were to remain out until the Mounted Infantry had captured *Kopje* A.[2] At dusk it was reported to him that the *kopje* had been taken, and that Kitchener's Horse were holding it, and he returned to camp. At 8.30 p.m. news having been brought in that some of Kitchener's Horse were in difficulties on *Kopje* A, I was ordered to send a battalion to their help. I sent six companies Gordons and two companies Canadians, under Lieutenant-Colonel Macbean, Gordon Highlanders, guided by Major Cookson, of Kitchener's Horse. They, however, lost their direction, and at daylight found themselves some five miles from the scene of action. Kitchener's Horse had, however, extricated themselves without help, killing several of the enemy and losing ten men themselves.

---

1. Killed at Doornkop a month later.
2. *Kopje* A was about five miles from camp.

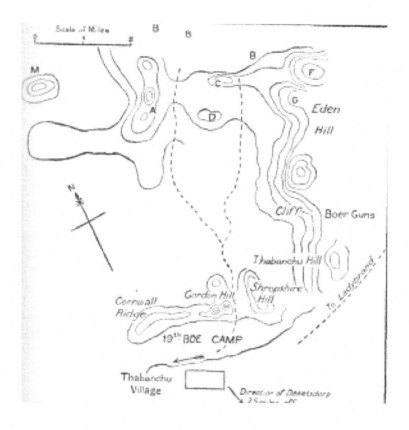

SKETCH OF THABANCHU

One company Duke of Cornwall's Light Infantry was sent to hold Thabanchu Hill day and night.

General French and the Cavalry Division arrived at midday and General Rundle and the 8th Division at dusk.

On the 28th April, in order to be ready to assist the Gordon Highlanders, and also to take part in a turning move on the north-east of Eden Hill with the mounted troops, the brigade (leaving one company of the Duke of Cornwall's Light Infantry on Thabanchu Hill and two companies of Gordons on Shropshire Ridge) moved out with the No. 2 Field Battery before dawn in the direction of *Kopje* A. By 7.30 a.m. the Shropshires had occupied the *kopje*, under cover of which I rode round the base of the hill with my staff, and, dismounting, left our horses and went forward to obtain a better view of the country beyond.

Suddenly a heavy burst of fire opened on us from Boers about 600 yards away, and, beating a hasty and undignified retreat, we betook ourselves to our horses, some of which had stampeded. My own horse was slightly wounded, and was the only casualty, which was very lucky, as we were under a really heavy fire for some minutes. At 7.45 a.m. the advanced parties on the eastern slopes of the same *kopje* came under a heavy fire from some *kopjes* 800 yards farther north.

Boers were seen moving up to occupy *Kopje* C, and the Duke of Cornwall's Light Infantry, supported by the Canadians, were ordered to occupy *Kopje* D, from which, with excellent practice at 1,100 yards, they soon dislodged the Boers with loss. It was apparent that the Boers were in considerable force at B, B, B, and also all along Eden Hill, and the 2nd Field Battery, helped up by infantry and drag-ropes, came into action on *Kopje* A, at 8.20 a.m.

By this time Ridley's Mounted Infantry were about *Kopje* M and to the north of it. Shortly after this Ridley signalled for me to support a movement of his against some Boers two miles off (beyond the left-hand B on the sketch), and I at once started, at 9.15 a.m., with four guns and two battalions, but hadn't proceeded far on my way when I was recalled by General French, as a Cavalry Brigade was commencing its movement past *Kopje* C with a view to working eastwards round *Kopje* F and Eden Hill generally.

The brigade and guns remained on *Kopjes* A, C, and D until 4 p.m., when the cavalry signalled back that several thousand Boers were trekking off along the Ladybrand Road. I then, leaving one battalion on *Kopje* A, ordered all the rest of my troops back to camp. Shortly after they had started, and before the Canadians, one company D.C.L.I. and one company Shropshires, had proceeded far, these last-named troops were recalled by General Hamilton to form a cordon on *Kopjes* F and G and along the high ground running from letter G towards the word "Cliff" on sketch.

These troops got into these positions about 5 p.m. A few minutes afterwards the Boers, who had been driven off by the Cavalry Brigade, seeing the latter retire, came on again in great force.

As I was uncertain about the geography of the position, and as I knew that the portion of it held by the Canadians (some 2,000 yards in extent) was commanded by the ground held by the Boers (they had fired on me), I feared that they might be rushed in the night, or that they might find themselves in an impossible position in the morning; I therefore found General Hamilton and recommended that they should not stay there the night, and further that the distant *Kopje* A, five miles from camp, should not be held by infantry throughout the night.

Hamilton directed that all should remain in position until after dark, and then withdraw quietly to camp. The companies of the Cornwalls and D.C.L.I, on *Kopje* G, just before dark, were engaged with Boers on *Kopje* F (some 900 yards off) and made them retreat; the Cornwalls on the north end of *Kopje* A also kept the Boers at a distance. In fact, the Boers retired some 3,000 yards, and the troops returned to camp after dark.

On the 29th the 8th Division and mounted troops were engaged north-east and south of Thabanchu with Boers who were quite aggressive and dropped shells into our camp. A convoy had been surrounded some eight miles to the south, and Brabazon[3] with yeomanry had been unable to extract it, so Rundle himself had gone off with two battalions, and before starting asked me to reinforce him next morning, which I promised to do. However, Rundle was successful, and that night my orders from Hamilton were to accompany him next day north to attack Houtnek, said to be held in strength. Before starting I had to exchange Shee's Battery for the 74th under McLeod, and to send back my *aide-de-camp*, Hood, sick to Bloemfontein, where he had a sharp attack of enteric.

Houtnek was a somewhat formidable position ten miles away. Although I did not know it at the time, this move was the commencement of the march of the army on Pretoria, the chief leaving sufficient troops behind him to deal with local troubles.

The country during the next day's march was fairly open as far as the road was concerned, but the latter was commanded in many places by high ground to the east, which was held by the enemy. The position we eventually attacked was visible at some distance, even the lower B B on sketch, but Houtnek stood higher still, and above all and visible everywhere was Thoba Mountain, some 600 or 700 feet above the plain. It was a remarkable hill, very steep at the western extremity of the position, where it fell straight into an open flat plain.

With front and flanks guarded by Mounted Infantry, the brigade, with the Shropshires leading, moved north, and later slightly west so as to edge away a little from the Boer positions. At 7.30 a.m. our right flank mounted-guard became engaged. This turned out to be the commencement of an important action which lasted until 4 p.m. next day. It was soon evident that the Boers were in force, astride our road, especially on both sides of Houtnek, and that more were moving there to reinforce.

Thoba Mountain, however, appeared to be only lightly held, and it was determined that this was the key of the positions, for it towered above everything else.

---

3. The late Major-General Sir John Brabazon, generally spoken of as "*Bwab*."

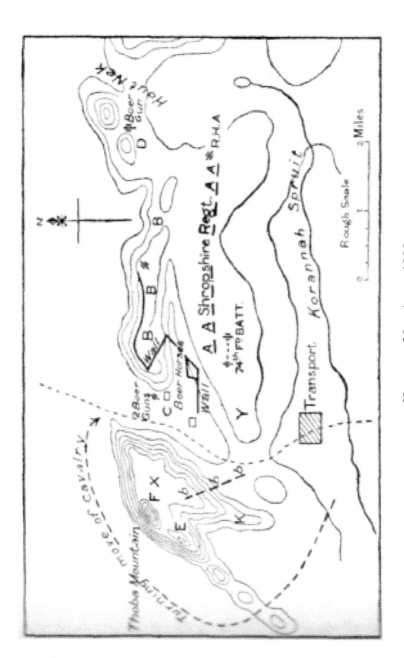

HOUTNEK, 30TH APRIL, 1900

By 10.30 a.m. the Shropshires occupied positions A, A, A, A, and engaged the Boers in front of them (shown B, B, B, mi sketch) distant about 1,800 or 2,000 yards, with a section of R.H.A. on their right flank and three Maxims interspersed about their line.

The 74th Field Battery was moved up behind their left, and came into action about 11 a.m. against the north end of Thoba Mountain, where the Boers were collecting. The remainder of the brigade was on the slopes behind them, and the transport was brought across Korannah Spruit, Watered and outspanned. The latter remained outspanned Until about 2 p.m., when shells fired some 8,000 yards away to our right rear landed amongst them, one after the other, lining damage and necessitating inspanning.

At 11.45 a.m. men of Kitchener's Horse were in evidence On the plateau of Thoba Mountain moving north, and I was ordered to reinforce them. I at once sent the nearest troops, namely two companies of the Shropshires under Major Dawkins, with Lieutenant-Colonel Macbean and the Gordon Highlanders close behind. By 1 p.m. these troops had reached the plateau, but not without a few shells from two guns hidden behind a wall near Farm C.

At 1.45 p.m. it was evident that Boers were moving up the northern end of Thoba and strongly reinforcing their men on that hill. I then, at Hamilton's direction, sent half a battalion of the Canadians to reinforce, following the same track as the other troops (b, b, b, on sketch). They came under an extremely heavy and accurate fire from the same two guns, and were fortunate in only losing Private Cotton,[4] who was killed.

At 2 p.m. a small patrol of Gordons under Captain Towse, with a few of Kitchener's Horse, were working along northwards by point X, and it was evident to us below that they were unaware that working southwards towards them was an overwhelming force of Boers—some 150 strong. This force[5] we had

---

4. The son of a prominent Canadian.
5. They turned out to be *Zaarps*, *i.e.* highly trained Transvaal Police.

seen for some time from where we stood near Y, and so regular were their lines and so unlike Boer movements, and like our own troops advancing, that they were within a few hundred yards of Captain Towse's party (which was at least 800 yards from his nearest support) before we realised they were Boers, and then the 74th Field Battery and R.H.A. guns poured shell into them at 3,400 yards.

We saw the forces, only about a hundred yards apart, suddenly discover each other, for both were approaching a crest line from opposite sides. It looked as though our small party must be annihilated, when these few men of the Gordons and Kitchener's Horse rushed forward and appeared to pour in a terrific fire before which the Boer lines recoiled and fled back. This gallant act saved us the hill. Had the Boers driven this small party back, our task of capturing the hill, difficult as it was, would have been more difficult. For this act I recommended Captain Towse for the Victoria Cross, which he got.

That scene is as clear to me today as when it happened twenty-four years ago. From where I stood in the plain with my commander we could see the whole of the side of the hill, and all that happened on it, and I have often wondered why that small brave force of ours rushed forward instead of back, and why they weren't all killed. It was soon evident that many of them were very much alive, for they maintained their position whilst the enemy withdrew partly down the hill again.

Nor shall I ever forget the pathetic sight in the evening, the arrival of the ambulance with the stricken Towse shot through both eyes; doubtful whether he would recover, but certain he would never see again, not a thought for himself, but plenty for his men, and those who had been with him, hoping that he had done his duty, and with it all so cheerful and apparently happy. Since then all his countrymen know that he has pluck and courage given to few men, and that in spite of his blindness he devotes his life to helping others, and especially ex-service men.

He spoke as quietly and lucidly as if he was in the best of health. He told me that when he found himself within forty yards of several Boers, who were supported by large numbers, they called on him to surrender, and he replied with the heavy fire which drove them off. He also spoke most highly of the behaviour of Kitchener's Horse, a few men of which were with him, and his last request before he went away with the wounded was that Sergeant Brunett, and Privates Dawes and O'Shaughnessy, of that corps, should be specially rewarded for the gallant way they helped him to keep the Boers at bay.

The Boers throughout the afternoon maintained accurate shell-fire from their two guns at C and a gun at D, and their rifle-fire all along their front was extremely heavy; but ours was also, and both sides maintained a terrific fire at times.

About 4 p.m., finding that we weren't making much progress on Thoba (we weren't trying to advance about A, A, A, A, as the Boers were behind walls and *sangars* with a smooth glacis of grass a thousand yards or more to their front), I was directed again to reinforce Thoba, and I sent up the other half-battalion of the Canadians, and went up myself to study the situation.

Night fell, and firing ceased. We were convinced that the job was a big one, unless we could turn Thoba by the west, and for that our mounted force was insufficient.

Hamilton accordingly wired for help from General French, and a battalion, the 8th Hussars, and one R.H.A. Battery arrived about 9 a.m. next morning, and the mounted portion, supported by our Mounted Infantry, commenced the turning move.

Soon after daylight on the 1st May firing commenced all along, and I went up on to the mountain to take charge of the operations. The Boers were still in possession of the highest peak of Thoba, F, and all the plateau to the north of it and a portion of E.

At 6.45 a.m. a company and a half of Gordons, under Captains Dingwall and Younger, worked forward, and established themselves on peak F.

The Canadians were sent from spur K, where they spent the night, to try and get spur E, which commanded them. They, too, only succeeded in establishing themselves on part of that spur, and did not get complete possession of it until 9 a.m. One half-company of the Shropshires, however, worked across between F and E at daylight, and established themselves there under a cross-fire. This section did extremely well, as they divided the Boers. They suffered severely, having ten casualties; but they never budged.

At 8 a.m. it was evident that the Boers were not giving up the struggle, as they were seen reinforcing the northern end of Thoba. At about the same moment the Gordons completely cleared peak F.

At 9 a.m. the Boers again turned all their guns on to our troops on Thoba for about three-quarters of an hour, and shortly after 10 a.m. I saw their guns from C inspan and move off.

At 11.10 a.m. I saw some twenty-eight wagons, evidently the Sterkfontein and Brightside *Laagers*, trekking east. It was then evident to me why the Boers had fought so tenaciously, and it was probable that the *laager* hidden behind Hill B B was large.

All this time there appeared to be a terrific fight going on with our Mounted Infantry and the East Yorkshire Regiment (the battalion sent by French) away to our right about Houtnek.

At 11.15 I gradually pressed troops forward along Thoba plateau, and at 12.30, knowing how desirable it was that the matter should be finished so that we might have a few hours of daylight to march into the plain, clear of the hills, I led a general move to sweep the plateau and a charge with fixed bayonets at the end of it.

The centre was formed by two companies of the Shropshires, under Major Austen, the left by a half-company of Gordons, and the right by Gordons. As we pressed forward the fire was heavy from the northern edge of plateau, but a few rushes, and then a final one with a ringing cheer, and the enemy were flying down the north side of the mountain, whilst we were merely out of breath.

At once Boers were in evidence, retiring hurriedly from along the whole position, and I signalled for the Shropshires and guns to advance from A, A, A, A to B, B, B, and for the transport to inspan; but Hamilton had already given orders.

By 3.30 p.m. the whole of our transport was safely moving through the pass, guarded by Gordons on the left, Shropshires and guns on the right, and the Mounted Infantry in front, and as we reached the northern end of the gorge we found Colonel Clowes, with the 8th Hussars, which had been completely round Thoba and done considerable execution amongst the Boers. We got settled in camp at Jacobsrust before dark. I had every reason to be satisfied with my new battery, which was very smart and efficient this day. Our total casualties in the two days' fighting had been forty-three.

Before descending Thoba I had seen five miles away in a north-westerly direction what looked like a British column on the march, and this proved to be the new 21st Brigade under Bruce Hamilton and Broadwood's Mounted Brigade marching to join "Hamilton's Force."

Chapter 13

Zand River, May 1900

We were glad to find next to us in camp the 21st Brigade, consisting of the Camerons, the C.I.V.s (Colonel Mackinnon[1]), 1st Royal Sussex, and my late battalion the 1st Sherwood Foresters, with my old friend Colonel H. C. Wylly in command. I found too another old regimental friend, F. Shaw, as Brigade Major. Two batteries, and two 5-in. guns, and Broadwood's Cavalry Brigade had also joined Ian Hamilton's force. Colvile, with the Highland Brigade, arrived and camped two miles off.

I heard from Ian Hamilton of the new organisation. The 19th and 21st Brigades were to form his Infantry Division under me—Spens of the Shropshires taking my place as Brigade Commander—whilst Colvile and the Highland Brigade were to be left behind to follow in rear as a sort of connecting file.

Lord "Bobs" plan was for his own, the main column, consisting of the 7th and 11th Divisions, to move straight up the railway *via* Kroonstad, whilst Ian Hamilton's force kept wide to the east *via* Winburg. French's cavalry to cover the main column up the railway as soon as his scattered troops could be collected.

On the 3rd May Ian Hamilton's force marched fifteen miles, camping north of Isabelfontein on the Winburg Road. Except an affair of cavalry near Fairfield Farm, in which one lancer was killed, the day was an uneventful one over the flat open *veldt*. We heard guns towards Brandfort, and, as we camped, saw about one thousand Boers occupy *kopjes* straight on our morrow's road—

1. General Sir Henry Mackinnon.

so we were prepared for opposition. A wire from the chief of staff at Brandfort indicated the possession of that place.

On the 4th May the force moved at 7 a.m., the Infantry Division being under my command: Bruce Hamilton's 21st Brigade led, followed by the 19th Brigade under Spens, K.S.L.I.

Soon after starting the mounted troops got in touch with the enemy, who occupied all the hills right across our road.

It was distinctly an interesting day. Our road lay through an open valley with low hills on either side, which were occupied by Boers, who had to be turned out of them before the main column could move forward at any pace. This resulted in a series of smart actions in which all arms were engaged, now on one flank, now on the other, and latterly straight ahead. Our attacks resulted in separating the enemy, and we had little difficulty in reaching our camp at Welkom Drift, twelve miles short of Winburg. Our losses were mostly with the mounted troops, who had thirty casualties, amongst which were Rose of the Blues, killed, and Lord Airlie, 12th Lancers, wounded.

It was apparent that the Boers intended no determined stand, and when the troops in advance moved on to the Vet River next morning, except for a few shots at our mounted troops they did not molest us. We saw columns of dust and large bodies of men with wagons trekking north and east. Unfortunately we halted outside Winburg to allow time for a message to be sent in under a flag of truce, which had the effect of allowing General Botha to clear out of the north end of the town as we entered the south.

Marching by moonlight, we moved on eight miles to Dankboarsfontein, where we halted for two days to allow the left column to come up, and then marched eleven miles to Bloemsplaats,[2] a splendid farm belonging to de la Plaats. It appeared to be a reserve for deer, as there were hundreds of them, which the men could not resist firing at, with great danger to their comrades—one man actually was hit.

General Hamilton went to see Lord Roberts some seven

---

2. The field of one of Sir Harry Smith's fights some sixty years previously.

miles west, leaving me in command of the force.

A Boer force was moving parallel with our right some 2,000 to 3,000 strong, and they attacked our right flank outposts, but were driven off.

At this time the north bank of the Zand River appeared not to be held by the enemy, but strict orders had been given that the force was not to cross. However, towards 2 p.m., seeing the Boers working westwards, north of the Zand, astride our next day's march, I gave permission for some of the Western Australian Mounted Infantry, under Major Moore, to try to seize the main drift. This they succeeded in doing on our side of the river only. The cavalry were to have crossed at 3 p.m., but by then the Boers were in too great force on the north bank.

This small party of Australians kept the Boers at a distance, and directly the sun set I sent the 1st Sherwood Foresters to the drift to entrench itself on both the north and south banks. This was very well done by this battalion, helped by the Royal Engineer sections of the 19th and 21st Brigades. The two 5-in. guns were placed in position after dark by Waldron,[3] the C.R.A. of the force, ready to shell the Boer position at dawn. Ian Hamilton returned after dark, approved of what I had done, and resumed command.

An hour before daylight on the 10th May the remainder of the 21st Brigade, under Bruce Hamilton, reinforced the Foresters in the bed of the stream.

The occupation of the riverbed overnight and reinforcing it before daylight in the morning saved the force from a serious action, as it appears that after midnight 800 Boers moved towards the riverbank, with orders to occupy it at the main drift, and to spread up and down stream, holding the banks; but, finding themselves forestalled, they were driven to occupy the river-bed at M (*vide* map) and between it and E, where, so far from doing us harm, they got held in the bed of the river by the Royal Canadians, one company Shropshire, and some Mounted Infantry, until their main position north of the river had been taken. Ac-

---

3. The man I had succeeded as Master of the Staff College hounds in 1887.

cording to prisoners' accounts, they were in such straits that they nearly laid down their arms, but managed instead to slip away in twos and threes up the bed of the river.

Having got the 21st Brigade along the river in the dark, I sent the 19th Brigade at daylight (leaving the D.C.L.I. in charge of the baggage) to move under Spens towards H and M, cross the river there if possible, and act in support of the right rear of the 21st Brigade.

For the time I kept the 76th and 74th Field Batteries under my own orders.

The Canadians leading, the 19th Brigade, approaching the Zand near M, came under a very heavy fire, and, as I mentioned above, held the Boers there until 2 p.m. At 7.10 a.m. a Boer gun opened from A, and shortly after a pom–pom from B. This latter appeared to be annoying Tucker's troops, for I could see the little shells bursting. I at once sent an *aide-de-camp* galloping to what we commonly called the "cow-guns," for they were pulled by bullocks.

He pointed out the stone wall behind which the pom–pom was; Waldron, with the first shot at 8,000 yards, knocked the offending weapon out, and directly after we saw the gun being removed; on examining the place later we found three Boers lying there, killed by the shell.

The 76th Battery came into action at 7.15 a.m. at H against the Boers at A, B, and C in support of the 21st Brigade, which was moving from the riverbed to *Kopje* D. At 7.45 a.m. I brought up the 74th Field Battery to take the place of the 76th, which I sent across the river by the drift to Bruce Hamilton at D.

The shell-fire of these two batteries and one of General Tucker's batteries at J, was most effective, and by 9.30 a.m. the attack of the 21st Brigade was gradually working up towards A, B, C, edging westwards slightly. I requested Spens to send a battalion to prolong to their right, and he sent the Gordons.

Shortly after this I asked for one of the corps batteries to take the place of the 74th, as I wished to send it forward to try to enfilade the ridge west of A.

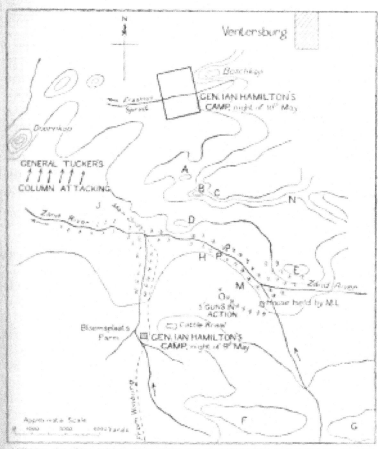

ACTION OF INFANTRY DIVISION OF HAMILTON'S COLUMN IN FIGHT
ON ZAND RIVER OF 10TH MAY 1900.

A = Boer gun behind wall opened at 7.10 a.m. Boers behind walls on slope.
B = Boer pom-pom shelling one of General Tucker's Batteries at J, made to
retire with three men killed by one shell from 5-in. guns at 3,000 yards at 7.45 a.m.
C = Very steep, stony kopje cleared by shell-fire of two Batteries at B and one
at D, when the Camerons occupied it with Gordons prolonging to their right.
D = Position of G.O.C. 21st Brigade, behind which he massed his Brigade,
which had occupied river-bed before dawn and launched them to attack.
M = Canadians holding Boers in river-bed and behind sangars at E. Boers in
force eventually shelled out at 1.30 p.m.
G = Boers (with guns) in force attacked 6th M.I. and especially Kitchener's
Horse at F, trying to get at our convoy. The M.I. were engaged all along spruit
from between F and G to M, F, J. Company Shropshire astride the Zand until
past noon prevented large numbers of Boers in river-bed from working down-stream.

The 82nd Field Battery was then brought up, and as it came into action a Boer gun from N at 6,000 yards range fired shell after shell into it, and into troops near it, without doing any damage, the Boer gun being soon put out of action by a 5-in. shell.

At 11 a.m. A, B, and C were in our possession. Boers in large numbers, with four guns, were visible retiring from the Doornkop in front of General Tucker, and some thousands were flying over hills towards Ventersburg. It was about this time that a determined attack was made on our rear-guard on *Kopje* F, and two guns were sent to reinforce it; and shortly after that Boers commenced escaping along the riverbank from P, P, under M, which they continued doing in small numbers until all their original 800 in the river, with the exception of those who had fallen to our shot and shell, had got away.

The fire on the Canadians had been very heavy, but we never believed, until after midday (too late to get any troops to surround them), that there were more than a few snipers in the river.

By 2 p.m. all had drawn off from the riverbed, and indeed from the south bank, and our rear was safe.

The casualties in the division only amounted to one officer and six men killed, eleven men wounded, and one missing: total, nineteen.

CHAPTER 14

Doornkop, Six Mile Spruit, Pretoria

The drift over the Zand River was very difficult, and, although our transport commenced crossing about noon, it was not until twenty-four hours later that the tail of it reached our camp, six miles from the drift. Our enforced delay, two days' halt on the 7th and 8th, had given the enemy time to get their transport away, and we only succeeded in capturing five wagons and sixty-nine prisoners.

The delay was apparently unavoidable, for French's cavalry was widely scattered when the advance from Bloemfontein commenced, and mounted troops were essential on our left flank and in advance of the left column, which, unlike our column, was deficient in them. Our own mounted troops occupied Ventersburg on the night of the 10th May.

Our next march was sixteen miles (mostly in the moonlight) to Twistniet.

French had bombarded the Boschrand (five miles from Kroonstad) and put the Boers to flight, but had had some stiff fighting, with about one hundred casualties. I was amused, during the day, by my orderly's apology for getting left behind. "My horse had a miscarriage," meaning she had slipped a foal.

Our next move was to Kroon Spruit, four miles from Kroonstad, from which Steyn fled to Lindley and set up the Free State Government there. The 11th Division camped north, and the 7th Division west of the town. French had gone west of the railway to cut the line north of the town, but was too late to get any rolling stock.

I rode in to Kroonstad to see Lord Kitchener about clothes and boots, etc., for the brigade. He was very cheery and accused me (pleasantly) of stealing a battery and deserting my late divisional general (Colvile)—both of which accusations had a smattering of truth in them.

We moved forward again, five miles east of Kroonstad, On the 15th May. Supplies were our great difficulty, as the railway was destroyed north of the Wet River, some sixty-eight miles off. A welcome reinforcement of six pom-poms and 1,000 Mounted Infantry joined our force.

Our direction was towards Lindley. All other troops halted at Kroonstad. Passing through Tweetpoort, we had on the 17th May a trying march, with five most difficult *spruits* for the wagons to negotiate. We halted for three hours at a bridge, over the Valsch River, and eventually bivouacked late at night east of Elands Spruit after a fifteen miles' march. The Shropshires with the last of the baggage were not in camp until 4 p.m. next day.

My force, consisting of the 19th Brigade and Roberts's Horse, was left in camp on the 18th May east of Elands Spruit to guard the line of communications whilst Ian Hamilton and the rest of his force moved into Lindley.

On the 19th, having received orders from General Hamilton to move back over Elands Spruit, thence to Quagga Spruit, I did so and met our convoy of supplies under Colonel Cholmondeley, with the M.I. of the City Imperial Volunteers, at Quagga Spruit, and started at daylight next morning to rejoin General Hamilton in the neighbourhood of Vellust. At 11 a.m., after marching some twelve miles, we viewed the head of General Broadwood's Cavalry engaged with the Boers south of the Rhenoster River, and joined him in quite a brisk action, but were unable to cross to the north bank of the Rhenoster, where the Lindley-Heilbron Road crosses it, until the 20th.

As we approached Heilbron on the 22nd May, the 19th Brigade leading, the cavalry reported a large commando with wagons leaving the town going north-west. I galloped to the front to see if the help of the Infantry Division was required. The cavalry followed the Boers slowly and cautiously, and a good deal of long-range fire with guns and lilies was exchanged, the Boers as usual fighting a splendid rear-guard action, in which they excel. Our guns, however, got at the Boer wagons, and eventually fifteen of them and seventeen prisoners were captured. We entered Heilbron, a pretty little town, where we obtained nearly three days' supply for the whole force, men and animals.

We got our sick and wounded into houses and prepared to stay a day or two and rest, but "No," orders came for us to march next day west to the main line. We left thirty sick at Heilbron.

The object of this move west was to surround Boers, but we all knew there were none to surround.

To avoid the left column we turned north and camped on Kromelboog Spruit at Arcadia on the 24th. I rode in to see Headquarters Staff, six miles and a half, to try to get boots, clothes, and medicines for men, but failed. Lords "Bobs" and Kitchener were most affable, and told me Ian Hamilton's force was to cross to the west next day and become the left column to continue up the railway. We heard that Mafeking had been relieved on the 18th and Baden-Powell promoted major-general.

Our orders were to reach the Vaal on the 25th, sixteen miles, but to take in supplies first from convoys which were expected. We, therefore, crossed to the west of the railway line and there outspanned, so as to leave the road clear for the advance, up the railway, of the 7th and 11th Divisions. Broadwood, with cavalry and Mounted Infantry, went on at 10 a.m. to seize the passage of the Vaal. We waited until 3 p.m. for the expected convoy of supplies, and then marched seven miles and halted for the night, hoping supplies would reach us ere morning; but they did not actually arrive for some days.

Entirely without forage, and with very short rations, we marched fourteen miles on the 26th to the Vaal, and crossed at a pretty wooded bend of this fine river. It was my forty-second birthday, an auspicious moment for entering the Transvaal.

We started again from Wildebeestfontein on the 28th May at

daylight. Hamilton having been sent for to see Lord Roberts at Meyerton Station, I was left in command of the force. I galloped ahead to join the cavalry under Broadwood,

and we occupied Cyferfontein, the cavalry and Mounted Infantry pushing on to hills three to five miles ahead, looking over the Klip River Valley. French was evidently engaged eight miles to our left front, but, although firing was fairly incessant all day, there was not sufficient to cause me to reinforce him, especially as he signalled at noon: "Boers in no strength, and retiring north-east." De Lisle reported 500 Boers crossing Klip River before him at 11.30 a.m.

The following is a paraphrase of my dispatch on the action of Doornkop, which was fought the following day :

On the 29th May Hamilton's force advanced from Cyferfontein—*via* Vlakfont, Rietfontein, to Zuurbekom *en route* for Florida, this westerly route being through open country and avoiding the formidable slopes of the Klip Riviersberg. This latter place was held in strength, and the enemy there were kept engaged by some of General French's mounted troops, supported by Broadwood's Cavalry Brigade, whilst the rest of French's force, keeping to the west, pushed on ahead of us.

About 11.15 a.m. this latter force was seen some two or three miles to the north of the Infantry Division (which was approaching Zuurbekom) and in pretty active conflict with the enemy, ending in our cavalry establishing itself on *Kopjes* A, B, and C (on sketch).

From the point of vantage thus gained the Boer position came in sight. It was hard to distinguish the features of the ground and where their main strength lay, but it was evident that they occupied many miles of front, some 3,500 to 4,000 yards from us, and several lines of forbidding-looking rocky *kopjes* of no great height or steepness, but with long, smooth, glacis-like slopes, without cover, leading up to them; and, what was worse, with all the grass burnt for a 1,000 to 1,500 yards in front of the position, thus rendering the khaki clothes of our advancing troops more conspicuous.

The Boer left was in greatest strength at *Kopje* E, but ran right down to Klipspruit Farm over rather lower *kopjes* than the one at E. Behind this position you will see on the sketch a long, narrow valley, which gave them perfect cover for operating from, and later on a covered way for retreating.

Overlooking this again was a long formidable spur with black rocky *kopjes* on it (D on sketch), and dominating everything at a considerable distance stood the Main Rand Ridge. The Boer right ran forward on a long ridge (*i.e.* the Doornkop and its spurs) and several *kopjes* lay in this direction, all of which were held. General Bruce Hamilton, with the 21st Brigade, arrived on the ground A, B, C, first, and immediately occupied those *kopjes* to free General French for a further turning movement to the westward of the Doornkop. To support him in this movement General French asked General Ian Hamilton that Broadwood's Cavalry Brigade and some Mounted Infantry might be sent after him, which was agreed to.

At 1 p.m., General Ian Hamilton having reconnoitred the position, decided that the Boers must be forced back and the direct road to Florida opened, one very cogent reason being that we were almost out of rations, and he hoped to get supplies at Florida. Accordingly he directed me to dispose the Infantry Division for attack.

Kopje E would undoubtedly have to be dealt with by the right brigade operating from A and B, and the question was, "Could the *kopjes* in the neighbourhood of D be attacked from C without settling with the Doornkop (*Kopje* F) *en route?*"

Bruce Hamilton, who was to operate in the western portion of the field with the 21st Brigade, thought that they couldn't, whereas I thought that they could.

Accordingly my orders to him were to converge towards l he attack of the 19th Brigade, and to try to avoid attacking the Doornkop, as I felt sure that the latter was too far off and would be cleared automatically when General French's turning movement had developed; and also that attacking it and *Kopje* E at the same time was more than two brigades could do without loss of touch.

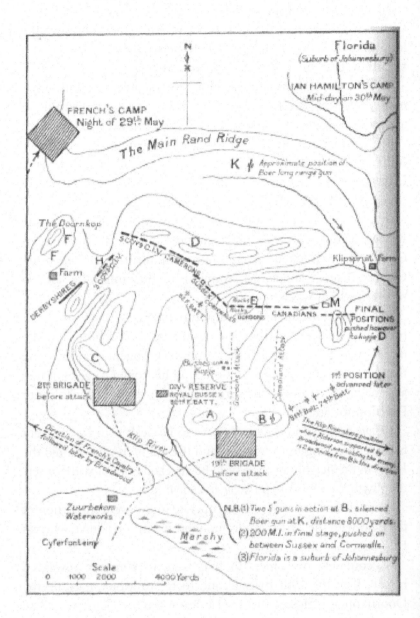

ACTION AT DOORKNOP

I took one battalion (the Royal Sussex) from the 21st Brigade and kept it as a divisional reserve between the two brigades.

About 2 p.m. the 21st Brigade, covered by their guns (the 76th Field Battery), was moving forward; and the 19th Brigade moved at 2.30 p.m.

The position of the guns and troops at the commencement and at the end of the action are shown on the sketch. The divisional artillery was distinctly slow coming into action and, at the time I ordered the infantry to advance, I was certainly given to understand by the C.R.A. that the guns were in action ready to open fire. However, the infantry was but little over 2,000 yards from the enemy when the first gun opened at 2.45 p.m.

At that hour also on receiving a signal from Bruce Hamilton that he was pushing half a battalion to clear the hills to his left (*i.e.* the Doornkop) I asked him to desist and work away from those hills towards the 19th Brigade. This he most skilfully accomplished. I had appreciated by that time that the enemy was in sufficient force at D and E to require all our men, and at 3.20 p.m. I sent up the reserve battalion (the Royal Sussex), with the lieutenant-general's permission, to connect the 19th and 21st Brigades in one continuous line of skirmishers extending some four and a half miles.

The 81st and 74th Field Batteries had advanced their positions at 3.15 p.m., as, owing to the smoke caused by the burning grass, it was impossible for them to observe. This was the case with almost all our artillery throughout the day. At about 3 p.m., seeing the 19th Brigade getting too far to its right, I sent an order to Spens to try to check it. This he did by sending his brigade major, Captain Higginson, K.S.L.I.

By the time this officer reached the firing-line of the Gordons the latter were under a tremendous fire, but he cantered along the line until he found the commanding officer, delivered his message, and rode back again. A little later, seeing the Gordons were getting too far ahead of the C.I.V.s, and that their left would be dangerously exposed unless something was done at once, I galloped forward myself and stopped them.

By dusk the enemy had been driven out of every portion of the field. They had made a determined and obstinate stand, turning their field-guns on the Gordons' extended line at 500 yards range, and remaining themselves in many cases until our men were within a few yards of them.

That they were in great force with a large amount of artillery I have no doubt. I myself mistook their retirement from the Doornkop and the *kopjes* captured by the C.I.V.s for General French's Cavalry Division.

The features of the day were enormous extensions of both attack and defence, and the attacks of the Gordon Highlanders and City Imperial Volunteers. The extended movements of this last-named corps compared favourably with some of our regulars.

The men were handled with skill by Mackinnon, and, in spite of determined opposition from several directions, he drove the enemy from every position with comparatively small loss. The attack of the Gordons was, however, a more formidable undertaking, and, as it took place under my eyes, I will add a few words of my own.

The long, glacis-like slope ended in a plateau, some 800 yards in depth, on which were three distinct lines of formidable natural boulders, behind which the enemy took up three successive positions as the Gordons approached. I must emphasise how effective, from the enemy's point of view, was the bare burnt ground. From the moment the firing-line reached it, each man stood out like a bull's-eye.

Some troops, with still 900 yards to go and several lines of rocks to clear of the enemy, would have hesitated; not so the Gordons. The commander of their firing-line, Lieutenant-Colonel H. H. Burney, a man of great coolness and dash, decided in a moment that the black ground must be got over as quickly as possible and the enemy routed, and so took place an attack of which even the Gordons may be proud. Lieutenant-Colonel Macbean pushed up one more company to prolong the firing-line to the left. Unflinching, the Highlanders went steadily on, regardless of thinning ranks, and capturing line after line of rocks, put the Boers to rout. In one hour and twenty minutes 4,000 yards of ground had been covered, and the main position was taken at 4 p.m.; but fighting continued until after dark, and so ended a hard day's work, an eighteen-mile march concluding with four hours' fighting.

The casualties in the division were 26 killed and 115 wounded. I deplored the death of Captain St. J. Meyrick, Gordon Highlanders, and that Lieutenant-Colonel Burney was severely wounded.

Owing to the Bearer Company being too far behind, it was long after dark before all killed and wounded were collected. It was extraordinary how most of the latter had escaped without wounds of a dangerous character. Many had been wounded several times; one man had six bullets in him, and, like all the rest of the wounded, was most cheerful and happy.

At dawn next day I pushed forward the 21st Brigade, with mounted troops in front of them, and occupied the Main Rand Ridge without opposition. We camped amongst the gold-mines by noon, some two miles from Johannesburg. As we did not move forward again for two days, we had opportunities of visiting that town.

We found there a curious mixture of untidiness and pretentious buildings. The whole place had an air of rowdyism, with its somewhat tawdry buildings and innumerable drinking-bars—but I only saw a very small portion of the town myself.

We marched, on the 3rd June, to Diepsloot (fifteen miles) and the next day to Six Mile Spruit (twelve miles), where we met the final opposition before Pretoria was in our hands.

This fight, in which all the divisions and mounted troops with Lord Roberts were engaged, was merely a picturesque rear-guard action, the Boers holding lightly a low range of hills on a wide front for some hours, whilst our artillery thundered and covered the deployment of our attacking infantry. As soon as the latter ascended the slopes of the position and our mounted troops threatened their rear, the enemy fell back.

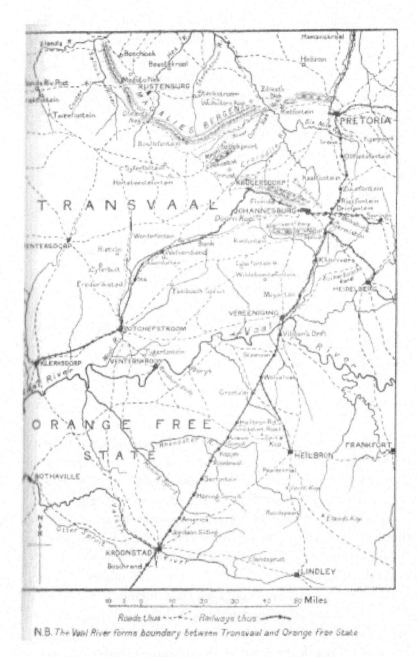

Roads thus ---·-·-·. Railways thus ━━━━━

N.B. *The Vaal River forms boundary between Transvaal and Orange Free State*

KROONSTAD TO PRETORIA AND PURSUIT OF DE WET

There was certainly some fighting, and Hamilton's force on the left flank of the attack had its fair share, but a detailed description is hardly required.

Pretoria was now in sight, some three miles off, and the days of "Hamilton's Force" were numbered. We had marched 380 miles in thirty-seven days, on eight only of which had we halted, and six of our fights might be classed as serious affairs—Houtnek (Thoba Mountain), Welkom, the Zand River, round Lindley, Doornkop, and Six Mile Spruit.

That night Colonel de Lisle rode up close to Pretoria and summoned it to surrender. The commandant came out and announced that General Botha would accept Lord Roberts's invitation to meet him next morning at 9 a.m. Accordingly by that hour we moved to within a mile of the town and on what became known as "Proclamation Hill" my division was drawn up in a formidable array ready to receive Botha. Everything was complete, except the one important ingredient, namely, Botha himself. He tarried and came not. We accordingly moved into camp west of the town and at 2 p.m. the town was entered in procession. All mounted troops of Hamilton's force had been previously ordered to the east of the town to support General Gordon's Cavalry Brigade. Accordingly Ian Hamilton was unable to attend the procession, and I had the honour of leading the troops by and sitting at Lord Roberts's right hand at the saluting point. My staff was a large one:

D.A.A.G. Gamble,[1] Intelligence Kirkpatrick,[2] Chaplain Southwell,[3] P.M.O. Colonel Williams (Australians), A.A.G. Inglefield.[4]

My troops:

C.I.V. Mounted Infantry under Cholmondeley; 19th Brigade (Spens); 74th Field Battery, D.C.L.I., Gordons, Canadians; then Colonels Flint and Waldron, C.R.A.s for R.H.A. and R.A., 81st,

1. Now Brigadier-General K. N. Gamble, C.B.
2. Now Lieutenant-General Sir G. Kirkpatrick, whom I had first met in Malta.
3. Now Bishop of Lewes.
4. Major-General F. S. Inglefield, C.B., D.S.O.

82nd, and 76th Field Batteries, also two 5-in. cow-guns; 21st Brigade (General Bruce Hamilton); and an ammunition column.

Bruce Hamilton and his staff, Shaw, Fraser, and Wilson, dined with me.

As the Boers were unable to take the many prisoners they had captured during the war along with them, they had to release them, and they were speedily formed into provisional battalions and used for defensive posts.

Lord Kitchener appeared early the next day, and ordered me to send Spens and the Shropshires with two guns by march to Irene, and thence by rail to Vereeniging—where Boers were threatening; he also told me the Boers were attacking the 4th Derbyshire Regiment, a militia battalion, at Kopje Station, eighty miles south of Johannesburg on the Rhenoster River. I myself was to command at Johannesburg, having under me the 15th Brigade, 74th and 82nd Field Batteries, Ross's Mounted Infantry, and the 19th Brigade less Gordons and Canadians, which were to remain as part of Pretoria Garrison.

On the 7th June Rawlinson brought me fresh orders to collect my brigade again, taking the Suffolks instead of the Shropshires. It was a big order, as the units were scattered miles apart and no one knew exactly where they were. However, by 3.30 p.m. the brigade, with two battalions R.A. and Colonel Cholmondeley and one company C.I.V. Mounted Infantry, were clear of Pretoria, and by 9 p.m. were camped ten miles off—three miles north-east of Irene Station, where I went to get orders from Ian Hamilton for the coming attack on Diamond Hill.

I was just moving off north-east at 9 a.m. next day with my force to join in the attack on the Boers, when Rawlinson appeared again with written orders from Lord Roberts for me to take charge of the line from Pretoria to Vereeniging, seventy miles, and to guard it at once with my Brigade and Colonel Ross's Mounted Infantry, some 500 strong. De Wet had been playing Old Harry down the line, capturing a militia battalion, the 4th Derbyshire on the Rhenoster, and two other posts on the railway, thus jeopardising our lines of communication on which we were entirely dependent for supplies; so we turned about and marched to Irene, where I left fifty Mounted Infantry, and 200 D.C.L.I. Owing to a difficult *spruit*, we didn't get very far that night.

Off at 6.30 a.m. on the 9th. Left Colonel Ashby and 200 D.C.L.I. at Olifantsfontein; then Major Harvey and fifty Lumsden Horse at Kaarlfontein; then 200 Suffolks and fifty Mounted Infantry at Zurfontein, and I finally camped the Brigade near Rietfontein after an eighteen-mile march.

I myself rode on to Elandsfontein, which I made my headquarters.

CHAPTER 15

Lines of Communication, Onrust and Olifants Nek

The events of the next month are not, I think, of sufficient interest to record in detail. There was plenty of hustle and bustle, due to the threats of an agile and brave foe to the lines of communication of the army, and when I add that there were about a dozen other generals sent in all directions, some with flying columns, others to repress specific threatening small bodies of the enemy, others to garrison certain towns, and all detached from their regular commands, some idea may be gained of how the chief had to upset his main plans and carry out fresh ones at a moment's notice.

There were almost daily attacks on some post or portion of the line for which I was responsible. My scheme of defence was to have, about every eight miles, a strongly entrenched post of 200 infantry, fifty mounted troops, and two guns, disposed to hold small works adapted to the conformation of the ground, and also to furnish posts at all important bridges.

The mounted troops were to scout wide of the line, and place Cossack posts on commanding heights throughout the day; and the infantry were to send patrols of six to eight men at irregular hours throughout the night to the station to the south of them, these patrols to return to their stations by train the next day. Thus every part of the line would be visited about every two hours through the night, and, as each patrol went from one station to the next, there would be no complication of patrols not meeting, and no fear of their shirking their duties.

No infantry patrol of less than thirty men under an officer was to go more than a mile or two from its post by day. Every post had to be in telegraphic and signalling communication with the next, and to have dispatch riders always ready.

A special siding at a central place (Elandsfontein) had to have reserve trains ready, and a force of 100 mounted troops, one battalion of infantry, and two guns were to camp alongside it, ready to entrain and move to any threatened point, the guns and light transport to be kept on the trucks.

For the first two days my charge extended only from Pretoria to Vereeniging, but the commander-in-chief was so pleased with the scheme that he wired me to take charge of the whole line from Pretoria to Kroonstad, and said that he had adopted it as a pattern for the defence of other railways. Although dashing attacks on my line were many and frequent, and often carried out by large numbers, no catastrophe occurred, and the traffic was never interfered with for more than a few hours from the time my system was in working order. I was, however, forced to order the destruction of farms near any breaks in the railway or telegraph as they occurred, and also the seizure of all horses, bicycles, and means of transport.

I was engaged on this work nearly a month when, on the 3rd July, Lord Kitchener ordered me to prepare a scheme to release my brigade, as Lord Roberts had wired, in the most flattering terms, that we could no longer be spared. I had, at the time, 9,000 men under my command, from which I had to extract the units of my brigade. They concentrated at Irene, and I handed over to General Chermside on the 9th July.

It appeared that the Boers had become active north and west of Pretoria, and quite a lot of small fights favourable to the enemy had taken place. Baden-Powell had entrenched his force at Rustenburg north of Olifants Nek, and the Boer General Lemmer was holding that *nek* or pass through the Magaliesberg.

1. Now Colonel Sir Percy Girouard, K.C.M.G.

Lord Roberts was anxious about the situation there, and also in the Brandwater Basin in the south-east of the Orange Free State, some ninety miles from Kroonstad, and came to the conclusion that until the Commandos in those areas had been dealt with he could not continue his main operations along the Pretoria-Delagoa Bay railway. To deal with the latter he had many of our best Generals—Clements, Paget, Broadwood, Bruce Hamilton, Macdonald, and Ridley, captained by Sir Archibald Hunter and Sir Leslie Rundle. They had enclosed important Boer forces in a particularly difficult country, and successfully rounded them up, except that the gallant and resourceful de Wet slipped out with 2,400 men over Slabberts Nek on the 15th July, and thus began the great de Wet hunt, in which I joined later on.

The chief's plans for dealing with the dangers west of Pretoria were as follows:

It seems that Baden-Powell told the chief that if a force would operate from the south against Olifants Nek, he would attack that place on the north side from Rustenburg, and so it came about that my hopes of two days' rest were rudely dispelled on the evening of the 9th July by the arrival of Girouard, R.E.,[1] the Director of Railways, with orders in Rawlinson's handwriting and signed by him to proceed to Krugersdorp and march thence with a small force against Olifants Nek.

To General Smith-Dorrien, Irene
Pretoria, 6.30 p.m., 9.7.00.
You will proceed by rail tomorrow morning with two battalions from Irene to Krugersdorp—without transport. At Krugersdorp you will get from General Barton two field-guns, one company of Yeomanry and transport for your two infantry battalions. You will march on Wednesday to Hekpoort (fifteen miles north-west of Krugersdorp). There you will be joined by the Greys and two R.H.A.

---

2. The owner of Sainfoin when that horse won the Derby.
3. 19th Coy. Imp. Yeom., 34 N.C.O.s and men, ten do. with Colt-guns sections. 2nd K. Shrop. L. Infy., 680. 1st Gordon Highlanders, 597. Two guns 78th Field Battery. With three ambulances and five days' supplies. On forty wagons.

guns. You should clear the country in the neighbourhood of Hekpoort and then march with the Greys to Krokodil-poort, sending back the two guns and company of Yeo-manry from Hekpoort to Krugersdorp. Keep us informed *via* Krokodilpoort of your movements—you should reach Krokodilpoort by Friday night.

By order,

H. Rawlinson, Lieutenant-Colonel,

A.A.G. for Chief of Staff."

My force started for Krugersdorp in three trains. Telegrams later than the above quoted order directed me to march to Ol-ifants Nek, thirty-nine miles off, and thirty-five miles west of Krokodilpoort. I was to co-operate with Baden-Powell. He would attack Olifants Nek from the north whilst I attacked it from the south. I replied that I had nearly fifty miles to march and Oosterheyzen's—a strong commando—to deal with *en route*, and could not possibly reach Olifants Nek until the 14th. I also remonstrated on the insufficiency of my force, and especially of my mounted troops.

I moved off at 7 a.m. on the 11th July with a ridiculously weak force: two guns 78th Battery, forty-five Yeomen of the 19th Company Imperial Yeomanry under Captain Sir James Miller,[2] and the Gordons and Shropshires. We had the most trying fight (to us) of the whole war, which is fully described in the follow-ing dispatch:

From Major-General H. L. Smith-Dorrien to the Chief of the Staff

Krugersdorp,

July 13th, 1900.

Sir,

I have the honour to report that on the morning of 11th July I marched off with force as per margin,[3] with orders to move to Hekpoort, where I should be joined by the Scots Greys and 2 R.H.A. guns, on meeting which I was to send back the Yeo-manry and two guns F. Battery to Krugersdorp.

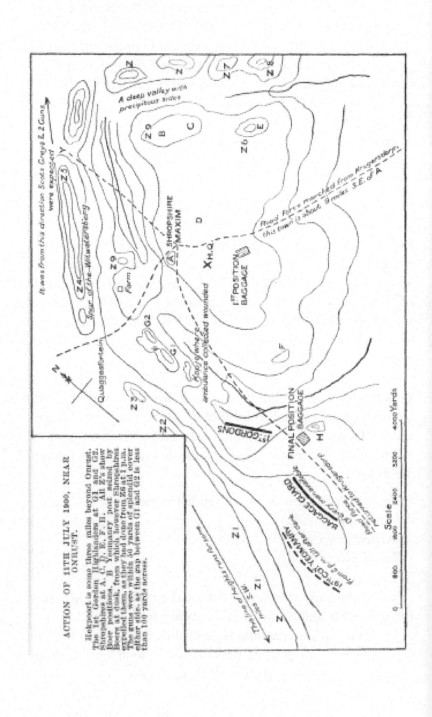

ACTION OF 11TH JULY 1900, NEAR ONHUST.

Heilbron is some three miles beyond Onrust. The 1st Gordon Highlanders at G1 and G2. Shropshires at A, C, D, E, F, H. All Z's show Boer positions. A, B Yeomanry post seized by Boers at dusk, from which, however Shropshires repelled them, as they had done from Z6 at 11 p.m. The guns were within 50 yards of epsilon-cover, either side, at the map between G1 and G2 is less than 100 yards across.

A deep valley with precipitous sides

It was from this direction Scots Greys & 2 Guns were expected

Your of the Watuerchberg

Z3

Z4

Z9

Y

Quaggasfontein

Z8

Z5

Z2

Z B C

Z6 E

A SHROPSHIRE MAXIM

Farm

D

X H.Q.

Road along where ambulance collected wounded

G2

G

G1 GORDONS

Z1

Z1

Boer Force marched from Krugersdorp, this town is about 9 miles S.E. of A

1ST POSITION BAGGAGE

F

I

FINAL POSITION BAGGAGE

BAGGAGE GUARD

19TH COY YEOMANRY from 3 p.m. till after dark

This line S.W. ran 1½ miles to the rear

Scale

0   800   1600   2400   3200   4000 Yards

After we had gone some nine miles and were in the neighbourhood of Onrust at 11.30 a.m., our small force of Yeomanry, which was all used up in a thin screen as well as in two flanking patrols of three men each far out from the baggage, was heavily fired on from the main Witwatersberg—Z4 on sketch.

The sketch gives a very fair idea of the nature of the country, which was quite the most broken and difficult of any I have come across in our operations in South Africa. The Witwatersberg itself, a precipitous and high range, faced us in front, and a continuation of it trended away from its western end in the neighbourhood of Quaggasfontein for many miles to the southwest, rendering it necessary to establish ourselves on it before an advance could be made in that direction.

The direct road to Hekpoort led over still more formidable country, and our right flank was commanded, at a distance of 2,000 to 3,000 yards from the road, by high ground shown as B and E on sketch; these in their turn were commanded by another series of four high *kopjes*.

Our scouts had found that the ridge Z1, Z2, Z3, to the south of Quaggasfontein, was unoccupied by the enemy, and I at once determined to try and seize it.

I therefore ordered the Yeomanry to proceed there at once, and sent off the Gordon Highlanders with the two guns with orders to open fire on Z4 from G2.

Shortly after, and when all these moves were in course of being carried out, I saw the enemy leaving Z4 in ones and twos, and galloping across the wide neck of ground towards Z3. But before they reached it the two guns, instead of going on to *Kopje* G2, had passed between G1 and G2 and opened fire at Z4.

I judged by their movement that the Yeomanry (who could easily have been at ridge Z3 before the Boers, had they known) were unable to see the Boers galloping up, and would be too

3. These casualties occurred at my H.Q. shown on sketch. This was very exposed and under fire all day, but we had no choice, for it was the most suitable spot from which to control the fight by signals.

4. General Barton was at Krugersdorp, and I was in direct signalling communication with him, and all my messages to the commander-in-chief had to go through him.

late. I therefore sent my *aide-de-camp* Hood to order the Gordons to advance no farther than Gl and G2 at present, and Dorrien-Smith to order the guns to withdraw from their exposed position.

This latter order did not reach Lieutenant Turner commanding the guns until fire had already been opened on him from Z2 and Z3 at about 900 yards range, and to convey this order Dorrien-Smith had to ride under a heavy fire up to *Kopje* Gl, leave his horse there, and walk under a shower of bullets out to where the guns were. Unfortunately, when the guns came into action the limbers, instead of remaining behind the *Kopjes* Gl and G2 close to the guns and under perfect cover, had withdrawn to 600 yards in rear, and when the order arrived to withdraw the guns the limbers could not be got up for some considerable time.

Just after sending off the Gordons and guns I requested Colonel Spens to send out two companies to the high ground at B a mile or more to my right, the remainder of the Shropshires to guard the baggage, which, directly the enemy opened on our scouts, I had ordered to park as shown in "1st position" on sketch.

At 12.45 p.m. I could see that the guns were under a very heavy fire, when suddenly a tremendous fire was opened on the transport from *Kopje* E Z6 at 2,500 yards.

I instantly ordered the transport to move farther to the west, and sent my staff off to carry out my instructions for repelling the attack. This was done in the very promptest manner, and within two or three minutes a line of skirmishers were advancing from the baggage against *Kopje* E and another from *Kopje* B, thus taking the enemy in flank. In twenty minutes our fire was so heavy and advance so determined that the Boers retired to Z8 and Z7, and we occupied E. It was during this phase that my A.A.G., Lieutenant-Colonel Inglefield, had one horse killed, and immediately after another wounded.[3]

It was about 2 p.m. when I signalled to General Barton[4] that I might have to retire, and saying I regarded such a movement as

5. As a matter of fact, they had been captured at Zillikats Nek that very morning.

undesirable, but that it could be avoided if he could send me any reinforcements. At the same time as I received his reply, saying he could not spare any, a message from the commander-in-chief came telling me that my operation was cancelled as the Scots Greys and two guns, whom I was momentarily expecting in the enemy's rear, had been counter-ordered.[5] The chief further directed that I should retire on Krugersdorp; this settled the matter, though, as will be seen, it was some hours before I could carry out the order. The enemy were on all the hills marked Z on sketch, i.e. a front of eight or nine miles which enveloped both our flanks, reinforcements were dribbling in all the time over the hills from the east, and it was impossible to say how many more were behind them. I accordingly issued orders to retire at 1.25 p.m., when Colonel Macbean, Gordon Highlanders, signalled that the guns could not be withdrawn, but that they could perfectly hold their position till nightfall, when the limbers could be brought up with safety.

Colonel Macbean's message caused me to cancel all orders to retire, and I moved the baggage to the high ground shown "final position" on sketch and distributed the companies of the Shropshires at A, D, E, F, and H.

Every available man from the baggage was utilised to cover the new position of the baggage and to support the Yeomanry and the Gordons at G1 and G2.

The Yeomanry, when they found the enemy had been too quick for them in seizing Z3, worked farther to their left, trying to gain a footing on the ridge; but wherever they tried the enemy were there to meet them. They were extremely well handled by Captain Sir J. Miller, and with their Colt guns were able throughout the day to prevent the enemy from descending on our left rear.

I will now return to what happened round the guns. After they had been in action about an hour all but three of the gunners had been shot, and of the limbers one, in endeavouring to remove a gun, had four horses shot and gave up the attempt, whilst the horses of the other had taken fright and bolted.

A party of the Gordon Highlanders with the unwounded gunners then manhandled one wagon under cover in spite of the heavy fire. More Gordons then, under the guidance of Captain W. Gordon (Adjutant, Gordon Highlanders), made a gallant attempt to remove the guns, but were unable to, Captain Younger and three men being killed and seventeen wounded in the attempt. Several instances of great gallantry occurred at this period in carrying wounded under cover, and vain attempts to drag away the guns.

At about 3 p.m. *Kopje* Z9 was occupied by Boers, and they poured a heavy burst of fire from it and a farm below it into the Gordons who, however, had built such excellent *sangars* that they suffered very little, added to which Major Doyle's company of the Shropshires, with a Maxim from A, very soon kept the Boer fire down, dropping some of their number.

Throughout the day the Boers made constant attacks against my right without success. Eight of the Yeomanry held *Kopje* B, and prevented the Boers coming up there until just dark, when I ordered them back.

The Boers then quickly appeared there, and opened a very heavy fire. Major Austin's company of Shropshires, however, instantly advanced from D, and drove them off. Directly dusk came on the Boers descended the ridge Zl, Z2, Z3 to within 300 yards of the Gordons, and their commands of "*Vorwarts*" could be distinctly heard.

At 6 p.m. the gun-teams were sent up to withdraw the guns. The moon was very bright, and the movement could be seen, and instantly a terrific fire was opened which lasted for twenty minutes and was eventually got under by the Gordons in their strong position. The Boers were clearly seen in clusters about this time, and suffered considerably, one being shot at 100 yards range; and from this moment they were content to be still.

I should mention that our ambulances, moving far away from troops, had been systematically fired at throughout the day, with

---

6. The men were so pleased with themselves that, on getting clear, and in column of route, they burst into song.

casualties amongst their mules, and were now back again at *kopje* shown on sketch.

About 8 p.m. all wounded had been removed, and the guns had gone back, and a general retirement to the baggage was commenced. This was most successfully carried out,[6] and, acting on the latest order from the commander-in-chief, the force returned to Krugersdorp, where it arrived at 4 a.m. on the 12th instant.

I must say a word in praise of the splendid way Lieutenant Turner, R.A., and his men worked their guns till almost every man was shot. Turner himself was one of the first to be wounded, but, although wounded a second time, he was actually firing the gun himself till the last moment, and when asking for help to bring away his guns he was wounded a third time, and had to go under cover; before doing so, however, he had caused the guns to be disabled.

The action of Captain W. Gordon (Adjutant, Gordon Highlanders) was something to be proud of, and he was awarded the Victoria Cross.

I cannot speak too highly of the way my staff worked. It can be seen from my account that every man, including servants and all with the baggage, were in the fighting line. I myself was alone with the signallers, near X, throughout the day. My staff were employed galloping with orders often under terrific fire, and it was largely due to their dash and promptness that I was able to beat off all attacks.

With less steady troops matters might have turned out differently. At one period the Gordons were getting short of ammunition, and it was impossible to get the carts close up to them; accordingly, in the coolest way, fourteen men of the Shropshires carried it across to them over a mile of ground under a very heavy fire, going one at a time. Our expenditure of ammunition was over 32,000 rounds.

Native accounts confirmed reports we had heard as we passed certain farms on the morning of the 11th, which were to the effect that we should be opposed by 1,500 to 2,000 Boers. That they were in large numbers I am sure.

Reports from Boer sources were that their casualties were between eighty and ninety, and that their general, Oosterheyzen, was wounded in the thigh.

After our strenuous twenty-four hours it was nice to get two or three days' rest, although there were many orders and counter-orders. The one which held was that Lord Methuen was coming with a larger force, and that I was to act under his orders, which were to make another attempt on Olifants Nek.

Lord Methuen's force had come by rail from Kroonstad in thirty-six trains, and had been enormously delayed owing to failures on the railway, and we were not able to move until the 18th July.

A mounted reconnaissance had gone out at 9 a.m. and had found the enemy all along the heights where we had fought on the 11th instant. Our right column consisted of 100 Yeomen, one battery 25th howitzers, the 1st Northumberland Fusiliers, the Loyal North Lancashires, and the Northamptons under General Charles Douglas; the left column, under myself, consisted of the rest of Lord Chesham's Yeomanry Brigade with two pom-poms, one Battery R.F.A., the Shropshires, and the 1st Gordon Highlanders of the 19th Brigade, with three ambulances and the Bearer Company of that brigade under Major Nicholl: Lord Methuen himself was in command.

The right column marched six miles, the left four and a half, and camped on Riet Spruit, about three miles apart.

The left column then made a wide turning movement to the left, and occupied the heights in the neighbourhood of Doornbosch, then, swinging to its right, covered the advance of General Douglas's force on to the range looking down on Hekpoort. The Boers made a feeble show of resistance, killing two of General Douglas's horses. The whole force looked down on the rugged country round Hekpoort, distant some two miles; then, swinging its right round, cleared some 200 Boers off the heights about Zeekoehoek, and camped at Vaalbank, a very pretty spot just at the mouth of the Zeekoehoek gorge. All reports showed the Boers as being active and handy, notably one Commando of 500 and two guns, which had passed through *en route* for Potchefstroom two days before.

Gradually drawing in to the main Magaliesberg range, we found a force of Boers astride our road, but they were driven off with slight loss to ourselves.

The gorge in the Witwatersberg on leaving Vaalbank, through which the river flowed, was a very picturesque one, cutting right through the range, which towered above the roadway on either side. Beyond was ridge after ridge of mountainous country. After driving the Boers away we passed over into a very fine valley in which our road turned farther to the west, and gradually drew in towards the Magaliesberg. We camped about two miles from this splendid range on the 21st, the day we reached Olifants Nek.

Douglas's Brigade was leading and we proceeded some four miles to Olifantshoek, getting into worse country every moment—a mile farther on, our Yeomanry were engaged and soon our guns were in action—Douglas's Brigade moving to clear the series of formidable hills to the left, whilst the 19th Brigade did the same on the right.

By 12.30 p.m. we had driven back the enemy and came in full view of the pass at Olifants Nek. The Boer force had been split in two, some 300 being driven away south-west by the Northumberland Fusiliers who passed over the bodies of five dead Boers and saw many more fall, whilst the rest, with two pom-poms, two Maxims, and twelve mule vehicles of sorts, fled up the pass under a very heavy but half-aimed shell-fire from our batteries. General Baden-Powell had been told to co-operate from Rustenburg, and we expected momentarily to hear his guns—at last tardily we heard three rounds, but it appeared afterwards that he had not got near enough, and all the enemy escaped with their wagons.

If he had only been able to get closer to the *nek* we should have caught them all.

Olifants Nek is a grand pass with a river running through

it, and we, after crossing it, passed at once into the Bush *Veldt* country—a lovely, well-treed country with high grass and rich orange-growing farms.

Our losses were some eight or ten casualties, of which I think five died.

It was originally intended that the 19th Brigade should return to Krugersdorp, but Lord Roberts had decided that it should remain with Lord Methuen for the present—so we settled ourselves down in our beautiful camp and prepared for a day or two's rest.

It was settled that we should spend the next few days hunting up commandos to the north-east of Rustenburg, but all was changed by news from Lord Roberts that de la Rey had cut the line and captured a train near Bank Station between Krugersdorp and Potchefstroom. Orders came at the same time to turn our attentions to de la Rey.

Accordingly, after numerous changes of orders, most of them unavoidable, leaving Kekewich, the defender of Kimberley, with the Loyal North Lancashires to hold Olifants Nek, Methuen's force started off and camped without incident at Wagenspud Spruit on the 23rd July. There fresh orders arrived for Methuen to pursue de Wet. The latter wily Boer had slipped away from Hunter, Rundle, Clements, and Paget, and, pursued by Broadwood, had cut the line near Honing Spruit, captured 100 Highlanders, burnt a train, and was moving on Potchefstroom.

Chapter 16

Pursuing De Wet

Lord Methuen's force was divided, and on the 24th July, one column under me, consisting of the 19th Brigade, Algy King's 20th Battery and Eric Smith's 10th Battalion of Yeomanry, marched south, to Hartebeestfontein—twelve miles west of our battle-field of the 11th at Onrust—whilst Lord Methuen with the remainder moved to Vaalbank.

My column had an uneventful march over a beautiful *veldt*, at first very hilly, but getting more open.

It was very noticeable how the climate of the Magaliesberg varied; north of that range the people had had no frost; south of it we found cold winds and frost most nights. On some farms we found fine orange-trees, which furnished an issue of fruit to the troops. Passing through Hartebeestfontein, we camped on the 26th July at Bank Station, near Methuen's force which had gradually closed in on us. We saw the train, wrecked by the Boers a week previously, and steps were taken to replace the rails which had been moved. Boer patrols were seen by our scouts on the Gatsrand, a prominent range which de Wet was to cross shortly.

Natives reported de la Rey, who had attacked the train, to be in those hills with 400 men and two guns, but that de Wet was still south of the Vaal.

Lord Methuen marched west, leaving me with two guns, two howitzers, an R.E. section, and the Shropshires to await an ox-convoy.

Lord Kitchener, with Hubert Hamilton and John Watson, came over from Krugersdorp to discuss the situation. He told us all the news—that we had got Middelburg and a lot of stores; that Generals Gordon and Hart were pursuing de Wet, who, with 400 wagons and 3,000 men, was twenty-five miles south-east of Potchefstroom about Rensburg Drift over the Vaal.

The famous de Wet Hunt was fast approaching our area. Should we be more successful than the many columns he had already eluded farther south? That question the following pages will answer. Never did a hungry pack of hounds pursue a tougher, more wily, or braver old fox.

Lord Methuen's ox-convoy having arrived on the 29th, I decided to march to Wonderfontein, eight miles.

An unconfirmed rumour on this day made out that affairs in China were serious, and that a large force under my old friend General Sir F. Grenfell was being sent. I, not wishing to be idle, and in case the Boer War should end sooner than expected, telegraphed to the War Office offering my services.

The next day we started at 5 a.m. and marched to Frederikstad—a long march of eighteen miles. We passed Welverdiend Station after seven miles, seeing a few Boers on the hills. Arrangements had been made for a large supply train to come in, and we had quite given it up when, just as we were choosing our camping ground, we heard it whistling behind a hill about a mile short of Frederikstad Station. It had met with a terrible disaster; the engine-driver, in spite of orders to the contrary, had come along twenty-five miles an hour and dashed through our advanced troops. The Boers had taken up a rail, and the engine and seven trucks were all in a heap, with injured and dead under the wreckage, fourteen killed and forty-five injured.

The positions of the camps, for there had to be one where the train smash had occurred, as well as the main camp a mile away, were selected that evening with more than usual care in case of attack. All reports, and wheel-tracks, showed that some 500 Boers with wagons had crossed the line two miles north-east of Frederikstad Station.

At 7 a.m. in the morning a Boer rode into camp on the railway, where I was myself, with a flag of truce from Commandant Liebenburg and demanded our surrender, or he would attack in half an hour. He was at once brought to me. I happened to be shaving, and between the sweeps of my razor demanded of "His Impertinence" what he required; but before he could answer the Boers opened a heavy fire on both camps, so without further parley I shouted to the escort which had brought him to me, saying: "Keep this man under a guard until we have driven off the enemy, and then we can shoot him at our leisure."

The main camp was splendidly situated, tucked close in under low hills which were strongly held, and Colonel Mackinnon, C.I.V.s, had been very prompt in meeting the attacks; but the Boers had worked boldly along the high ground, and were firing, at quite a short range, on the C.I.V.s covering the camp. It was here the latter had their losses. Our guns were in action, guarded at the time of attack by Yeomanry, and quickly reinforced by two companies Shropshires, and the results were never in doubt. After one and a half hours the Boers retired, and I sent guns and Yeomen in pursuit; but I had to stop them on seeing mounted men approaching from the south, which afterwards turned out to be the escort to a convoy coming to us from Lord Methuen. It was under command of Major Leverson, R.E., and had been fighting all the way.

Directly the attack opened I had signalled Methuen at Potchefstroom, thirteen miles off, to come and take the enemy in rear, and later on I caught him with another signal that the Boers were retiring north-west towards Ventersdorp. He succeeded in catching them and completing their discomfiture with shell and rifle fire.

I am unable to say how far the Boers suffered, or what their exact numbers were, but they were commanded by Liebenburg, and I don't think the total force which attacked me and the convoy was more than 500 and two guns. My force was Shropshires, C.I.V.s, 140 Yeomen, and one section 20th Field Battery.

As soon as the attack was driven off I moved out to help in

Major Leverson's convoy; on our way in, and about where the Boer line of retreat cut the railway line, we found the bodies of two Englishmen and three natives riddled with bullets and much battered about. We heard afterwards that on the previous night an unarmed party of one Corporal, R.E., one man R.W.F., and three natives on a trolley had been brutally murdered by some of Van Kraan's followers, the evidence chiefly pointing to one Abram Bezeidenhout. As a reprisal, the farms of Daniel Pilser and Jacob de Bruins were burnt.

Next morning, my wrath against the Boer emissary having subsided, I thought it advisable to let him go for propaganda purposes; so, telling him of Prinsloo's surrender with 5,000 men, of which I had just heard, I had him conducted a few miles out and turned loose.

The debris of the train kept Lieutenant Thomson, R.E., and his men, with fatigue party and 160 bullocks, busy, and it was not until the next day that all the bodies were got out—whilst Major Leverson repaired the destroyed railway bridges. The farms of F. Wolmerans and Piet Bezeidenhout, junr., were burnt, and, as a further reprisal for the murder, and also for wrecking the train, the following farms were burnt: (1) Therence Dryer, (2) P. Briedenbach, (3) T. G. Briedenbach, (4) De Bruins' forage store.

I sent half the Shropshires, a section 20th Field Battery, and the 43rd Imperial Yeomanry, under Colonel Spens, to garrison Welverdiend Station, while the clearing of the railway line and repair of bridges proceeded. The next day or two we were fully occupied getting supply columns backwards and forwards between Bank Station and Potchefstroom, as the Boers were pretty active.

I heard early on the 8th August that Methuen had been fighting de Wet the day before and had driven him north-east from Tygerfontein towards Lindeque, and so wired Lord Roberts the situation and got his reply to concentrate at Bank Station. I remonstrated, as I feared leaving a gap open at Frederikstad. I recalled all the troops which had guarded the train towards Potchefstroom and ordered back the empty train with two companies of Shropshires. It was an anxious day as I had no engine and everything depended on the return of the train to move my supplies. At last, at 7 p.m. it appeared, and I heard by telegraph that Potchefstroom had been evacuated. We marched at 9 p.m., escorting a train of sick, wounded, and supplies to Welverdiend. Glorious moon, but very cold; we walked all the way, fourteen miles. Spens and his force marched from Welverdiend to Bank Station, reaching the latter in the small hours of the 9th. During the afternoon I had destroyed all the bridges across the Mooi River so as to hinder the passage of the Boers from west to east.

We arrived at Welverdiend at 3 a.m. on the 9th, and I wired Lord Roberts suggesting the danger of leaving a gap for de Wet to pass through if we all moved to Bank; but he would not consent and we marched at 9 a.m. with the train, and reached Bank, sixteen miles, at 3 p.m., an ox-convoy and Shropshires arriving at 6 p.m.—a good march; half the Shropshires had done forty-three miles in thirty-two hours, and all the rest of my force, C.I.V.s, Bucks and Suffolk Yeomanry, the 20th Field Battery, had done thirty miles in seventeen hours. During the afternoon two trains with supplies and the whole of West Yorkshires under Major Fry arrived; during the night our extra transport marched in from Krugersdorp.

The West Yorkshires had brought tents with them, and the commanding officer asked where he should pitch them. I explained to him that it was only in Buller's pampered Natal force, from which he had come, that luxuries could be indulged in, and that we had not seen a tent for many months, and further, moved too rapidly to make use of them. But I found these tents a very useful reinforcement—for we had not enough troops to block all the line with a view to preventing de Wet going north, so we pitched three or four small camps from these tents at intervals of three or four miles along the railway. The Boers, seeing these new camps, would naturally suppose they were occupied, and their difficulties of crossing the railway would be increased; and so it proved.

If the West Yorkshires ever felt the loss of tents they certainly never showed it, for as a hardy fighting unit I have never known a better.

The 10th of August was a day of constant wires. Lord Roberts wired that Kitchener, with Broadwood, Little, Ridley and Hart, were about Lindeque pursuing de Wet with Methuen on his left flank, de Wet going straight for our station (Bank); this latter I felt sure was doubtful, as I knew he would not run his head against us, but felt that if he saw us moving west he would be prepared. Accordingly I planned and carried out a move after dark, namely, Spens with Shropshires in the train, two guns and ninety Yeomen to Welverdiend, Mackinnon with C.I.V.s, two howitzers, 86th Field Battery (which had come from Standerton with the West Yorks) under Captain Woodcock, and fifty Yeomen to Wonderfontein. Colonel Sandwith, late in the afternoon, reconnoitred with his yeomanry and got driven back to the railway line. Small parties of Boers were seen all day moving west along the north side of the Gatsrand.

At 1 a.m. next day a most important dispatch from Broadwood told me that he, Ridley, and Little were at Weltervredend and Methuen at Taibosch Spruit, also that de Wet's wagons were crossing the Gatsrand on the night of the 9th for Bank. I at once informed Broadwood that I was sure he would go farther west, and asking him to bring his right shoulder up, sent order to Spens to move to Doornfontein and Mackinnon to support him, saying I would follow with the West Yorks and the 6-in. gun.

This latter, mounted on a railway truck, had arrived the day before from Elandsfontein. I wired a full report to Lord Roberts, and at 5.15 a.m. myself and staff lay down for twenty minutes' rest, when we had breakfast. Then, sending off half the Yorkshires and the train, I started myself with Yeomanry and baggage towards Welverdiend; just before starting we heard Mackinnon's howitzers firing at what turned out to be fifty Boers north of the railway. After twelve miles we became sure that de Wet was farther west, and I ordered the other half of the West Yorks, two guns, and the rest of the Yeomen, with all transport, to march from Bank, and they reached Welverdiend during the night. I myself started to join Spens and Mackinnon near Doornfontein. Too late, alas! De Wet had crossed the line three miles west of Welverdiend at 1 a.m. The only hope now was to block the passes through the Magaliesberg range. I then ordered concentration at Welverdiend Station. We found train loaded with sick from Potchefstroom stopped by a broken culvert one mile west of Welverdiend. It had had sundry adventures, having been two days coming twenty-six miles, and having been stopped by de la Rey and 500 Boers. We had heard the explosions of the culvert being blown up by de Wet the previous evening.

Lord Kitchener, with Broadwood's, Ridley's, and Little's Brigades, arrived at Welverdiend during the evening. Lord Kitchener, myself, and our staffs dined together in the station. We heard some shelling during the afternoon over the Gatsrand. Methuen, with his troops and the Colonial Division, went to Frederikstad. Half the C.I.V.s under Albemarle, with two empty trains, returned to Bank during the night. It had been a terrible day of wind and dust.

On the 12th August Ridley, Broadwood, Little and myself, after loading up supplies, started about 9 a.m. Hart's column of five battalions, guns, etc., which had pursued de Wet from the Vaal, marched in at 8 a.m. Thomson's Royal Engineers were left on the railway to repair the culvert.

It was very pleasant to see my Regiment, the Sherwood Foresters, and also the Canadians, again; both had arrived with Hart, and gave me a warm welcome. I and staff remained at Welverdiend till noon to make arrangements and see fresh supply trains in from Krugersdorp.

At 11 a.m. (the 12th August) Methuen's guns were heard going hard near Cyferbult, and they continued all day, getting farther and farther north; our own mounted troops went very slowly. The drift at Rietvlei over Mooi River was awful, and it

1. *Vide* plan, which shows how much shorter the road is to Olifants Nek from Commando Nek, north of the Magaliesberg.

took our wagons till twelve next day to get over. I myself was on and off near the drift all night, barring one hour and twenty minutes which I took for sleep.

Lord Roberts wired the previous night that Ian Hamilton was to reach Hekpoort (from Commando Nek) today, *en route* for Olifants Nek. This meant his approaching Olifants Nek from the south.[1] I immediately sought out Lord Kitchener and implored him to wire the commander-in-chief begging him to direct Ian Hamilton to keep on the north side of the Magaliesberg so that he might seize Olifants Nek from the north; but he refused. It was therefore a certainty that Olifants Nek could not be blocked, since Lord Kitchener had informed me that the garrison placed there by Lord Methuen had been removed. From this moment all hope of stopping de Wet vanished from my mind.

On the 13th August we started at 3 a.m.; the ox-convoy followed at noon. We halted at Cyferfontein to water and reached Klippan, twenty-six miles, at 4 p.m. The men marched splendidly. Reports as to de Wet's movements were conflicting. Methuen with Chesham's Yeomanry were doing splendidly, whilst our mounted troops were still going slow. Ian Hamilton signalled from Zekoehoek that Boers were at Boschfontein, so it was evident he had come too much south and could not be in time to seize Olifants Nek.

From the 14th to 25th August I merely give extracts from my diary.

14th August.—Marched at 6 a.m. *via* Grondfontein, Rietfontein to Syferwater, fourteen miles. Bernard, with ox-convoy, arrived at Klippan 6 a.m. Our mounted troops were engaged; a few casualties, de Lisle wounded. They only encamped a few miles ahead of us. Fine, picturesque, broken, wooded country. Lord Kitchener at last feels de Wet has escaped. As a matter of fact, we heard he crossed Olifants Nek this evening. The authorities have made a mess of it in not ensuring Olifants Nek being held, and the war may be prolonged six months in consequence.

News that Colonel Hore, with 300 Rhodesian Horse and

Bushmen, is holding out on Elands River at Brakfontein. Lord Kitchener decided to go to relief with all his force, abandoning the pursuit of de Wet; very sorry for Methuen and Chesham. The Yeomanry and Colonial Division under Dalgety have done magnificently, and if only properly supported by Lord Kitchener's mounted force, most of de Wet's force must have been caught.

Overheard by camp fire, Shropshire Regiment: "'Ere we are again, mate, off on another blooming trek, 'alf rations and full congratulations."[2]

15th August.—Marched at 9 a.m., fourteen miles. I saw Ian Hamilton, whom Kitchener left to make his own plans with Lord Methuen. Men marched awfully well. Two Canadian Mounted Infantry captured four Boer scouts, the Head of the Free State Intelligence, six horses, and one Cape cart. News that Hore still holding out, so we should relieve him tomorrow. I believe my nephew, Arthur Dorrien-Smith, of the Rifle Brigade, is with him.

16th August.—Marched at 4 a.m., got to Tweefontein at 6 a.m., six miles. Found mounted troops just moving off, great confusion of transport. Halted my force to let others get clear till 9.30 a.m. as I heard that Boers had retired from Hore's position, and there was no urgency for our pressing on. Reached Brakfontein, seven more miles, at 12.30 p.m., and encamped on a charming spot by a stream. We found Arthur Dorrien-Smith among the relieved force, very fit and cheery. They had been besieged since the 4th. During their first two days they had had 2,000 shells pitched into them, and had had almost all their animals killed.

They only had one wretched little 7-pounder, with 100 rounds, which were soon expended. The position all round taken by Boer guns and pom-poms fired straight into their force. One night the Boers had brought guns within 2,000 yards, but had to stop firing, and were unable to withdraw them until after

---

2. I heard afterwards that the last five words were generally used to describe myself.

dark, owing to a heavy rifle-fire—a good instance of the power of modern long-range musketry-fire. Our casualties during siege had been about seventy. We found plenty of rations for men, and, thanks to Arthur, lots of rum. Up to now troops had never had more than three-quarters rations since leaving the railway.

17th August.—Busy all the morning finding out about the roads, as Lord Kitchener was bent on going north, by Boschoek Pass, in two columns. I persuaded him that the road was impracticable, and he reluctantly gave in, and ordered us to march back the road we came; but, on hearing that Methuen had taken the Mogato Pass, he directed that my force, with Ridley, should go that way, Methuen going west to Zeerust, Broadwood and Hart going back the way we had come up the Hekpoort Valley.

18th August.—Leaving Little's Brigade for Methuen to pick up at Elands River, and Broadwood to move south-west to join Hart, we started at 4.30 a.m., Ridley's Mounted Infantry covering us. Great confusion owing to want of orders for the march. Lord Kitchener himself commanding our column. After thirteen miles through very rough country, we reached Ebenezer, where we met Lord Methuen's force at 11 a.m. and outspanned for two or three hours, ox-convoy for longer. Methuen and Ian Hamilton had attacked Mogato and Olifants Nek Passes respectively yesterday, and had taken them, with slight losses. We marched at 2.15 p.m. five miles to Coster River, where we bivouacked. Ridley, who was three miles off on the Selous River, reported large force of Boers had reoccupied Mogato Pass. Animals very hungry, as we had almost no forage, but got a little from the country. Total march eighteen miles, troops not asleep until midnight.

19th August.—All astir at 2.30 a.m. and off at 4 a.m. over Mogato Pass, Which was not held. A very picturesque pass, road fairly easy from west, but steep down the east side. Infantry and guns reached Rustenburg at 1 p.m. all pretty tired, transport not in until later, and ox-convoy with the rear-guard not till 2 p.m. We enjoyed our afternoon in a pretty little town of gardens and orange-groves.

Ainsworth, of Durham L. Infry., and Lambert, lately commandant of Klerksdorp when that place surrendered, joined us, having just escaped from de Wet. The latter had gone through Olifants Nek, and it was clear if that pass had been held he would almost certainly have been captured. The Boers had fully expected to find it held.

A dispatch from Lord Roberts that de Wet was ten miles from us and near Commando Nek yesterday, and was being pursued by Ian Hamilton, caused the hasty dispatch of Ridley's Brigade in that direction at 5 p.m., so off he started with his tired men and horses.

On the 20th we marched eleven miles, and on the 21st twenty-four miles, making seventy-four in four days.

Prisoners reported de Wet at Zoutpan. We saw the Boer Scouts on the top of the Magaliesberg, and they fired at our men. Scenes on rear-guard were most pitiful, weary men all along the road, and over a hundred transport mules dead.

22nd August.—Astir at 3.30 a.m.; we were just starting for Commando Nek when orders came from Lord Roberts for a move to block the drifts north of us on Krokodil River, as de Wet was reported there; so back I turned with Colonel Legge, 300 Mounted Infantry, four R.H.A. guns (P Battery) under Sir G. Thomas, the Shropshires, West Yorkshires, and King's 20th Battery, and marched for Beestekraal. We reached Mamagali, twelve miles north of Wolhuterskop, and eventually got to camp by 8 p.m. Our march was over a rough winding road through an extremely picturesque, rocky, *kopje* scenery.

Patrols reconnoitred the drifts of Krokodil River. About 9 p.m. a dispatch-rider arrived, informing me that Baden-Powell and Paget were engaging Grobler's rear-guard near Pienaars River north of Pretoria, some twelve miles north of Hamanskraal, that a colonel and five men of Protectorate Regiment had been killed and others wounded, and that we should march on Hebron.

23rd August.—At 2 a.m. another dispatch-rider brought orders to move on Pretoria. A Boer force was reported to have come by Krokodil drift north of Wolhuterskop crossing road five miles west of that *kop* for Piet Kruger's farm and across Magaliesberg to Hekpoort before daylight yesterday. I doubt the truth of it, but wired it to Lord Roberts. Certainly Theron's scouts have gone in that direction, and natives insist that de Wet himself has gone with them. We moved towards Commando Nek, but after some hours' trek had to retrace our steps to our last night's camp.

24th August.—Astir at 4 a.m. and off 5.15 a.m., through an extremely beautiful wooded country, with the Magaliesberg overhanging the road. After five miles we passed over Commando Nek, held by the Border Regiment, where we breakfasted with Major Pelly and the Borders, our old Malta friends; then, crossing the Magalies River half a mile farther east by a bridge, we passed, three miles farther on at Rietfontein, the King's Own Yorkshire Light Infantry under Barter[3] with two 4.7 guns under my A.A.G.'s (Inglefield) brother. The duty-of this force was to watch Zillikats Nek, which opened some two miles north of them, and in which on the 11th July the Scots Greys and Lincolns had met with a serious reverse. We formed our camp three miles farther on, having completed twelve miles and being still some twelve miles from Pretoria.

25th August.—A bitterly cold morning. March at 5.30 a.m. Found it was fifteen miles to Pretoria, where we camped on the race-course, having marched 116 miles in the last seven days and 245 in the last eighteen days, on two of which only had we halted.

Lord Roberts had gone to Belfast. News that Buller had fought yesterday near Carolina, losing a company of Liverpool Regiment. A plot to kidnap Lord Roberts ended by the instigator, Hans Cordua, being shot here yesterday. The whole country is being divided into districts. My Brigade reconstituted, i.e. the original Shropshires, Gordons, Duke of Cornwall's Light Infantry, with West Yorkshires instead of Canadians. Brigade ordered

---

3. Lieutenant-General Sir Charles Barter, K.C.B., K.C.M.G., C.V.O.

to join Lord Roberts at Belfast with 20th Field Battery by rail. D.C.L.I. went today. Gordons pass through tomorrow from Krugersdorp. The Boers, with big guns, hold a large position near Belfast.

CHAPTER 17

Buller and Komati Poort

In the midst of orders and counter-orders the Brigade en-
trained for Belfast during the next four days. The railway staff,
hustled by Head-quarters, were having a harassing time of it.
While waiting for trains I had an hour's talk with Ian Hamilton,
who arrived from the north on his way east. It appeared that
his force had suffered, too, from a want of dash in his mounted
troops.

We arrived at Belfast,[1]120 miles from Pretoria, bitterly cold,
on the 31st August. I lunched with Lord Roberts in his railway
carriage, and found my Brigade had been again changed, and was
to consist of Gordons, Royal Irish (18th) under Guinness, and
the Royal Scots, under Douglas; I fought for, and got a promise
of, the Shropshires, too. I also had the C.I.V.M.I. (Concannon, a
pushing leader), 1 Sect. R.E., 20th Battery R.F.A. (King), etc.

The Transvaal was annexed on the 2nd September, on which
day the Boers burnt trains at Klip River and Holfontein, and Ladybrand was attacked and summoned to surrender—altogether
a fine opening day in our newly annexed country. The situation
was not made rosier by an urgent wire from Buller saying that
his advance on Lydenburg was opposed, that he was confronted
at Badfontein, just north of Crocodile River, by a position as
strong as Laing's Nek, and that he wanted help.

I found myself again under Ian Hamilton and we started at

---

1. Belfast is 6,400 feet above the sea, the highest plateau in the Transvaal, though
there are several peaks higher.

6.30 a.m. the next day, towards Dullstroom, to help Huller. The oxen were weary after seventy-six hours in the train, without food or water, and transport got along badly in consequence.

At 1.30 p.m., as we were approaching Swartz Koppies (distant twelve miles), a Boer gun (4-5 howitzer) opened fire and landed shells in the middle of the extended Royal Scots. The C.I.V.M.I., with great dash, seized a commanding hill, the 20th Field Battery was brought up and came into action, and the Royal Scots advanced on a wide front. The Boers soon retired and took up another position 5,000 yards farther on; we camped, however, and got comfortably settled before sundown. The Boers tried to burst shells in our camp, but could not quite reach it.

The C.I.V.M.I, were only forty strong, and we were to have been joined by a cavalry brigade of Buller's this evening, but it didn't appear—it was the 2nd Cavalry Brigade under Brocklehurst, and camped ten miles short of us.

We resumed our march at 6.30 a.m. (4th September), and directly we showed our noses out of camp the Boer gun opened on us and delayed us nearly an hour whilst we got up our 5-in. cow-guns to reply. The Boers soon retired on Dullstroom, disputing every *kopje*; our small mounted force of C.I.V.s under Concannon did extremely well, pushing back the Boers' sharpshooters with great dash without delaying the column. The 20th Field Battery and Rouse's pom-poms also did useful work. We had cleared Dullstroom of the enemy and occupied heights behind it by 11.15 a.m. and halted to rest animals and feed men till 2 p.m.

Then the 18th Hussars, which had arrived meanwhile, took up the scouting and we moved on without incident till we reached Palmietfontein, where we halted for the night in a very hilly and well-watered country with piquets on distant hills, and Boers two miles and a half to the east.

There was a dense fog the next day, and in consequence we could not start till 7.30 a.m.; an awful road, with very heavy gradients, beautiful mountainous country, with any amount of clear rapid streams. Very few Boers seen, but a certain amount of

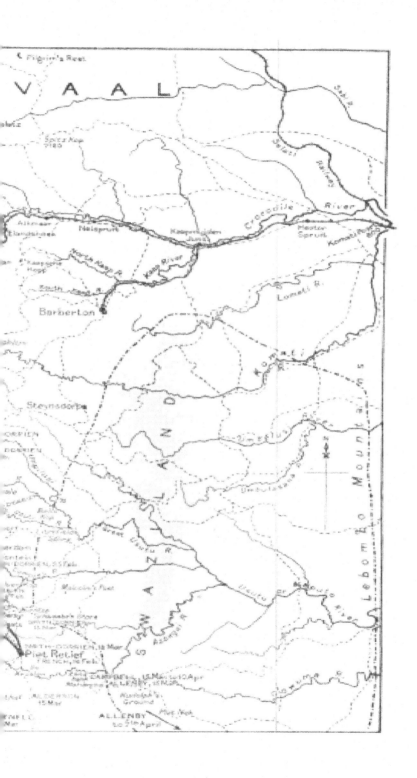

sniping. We camped at Wemmerskraal, in the hollow, surrounded by mountains which had to be piqueted, and got signalling communication with General Buller, whose guns we heard from 8 a.m. as he attacked the Boers' left. One important hill (Wemmershoek) above Zwagershoek, six miles off, commands the pass we had to go through, so I sent on half the Royal Scots, under Major Douglas, at 8 p.m. with six C.I.V.M.I. to seize and hold it by moonlight.

6th September.—Cavalry started at 6 a.m., with our force following. After six miles we entered a regular Tirah gorge, and our wisdom in sending the Royal Scots to occupy Wemmershoek overnight was evident. The pass was four miles long, and the Boers were sniping from every hill. My old piqueting experiences gained in Tirah came in, and the Boers were unable to get a shot, into our convoy, only one man being wounded. When we were clear of the pass we had turned the strong Boer position in front of Buller at Badfontein,[2] and at 1 p.m. got a signal from him that the Boers had retired and he was moving up the main Lydenburg road towards the town and had reached the neighbourhood of Rietfontein. At 5 p.m. after a very tedious march for animals over a winding road, full of drifts, we camped north of Spitzkop, six miles from Lydenburg.

General Buller came to our camp to see General Hamilton; the troops cheered when they saw him; he decided on concentrating at Lydenburg next day.

7th September.—We moved from our lovely camp at Spitzkop at 6 a.m., our rear-guard being engaged with small parties of the enemy. We collected cattle *en route* under fire; and camped south of the town, under trees by a farm, where we lunched. Shortly after a pleasant snooze was disturbed by Long Tom shells bursting over the camp fired at a distance of over 12,000 yards (*i.e.* seven miles). Almost the first shell killed two Royal Irish and

---

2. Our being brought from the west of Pretoria to help Buller was quite unnecessary, for he had plenty of troops, and. could perfectly easily have turned the position himself if he had shown any initiative.

wounded another. An incessant and accurate fire was kept up all the afternoon, of which my camp was the centre; later on shell after shell burst over my tent, and one bullet came through it and embedded itself in the ground within three inches of my foot, whilst I was tubbing. Ian Hamilton had gone to stop in the town, so I ordered out the 5-in. guns, and rode into the town myself to see General Buller.

It was a stormy, windy evening, and looked like rain. We got orders to move at 7.30 a.m. next day to attack Paardeplats, the Boer position, the highest point of which, the Mauchberg, is 8,720 feet above the sea.

8th September.—All ready to move off at 7.30 a.m. Leaving Colonel Guinness, two guns, and half the Royal Irish, we moved north of the Machadodorp road by 8 a.m. and awaited Buller's orders to attack. The Long Tom was playing on us, and one shell knocked over sixteen men of the 2nd Gordons in Buller's force; we waited until 10 a.m. before Buller allowed us to move.

The problem before us was to climb the Mauchberg, to the top of which a certain number of Boers had retreated. The top was probably 3,000 feet above where we were, and it must have been eight to nine miles to the top the way we went. We had a ridiculously large force for such a small operation. In addition to Ian Hamilton's force there were Buller's troops, consisting of at least one division and a cavalry brigade. It was certainly an interesting day, and there was plenty of firing—but it is not worth describing in detail. When we eventually reached the top a dense fog came on, and we could see the Boers as they galloped away, and disappeared in it. It was a hard day for troops, as I reckon by the time we got back to camp twenty miles had been covered. The best part of the day was the nine-mile walk down the mountain, for it was intensely cold and the descent warmed one's blood. The position and the attack on it was very like that on the Sampagha Pass in the Tirah expedition.

The end of the fight was like the end of an Aldershot Field Day, crowning the position being followed by firing at the retreating enemy, and it was made more like it by the arrival of the staff officer, who touched his hat and said: "March back to camp, please, sir."

The total casualties in our whole force were under twenty-five, and thus ended a day illustrating how a sledgehammer can be used to crack an eggshell.

Buller now decided he could do without our help, so we started off at 6 a.m. on the 9th September *en route* for Machadodorp. We marched about ten miles and saw the position which held up Buller and caused our being sent out to help him. It was undoubtedly strong to look at, but turnable, and bringing up our force to assist ought not to have been necessary.

We arrived at Helvetia on the 11th September and found the Manchester Regiment as garrison there, and Stephenson's 18th Brigade of Warwicks, Yorkshires, Essex and Welsh, which moved off in the evening eastwards. Pole-Carew was moving near Nooitgedacht on the railway with Hutton somewhere handy, French being near Carolina. We awaited orders; the 19th Brigade had completed 1,215 miles on foot.

Lord Roberts having had to go into Pretoria to answer questions before the Hospital Commission, "Lord Romer & Co.," it was evening before Ian Hamilton could get orders, so we enjoyed a welcome rest at Helvetia.

Then orders came in for us to move on Komati Poort, so next morning we dropped down from the high *veldt* over 2,000 feet to Waterval Onder. This was a very interesting spot. It is an important railway depot at the foot of the cog railway, connecting it with Waterval Boven on the high ground. The Boer Headquarters had been there, before moving thirty miles farther east to Nelspruit, which latter President Kruger had left only a day or two, and rumour had it that he had already embarked on a French ship at Lourenço Marques.

Unfortunately Pole-Carew's division was ahead of us, so we got a very limited amount of the stores left by Boers, but were able to purchase a few of Kruger's plain unmilled sovereigns from the local hotel-keeper.

The place was full of yarns, such as—that the Boers were pinning their faith on the French, to whom Kruger was journeying, to arrange their independence; that the result of the pending American elections was bound to be in their favour; that the patience of the people in England would soon be exhausted—and so on.

The march to Komati Poort always struck me as another instance of using a sledge-hammer to crack an eggshell, for the number of columns and troops employed was very large and the enemy very few. The country, however, was most interesting, and some of the scenery magnificent. The roads were difficult, and some of the gradients immensely steep—notably the one up the Kaapsche Hoop. This really was a most formidable hill, said to be 2,000 feet above our previous camp. It was some fifteen miles beyond Nooitgedacht, where many of our men had been kept prisoners, and it required an elaborate system of large fatigue parties to work our wagons to the top. One was rewarded, when one got there, by a really magnificent view. South-east one saw the town of Barberton, twenty miles off, on the far side of the Kaap River, and picturesquely situated under considerable heights. Due east one looked down the valley of the Crocodile River, wending its way to Komati Poort, about eighty miles away. Some twenty miles north the Spitzkop was visible 7,000 feet high, an outpost from the higher Mauchberg, where we had fought on the 8th, and round which Buller's troops were still operating.

Of fighting there was very little, for there were not enough enemy to go round with our large numbers. In front of Ian Hamilton's force—always one day ahead—was the 11th Division, and away to the right, Hutton's Mounted Infantry and French.

Each day we got on to lower ground, but had many climbs and descents and river crossings, and at last we reached bottom, where the climate became almost tropical.

On the 21st September orders arrived for Hamilton's force and Pole-Carew's Division to press on to save the rolling stock collected by the Boers at Komati Poort from being burnt, and also to try to capture a 6-in. gun, as the chief wanted one to take to England with him.

French and Hutton were given other roles. The low country we had now got into was certainly no place for horses. It was bare and inhospitable, with a peculiarly forbidding-looking yellow-stemmed tree in evidence wherever one went —an uncanny-looking tree suggesting, though I cannot say exactly why, fever and snakes.

On the 22nd we found Lord Kitchener at Kaapmuiden Station, generally having a look round and imagining he was creating order out of chaos—and doubtless he was right, though his methods were apt to be upsetting to a mere commander of a small body of troops. Two days later, I see I record in my diary, arriving at a broken railway bridge, when I commenced to take steps to have it repaired Lord Kitchener appeared, and I disappeared. Now this was not done in any spirit of disrespect for him, but he was apt to issue instructions to the nearest person to him, quite oblivious of the fact that that particular person's duties might lie in another direction.

On the 24th September Pole-Carew occupied Komati Poort, and Ian Hamilton's force arrived next day.

We had marched about 140 miles in thirteen days, which, compared to what we had done after de Wet, sounds nothing; but the conditions of the country, necessitating much manhandling of wagons, and the climate combined, had been most trying to the men.

We found masses of material at Komati Poort, which for the uninitiated I will record is on the Portuguese frontier, which could not be crossed by the belligerents. There were many miles of rolling stock visible up the Selati branch railway which ran north, just inside the Boer frontier. It was said, at the time, that there was sufficient to make up 130 trains, and it certainly stretched farther than the eye could see. The only 6-in. Boer gun we could find had had its muzzle blown off, but the remains were taken as a trophy, I believe for the commander-in-chief

I was not able to get away from Komati Poort until the 13th

October (nearly three weeks) and then I moved off west.

There was an immense amount to be done before the trains could be moved off to Pretoria, for so many bridges had been blown up, and so much of the line destroyed; but it was evident there was no object in keeping such a large force as we were idle.

The only Boers were 1,000, over the frontier, and they had expressed a wish to surrender. The work was hard, and the climate very trying; but one got a certain amount of breathing time for seeing old friends.

The 28th September was the King of Portugal's birthday, and a ceremonial parade was held under Pole-Carew to salute the Portuguese flag. I remember how smart all the Portuguese officers looked in their blue full-dress uniform and white cock's feathers and decorations, compared to our somewhat war-worn uniforms.

That evening the Guards Brigade commenced moving by rail to Pretoria. General Pole-Carew went on the 30th September and Ian Hamilton and Staff on the 1st October, leaving me as commandant of Komati Poort. Lord Kitchener with his Staff did not go until the 4th October, and then I was left alone in my glory, as head charwoman, to complete the sweeping up, and I must own I rather enjoyed it, for there were plenty of good fellows to associate with, and I was my own master.

The battalions left with me were the Royal Scots and the Gordons—the Royal Irish had gone off to Belfast on the 30th —and I see in my diary the names of Colonel Dorman and Mayor Sawyer, R.A.M.C, C. B. Thomson, R.E., O'Callaghan (Royal Irish), Major Foster, R.A., who had been with me at Athlone in 1878, Major Graham Thomson, R.E., Douglas, Moir, Bode (Royal Scots), Macbean, Burney, Crawford, Gardyne, Ogsdon, Lockley of the Gordons, Rouse, R.A., Walker (D.C.L.I.) and Steinacker. The last two had been on a raid up the Selati River, and Gardyne had, I think, been with them, and they told thrilling tales of how lions had prowled round their *zeribas* each night, and had actually killed one man (Smart) and removed animals from the middle of their camp.

Steinacker was a hard-bitten Colonial, who commanded a force called after himself.

Our chief interest whilst at Komati Poort was in reports such as that Lord Roberts was to be commander-in-chief at home, and was to be succeeded by Lord Kitchener in South Africa; and of the elections which were taking place at home in favour of the Government.

At last an order arrived for me to return post-haste to Belfast, to resume command of a mobile column, which was to consist of the Gordons, the Shropshires, half the Suffolks, the 34th Battery Royal Field Artillery, two pom-poms, two 5-in. guns, some mounted troops, with ammunition and supply columns; and on the 13th October, a very hot day—107° in the shade—I put myself into a train. Just before starting I heard that the C.I.V. were to be sent home, and sent Mackinnon a wire expressing my appreciation of their services. It will be a suitable place here to record that the removal of the C.I.V. and the Imperial Yeomanry caused a good deal of feeling amongst the Colonial Troops, which was so admirably expressed in a parable written by a Canadian officer—a copy of which he sent me— that I reproduce it here.

THE PARABLE

There was a certain man whose name was John Bull, and he had five sons. And three of them went into a far country, where they prospered exceedingly, and begat children, so that their seed was as the sand upon the sea-shore for multitude, and the names of these three were Canada, Australia, and New Zealand.

But the other two sons abode in their father's house—and they were as the light of his eyes, they and their children's children. And the names of their children were C.I.V. and I.Y.[3]

And it came to pass that there was much work to be done in the fields of John Bull, and he was vexed exceedingly, yea, in sore straits, inasmuch as the work was great and his labourers were few. And the children of Canada, Australia, and New Zea-

3. City Imperial Volunteers and Imperial Yeomanry.

land, when they heard of these things, took counsel together, and said, "Behold now, this John Bull, our father's father, he is in sore straits because of the work which he hath to do, and he hath only one hired servant, one Tommy, to accomplish the labour wherewithal. Shall we not therefore go to him and say, 'Lo, we are of the seed of thy loins, and verily blood is thicker than water; let us therefore work in thy fields for a season, until such times as the labour is so far accomplished that the rest may be done by Tommy, thine hired servant.'"

And they sent messengers to John Bull, and told him, and he, when he had heard these tidings, was glad exceedingly, and waxed vainglorious among his neighbours, saying unto them, "Behold now my children's children, how when they hear that I am in sore straits, they come and labour in my fields, yea, they make themselves even as mine hired servants, that my work may be accomplished."

And the children of Canada, Australia, and New Zealand tarried not, for the need was pressing, but left their homes, their wives and their children, their flocks and their herds, even all that they possessed, and hastened unto the fields of John Bull.

And John Bull made them even as Tommy, his hired servant, and set over them as overseer one Roberts, a just man, and of good repute, so that the fame of his uprightness had reached even unto the countries of Canada, Australia, and New Zealand.

And the children of Canada, Australia, and New Zealand rejoiced, and were exceeding glad that such a one had been set over them.

And the striplings C.I.V. and I.Y. did John Bull also send out, that they might labour in the fields with the children of Canada, Australia, and New Zealand, and with Tommy, his hired servant.

But they did come into the fields clad in purple and fine linen, yea, in splendid raiment, for they understood not the manner of work whereunto they were called: and they skipped about like fawns, yea, even as the young of the wild ass disported they themselves. Nevertheless, did Roberts the overseer continually send tidings unto the house of John Bull, saying unto him, "Behold, the young men C.I.V. and I.Y. whom thou didst send out to labour in thy fields, the work which they do! The young men, the children of Canada, Australia, and New Zealand, and Tommy, thine hired servant, they do labour exceeding faithfully; but their work which they do is as nought compared with the work of the young men C.I.V. and I.Y. Verily they 'will not be denied.'"

And when the children of Canada, Australia, and New Zealand, and Tommy, his hired servant, heard these things they murmured among themselves, saying, "Have we not borne the burden and heat of the day, while the young men C.I.V. and I.Y. have disported themselves? Is it therefore meet and seemly that this Roberts should send these tidings continually to John Bull?"

But, having bethought them, they took counsel together concerning the matter and said, "Lo, are not the young men C.I.V. and I.Y. as the light of his eyes unto John Bull, and shall not the tidings of this Roberts concerning them be pleasing in the ears of the old man? Let us therefore have no bitterness in our hearts, but let us rather labour the more faithfully, so that when all is accomplished John Bull himself shall see what manner of work we have done."

And they said with one accord, "So be it," and they did murmur no more, but did labour exceeding hard.

But when the day was far spent, and the evening drew nigh, and the work was well-nigh done, John Bull did send messengers unto Roberts, even unto the overseer, saying Unto him, "Send now to my house the young men C.I.V. and I.Y., that I may make merry with them according to the great work which they have done for me. I have prepared a feast for them—meat and wine—yea, the flesh of the turtle, and the wine of the country which is called Champagne, which foameth when it is poured into the vessel. But the young men, the children of Canada, Australia, and New Zealand, let them remain in the fields with

Tommy, mine hired servant, that they may finish the labour, even unto the last jot and tittle."

And Roberts did with the young men even as John Bull had commanded him. Now when the children of Canada, Australia, and New Zealand heard these things they were exceeding wrath, and their hearts were full of bitterness, and they said one to another, "Why hath John Bull entreated us thus shamefully? Have we not left our wives, our children, our flocks and our herds, yea, did we not leave our own fields untilled that we might hasten to labour in the fields of John Bull? And now that we have laboured exceeding faithfully all the day, and the work which is yet to do can easily be done by Tommy, even by the hired servant—for unto this end is he hired—behold, we are left in the fields, while John Bull doth feast and make merry with his young men C.I.V. and I.Y.

In the fullness of time it may well come to pass that John Bull shall again be in sore straits by reason of the work which is to be in his fields. How then shall we answer him when peradventure he may say unto us, 'Come over and help me that I may accomplish the labour whereunto I have set my hand'? Shall not the bitterness of the dirt which we have eaten abide in our mouths? How then shall we answer him?"

And they cried with one accord, "Thus shall we make answer unto him: 'Aforetime, when thou wast in sore straits, and troubled exceedingly, did we not leave all that we had, and labour for thee, and thou didst shamefully entreat us? Now therefore do thine own work, as best thou mayest, even thou and thy young men, C.I.V. and I.Y. who shall abide with thee, for we have work of our own to do, fields to till, and flocks to guard, and we leave them not lightly anymore.'"

CHAPTER 18

Belfast

I only reached Belfast, 130 miles from Komati Poort, at mid-day next day (the 14th October) and at once set to work to collect the scattered units allotted to my force; but it was not until the 18th October that I was able to wire to the chief of staff at Pretoria that I was complete in everything, except mounted troops. That day information reached me that the Boers under Botha and four other commandants were massing in the Dullstroom-Witpoort district.

Receiving orders to proceed to Pretoria, I arrived there after a lengthy and sketchy railway journey of two days (trains were not allowed to run at night) on the 25th October, just in time for Lord Roberts's farewell parade which took place the same afternoon. This was quite a fine sight. In addition to a number of troops marching by, the chief presented ten Victoria Crosses. I watched from a balcony overlooking the square with Kendal Franks, Windham, Creighton, and Father Rawlinson.

Next day Lord Kitchener informed me that he must get me off the Line of Communications to active offensive operations against the enemy.

It happened so often that troops were suddenly seized on by a higher authority, and sent off to carry out some duty outside their general's command, that one never felt safe: a curious illustration happened here.

For Lord Roberts's farewell review, representatives of all corps within a reasonable distance were brought into Pretoria, and amongst others from my command three companies of the Royal Irish, under Major Hatchell, had reached the capital with orders to return at once to Belfast; but I found they had been commandeered and ordered off to reinforce Rustenburg, about sixty miles in the opposite direction, where some trouble from the enemy had arisen. By protesting I got them back a few days later.

General Lyttelton, in command at Middelburg, with his Chief Staff Officer C. McGrigor, came to see me at Belfast on the 29th and arranged an operation for my flying column. This latter had been augmented by the 5th Lancers under Fawcett, the Royal Canadian Dragoons (Lessard), the Canadian Mounted Rifles (Evans), and the Queensland Mounted Infantry (Chauvel).[1]

So far I had confined operations to raids on farms known to be centres of hostile activity, and to reconnaissances, but the arrival of so many mounted troops made it possible to design a larger enterprise, and so, as it appeared that much of the interference with the railway was traced to a *laager* at Witkloof, some eighteen to twenty miles due south of Belfast, I called commanding officers together on the morning of the 2nd November and explained a raid I had planned for that night. It rained hard in the day, but as it cleared at sunset we started off in two columns as soon as it was dark, when, thanks to the weather, not only did our raid fail, but we experienced the most abominable twenty-four hours imaginable.[2]

Two columns marched, one under myself, *via* Bergendal, along the ridge south to Frishgewaadgt; the other, under Lieutenant-Colonel J. Spens, *via* Leeuwbank, to Van Wyks Vlei, starting at 6 p.m.

It was raining slightly when the column started, but shortly afterwards the rain came down in torrents and a bitterly cold wind blew. As, however, the columns were miles apart and they

---

1. Lieutenant-General Sir H. Chauvel, who commanded a Mounted Division in Palestine in the Great War.
2. There is no special sketch for this, but the operation can be followed on the sketch illustrating the action a few days later.

were acting on a preconcerted plan, neither could turn back. Both columns at times had great difficulties in keeping the track, but the guiding of the two columns was deserving of all praise. When dawn broke my column was close to Welgevonden, and the Canadian Mounted Rifles became engaged with the enemy, whilst the main column, screened by the 5th Lancers, leaving Frishgewaadgt to its right, crossed a stream and worked along to a point south of Van Wyks Vlei. On approaching the latter place Boer horses were seen, knee-haltered, and shortly afterwards a lot of Boers ran out of the farms, manned some rugged *kopjes* and opened fire, compelling the 5th Lancers screen to fall back slightly. It was now about 6.30 a.m., and although I had sent several orders to the Canadian Mounted Rifles to join us, I heard them still firing heavily near Welgevonden.

It appears that on going on to those heights in the morning they had seen several Boers coming out of their farms in the valley below, and had opened a heavy fire at close range, knocking over men and horses. The ground was extremely rugged and broken, and the Boers worked up fairly close, when a sergeant of the C.M.R. lost his horse—Major Saunders, C.M.R., then gallantly rode out, and, in bringing away the sergeant on his horse, the latter was shot; then, as both proceeded on foot, Major Saunders was wounded and crawled under heavy fire behind a stone. Lieutenant Chalmers then advanced to help Major Saunders, but was told by the latter to return and leave him there. This Lieutenant Chalmers did, but again gallantly advanced to the help of his commanding officer, when he was shot dead.

When the Canadian Mounted Rifles eventually rejoined us it was 7.30 a.m., and Colonel Spens' column had appeared, according to plan, to the west of Van Wyks Vlei. This column had been delayed by small parties of Boers, getting one man wounded. Our transport, which I had left under a special escort to come out later by the direct road *via*, Vogelstruispoort and Blyvooruitzicht, now appeared three miles off, having left Belfast at daylight. The whole force was wet through and the men perished with cold wind and driving rain; three horses had succumbed to the rigours of the climate, and the infantry, marching in wet great-coats, had all done fourteen or fifteen miles. The main laager at Witkloof was still three or four miles off, and to attack it meant that the force must bivouac out.

I was convinced that this would mean very serious sickness and probably loss of life from cold and exposure, and so I ordered the transport back to Belfast and both columns to march north to the same place by the shortest road.

Colonel Spens' column, which was farthest north at the moment, took the road first, and my column followed as rear-guard. No Boers were in view.

My rear-guard consisted of a squadron of 5th Lancers, two guns 84th Battery and two companies Gordons. As we were crossing the spruit just east of Blyvooruitzicht I heard heavy firing by the rear-guard on the ridge behind about Eerstelingfontein.

The 5th Lancers, hampered by sword and lance, and with a short-range carbine, were no match for the long-range Mausers, and had to retire behind the Gordon rear-guard.

As the rear-guard fought its way back across the spruit, all our guns, the pom-poms, and Royal Canadian Dragoons machine-gun, which had joined from Colonel Spens' column, opened a heavy fire. The Boers, who were never more than 150 strong, exposed themselves in the boldest manner all along the ridge; in one case one of them was shot within fifty yards of a Gordon.

But the Boers never had a chance, and after an engagement of some two hours they desisted from following.

The force was back at Belfast by 5 p.m. after marching twenty-eight miles in twenty hours. The cold really was awful; men and officers were shaking all over. Many got ague. I myself had to lie down in my blankets, and it was an hour before I could use my fingers sufficiently to wire to Lord Roberts an account of the operations.

It was very pleasing to receive a most charming reply of sympathy; but we were all grieved to hear that Miss Roberts[3] was dangerously ill with enteric at Johannesburg, and that her father had had to hurry off there to see her.

The weather continued very bad, and to keep ourselves warm we actually engaged in the homely game of rounders. Of course, we were all itching to have another go at our friends at Witkloof and Leliefontein in the valley of the Komati River, west of their stronghold in the township of Carolina, and, the rain having stopped, the small hours of the 6th saw us heading again in a southerly direction. To describe the subsequent operations I give a paraphrase of the official report I sent in at the time.

I marched with a force as per margin[4] on the 6th November, at 3.30 a.m. Our object was to destroy the farms which the Boers used as outposts and camps when they fought on the 2nd inst. as well as to clear their *laagers* from Witkloof and Leliefontein.

The Boers opposed us first at Eerstelingfontein at 7.40 a.m. From this point they hung on our front, flanks, and rear like Cossacks, but our advanced guards, commanded by Lieutenant-Colonel Spens, steadily forced them back across Van Wyks Vlei, until they stood at an immensely strong position along the Komati River, extending from Witkloof to Leliefontein. There they made a most determined stand. The Shropshires held them in front and along the Witkloof itself.

Four companies, over perfectly open ground, worked up to within 500 yards of the position, and there maintained themselves for over three hours under a very heavy fire. The supply of ammunition was particularly difficult, and great gallantry was shown in carrying it up, and also in removing the wounded.

Our artillery was distributed along the front, one section of the 84th Field Battery under Lieutenant C. Twidale being in po-

---

3. Now Countess Roberts.
4. One Squadron 5th Lancers, Royal Canadian Dragoons, Canadian Mounted Rifles, 250 mounted men in all.
One Sect. Royal Canadian H.A. guns.
Two Sects. 84th Field Batty., 2 5-inch guns.
S. Section pom-poms. 900 Infantry (Suffolks and Shropshires).
One Section R.E. Bearer Company.

sition on our left and fighting under a heavy fire at 1,400 yards range for over an hour. It was most difficult to reconnoitre and find how to turn the position, as riflemen met us everywhere.

At 2 p.m. I sent the Canadian Mounted Troops with their two R.H.A. guns supported by the two pom-poms and two companies of the Suffolks, the latter under Major Lloyd, to work round the Boer left.

The Suffolks were particularly well handled, and at 4 p.m. had outflanked the left of the Boers facing the Shropshires. The result was that the Boers evacuated their position along the whole line and retired across the Komati.

Throughout the day the Boer convoy, which consisted largely of Cape carts, had been crossing the river and were working

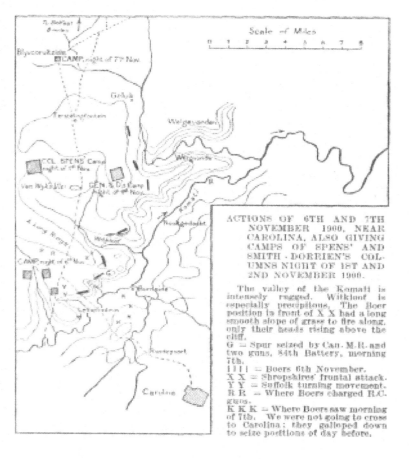

ACTIONS OF 6TH AND 7TH NOVEMBER 1900, NEAR CAROLINA, ALSO GIVING CAMPS OF SPENS' AND SMITH - DORRIEN'S COLUMNS NIGHT OF 1ST AND 2ND NOVEMBER 1900.

The valley of the Komati is intensely rugged. Witkloof is especially precipitous. The Boer position in front of X X had a long smooth slope of grass to fire along, only their heads rising above the cliff.

G = Spur seized by Can. M.R. and two guns, 84th Battery, morning 7th.

I I I I = Boers 6th November.

X X = Shropshires' frontal attack.

Y Y = Suffolk turning movement.

R R = Where Boers charged R.C. guns.

K K K = Where Boers saw morning of 7th. We were not going to cross to Carolina; they galloped down to seize positions of day before.

their way up several roads towards Carolina, and it was in order to get them away that the Boers had hung on with such determination. These wagons collected behind a hill distant some 9,000 yards, at which range our 5-in. guns, after shelling for a considerable period, succeeded in driving them out and making them take the road to Carolina.

Throughout the day signal fires had been springing up in all directions.

Having cleared the position the force moved on along the high ground, and camped at sundown just west of Leliefontein. Our casualties were six killed and twenty wounded, mostly Shropshires, who had fought most gallantly.

The large numbers of the enemy decided me that to move on Carolina next morning in such a country would be risky, but to make them think such was our object I, after driving them off, moved on and camped at Leliefontein. Next morning at 7.30 a.m., instead of crossing the Komati, we turned east along the north bank.

At once several hundred Boers galloped back to seize their old positions on the Komati. Now it was my invariable habit to detail each day a special small mobile reserve under my own orders, and today it consisted of fifty Canadian Mounted Rifles and two guns of the 84th Battery under Colonel Evans and Major Guinness respectively, and I ordered this reserve to gallop straight for the key of the position, *Kopje* G on sketch. It was an exciting moment, for I knew dismounted Boers were climbing up the far side. The reserve had nearly two miles to go; but they simply raced for the hill, and were just in time to get into action with rifles and guns and hold some 300 Boers in the riverbed whilst the 5-in. guns at the same time did splendid practice at masses of Boers in the open coming down the slopes from Carolina.

As the Boers were working east and north down the Komati I sent orders to Colonel Spens, commanding the advance guard, to seize the high ground at Van Wyks Vlei, which he did with the 5th Lancers and one section of the 84th; Lieutenant-Colonel

Lessard, with the Canadian dragoons and two Royal Canadian guns under Lieutenant Morrison covered the rear. Three companies of the Shropshires were sent to support Colonel Evans and Major Guinness in their position overlooking the Komati, G on sketch. Under cover of these positions the baggage moved steadily away towards Van Wyks Vlei.

From the moment the baggage began to move from camp the Boers showed themselves everywhere round the rearguard. The latter, most ably commanded by Lessard, Royal Canadian Dragoons, displayed the greatest gallantry. The two guns Royal Canadian H.A. were continuously in action against small parties, at one time working singly in positions a mile apart.

At about 10.30 a.m., seeing the baggage and infantry were at a safe distance, the rear-guard began to fall back. As they did so the Boers became more and more aggressive, but the fire of the two guns and the bold front of the dragoons kept them at a distance. However, the Boers, being thoroughly conversant with the ground, at length collected in a winding depression, and, thinking they had their opportunity, some 200 charged out on their horses, firing as they came, their object being to get the guns; but Lieutenant Cockburn and his troops, Royal Canadian Dragoons, sacrificed themselves, and those who were not wounded or killed were captured; but their action enabled the guns to retire to a safer distance.

The next two hours a running fight was kept up, and at 1.30 p.m. the Boers again made a determined effort, galloping up to within 200 yards of the guns, to be driven off by another determined stand of the Royal Canadian Dragoons under Lieutenant Turner. It was at this period that the Colt gun, which was doing splendid work covering the retreat of the guns, was almost surrounded by Boers; the horse was blown, but Sergeant E. J. Holland, who was in charge of it, with great presence of mind detached the gun from the carriage and rode off with it. All this time the fire of the Boers, being mostly from the saddle, was wild, and our losses in consequence were abnormally few.

This last attack seems to have satisfied the Boers that they had better keep at a respectful distance, for from this time on they never came within 2,000 yards; but this they did several times in masses and came under heavy shell-fire. They never again seriously molested us; in fact, I think only one casualty, Lieutenant Elmeley, Royal Canadian Dragoons, occurred after this. The force camped at Blyvooruitzicht at 4 p.m.

Sixteen Royal Canadian Dragoons were for some hours in the hands of the Boers, who behaved splendidly towards them. They report that they appeared in anything but a state of demoralisation, that they had excellent horses, and that almost every man had two horses, two rifles, and a black man to look after them.

The Boer idea had been to hide part of their force in the indescribably broken ground on the west side of the Komati until our force was committed to crossing the river towards Carolina. Luckily we did not do so, for our force was numerically weaker than the enemy, and infinitely so in mounted troops. I was convinced that it would be courting disaster to attempt to cross to Carolina and Ermelo against these determined commandos, except with two strong columns, each having at least 500 mounted riflemen.

At the same time I was satisfied that their heavy losses on those two days tended largely to prevent repetitions of the bold tactics they had shown.

It was reported that amongst their killed were General Joachim Fourie, Commandant H. Prinsloo (the de Wet of these commandos), and Field Cornet D. Lange, commanding No. 1 Ward of the Carolina Commando. The deaths of the first two were confirmed later on.

The Royal Canadian troops deserved well of the Empire this day, and I recommended four for the proud distinction of the Victoria Cross—Lieutenant H. Z. C. Cockburn, Lieutenant R. E. W. Turner,[5] Private W. A. Knisley, and Sergeant E. Holland— and Lieutenant E. W. B. Morrison,[6] for special distinction for the

---

5. Lieutenant-General Sir B. E. W. Turner, V.C., K.C.B., etc.
6. Major-General Sir E. W. B. Morrison, K.C.M.G., C.B.

coolness and skill with which he handled his guns.

The following telegram sent by me to Lord Kitchener, referring to the action just described, illustrates what respect I had for our enemies, and that there was good reason for my admiring them.

9th November.—The ambulance I sent back night of the 7th, to bring our wounded left in Boers' hands, arrived here last night. Our wounded all report Boers were educated men, and well clothed, and that there were three Commandos under Prinsloo, Grobelar, and Fourie. Many were quite boys, and all said they would fight until they were killed. Our doctor, who delivered letters from me thanking them for their chivalrous behaviour to our wounded, described a most interesting conversation with a highly educated Boer.

The latter spoke quite openly, and said that the war was due to Rhodes, much more than to Chamberlain. He then said how unlucky they had been that day, as both their General Fourie and Commandant H. Prinsloo had been killed. From all sides it seems that burning farms rankles in their minds.

The fine behaviour of these men is quite remarkable. In one case Lieutenant Bliss, Canadian Mounted Rifles, was captured just coming away from a farm we had burnt by the owner and twenty-five Boers. They merely expressed their disapproval of his act, disarmed him and let him rejoin us in the middle of the fight. They seem to think they are fighting for their land, and that if they surrender they will never get their properties back.

It was on the morning of the 8th November that we got back to Belfast to find orders for all the mounted troops, except the 5th Lancers, to be dispatched to Pretoria and Barberton.

The news otherwise was good and yet bad—good, in that de Wet and Steyn had been severely handled near Bothaville from combined operations by Major-General Charles Knox, De

Lisle, Le Gallais and Ross,[7] but bad, in that the gallant Le Gallais had been killed, and my old friend Watty Ross very dangerously wounded.

As the enemy continued to destroy the railway, I continued the policy of raiding and burning farms, which were being used by the raiders as jumping-off places. I sent out to warn them that the next time the line was interfered with I would sally forth and lay low Witpoort and Dullstroom, some twenty miles north of the line, at both of which there were flour-mills said to be working day and night on behalf of the enemy.

On the 13th November, a further transgression having occurred, my flying column left for the rich Steelpoort Valley, in co-operation with another column sent out by General Lyttelton from Middelburg.

I have related how, on a previous occasion, I had found mounted men, carrying sword, lance, and carbine, at great disadvantage with the agile Boer, armed with a long-range rifle only, and I had obtained permission to substitute a long rifle for the other weapons carried by the 5th Lancers; and, as the rifles had not arrived, I gave them the choice of coming without their lances or remaining in camp, and was glad when they selected the former.

At 7.30 a.m. Boer outposts opposed us and at 9 a.m. a very smart engagement on Langkloof heights took place in which Lieutenant Keogh, Connaught Rangers, and his detachment of 3rd Mounted Infantry, did exceedingly well. Whilst the mounted troops on the heights were driving back the Boers, the main column and transport had to turn west down into the Steelpoort Valley. All day we struggled on over terribly boggy drifts.

We passed some very fine farms, and gave notice that in ten days they would be burnt if the owners had not come in.

The Steelpoort Valley is extremely rich in crops. It is several

---

7. Brigadier-General Sir W. C. Ross, K.B.E., C.B., etc. Although he lost his lower jaw he lived to do a lot of work for the Empire, and eventually in the hour of her great need came back to the army and commanded a brigade in the field throughout the 1914–18 war.

miles wide, and we saw Boers driving off their stock and some sixty wagons towards Roos Senekal.

On the 14th November we commenced at 5 a.m. getting wagons across a boggy *spruit*, and the column was not able to march until 7 a.m. The Boers held a strong position across our road a mile and a half from camp, out of which the mounted troops soon turned them.

About five miles farther on they took up a very strong position at Welgevonden, to occupy which they came out of several very fine farms. As a lesson to them that they could not use farms to assemble in, I ordered them all to be blown up and burnt, right in front of the Boers, and before we turned them out of their position.

They drove in our mounted troops all along the line. Lieutenant Howard,[8] Royal Canadian Dragoons, however, remained with his Colt guns close to the position, which was a very strong one. I therefore concentrated all the guns on what I considered the key of the position, and, sending the mounted troops wide to threaten the Boer right, dispatched three companies Royal Irish and two companies Gordons to attack the point, covered by a heavy shell-fire. The hill was so steep that most of the ground was dead, and the attackers carried the position without much difficulty.

Whilst the main body camped I went on with the mounted troops to Witpoort. A few Boers fired from the hills round, but the mounted troops kept them at a distance, whilst the mill was blown up and a certain number of houses burnt.

To mislead the Boers as to our movement on the morrow I spread reports that we should pass through Witpoort.

We started early on the 15th, up a narrow valley south-east, which took us on to the high ground just north of Witbooy and thence to Swartz Koppies, where we camped. We had, by our reports in Witpoort on the previous evening, and by the

---

8. Known as "Gat Howard," a very fine American and a rich man who had come out merely for the love of fighting. I regret to say he was killed serving under General Alderson in the Eastern Transvaal later on.

direction of our mounted troops at 4 a.m., quite misled the Boers, who all assembled in the rough ground about Witpoort to meet us. Consequently only a few snipers opposed us, but others later came up from Witpoort, and gave a company of the Gordons a good deal of trouble. Three and a half miles after starting the force came out of the valley on to a narrow commanding ridge with strikingly broken and deep valleys on both sides. The mounted troops then found themselves overlooking the valley of Witbooy, and, driving off the Boers with our guns, we captured 800 sheep and 200 cattle and two prisoners.

The next day, leaving our camp guarded by four companies and two guns under Colonel Macbean of the Gordons, we marched at 4 a.m. for Dullstroom. Having destroyed the mill at Dullstroom and many other houses, the force returned to camp at Swartz Koppies.

On the 17th November the force returned to Belfast, the mounted troops moving wide to the east; a few Boers followed and fired odd shots.

The actual result, besides the destruction of several farms, was the important levelling of the flour-mills at Witpoort and Dullstroom. We had found both of these were in full swing. At the former 300 bags of flour and wheat were destroyed, and reports said that wagons were frequently moving between the mill and Roos Senekal. We actually captured 167 oxen, 809 sheep, thirty-nine horses, and nine wagons. All the Boer Commandos which had been working south on to the high veldt had been driven north into less healthy climes again. These destructive raids can hardly be described as enjoyable, for it is hateful to burn farms and render people homeless; but the aim and object in a campaign is to win it, and win it quickly, and the more soft-hearted one is, the longer will the war last, and the larger and greater will be the sufferings caused by it.

The rifles having arrived, the 5th Lancers set to work to carry out a course of musketry. Now followed a time of comparative quiet, as my wings were clipped by the removal of most of my mounted troops. All the Canadians departed, much to my regret, and I was left with barely sufficient for ordinary patrols and small posts for safeguarding the line. Small raids were continued, and one or two larger ones under Macbean of the Gordons and Spens of the Shropshires respectively; but on the line itself there was plenty of activity.

It was trying to have to remain inactive, and I am afraid Lord Kitchener hardly blessed me for incessant requests for more mounted troops.

I devoted a good deal of time, however, to strengthening the posts held by the outposts all round the somewhat extended position we had to occupy about Belfast, and this was to stand us in good stead later on.

We got a little shooting and polo, and one of our amusements was schooling our horses over a steeplechase course we had constructed.

Meanwhile the Boers were becoming more and more aggressive, annoying my outposts, and on the 6th December a party of one hundred attacked Colliery Hill, two miles out; but got repulsed with loss.

Some of them came in occasionally under a flag of truce. I was interested in two of them: Mr. J. F. Pretorius and his brother-in-law, Maynard, a Pretoria lawyer, educated men, who said they were Progressionists and averse to war, and had always opposed Kruger, but intended to fight to the bitter end—an illustration of principles having to give way to patriotism—for which I admired them. Generals Louis Botha and J. Smuts used to send in requests, too, under flag of truce, and one always endeavoured to comply with them; for the days of chivalry were then still in being.

On the 15th December we heard the bad news of Clements having been driven back by Beyers and de la Rey, at Nooitgedacht, west of Pretoria, with a loss of four companies of the Northumberland Fusiliers, the total casualties amounting to 600, amongst which several fine officers were killed—Legge, Atkins, Murdoch, and Macbean. Clements was afterwards blamed, and I am not prepared to dispute the weakness of his original disposition; but so much was I impressed by the stories of his wonderful achievements when he was faced with disaster, that in July 1901, when H.M. King Edward VII commanded me to go and see him, I took the opportunity of telling His Majesty what a grand fellow he was, and how proud his friends were of him.

De la Rey's triumph was short-lived, for General French was sent to that district with large numbers of mounted troops, and soon re-established the British control of the Magaliesberg range.

On the 18th I was ordered to take over the Lines of Communication from Pretoria to Komati Poort temporarily, and moved into Middelburg, and took over from Lyttelton, who was going away for a fortnight.

They were quite a jovial party in Middelburg, and besides a good deal of polo we actually indulged in concerts and a dance. However, things were by no means peaceable, for the line was cut daily, and posts were crying out for help, resulting in a great deal of movement of reinforcements by rail and road from place to place. Amongst others, Colonel Reeves, commanding at Machadodorp, was in trouble, and at length the sad news came that one of his posts at Helvetia had been rushed, with the loss of 250 men, mostly prisoners, and a 4.7 gun. Eventually the Boers released the prisoners, as they could not guard them, and all that was left to them was the 4.7 gun, for which they had no ammunition. An amusing story about Reeves may relieve my *Memoirs* at this point.

When we were at the Staff College together—fifteen years previously—I had bet him forty pounds to one pound that I should not be married in ten years. I was only reminded of the bet, when the ten years had expired, by the receipt of a cheque for one pound, and on finding him under my command I had sent him a cordial telegram, concluding with the words "What price matrimony now?" A question he never answered. I admit it was a wrongful use of the official wires, but such amenities tend to lighten the monotony of incessant business communications.

On the 28th December General Lyttelton returned, and I resumed my command at Belfast.

The Boers, pleased with their success at Helvetia, decided on a raid on a larger scale, and an extraordinarily bold one, considering they only had 3,000 men available. It appears to have been Louis Botha's plan. Viljoen was to attack from the north, C. Botha and Smuts from the south, and the places selected were Machadodorp, Dalmanutha, Belfast, Wonderfontein, and Pan—all railway stations—and the night of the 7th January 1901 was the one selected for the enterprise.

It was a desperate night for such an operation, for an impenetrable fog, driven along by a considerable wind, accompanied by a drizzling rain, made it impossible either to see or to hear, and, in spite of their intimate knowledge of the ground, I still wonder how the Boers, in each case, succeeded in moving straight on their objective.

The railway station at Belfast, with our depôts and stores, was not easy to guard, owing to the shape of the ground. It was in a hollow, surrounded by commanding hills, all of which had to be held, involving a perimeter of fifteen miles. To hold these hills, guard the guns and town, and furnish a reserve, there were only 1,300 infantry and 460 mounted troops—the latter, being fully occupied during the day, could not take part in holding outposts at night, and the only infantry available for reinforcing any part of the outposts were one company Royal Irish and forty-three Shropshires. I was in telephonic communication with the main outposts.

I often think of the weird and unpleasant experiences of that night. I admit having felt a good deal of anxiety, but I knew the posts were strongly entrenched, and hoped they would hold out, and that no commando would, out of the fog and mist, hap on my guardless Head-quarters (for I had to part with my own escort) and carry the G.O.C. and his staff off to Carolina as a trophy.

At midnight precisely a tremendous burst of fire was heard at the Monument, which continued for half an hour. The Monument is two miles from the centre of the town, and was held by eighty-three Royal Irish under Captain Fosbery of that regiment. Shortly after, heavy firing was heard three miles in the opposite direction at the Colliery piquet. I heard from both on the telephone that they were heavily attacked. The Colliery was held by Shropshires. Very shortly after the south-west and south-east piquets, held by Gordons, were attacked with great determination, whilst a fire was poured into the Mounted Infantry piquet holding the drift at the north of the town.

Thus the circle of attack was complete. After about twenty minutes I failed to get answers on the telephone from either Colliery or Monument Hill, and I found out afterwards that the wires had been cut, but I heard from the Gordons throughout the attack.

I had only the one company Royal Irish, and the forty-three men, Shropshires, available for reinforcing on the north of the line, and the Gordon Highlanders had already reinforced their piquets with every available man. At about 12.30 a.m. the firing at the Monument ceased, and soon after Colonel Spens, who had been reconnoitring that way with his small party of forty-three men in the dense fog, came back to say a man had run in and reported the Boers had overpowered and captured Monument Hill, and he at once volunteered to go and find out himself. Mauser firing was still going on from the rocks round the Monument, but not at the post itself. He most gallantly worked himself right up to the barbed wire fence, within sixty yards of the tents at the Monument, and could see the Boers busy looting. He had ascertained that there were two small outlying piquets of the Royal Irish still holding out, but he knew that when daylight broke they would be captured by the very large force of Boers, so he most discreetly withdrew them.

About 1 a.m. the firing at the Colliery ceased, and a patrol I sent out from the 5th Lancers returned about 3 a.m. and reported that a small post of the Shropshires had been overpowered, but that the attack on the main work had been driven off. The Gordon Highlanders reported having repulsed their attack, after a desperate fight, at about 3 a.m., but firing continued until 3.30 a.m.

The attack on the Gordon piquets was made by the Ermelo and Carolina Commandos, by at least 500 men. They brought up stones with them and placed them some two or three yards apart in a circle all round, and only forty yards from the south-west piquet commanded by Lieutenant McLaren, Gordon Highlanders, and poured in a deadly fire after breaking down the outer circle of barbed wire. The defence of this post was a thing to be proud of, and five dead Boers were found within thirty yards of it.

One small post of the Gordons, of twelve men, was rushed; after firing 198 rounds and getting four of their number knocked over, they were completely overpowered by 200 to 300 Boers.

In the attack on the Monument the Boers were undoubtedly led by someone who knew the ground. There was one point slightly weaker than the rest of the defences, and there they came. That very evening, at sundown, I had seen Captain Fosbery post his night piquets, and he remarked to me how strong the defences were and how safe he felt inside them; but neither he nor I could have reckoned on such a desperate attack, breaking down what appeared to us impenetrable fences of barbed wire.

The Royal Irish on this post had thirty-nine killed and wounded out of a total of eighty-three, which is sufficient evidence that the defence was a fine one.

I will now turn to the post at the Colliery which was held by twelve men of the Shropshires, and seven men of the Mounted Infantry, under Lieutenant Marshall. This post was attacked by a large force, and amongst them 200 of the Staats Artillery. It was a strong post, but not so strong as some of the others, and had the fatal drawback of being too large for its garrison.

I cannot speak too highly of the determination they showed— they fought for an hour, at the end of which time they had Lieutenant Marshall and nine out of the twelve Shropshires killed and wounded; the Boers then rushed in and seized them, taking away the seven Mounted Infantrymen (four of whom were reported wounded) and three Shropshire Light Infantry, in addition to six Shropshire Light Infantry holding an outpost of the main work.

From good evidence I gathered that the total Boer force attacking Belfast was 2,000, those to the south being under Louis Botha and those to the north under Ben Viljoen. Both forces had guns, three to the north and five to the south, to be brought up, I concluded, in the morning if successful.

The attacks on Wonderfontein, Nooitgedacht, Wildfontein, and Pan, all garrisoned by the Royal Berkshires, were repulsed in a most gallant fashion.

Dalmanutha and Machadodorp, the next stations east of Belfast, were heavily attacked at the same time.

The behaviour of the troops, scattered about in their small posts, isolated in the dense fog, and surrounded by overwhelming forces of the enemy, was a thing to be proud of. It was pleasant to hear the way the Royal Irish spoke of their late Captain Fosbery. It appeared that he had no thought except the safety of his post and his men, and in the defeat of the enemy, and whilst going through the open to the main work, in the midst of the Boers, to see how matters stood, he died a hero's death.

No. 3733, Private J. Barry, of the Royal Irish, who sacrificed his life to damage the Maxim before it was taken by the Boers, would have been recommended for the V.C. had he lived. When he saw all his comrades killed and wounded and the gun surrounded by Boers, he seized a pick and commenced to smash up the breech of the gun. The Boers threatened him, but he continued until he had rendered the gun useless to his captors, whereupon the Boers, robbed of their spoil, shot him dead. Truly poor Barry died a noble death for his country's good.

The Boers found in his pocket a letter containing a sovereign addressed to his wife. This they afterwards gave back to one of his comrades, and it was sent home to the poor bereaved woman.

The 5th Royal Lancers did some very plucky patrolling; one

of the incidents is well worth mentioning. When the Monument Hill was attacked Corporal Forbes, of that regiment, went about a mile and a half in the dense fog up to where he heard the firing. He went right into the camp and found the Boers in possession of the tents. He managed to pass himself off as a Boer, got away as quickly as he could, and came straight to me and told me that the post had been captured, and that he had seen some 18th Royal Irish men lying there wounded amongst the tents. This was the first news that reached me of the Hill being in the Boers' hands.

The total loss to the force that night was 171, of all ranks. From reliable sources we heard that the Boer losses were in excess of these—we knew of fifty-eight killed and fifty wounded, the latter figure was more likely to be one hundred—and we heard that the Boers had come to the conclusion that night attacks were not a good thing. They had made up their minds that all our troops would be asleep, and that they would capture every place.

It was this attack which decided me that native listening-posts would be an advantage for giving warning, and I asked to be sent some, emphasising that they should not be locals known to the Boers, nor town-breds, but Basutos or Zulus fresh from the jungle.

CHAPTER 19

A Sweep to the Swaziland Border

The following three weeks brought us nothing of great importance, but the troops were kept busy with raiding, escort work, small local expeditions, and strengthening defences.

The Boers made themselves very inconvenient, to say the least of it, for although they never again made an attack in force, they were frequently sniping our outposts and interfering with trains; hardly a day passed without their wrecking a train or blowing up a portion of the line.

One day (the 23rd January) they actually blew up the line in front of Lord Kitchener's train, and prevented his getting to Middelburg to interview General Lyttelton. It became a custom to put a truck or two laden with coal or stones in front of the engine to bear the explosion and save the engine. Their activities against our line of railway were so marked as to make the chief suspect that Botha's object was to distract attention from happenings elsewhere.

New Boer leaders were in evidence in the Orange River and the Cape Colony, and matters were becoming serious. News also came in of a considerable concentration south of our line in the Carolina-Ermelo-Standerton direction.

To gain a little more information as to what was taking place in our neighbourhood, I was directed to collect a force at Wonderfontein and move on Carolina, and at the same time Lyttelton was dispatched to assume control of operations in Cape Colony.

The Boers were doing a lot of communicating with us by flag of truce. On the 18th January I received a letter from Louis Botha complaining of our using expanding cartridges, enclosing me one of them. It was an ordinary cartridge, the bullet of which had been cut across with a knife, which proved nothing. On the 20th one "Bester" and another Boer came in from Ben Viljoen.

I think they were hopeful that the war would soon end, and were encouraged by the conciliatory messages sent out from our army head-quarters. Peace Delegates, too, had actually gone out to see Botha, and he himself had been invited to come in and discuss matters. The following extracts from a letter I wrote at the time may be of interest.

Belfast,

22nd January 1901.

The above date will bring back to you, as it does to me, an eventful day in my life, 'Isandhlwana.' I have had some most interesting communications with Generals Louis Botha and Ben Viljoen lately under a flag of truce. It is curious that their tone is much more civil since their attack on this place was repulsed. Ben Viljoen used to be very rough to our prisoners, but now he is quite the contrary. He sent in one day to say if there were any letters for the prisoners he had taken he would be glad to give them to them. I sent them out with a letter of thanks and asked if I could send him anything as a return for his courtesy. He asked for some claret, and I sent him two cases a day or two later. He sent me a Kruger sovereign, which he wished me to keep as a keepsake and to have engraved, 'General Ben Viljoen to General S.-D.'[1] I take this as a sign that he is hedging, and that the Boers really are considering the question of ending the War.

By the evening of the 24th my force was collected at Wonderfontein ready to move, and a very fine force, too, of about

---

1. This I had done and made into a bracelet for my mother.

5,000 fighting men.[2]

The Boers were buzzing round us like flies, and finally on the 25th, at the end of an eighteen-mile march, they took up a strong position in the riverbed at Twyfelaar. An infantry attack, in which the Suffolks bore the brunt, and a skilful turning movement by Colonel Henry, forced the Boers to retreat.

Our next day's march, which was opposed all the way, took us to Carolina itself, which we occupied at 1 p.m. This township had been the centre from which most of their raids on the railway had been launched, and it was gratifying to have secured it. The Boers had evacuated it in good time, for eighty wagons, too far off to secure, were seen trekking off towards New Scotland.

Having secured Carolina, I was anxious to remain there, knowing that it would be a good jumping-off place for a big sweep which the chief was planning, and further that to withdraw must involve casualties in rear-guard work. But I received peremptory orders to return to Wonderfontein.

But next day, the 27th January, we had continuous fighting,

---

2. The Mounted Troops, under Colonel Henry, were:

5th Lancers	300	Major King
18th Hussars	200	Major Laming
19th Hussars	50	Captain Bramley
3rd Mounted Infantry	345	Major Anley
Imperial Light Horse	380	Lieutenant-Colonel Duncan McKenzie

The Artillery, under Colonel Bell-Irving, were:

4 guns, 84th Battery	Major Guinness
2 guns, 66th Battery	Captain Stapleton
2 guns, 83rd Battery	Major Guthrie-Smith
S. Section—2 pom-poms	Major Rouse.
P. Section—1 pom-pom	Captain Poole
1 horsed 5-inch gun	Major F. A. Curteis
2 bullock 5-inch gun	" "

Infantry Brigade, under Colonel J. Spens:

Camerons	Major Malcolm
West Yorks	Major Fry
Essex	Major Brown
Suffolks	Lieutenant-Colonel Mackenzie

Also an Ammunition Column under Major C. B. Simonds, two Field Hospitals under Major Julien, two Bearer Companies and fifty Shropshire Mounted Infantry and thirty Gordons as Divisional Head-quarters Troops.

304

and, unfortunately, the rain was heavier than ever, a sea of mud delaying our transport, and affording just the delays which gave opportunities for attacks on our rearguards. The lightning at times was very vivid, and three men were killed by it and fifteen Gordons injured in our five days' expedition.

It was always a case of trying to deceive the enemy, as to the direction we were taking, long enough to get our transport under way. Coming away from Carolina, troops were sent towards Ermelo, whilst the transport and escort moved direct to the drift over the Komati on the Wonderfontein road, and, if it had not been for the tremendous thunderstorms which delayed the wagons, we should have got away without casualties. As it was, we had seventeen—an excellent officer, Lieutenant McCaulay, of the 3rd Mounted Infantry, being mortally wounded. The Boers really were very brave and daring.

Hearing several wounded of ours had been left in Carolina, I sent back ambulances and two doctors under flag of truce. The Boers behaved very badly and actually kept three ambulances, twenty-five horses, and all medical appliances. The doctors, on return, reported 2,000 Boers with Louis Botha and J. Smuts as back again in Carolina and very confident.

The orders and counter-orders were very trying. At one time, when halfway to Wonderfontein, I got an order to return to Carolina; turning back, I had marched some distance when, as a result of the telegrams I had sent urging the inadvisability of returning, a fresh order came from Lord Kitchener, saying some ass (I wonder who?) had given me the wrong order, and he agreed with me that no advantage would be gained by returning to Carolina. This ass (whoever he was) cost us quite a lot of casualties. We eventually reached Wonderfontein on the 30th.

So far my force had been used by the chief to occupy the attention of the enemy, and keep them occupied in the northern area of the stretch of country bounded by the two railways from Pretoria, *i.e.* the one to Natal, the other to Delagoa Bay, in order to allow another and more important move to develop undisturbed. This was a plan to sweep up the whole of this area by several columns, with a view to hemming the enemy in or forcing them over the eastern frontier of the Transvaal into Swaziland or Zululand. (See map)

By this date the sweep was moving east, and four columns had already passed the line Greylingstad–Balmoral, and thus were still some seventy miles from Wonderfontein.

To convey an idea of the sweep to the mind of the reader, I would ask him to look at the Eastern Transvaal map, where the places reached on the 4th February are marked.

Eight columns in all, under General French, were being employed; five of them, distributed between Pretoria and Heidelberg under Alderson, Knox, Pulteney, Allenby, and Dartnell,[3] in that order. Alderson's being the most northerly moved east on the 28th.

The stops on the north were two of the eight columns, under Pitcairn Campbell[4] and myself, at Middelburg and Wonderfontein, on the Pretoria-Delagoa Bay railway, and the eighth column was thrown forward on the extreme right or south to Greylingstad under A. E. W. Colville, on the railway to Natal.

Campbell and I were to remain stationary but observant until the sweep came opposite our respective stations, when we, too, were to get on the move.

It was whilst we were waiting that the sad news of Queen Victoria's death reached us; but we could not help being amused by hearing that one of the first acts of King Edward VII was to make the German Emperor a Field-Marshal, on which the latter had retaliated by making our King an Admiral in the German navy.

Campbell's column started from Middelburg on the 1st February, and next day they had some heavy fighting, losing seven killed and ten wounded, but successfully drove back the Boers and camped at Roodepoort. The other columns were steadily driving Botha back on Ermelo.

---

3. Now Lieutenant-General Sir E. Alderson, Lieutenant-General Sir W. Pulteney, F.-M. Lord Allenby, and Hon. Major-General Sir J. Dartnell. 4. Now Lieutenant-General Sir W. Pitcairn Campbell.

On the 3rd February my column, which was the strongest, moved to our old camp at Twyfelaar practically unopposed, though Campbell away to my right had some quite brisk and successful scrapping. The country, owing to continuous rain, was in a worse state than when we were there a few days previously.

As mine was the strongest column and the one nearest to the northern railway, I had to escort supplies for some of the other columns, and altogether had 500 wheeled vehicles—a large charge, entailing many hours' marching each day. Watercourses were frequent, the drifts across them were muddy, and to pass all our transport over one was often a matter of hours.

In order to prevent the enemy living on the country we had orders to destroy all the growing crops, as well as all cattle we could not drive along with us. This was a heavy and disagreeable job, but it had to be done, and each day acres and acres of crops were laid waste (with bayonet and sword) and thousands of sheep were slain.

Again on the 4th February there was no opposition worth mentioning, and Campbell wired that he was in touch with Alderson's and Knox's columns away to his right.

The 5th February, too, was a more or less uneventful day, though there was considerably more skirmishing, and, from some very commanding ground we had to cross, large convoys could be seen in the far distance, fifteen miles away, trekking off from the direction of Ermelo on the Amsterdam road. That night we camped at a small township called Bothwell on the edge of Lake Chrissie. It was a lovely night but inclined to be foggy, and I carried out my usual custom of selecting the outpost line and visiting every post before settling myself in camp.

Bothwell was a pretty place, just a church, a store, and hotel, kept by one Campbell, and three British families, the Boer families having fled.

I was roused at 3 a.m. on the 6th February by a terrific fire; moonlight—but a dense fog had descended. Horses, and, I am ashamed to say, men too, were stampeding everywhere—many from the interior of the camp rushed in amongst the trees by my camp; two groups in groves sixty yards apart fired at each other, each thinking the others were Boers, luckily without damage. The rattle of bullets everywhere was deafening, especially on the tin roofs around us. It took Spens and me all our time to make the men round my own camp cease firing, and they actually mistook us for Boers and called "Hands up!" to us. Luckily they shot too badly to hit us. The outposts behaved splendidly, as the attack was a very determined one by 2,000 Boers.

This does not sound a very creditable performance, but it was the rush of the horses, really most alarming, which created the temporary panic, and not the firing.

It appears that the Middelburg, Ermelo, and Krugersdorp Commandos, under Louis Botha and J. Smuts, consisting of some 2,000 men, had under cover of the fog attacked the camp opposite the outposts of the West Yorks. Their advanced troops had got within 100 or 200 yards before opening fire, having crossed the valley west of the camp, whilst their supports opened fire from the far side of the valley at a range of 800 or 900 yards. The first burst of the fire was so close and so loud that the horses of the 5th Lancers stampeded. They circled round like mad things, at one time dashed through the outposts, and on returning afforded an opportunity to the Boers of rushing in under cover of them— an opportunity they bravely took.

The fighting on the outpost line was of a determined nature, and although severe where the Suffolk piquets stood, the brunt of it fell on the West Yorkshires, who enhanced that night the fine reputation the Regiment already held for bravery and determination. The nerve and steadiness they showed were particularly commendable as there were amongst their piquets several young draft whose *baptême de feu* it was.

Under cover of the returning horses the Boers got close to two of the West Yorkshire piquets, almost all of which were killed or wounded at their post. Spens, who had gone out through the fog to where the firing was heaviest, the sort of place he seemed to select for himself in all fights, seeing this onrush, at once sent up a support under Lieutenant Cantor. Just in time; although unfortunately Cantor was killed, and all his support killed or wounded, except Colour-Sergeant Busher. However, the Boers were stopped from penetrating the outpost line, and gradually withdrew, and in about three-quarters of an hour their fire slackened, and in another half-hour ceased altogether.

I will now describe an incident of audacious bravery in the cause of duty. As the Boers were about to launch their attack a Canadian scout, sent by French with a dispatch for me, arrived in the middle of them. He at once gripped the situation and lay low, and as the Boers advanced he advanced with them, and before the firing ceased he appeared before me and, saluting, handed me the dispatch with as much unconcern as though it had been an Aldershot field-day. I asked him how he had got through, and he told me, and when I asked how it was he had not been discovered, he said at one moment in the advance he noticed a Boer looking at him rather interestedly, and as dead men tell no tales he had pushed the muzzle of his carbine into his back and pulled the trigger; but, excepting that incident, nothing unusual had occurred.

Needless to say, I brought his conduct to the notice of the general.

Unfortunately, thick mist still prevailed, and we could not ascertain even the direction of the Boer retirement. However, at 6.30 a.m. it cleared slightly and I sent off Colonel Henry with all the mounted troops in pursuit. But although they caught them up sufficiently to harry them for many miles with shell-fire, they were unable to do more as the enemy were as well mounted as themselves.

Our losses in horses were fifty-four killed, about the same number wounded, and over 200 lost. I am convinced that, except for this stampede of horses, our casualties would have been very light. The Boers had a very bad time. A few days after we found a record in a farm giving twenty-eight killed, and an unknown number wounded.

I found the telegraph between Lake Chrissie and Ermelo in

working order, and got into communication with French at the latter place, when we did a lot of wiring about future plans. I wanted to push on at once, but he told me to wait.

There was a slight rearrangement of troops which placed Campbell's column under me, and the sweeping movement proceeded. The weather conditions were not good; at times our faces were blistered by the sun, but generally it poured with rain. I have vivid pictures in my mind of the Camerons, all stripped, crossing the Umpilusi River with the help of ropes, and carrying tents on their heads; of listening, in the night, to the roar of the Umbenoni, and wondering how the men, without tents, would keep alive; and of cleverly-devised bridges made by Thomson, R.E.[5]

When we left Bothwell (the 9th February), we could see a few Boer wagons north-east of us, and Henry signalled that he saw more, and was pursuing them with mounted troops. We reached the Umpilusi River soon after midday and found it in flood, and impassable, but we could hear Henry's guns, and soon after I got news of a great capture.

Colonel McKenzie, Imperial Light Horse, had headed a Boer convoy, twenty miles from Bothwell. Most of his troop horses were blown, but he, with two officers and eleven men, made a dash at the head of the convoy. There was a good deal of firing, and some 200 Boers escaped, leaving five badly wounded and thirteen prisoners in our hands, as well as two killed on the ground. It was a magnificent piece of work on McKenzie's part. Our total capture was twenty-one prisoners, 4,000 splendid cattle, 14,000 sheep, fifty to sixty wagons, and fifteen carts.

Luckily we were close to the telegraph wires from Ermelo to Steynsdorp, on the Swaziland border, and I was able to get through to French. I urged that Alderson, from Mooifontein, be pushed forward to help Campbell, as there were numbers of wagons and cattle south of the Umpilusi, unable to cross for the flood.

The indefatigable Thomson made a bridge which enabled us

5. Now Lord Thomson, in the late Labour Ministry.

to cross the river. By the end of the next day I had over 20,000 sheep. My orders were not to leave any food for the Boers, but how to drive these flocks and herds along was a puzzle. I showed transport officers and conductors how to make a wagon laager to put the cattle in, on a pattern learned in the Zulu War. It was no good. Before we moved on we had to slaughter 15,000 sheep.

At nightfall we had a further capture of 23,000 sheep, and over 4,000 cattle.

French's orders were always very clear and well worked out. Our seven columns—Dartnell, Allenby, Pulteney (French was with Pulteney), Knox, Alderson, Campbell, and myself—were sweeping the country, capturing an enormous amount of cattle, wagons, an d a certain number of prisoners and gradually enclosing the country from Amsterdam to Pietretief, and hemming in the Boers on the Swaziland border.

On the 14th February we marched through a remarkable narrow, winding defile, four miles long, mostly along the bed of a river, into a plain, where stood Amsterdam, a small town of some thirty houses, prettily nestled against the hills.

Mr. David Forbes, a fine old Scottish laird, came in with his family from his farm, "Athole," to join our camp.

A deputation of Swazis also came in to inquire how their Queen ought to treat Boers who took refuge in their country.

We obtained a lot of horses, mostly unbroken, from Messrs. Forbes, Buchanan, etc., which we commandeered for mounted troops.

Lord James Stewart Murray, a lieutenant in the Camerons, had a warm meeting with Mr. Forbes, whose home was near the Duke of Atholl's estate in Scotland. I and my *aide-de-camp* called on the Forbes family, living amongst their wagons. Mrs. Forbes and the three daughters were very nice people, and distinctly clever. Miss Forbes told us what a trying time they had had all the war, living in the midst of the Boers, who made themselves most unpleasant, and spread nothing but stories of British defeats.

They say that the only person who was always full of confidence and cheered them up was a Zulu servant they had had ever since the Zulu War. He had fought against us at Isandhlwana and Ulundi, and was much impressed with the bravery of British troops and the straight dealings of the British nation. When he was told the Boers were beating our people, he refused to entertain the idea for a moment, but said, "The British may be slow, they may lose heavily at first, but they'll come and sweep all the Boers before them;" and the day our columns appeared he was full of glee and said, "There they are; didn't I tell you the British would come?"

When the Boers spread stories of the British troops having run away, he would say, "Impossible; the British troops may all be killed, but they can't run away." He used to talk of Isandhlwana, and how all our men had fought and died there, and used to say he couldn't understand why we had classed it as a victory for the Zulus, as never in any battle had they suffered such fearful losses. I particularly wanted to see this interesting person, but somehow I was so occupied that I let the Forbes family go away with a convoy on the 17th to Pietretief without seeing him.

French reached Pietretief on the 16th February up to his arrival the Boers had been talking to us on the telephone, and when they cleared out these curious people left the wire in working order, so I was able at once to talk to French by telegraph, and I got leave from him to get rid of all Boer prisoners and families, captured cattle, and my sick and wounded, by sending them into Pietretief.

Judging from his communications, French was puzzled as to where the Boers had gone; and I was not surprised.

I wrote and dispatched a letter to the Swazi Queen, having been coached in Swazi etiquette by the Forbes family. They spoke Swazi fluently and knew the Queen and chiefs well. The Queen, only three weeks before, had offered to send an *impi* (army) to take them safely into her country. Having informed the Swazi Queen, whose official title is *Inhlovogasi* (*i.e.* Queen Elephant), of the death of our Mother, the Great White Queen,

I went on to say that I had sent her 1,000 sheep and fifty black oxen. It appeared that in war-time black was the proper colour; also, as the Boers had a short time before sent her twelve oxen, I had to go a bit better, and, as I had several thousand captured from the Boers, I could afford to be generous.

I then went on to tell her that she must allow no Boers in her country, and, should any be there with their wagons and cattle, she must direct her people to seize the wagons and cattle for themselves, and send the Boers as prisoners to the nearest British post.

In conclusion, I inquired after her Majesty's health, and subscribed myself as one "H. L. S.-D.," commanding British troops on the Swaziland Border. Although the Swazis were most friendly and ready to join in our fights, they did not show any sign of action on their own account. In fact, they were sitting on the fence, and making sure first that there wasn't still a Gladstone in England to hand back the country to the Boers.

On the 18th February, another wet, misty morning, when operations were impossible, Alderson wired that poor gallant Major Gat Howard of Canadian Scouts had been killed near Schwaabe's Store on the Swaziland border—a great loss to the army.

French consulted me about a move south. I recommended taking our time, and leaving no corner unsearched, removing every family and destroying every crop. I suggested my force moving south as soon as I had cleared this district. I also urged that he should ask the chief to confiscate the farms of all Boers still fighting after a certain date, and to sell the farms to defray the expenses of the war.

I had advocated this with Lord Kitchener some months before, and, to prove my idea was a correct one, two influential farmers told me that Louis Botha had told them that only two things would end the war at once, one being the capture of Steyn and de Wet, the other the confiscation of land; but of course, a commander-in-chief cannot possibly listen to all the suggestions he gets, or he would soon come to grief.

FULL TEAM OF OXEN PULLING

THE HEIR TO THE THRONE OF SWAZILAND

That the Swazi Queen was taking an intelligent interest in affairs was indicated by my receiving a letter from her Majesty, addressed to Lord Kitchener, which I am not at liberty to quote.

On the 19th February we had a very successful round up, actually on the Swaziland border. I had a carefully-worked-out plan, and, moving in four columns, everything went right. We covered a lot of ground, some of the mounted troops covering forty miles; thirty-one Boers, thirty-one wagons, and just under 8,000 cattle, sheep, and horses were secured.

The Swazis thoroughly enjoyed our operations, about this time, joining in with our troops, firing at the Boers, and carrying off for themselves cattle and Boer rifles.

The heir to their throne joined us one day, bare to the waist, the usual garment of animals' tails round the middle of his body and a British billycock on his head, in which turn out he fired a 5-in. gun with great glee.

One of our great difficulties was supplies, as convoys were held up by bad weather, roads, and flooded rivers. Luckily *mealies* and fruit were all just ripe. I collected coffee-grinding mills from Boer farms and established a factory formed of wagons and wagon-sails, wherein to grind *mealies*, and was able to give everyone half a pound of *mealy* meal to make porridge with. We had heaps of splendid sheep and cattle, so with good soup, porridge, fresh *mealies* as a vegetable, and peaches, of which there were great numbers, we got along all right.

The rain was never-ending, the ground became a quagmire, wagons were up to their axles in mud, and for days together movement was impossible.

French wired on the 24th February to say he thought our rations had reached Luneburg, between the Intombie and Pongola rivers, and he hoped to bridge or raft the Intombie and get rations into Pietretief on the 27th, on which day he wished me to take up our new positions, namely, Campbell's column at Schwaabe's Store, myself at Pietretief, and a post of one battalion, two guns, and 150 mounted men at Zandbank, close to the Swazi border; Alderson was to move at the same time from Rustplaats to Marienthal, and the other columns to go farther south on the Swaziland border. Later I directed Campbell to go to Zandbank instead of Schwaabe's Stores, on hearing from French that a lot of Boers and wagons had trekked south and east to the Zululand border. He also wired that a Boer had come in and surrendered, and said that ten days ago, when we were approaching Bethel, Louis Botha had addressed the burghers and urged them to fight for their independence for six years, as the Americans had done. A burgher then asked him how they were going to live, as the British were destroying all the food-stuffs, and he replied, "Trust in the Almighty." This was too much for the burgher who had asked the question, and he went straight and surrendered to the British; showing that his faith was not very deep-seated.

26th February.—French's last order involved crossing the river Compies, which was rapid and in flood, but we managed to get over by noon, i.e. seven hours. Duncan McKenzie, as usual, was the life and soul of getting wagons and animals across; several men and horses were swept away. In one case McKenzie most gallantly leapt into the torrent and saved a man and two horses.

Getting our sheep across the bridge was most amusing. The men also threw them into the river and saved them on the other side. Only a few got drowned, and one horse. The mules were very obstinate; they hate water.

The Boers showed in considerable numbers. A flag of truce came in from J. Smuts, asking what I had done with two flag of truce men who came into Amsterdam. I replied saying it was evident they came to spy (couched in less plain language) and told him I should make prisoners and keep all flag of truce men who came in again on frivolous pretences. We started from south of the river at 1 p.m.—not having any grain we were bound to give animals plenty of time to graze. Boers kept following up, and we had a certain amount of shell and rifle fire but no casualties. In the evening Campbell was only five miles off, being unable to cross the Shela River, but hoped to do so in the morning.

French wished me to move to Derby, ready to enter Swaziland if necessary. I requested Campbell to try to reach Pietretief next day. Twelve months ago we were lying in wet trenches previous to the final and decisive assault on Cronje.

27th February.—-Tremendous dew and thick mist I postponed march to 6.30 a.m. as I feared our cattle might stray in fog. We took five hours crossing the Shela River, and after a trying march over boggy ground camped at Derby. Whilst marching we saw Campbell's column just across the river and Alderson's camp of tents at Rustplaats. Other columns had no tents, but bivouacked.

By way of destroying enemy food, the Infantry Brigade cut down a huge field of *mealies*. We stayed a few hours in a shady garden, and whilst there communicated by wire with French and Alderson. We got into camp at Derby, which is practically Schwaabe's Store, on the Swaziland border, at 5 p.m. Fine commanding ground looking down into Swaziland. Alderson rode over from Rustplaats, four miles off, to see me. French wired that de Wet had been defeated trying to enter Cape Colony.

28th February.—I sent off Henry with pom-pom and 200 men about twelve miles into Swaziland due east, to strike a road which runs north from Mahamba police station to Bremmersdorf, or Litchfield's Store, as I heard this road was being used by Boers to break back into the Transvaal. I wired to inform French, who replied that it was a grand move, as Allenby from the south reported Boers and wagons moving up that very road. This I signalled on to Henry, who replied that he was in very difficult country and considerably opposed. I signalled back that I would send him reinforcements and food, but that he must remain out and push south tomorrow; and I wired French asking that Allenby might push north. Later on Henry signalled that he had captured Prinsloo and Van Dyk (two officers of the Pietretief Commando) and had wounded two other Boers. Alderson moved from Rustplaats to Pietretief, and my wire was cut about 6 p.m.

1st March.—French sent me seven welcome wagons of biscuits, groceries, and bread—some of the latter was so impossibly heavy that I could not resist sending the following satirical telegram to the Director of Supplies at Pietretief: "Many thanks for bread; one sort is excellent, the other is causing heavy casualties. You might use your influence with the lieutenant-general to send large quantities of the latter to all Boer *laagers*, for I am convinced that such a measure would hasten termination of the war, as long as they don't use the bread as projectiles."

By 6.30 a.m. Henry had moved six miles south from his last night's camp, and could be seen some fifteen miles off, apparently closing on a Boer convoy. It was quite exciting, especially as the sun failed, and for hours our helio wouldn't work, and we didn't know what had happened. The last we had seen were wagons going into a dip, and horsemen galloping about. About 10 a.m. Campbell, marching from Pietretief to Zandbank, signalled that Englebrecht, commandant of the Pietretief Commando, with some twenty or thirty burghers, had surrendered to him. In the afternoon the sun came out again, and I gathered from Henry what had happened. He had captured all Englebrecht's convoy, consisting of fifty-six prisoners, twenty-four wagons, 1,200 cattle, and many sheep. It appears that when Henry attacked the head of this convoy yesterday Commandant Englebrecht, with twenty or thirty of his men, fled and surrendered to Campbell in hopes of saving his wagons and cattle; but too late, as Henry had captured them in fair fight.

I wired telling French I had ordered Henry north to guard a tract of country between Compies and Assegai rivers, and I asked him to send Allenby to guard the same district from the south, as there were many wagons and Boers in this district, remarking that with these points guarded they must be our prey eventually, as the country was so bad they could not get away east. French agreed and thanked me most warmly for my skilful co-operation with him throughout. He also said that Louis Botha had asked Kitchener to meet him at Middelburg to discuss means to end the war, and Kitchener had agreed and gone to Middelburg.

Henry's total capture amounted to sixty-five prisoners, twenty-seven wagons brought in, five destroyed, and one Cape cart, over 2,000 cattle and 2,000 sheep, one Boer killed and two wounded; our casualties nil. A small convoy of rations reached us from Pietretief, also the sad news that the Assegai River had risen again, thereby stopping our rations coming up.

3rd March.—I sent Colonel King, 5th Lancers, with a force to punish some Boers who sniped Alexander yesterday, and to clear a mill of grain and destroy it. Instead of our punishing Boers they punished us—there were only about eight of them hidden in rocks, and they remained hidden, allowing us to take forty sacks of grain and destroy the mill, and then, when most of our force had gone, crept up to a small party of 5th Lancers and wounded four of them. Lieutenant Dugdale, 5th Lancers, behaved very bravely and brought away two of the wounded men under a heavy fire, one on his own pony and one on a wounded horse, for which I am recommending him for a Victoria Cross.

4th March.—Henry moved north to a point on the Mahamba Road, ten miles due east of this. He signalled that Swazis had located Boers and wagons fifteen miles east of this. I wired scheme for capturing them to General French, which he approved. I also wired news of cattle on Assegai River to Campbell and Allenby.

5th March.—Received orders from General French to meet him in Pietretief and discuss future operations. He wished me to command all columns north of Pongola River, with my headquarters at Pietretief, whilst he cleared the south-east corner of Transvaal up to Zulu border.

The Swazi Queen has called out her *impis* to attack the Boers, and clear them out of her country.

Pouring rain and awful weather day after day; most depressing, and the poor men with no tents and only half rations.

We have not much news of the outer world, but hear of a big reverse, said to have taken place in Uganda, 380 casualties, a Colonel Maitland amongst the killed. We hear honours are coming out. I hope I may be made a real major-general. I wish this war would end, as so far I have not been found out in any glorious mistakes, and should like to "stand," as one says at cards when one has a fair hand and doesn't care to risk taking more for fear of losing everything.

CHAPTER 20

Pietretief

The country was in an awful state, and rains were continuous. I saw French in Pietretief; he was cheery and hopeful. His operations had been most successful, and he was much pleased with my share in them. He told me that in future I was to command more than half his force, consisting of my own big column and the columns of Campbell, Allenby, and Knox, and that he would leave me to work out, in my own way, all operations north of the River Pongola, which runs west and east, about twenty miles south of Pietretief.

He had little news at this date, 6th March, but what he had was satisfactory: de Wet had been hunted out of Cape Colony, losing all his guns and transport; Colonel Bullock had reached Pietretief with a convoy by the good road from Volksrust, *via* Wakkerstroom; but Burn Murdoch was still on the south side of the Elandsberg.

Meanwhile the Swazis continued, in a most unneighbourly manner, to attack our brother Boers, and succeeded in driving them out of Swaziland, which saved us a good deal of hunting about in bad country; while our operations continued to yield a small but steady return of prisoners and cattle.

The weather did not improve, and rain was incessant, so occasionally we amused ourselves (self, Colonel Spens, and the *jeunesse dorée* of our respective staffs) by playing hopscotch, as I used to do on wet days in the schoolroom at home. Colonel Spens was very unfortunate at this game.

Having received orders to move on to Pietretief we did so on the 15th March. A rumour was current about this time that Lord Kitchener had had a satisfactory interview with Louis Botha, that the mine shares had gone up, and peace was a certainty. But a wire from Lord Kitchener, dated the 16th, which came part of the way by runner, informed us that Botha had refused all terms; also that he wanted troops as soon as possible—so that the momentary vision of getting some hunting in England this season vanished.

General French left on the 21st March, going towards Vryheid, and we rode with him four miles to the bridge over the Assegai to say goodbye.

Thanks to the enterprise shown by Campbell and Allenby, operating in the difficult country south-east of Pietretief into the valley of the Pongola, I never had a moment's anxiety. There were, however, some minor troubles with convoys. I find I note that on the 25th I received a dispatch from Colonel Bullock, telling me his convoy of supplies from Volksrust, which had met with slight opposition, was seventeen miles out. After a busy morning I rode out to meet it, but, owing to the difficulties of the road, we only got fifty out of a hundred and forty wagons across the Assegai bridge before dark. The supply people had done us badly, and only sent half the amount of rations required; consequently I had to make new plans and many calculations, ending in my deciding to send my D.A.A.G. Scott to Volksrust, and to send an escort under Colonel Mackenzie (Suffolks) with two guns, one hundred 5th Lancers and fifty Imperial Light Horse to bring in the next convoy from Castrol Nek, whilst Colonel Bullock remained there to bring in the succeeding convoy on its arrival from Volksrust.

On the 27th I got orders to march back to Belfast when all was clear south, and at the same time was told that the chief wanted the Camerons by the 4th April at Volksrust. I remonstrated with the chief for taking away the Camerons, and told him I must have more remounts. I also wired him plans for my move north, and asked him to have a column ready on the northern line as I approached to act under my orders. He refused me any more remounts, and I replied that the whole of my three columns would be reduced to 2,000 infantry, a sufficiency of guns, and 1,600 mounted troops, the latter one-third on foot, one-third on horses that could not go out of a walk, and that unless I got more remounts and a lot of fresh mules my operations would have to be very limited. However, I got no change in reply, and so my last hope of making a success of my northern move disappeared.

There was, at this time, disgraceful behaviour going on somewhere, and the men in the field had to suffer by short rations in consequence. The biscuits sent to us were terrible, and also the shortage in rations—each 56 lb. tin of coffee was always 12 lb. short, and each 70 lb. bag of sugar 17 lb. short. "The most serious matter is the shortage of 54,000 lb. of oats, as our horses are already half-starved."

On the 30th March I noted:

Wettish morning. At 1.30 p.m. got a report that large Commando north of St. Helena threatening our convoys half-way between this and Wakkerstroom. I wired Campbell to send a hundred mounted men at once, and sent off Major Malcolm, Camerons, with four companies, two guns, and fifty Imperial Light Horse to make a forced march to St. Helena, and wired everyone to tell them what I had done, especially Bullock, directing latter to see Mackenzie through from Mabohla to St. Helena (a distance only of twelve miles) and then to return for next convoy, which I would again meet and see safely through.

This leaves me with a minimum of troops in here. French with Pulteney at Alsboom, Dartnell near Toovernaarsrust, Alderson about Tochgevonden. These three places are on or towards the Zululand border some sixty to seventy miles south of Pietretief. Some 1,300 Boers with wagons were retiring east before these columns, hoping to get across the Pongola at Langdraai Drift; but I had got Allenby blocking that drift until the 6th April, on which date I hoped to move north.

31st March (Sunday).—Too much work to get to church; at 12.45 a.m. Campbell wired he heard of Boers and wagons crossing drift at De Kraalen between Zandbank and Pietretief. With great promptness he sent at 2 a.m. twenty-one King's Royal Rifles Mounted Infantry, supported by fifty 18th Hussars and one company Leicesters, who got to the drift and surprised the whole party—only thirteen Boers got away. Total capture twenty prisoners, thirteen rifles, seven wagons, one cart, six horses, three mules, and 503 cattle.

Allenby captured one 15-pounder gun and two pom-poms at Langdraai Drift, also some wagons, cattle, and prisoners. French wired that he hoped I would go north as soon as arranged, to which I replied, "All right."

Just before dinner got two most startling wires from Colonel Bullock, saying enemy so strong on road that he did not consider it safe to send convoy and was keeping it. Considering he had about 1,200 troops, and that there were a further 500 under Malcolm on the road he is marching along at St. Helena, only twelve miles away from him, I could not see his difficulty, and directed him to send convoy oft at once and see it safely through to St. Helena.

5th April (Good Friday).—Fresh orders from French. The bulk of Boers near him gone south, and he is going after them, taking Knox away tomorrow from P. P. Burg. The wire is sure to be cut then, and my columns will have no communication with the outer world. I wired Allenby (or rather signalled and sent by runner through Campbell) to withdraw from Langdraai on the 7th, Campbell to come in here on 10th. I hope to be able to start north on 14th.

Owing to the saturated state of the country it took thirteen and a half hours for nineteen lightly loaded wagons to go twelve miles to Zandbank today.

6th April.—Boers with thirty wagons reported at Altona and Kortnek on the Pongola, forty-odd miles south-east of Pietretief.

French wired that he had undoubtedly driven 1,200 Boers south of Vryheid and was moving Knox at once from P. P. Burg, so that with him, Dartnell, and Alderson he might form a line across southern triangle of Transvaal.

7th April.—Knox wires he is moving, so I expect wire may be cut any time. I wired French saying that, as so many Boers were still south, I thought it a great pity that I should move north at present, but that I should come down and help him bottle the 1,200 Boers. It will be a great pity not to do the thing thoroughly. Reply from French thanking me for offer of help and saying that he and chief consider enough has been done down south. I only hope they may not find themselves mistaken. I should like to take another month about it.

De Wet and Steyn were reported on our road north with the Ermelo and Carolina Commandos, about twenty-four miles off.

I much fear that we are leaving a lot of work unfinished by our move north, and am sorry the authorities won't listen to my opinions. There are a lot of Boers about down here, and unless a very unexpected peace takes place this part of country will have to be visited again. I should like all columns to work about here for another month at least. I also want to level every house. The houses will all be occupied during the winter and keep the Boer out of the cold. It would actually pay us, by ending the war so much sooner, to destroy every house and build them up again at our expense when the war is over.

However, conciliatory and kind measures are still the order of the day, and so the war must be prolonged and the poor troops kept at it. I find that out of my total of 1,838 mounted troops with the three columns 677 are on foot, and the remainder on enfeebled horses, so we shall hardly make a good show if hard pressed; but Lord Kitchener says he is quite unable to provide any remounts. The mounted troops consist of the Carabineers, Scots Greys, 5th Lancers, 18th Hussars; the King's Royal Rifles Mounted Infantry, the 3rd Mounted Infantry, the 2nd Imperial Light Horse.

However, we moved on Sunday, 14th April.

Campbell and Allenby started at daylight to clear our front, turning off our road five miles north of Pietretief to Idalia. I had made them as mobile as possible. They had 750 men fairly mounted, and 1,200 infantry, and all sorts of guns, and only rations for six days. They moved on the exposed flank, and I took all the heavy ox-convoy with me, and left them unhampered to strike. I was much impressed with Allenby as a fine specimen of an Englishman: he looked twenty-four instead of nearly forty.

We started at 7.30 a.m.—only eleven miles to Shela River. The Royal Engineers (Addison) threw a pontoon bridge across, but the drift worked badly, and what with that and a Weldon trestle breaking, we still had 200 wagons south of the river at dark, and there being no moon we could do no more. Our outposts in consequence had to be somewhat extended. Campbell's scouts, in approaching Krom River (Field Cornet Van Royan's) farm, had had a Scots Grey shot dead, and the Boers sniped from the farm. As a punishment, I blew up and burnt the farm. Two hundred Boers had gone north out of the farm with three wagons. Campbell camped in view of us, and appeared to be six or seven miles off and on a farm called Idalia.

15th April.—Commenced at dawn crossing ox-convoy over Shela. Started half force and mule convoy at 8 a.m. up the long slope to Panhilt. All went well until, having surmounted the hill and marched some ten miles along the top of it, the ground began to give way and wagons got bogged everywhere. We had to camp five miles short of our goal, and after dark a lot of the first half of wagons were still bogged, and the ox-convoy parked three miles back. It bids badly for future marches. The country is absolutely rotten. In this curious country the bogs are always on the top of the highest hills. today we rose some 700 feet, and when we reached the summit got hopelessly bogged. We saw about 120 Boers—thirty fired at our advanced troops across the Compies, but soon made off in the direction of Amsterdam—three wagons of theirs went the same way this morning and six more to Bankkop. Campbell signalled difficulties of ground also on his side, and camped at Springboklaagte—north of Compies. Luckily cloudy, cool day for animals, splendid grass.

16th April.—Truly a sad day. By nightfall only ninety ox wagons had got across the three miles of boggy ground, leaving 130 almost where they were last night—under guard of 5th Lancers, half West Yorkshires and two guns. The ninety wagons escorted by half West Yorkshires remained at our last night's camp. The 3rd Mounted Infantry, 2nd Imperial Light Horse, and mule supply party crossed Compies four miles from last night's camp by a pontoon bridge. The Suffolks, guns, and head-quarters camped just south of bridge.

Campbell found his crossing of Compies difficult and had to make a bridge. He signalled that J. Smuts, Botha, and Oppermann were near Beginderlyn on the Vaal, and later that a large Boer Commando was moving on Carolina. A native came in and reported J. Smuts with 150 men at Lake Chrissie, that he was tired of being a general and anxious to give in, and that English occupied Carolina on 13th—all untrue. I think chief would have told me had he intended me to occupy Carolina— my orders being to keep to the west of it.

The accounts I have so far given of our daily marches towards the Pretoria-Komati Poort Railway are typical of the remaining eleven days it took us to reach our objective, and it would be wearisome to give in detail the story of each day. The Boers, though continually worrying us, caused no serious inconvenience. Allenby's and Campbell's columns, whose guns we heard frequently, moved *via* Ermelo on Middelburg, whilst I with the main column kept parallel with them to the east on Wonderfontein.

Both movements are clearly marked on the map of the Eastern Transvaal. All three columns reached their destinations on the 27th April. On the 22nd April I had received a message by helio, saying I was to proceed to India at once as adjutant-general and to report myself to the chief at Pretoria as soon as I reached the railway; so I realised that, unless I could persuade Lord Kitchener to keep me until the war was ended, I should have no more enjoyable treks.

On arriving at Wonderfontein on the 27th April I received a wire from the military secretary saying that I was to take up my appointment very shortly, and one from the A.G., Pretoria, to say that I was promoted major-general from the 11th February 1900, which was splendid. I left for Pretoria on the last day of the month, and stayed with Lord Kitchener, who informed me that I was to get away home at once, en route for India, as Lord Roberts would not hear of my remaining on in South Africa.

CHAPTER 21

India, 1901-1907

Leaving Wonderfontein on the 30th April, I went to Pretoria and stayed with Commander-in-Chief Lord Kitchener, for a week; and a very pleasant week it was, settling up business connected with the war, and concluding with a most cheery dinner, at which I met Sir Bindon Blood, Jimmy Spens, Marker, Hubert Hamilton (both the last two being killed in the first few months of the 1914-18 war), and John Maxwell, then Governor of Pretoria. Our host was in great form, and full of confidence as to the progress of the war, and after a merry game on the billiard-table in which Lord Kitchener took a prominent part, I took my leave and slept in the train, starting for England at daylight next morning.

After a most enjoyable journey—for friends met me at almost every station—Capetown was reached in three and a half days—a long time, but until the war area was cleared trains could only move by day. I stayed at the Mount Nelson Hotel, concerning which numerous legends of beautiful ladies and wild revelries had reached us in the field; but I am bound to say that, although I had to spend five days there until my ship, the *Norman,* was ready to sail, nothing occurred which could have stirred the feelings of the most sensitive and puritanical of critics.

I reached England on the 31st May, and was given a most kindly reception by Lord Roberts, the commander-in-chief, when I reported myself to him next day at the War Office. After that interview I went to my home at Berkhampsted, where I was given such a royal reception that I almost began to think I had done something to be proud of. My mother and thirteen brothers and sisters were at home to greet me. The change and the complete holiday were welcome to me, and it was very enjoyable being able to go where the spirit moved me during the next four months.

Many years had passed since I had been free to attend the annual festive gatherings such as the Derby (Volodyovski won), Ascot, Henley, Lords, etc. There were certainly rather too many big dinners and too many speeches, but a good deal of sport, shooting and cubbing, before I embarked in October to take up the adjutant-generalship in India—a more important post in those days than it is now; for then there was no chief of the staff, and the adjutant-general was the senior staff officer responsible for both the training and discipline of the army. I was most graciously received by H.M. King Edward VII at Marlborough House on appointment.

There were two incidents worth recording which occurred just before leaving England, both of which gave me a shock. The first was seeing an announcement in the papers of my engagement to be married, without a vestige of truth in it, accompanied by pictures of myself and the young lady; and I was sorry for her.

The other was a more serious affair. At a dinner given in my honour I had been challenged by a well-known and highly respected Member of Parliament to suggest an organisation for our land forces, which would secure a reserve adequate in quantity and quality for meeting the sudden outbreak of such a war as was then going on in South Africa. I, in all simplicity, and quite unaware of the presence of any of the Press, outlined a scheme involving a form of compulsory service for home defence. Roughly my plan was to treat the Militia as our basic reserve, and to ensure its ranks being full by enforcing the Ballot Act (then in abeyance), the exemptions to be men who joined the regular army and volunteers who contracted for a fixed period of years, during which they would submit to a much higher standard of training than was in vogue at that time. It never struck me that I had said anything outrageous, and I went to bed and slept the sleep of the just. Next day I was surprised to receive a telegram from Adjutant-General "Kelly-Kenny," saying the chief wished to see me at once.

On being ushered into the presence of our beloved chief, he, evidently much perturbed, but without departing from his usual kindly manner, demanded why I had so far forgotten my position as a general on full pay as to advocate publicly the introduction of compulsory service. Lord "Bobs" went on to say that he held in his hand a wrathful letter from the Secretary of State for War, and there it was, eight sides of notepaper, saying that in consequence of my misbehaviour the Government was seriously considering whether my appointment as adjutant-general in India should not be cancelled. My first feelings were those of intense indignation on his account, and I expressed my deep regret to the chief for having done anything which should have caused such a letter to be written to him, but at the same time pleaded I had done nothing to warrant such a letter; that I had been forced to accept the appointment in spite of my requests that I should be allowed to remain in South Africa until the war was over; that I had still no wish to go to India, and under the circumstances I hoped the Government would find someone else for the post.

Seeing me taking matters so seriously the little chief got up, and putting his hand on my shoulder calmed me down, saying he would explain matters to the Secretary of State. Instantly my wrath vanished, and I was ashamed of my vehemence. Who could resist the magic persuasion of that wonderful personality—so gentle and so considerate and yet so firm and determined when occasion demanded? He is still my ideal of what a leader, patriot, friend, or enemy should be. I include "enemy," for it wasn't in him to take a mean advantage. Is it possible that the little man's leniency was due to his innermost promptings? for who can forget his splendid patriotism when in later years, instead of taking the rest so fully due to him, he, as the voice of one crying in the wilderness, urged in public speeches and in articles that some form of compulsory training alone could secure the safety of the nation.

Passing over my voyage to India in the P. & O. *Arabia,* I duly took over the adjutant-generalship in Simla on the 6th November, and was fortunate in finding as commander-in-chief one of the most delightful men I have ever served under, General Sir Arthur Power Palmer. He was a cavalry soldier of the Indian army, and had been general in command of the Punjab army, but when the commander-in-chief in India— General Sir William Lockhart—became too ill to carry on his duties, had been appointed to officiate for him—and, although Sir William Lockhart died in March 1900, Sir Power was never confirmed as commander-in-chief, but continued to officiate for three and a half years.

There was no question of his suitability, but the custom being that the appointment should be held alternately by an officer of the Indian and Home armies, the authorities decided, as General Lockhart was of the Indian army, it would be just not to fill up the appointment permanently until a home army man was available. The man they had in their eye was Lord Kitchener, and, it being beyond their ken that the Boer War would drag on as it did year after year, the unfortunate Sir Power was never confirmed, but was made use of as a stop-gap until Lord Kitchener, having settled with the Boers, was free, and this did not occur until the autumn of 1902.

It really was a very difficult position for him, especially with the constant interference of the Military Department— which had such extensive powers that they were able to interfere not only with measures involving expenditure, but with changes necessary to conform to the latest experiences of modern war. It will be as well to explain briefly here that the functions of the Military Department should have been the same as those of the Secretary of State at home in his civil capacity, and should chiefly have been concerned in controlling expenditure and in shaping the policy in regard to the size and organisation of the army decreed by the Government in power.

To illustrate this, I will mention one instance out of several which came under my immediate attention. The Indian Cavalry Regiments had, in addition to their complement of horses, eight camels each. These latter were employed for orderly duties, long distance dispatches, and in other ways to save the horses. It struck the commander-in-chief that it would be all in the cause of economy and efficiency if the establishment of camels could be increased from eight to sixteen per regiment, and the number of horses correspondingly reduced. There was no doubt about the economy, as camels were cheaper to buy and cheaper to feed, and regarding efficiency the question was put to every Indian Cavalry Regiment in India, and the replies without exception were strongly in favour of the proposal.

Sir Power had been a cavalryman all his life, and had served in several campaigns as such, and there is no doubt that on such a question his advice should have been paramount, especially as not only was no increase of expenditure involved, but the contrary. The Military Department, however, had become so powerful that such questions had to be referred to them—lo and behold! the project was returned with a brief minute signed by a captain in the department, saying the Government of India did not agree that the change proposed was desirable. Unfortunately, such inferior beings as soldiers loomed small in the mind of the Viceroy, and the Military Department knew they could count on his support, so the matter had to be dropped.

Now I had been selected and sent out to my high appointment by Lord Roberts, as he considered I had assimilated the requirements of modern warfare sufficiently to be in a position where my advice and recommendations would tend to raise the efficiency of the army in India. I very soon realised that an officiating commander-in-chief, with a hostile Viceroy and predominant Military Department, had not the requisite power to insist on the necessary reforms. I was devoted to my chief, I had a delightful staff to deal with, especially do I mention my Deputy Adjutant-General, Beauchamp Duff, later himself commander-in-chief in India, and yet I asked myself "Are you fulfilling the role Lord Roberts selected you for? Are you pulling your weight?" and could find only one answer, and, after struggling for eleven months, flapping against the bars of my cage, I decided finally that my position was intolerable, that I was drawing pay under false pretences, and I tendered my resignation—but I am anticipating, and will now return to my story.

By joining the commander-in-chief's staff, I had inherited a very delightful life. Simla was full of pleasant people, the chief hostess being the chatelaine of Viceregal Lodge; quite one of the most beautiful and agreeable women it has ever been my good fortune to meet. Then amongst my friends were the quartermaster-general and his wife, General and Mrs. Henry, and Franklin the Viceroy's medical officer, who afterwards, at the head of the Indian Medical Services, became Sir Benjamin. He and Lady Franklin were friends of mine when at Jubbulpore in the early nineties. I must not omit a very distinguished and capable officer, who with his wife became life-long friends of my wife and myself. I refer to General Sir Edmund and Lady Barrow.

I, too, had obtained a particularly nice house, "Balquholly," and everything was *couleur de rose,* excepting my efforts at improving the army. Amongst the most fascinating features of Indian life are the winter tours—and only a fortnight after taking up my duties my chief proceeded on a tour of inspection of Imperial Service troops. These troops were those maintained by the several native chiefs, but trained under the guidance of British officers and available for the defence of the country—though they have actually fulfilled far wider duties and have come to the help of the Empire most ungrudgingly in all parts of the world —and well may we be proud of their achievements.

The commander-in-chief had already visited a few native states before I joined him at Bikanir on the 23rd November. This was my first experience of the regal hospitality of our Indian chieftains. The Maharajah, a charming and cultured young man of twenty-one, who is now so well known personally in England, and has over and over again proved himself one of the pillars of the Empire, had just completed a new palace, and was, under great difficulties for lack of water, laying out the grounds. It looked rather a hopeless task then, for sand appeared to be the main component part of the soil, but I hear that, in spite of this, nature has been defeated and that the palace is now surrounded by gardens and grounds of very considerable beauty.

His Excellency was accompanied by Lady Palmer, his Military Secretary, Lieutenant-Colonel de Courcy Hamilton, who became a personal friend of mine, and four *aide-de camps*, one of whom, George Barrow, was to make his mark later as a commander in the field, and is now Lieutenant-General Sir George Barrow, holding a high command in India.

We were guests of the Maharajah for ten days, and a right royal time we had of it. The inspection of H.H.'s troops, consisting of infantry, Transport, and a very fine Camel Corps, only occupied a comparatively small part of our stay, and there was sport of all sorts—pig-sticking and polo, shooting duck, partridges, and the Imperial Sandgrouse. This latter is one of the finest sports in the world. The guns are placed just after dawn not far from water to which it is the habit of the birds to fly in the early morning from the desert and waste land, where they have spent the night.

The Imperial Sandgrouse is a beautiful bird, and flies straight and fast, and in a good season 2,000 birds have been killed in a morning. Unfortunately they were scarce that year, and our daily bags did not run to much over a hundred.

His Highness's Palace at Gujneer, some sixteen miles off in the jungle, was a particularly interesting spot, and feeding the wild pigs there was a sight never to be forgotten. The spectators having been placed on a raised platform, calls were sounded, and ere many minutes had passed pig began to show themselves in ever-increasing numbers until quite a large number had collected, coming boldly on to the very foot of the platform, when they were fed. There they were within a few feet of where we stood—all sizes, from magnificent old boar with fine glistening tusks down to small families, only a few weeks old. It was a unique opportunity for seeing this splendid denizen of the forest in his native home, and I am glad to have had it. They all looked so peaceful, and yet I knew from my experiences, pig-sticking, that they were about the most dangerous and bravest animals which roam the Indian jungle. I had had a personal experience of this only a few days previously, when we were partridge shooting. We were walking in a long line of guns and beaters through a Kerinda bush jungle, and I had approached within three yards of one of these dense bushes, when suddenly, and without any warning, a magnificent boar rushed from it straight at me—whereas his line of least resistance, had he wished to escape, was in the opposite direction. Mercifully for me, I was just able to jump on one side, though he brushed my leg and nearly carried me off my feet. A coolie, one of the beaters behind me, was not so fortunate, for his thigh was ripped right open, and when we left Bikanir it was doubtful if he would live, though we never heard afterwards how he fared.

All good things have an end, and we were sorry when the 2nd December arrived and we moved on to Jodhpore. There, as ruling chief, we found a man whose name spells chivalry and all that is highest and noblest in the human race to every Englishman who knows of him or who ever had the good fortune to know him personally. I refer to H.H. Maharajah Sir Pertab Singh. The reputation of Sir Pertab, his bravery, his adroitness at every form of sport, and especially at pig-sticking and polo, and his wonderful stories, so modestly and picturesquely told, are too well known to warrant embarking on here. Nor is it necessary to describe his unfailing help to the Empire both by personal service and supplying of troops, the last occasion being the Great War, when he, an old man, personally accompanied our armies in France. Alas! he has gone, and we shall never see his like again.

It is needless to remark on the warmth of his welcome, or the excellence of his troops. The whole party were put up at the Residency and enjoyed the hospitality of two very charming people, Captain and Mrs. Erskine.

That night they gave a state banquet, and next evening, after pig-sticking and polo, in which I had not time to participate, we started for Ulwar.

Our stay there was again full of interest. The Maharajah was a handsome, smart, and particularly agreeable young man, looking every inch a *Sahib*.

On two days the whole party, except myself—for I couldn't spare the time—indulged in tiger-shooting, and Sir Power bagged the only tiger. The parade of the troops, consisting of cavalry, infantry, and transport, gave a very favourable impression; but what appealed to me most was the stud farm, and this is worth briefly describing.

The principal object of this farm was to provide young and active horses for cavalry remounts. It consisted apparently of a large extent of grass land divided up by small fences, where mares and foals were allowed to roam it will, though brought in and shut up in paddocks at night. It was the method of bringing them in which was inspiring. The fences I have referred to were so arranged in parallel lines, some hundred yards apart, that animals coming from the far end of the farm to their paddocks and feeding boxes in the evenings were bound to jump them.

Feeds were only given after the cavalry "Feed" call had been sounded on the trumpet, so all the mares had learned what that call denoted. On being let out of the paddocks in the early morning, mares and foals were driven to the far end of the farm through a line of gates, left there for the day and the gates closed. One evening we went to the paddocks, from which the ground rose before us in a long, steady slope visible for about a mile, when the horizon was reached and beyond which we could not see. It was on these slopes right down to within a few yards of the paddocks that the parallel fences were placed.

Not a horse or moving object was to be seen when the order was given to the trumpeter to sound the feed, which he did in loud, clear notes in the direction of the slope I have mentioned. After an interval of a few minutes mares appeared over the horizon, galloping in from all directions, followed by their foals.

Over the fences they came, one after another—some 200 to 300 of them—a very beautiful and thrilling sight, until, negotiating the last fences, they drew up, blowing, snorting, whinnying and neighing, asking for admission to their paddocks and their "grub."

The fences were of course very small, but it struck me as an admirable way of training young stock to use their legs and to take to leaping obstacles from the real love of it.

After two nights at Ulwar we moved on to Gwalior, rather doubtful if we should not have to change our destination, for the chief had had a somewhat disconcerting telegram from the Viceroy regarding the Waziristan Blockade, the only military operation then on hand, and about which I shall have more to say later. However, we fetched up at

Gwalior all right at 8 a.m. on the 8th December, and were accorded a wonderful reception—really magnificent. Sir Power's half-sister, Mrs. Schneider, with Colonel and Miss Schneider, joined the chief's party that same night.

In the Maharajah, H.H. Sir Mahdo Rao Sindhia of Gwalior, the head of the Mahratta house of Sindhia, we met a very remarkable and striking personality, the embodiment of intelligence, energy, and mechanical knowledge, with a zeal for studying every modern invention, so that he might be in a position to develop his country on the most modern lines and by his own knowledge. He was then only twenty-four, but was already an impressive and interesting man, and one who, whilst free from any signs of superiority and almost simple in his cordial and cheerful manners, left no doubt in one's mind that he was the mainspring of his State and a born ruler.

We were guests in his gorgeous palace, and were kept fully occupied for the three days we were there—state banquets, receptions, a dance, tiger-shooting, pig-sticking, though again I had to content myself with office work. The commander-in-chief again shot the only tiger bagged, and was accompanied by his niece, who thus was in at the death of her first tiger. She was the young lady who was subsequently responsible for building the most important milestone in my life by becoming my wife and bringing perpetual light and happiness into it.

The more serious part of our visit was taken up by parades and field-days. The latter were remarkably well carried out. The troops were well drilled and moved smartly, and a very considerable knowledge of our modern ideas of handling forces was shown. This, it appeared, was mainly due to the soldierlike qualities of the Maharajah himself, for his guiding hand was apparent everywhere. One day he had a ceremonial parade of 4,000 troops, and the road leading to the parade was lined by Mahratta horsemen in the old-style fighting dress of a hundred years previously, bright coloured and flowing garments—and the arms of the time—such a picturesque setting.

His Highness commanded the parade himself and received the commander-in-chief with a salute at the head of his troops, when guns belched forth their greeting and swords were lowered and rifles presented. Another day he held a very realistic field-day, at which, although his infantry were only armed with the old brown Bess and artillery with smooth-bore guns, he assumed that the weapons were the long-range ones of modern date and worked them accordingly, using large extensions and dispersion of guns. He had sent one force out fourteen miles overnight to bivouac, and quite a practical and instructive field-day was the result.

Another day he gave us sports with a mimic fight *à la* Military Tournament at Olympia, but surpassing anything I have ever seen there owing to the extent of ground and the numbers employed. It must have taken months of preparation, for a fort had actually been built of light material, and this was attacked, stormed, and eventually, having caught fire from the shells, was burned to the ground just as daylight departed, the flames in the gathering darkness making a very impressive scene. This up-to-date Prince also showed us vast workshops in which he toiled with his own hands, and took some of the party in his miniature railway, driving the engine himself.

From Gwalior the chief had intended to go to the Army Rifle

Meeting at Meerut, but the Viceroy, who was anxious, though why to us was not apparent, about military affairs in Waziristan, insisted on his going to Calcutta. Sir Power, therefore, sent me to Meerut to represent him. The general commanding in Bengal, Sir George Luck, and the general commanding the Meerut District, Sir Donald McLeod, were both there, the guiding spirit being Colonel Woollcombe, a first-rate officer (later Lieutenant-General Sir Louis Woollcombe, commanding a division in the Great War).

The Rifle Meeting ended, I wended my way to rejoin my chief in Calcutta, where army head-quarters were established for the cold weather, and settled down to serious work, which was only interrupted by such events as races, horse-shows—at one of which I took three first prizes with a charger—entertainments, and functions at Government House, etc. These latter were splendidly organised and most regally carried out, though tight full dress, which was *de rigueur,* was hardly conducive to comfort. A propos of this, my old native servant remarked one evening, as I was departing for a state banquet: "*Sahib*, where do you find room for your dinner?"

I saw a good deal of my future wife during this period, but was not given the *coup de grâce* until an eventful dance in the Gunners' Mess in Bangalore on the 29th January— to which I refer later.

The chief had not visited Burmah for some time, and had made his plans to inspect that command as his spring tour, but there again it was a case of "Commander-in-Chief *propose, et* Viceroy *dispose,*" for he was told that, as the Viceroy himself wished to visit Burmah, the commander-in-chief must give up the idea, the reason given being that the burden of entertainment expenses would fall too heavily on the good people of Burmah if two high personages were to visit the country in the same season—so he had to make fresh plans.

There is no gainsaying the fact that Lord Curzon was a powerful Viceroy and made a great mark in India, but those who served under him would hardly say that his methods were always soothing; but it was no good resisting him, and a fresh tour to take place in the Madras command had to be arranged.

On the 12th January, His Excellency started for the Madras Presidency so as to be present at the Secunderabad manoeuvres under General Sir Jocelyn Wodehouse—a distinguished soldier who had seen many campaigns, and a very old friend of mine.

The chief was accompanied by the same staff as before, with the addition of the Q.M.G., General Henry, and also by Mrs. and Miss Schneider.

The manoeuvres lasted some days, but there was no incident of sufficient interest to describe in these pages. Briefly, we visited Hyderabad and Bellary, where Sir Power inspected the camp of Boer prisoners, and thence went to Madras, and were most hospitably entertained at Government House by Lord and Lady Ampthill.

Thence we went to the Simla of the South, the hill station of Ootacamund in the Neilgherries, 8,000 feet, remarkable for rolling downs of verdant green, which are taken full advantage of in the hunting season; perfect roads; an ideal climate—never very hot or very cold—with a wealth of flowers and trees which did one good to see. Here we found General Sir George Wolseley, brother of the distinguished Field-Marshal Lord Wolseley, installed as commander-in-chief of troops in Madras.

After that Sir Power inspected the Bangalore troops, and it was then the incident happened which changed the course of my life—not for the worse—and which I have already mentioned. These were otherwise very busy times, for there were a great many military stations and numerous bodies of troops to be inspected.

In the course of our peregrinations we went to the Kolar gold-fields in Mysore, and were taken down a mine by its most cordial manager, Mr. Hancock. He showed us the whole process of extracting gold from quartz.

It might be inferred, from my story, that amusements were the main occupations on a tour of this sort; but Sir Power was a very earnest worker, and, with his vast experience of the Indian army, had effected many valuable reforms, and now was bent on supplanting the softer races which largely formed the Madras army by hardier and more warlike men from the north. His inspections during this tour were, therefore, of a very scrutinous and careful nature.

Poona was our next port of call, and there General Sir Robert Low, on whose staff I had been in Lucknow in 1894, was the reigning military authority, and it was very pleasant being again under his roof. I will not weary my readers with more detail, for the round of inspections and functions was much the same at one place as another.

Lord Northcote was the Governor of Bombay, and he and Lady Northcote showed us all much hospitality.

We then worked up-country to Jhansi, Agra, Delhi, Bareilly, Shahjehanpur (where we inspected another camp of Boer prisoners), Lucknow, Cawnpore, and the tour ended by our return to Calcutta on the 23rd February.

The tour, from my point of view, had been very valuable, for I had met a large number of units and been able to feel the pulse of the army. When I had first arrived in India I had heard many stories of the unsympathetic attitude of the Viceroy toward the army, and I am bound to say I regarded them as exaggerated. The stories were to the effect that the Viceroy regarded the army as an inferior profession; that he missed no opportunity of showing the low opinion he held of the intellect of officers, or his conception of the rank and file as a rowdy and licentious body, and that his mind was so saturated with such views that misunderstandings between soldiers and natives were certain to be judged as due to the bullying nature of the soldier.

The only confirmatory evidence I had of these stories was the fact that soldiers had almost completely abandoned an amusement dear to their hearts, namely, going into the jungle for a few days' sport. It appears there had been a few *fracas* resulting in sweeping condemnation of the soldiers when the latter were firmly convinced that the natives had been the aggressors. It was said, rightly or wrongly, that matters had reached such a pass that the natives had jumped to a conclusion that they would be certain of the Viceroy's support and had become so aggressive that soldiers had abandoned their sport, feeling that the risk of being set upon and put in a false position was too great a one to take.

At every military station visited by the commander-in-chief in the course of his tour, it was customary for commanding officers to pay a personal visit to the adjutant-general, and it was from these visits that I became convinced that there was some foundation for many of the stories I had heard, and that the feelings of injury amongst the British troops were very deep-seated.

One commanding officer of an infantry battalion—I won't mention names—made a request that his battalion might be selected to attend the Delhi Durbar fixed for the end of the year. I told him the chief consideration would be economy, and that if at that time his battalion should be quartered a long way off it would only be selected if its record particularly connected it with wars in India. The colonel regretted that they had no claim on that score, but expressed a hope that as it was to be an occasion for ceremonies, and new colours were due to the battalion, they might be allowed to come to Delhi so as to receive them at the hands of the Prince of Wales. I replied that, as such picturesque ceremonies would brighten the proceedings, I would lay his request before the commander-in-chief, but that the report of H.R.H.'s coming was untrue; I added that this would make no difference since His Excellency the Viceroy would be asked to present the colours. I shall never forget the man's face. He did not speak, but he looked aghast.

At once the stories I had heard flashed through my mind, and I blurted out, "Surely things are not as bad as that."

To which his reply was: "If we have to receive our new colours from the Viceroy we would rather not go." Further experiences on that tour and subsequently convinced me that other units had much the same feelings of resentment.

It is no satisfaction to me to refer to these unpleasant stories, but on behalf of my late chief and of the British army in India at that time I feel it is only just to record a deeply seated feeling of grievance which then permeated the British army in India, due to one person, and one person only.

I do not for a moment imagine that Lord Curzon was aware of it—a masterful, self-centred man with no one to say him "Nay" would not pause to reflect that any attitude of his could be open to criticism, or that cutting and disparaging remarks and minutes from the head of a great Government cannot be answered, but do all the more harm on that account, for the iron enters far deeper into the souls of the people reflected on when no reply is possible.

I have no personal grievance on the subject, for both the Viceroy and Lady Curzon showed great kindness to my wife and me both before and after we were married, but these official grievances did much towards spoiling my enjoyment of a high appointment and loomed large in my decision, taken a few months later, to resign it.

On the 20th March, my fiancée and her parents started for England, and I did not see them again until I went there myself six months later after tendering my resignation. Nothing more worth recording happened, and the 1st April saw head-quarters back in Simla for the hot weather.

Life in Simla consisted of heavy office work, relieved—or shall I say handicapped?—by dinners, dances, races, and a horse-show. I was on the whole successful at the last two, for I had collected quite a useful stud, winning several races and the jumping at the Horse Show, riding my pony Muskerry.

I remember the arrival of the thrilling news on the 31st May of "Peace in Boerland." This indicated to me that the end of my connection with my beloved chief was in view, since Lord Kitchener, already designated, would soon be free to succeed him. Then, on the 24th June, came the alarming news of King Edward's illness and the postponement of his Coronation, and in consequence the instructions already issued to the army for ceremonies of joy to commemorate the Coronation had to be redrafted so that the parade services should take the form of prayers for the King. The Coronation day had been fixed for the 26th June, and it was sad that instead we throughout India were that day praying that the life of the King might be spared.

The whole of Simla, from His Excellency the Viceroy down, attended a service in full dress. It was a service fitted to the occasion, so simple, so solemn, and so earnest. The sermon preached by Bishop Lefroy, the bishop of Lahore, could not have been more eloquent and appropriate. Without any specific text he described the sad circumstances which had brought us together in words which touched the hearts of all present, laying stress on the saying that man proposes and God disposes as particularly applicable.

The bishop was a man peculiarly fitted for such a solemn occasion. There was naturally a saintly air about him, he had an appealing and refined voice, a power of expression in beautiful, simple, and earnest language, and erudition and eloquence of a standard which very few have reached. There were only two hymns during the service, No. 375, "Great King of Nations, hear our prayer," and No. 165, "O God, our help in ages past." There was, however, nearly a grave omission, but the situation was saved, for I saw Lady Curzon whisper to the Viceroy, and an *aide-de-camp* dispatched to the rector with the result that the *National Anthem* pealed out, and then the whole congregation sang "God Save the King."

I believe every one present was stirred to the depths by the beautiful and solemn service. I know I was.

Throughout India as throughout the Empire people of all religions held services and joined in earnest prayer for the King's recovery, and "From that moment he began to amend."

I have mentioned the existence of what are known as "Bazaar Rumours" in writing of my experiences in Egypt, and it really does seem that "Coming events cast their shadows before," and that the latter are seen in native villages in a most uncanny way; an illustration of this occurred in connection with the King's illness, for two days before the telegram announcing it came, I was actually told that the common talk in the bazaar was that the King would not be crowned then.

Although there was no monotony about my life in Simla, which, on the contrary, was full of interest and largely taken up in wrestling over necessary reforms in which I was often blocked by the Military Department, there is little of sufficient interest to record. I see from my diaries the joy brought into my life by the arrival to stay with me of a friend, reliable in peace or war, and with it all so clever at his profession, and whose gallant work in the field when attached to my battalion in Tirah (1897-8) I have already expatiated on—Colonel C. Manifold (now Major-General Sir Courtenay Manifold) of the Indian Medical Service. He had just returned from eight months' explorations in the wilds of China—a man of initiative and originality, who did not let the grass grow under his feet.

I must refer briefly to my official life at this time. I cannot say I enjoyed it, as I found it often vexatious and irritating. I hated to see my chief snubbed on every possible occasion, and his efforts to improve and modernise the army set at nought. The tone of the minutes on his recommendations was hurtful and trying, and, as one disagreeable incident succeeded another, I was rapidly beginning to realise that I should never be able to pull my weight or fulfil the role for which I had been sent out, and that the resignation of my appointment could not be long postponed. I will describe two incidents which finally decided me to put up with it no longer.

The one was in connection with the "so-called" Waziristan Blockade—I say "so-called" because it was for all intents and purposes as much a frontier campaign as many which had preceded it.

The Viceroy, however, possibly wishing it to be said at the end of his Viceroyalty that he had been able to control the wild tribes on the frontier without recourse to a campaign, had decreed that the operation was to be regarded as too insignificant to be called a campaign, but was to be dubbed a "blockade." In support of what I have said, I quote from a very charming and eloquent speech made by the Viceroy at a dinner which he and

Lady Curzon were giving to Sir Power and Lady Palmer at Vice-regal Lodge on the 19th March 1902:

> We have not, it is true, supplied him with any wider field of warfare in India itself or on its borders than a brush with the Mahsud Waziris, but I daresay that he may not have been sorry to escape another Tirah, and the energies which might have been dissipated on that most unprofitable of all undertakings, a frontier campaign.

And, although not relevant to this point, as an indication of the somewhat unpleasant experience Sir Power had had on the Viceroy's Council, I quote from part of his witty speech in reply, wherein his meaning is thinly veiled:

> I consider it a high privilege to have been a member of your Lordship's Council, and wish I could have been appointed to it at the age of twenty-five, as I look on its teaching as a most liberal education." (Laughter.) "Any intolerance or diversity of opinion that a man may feel on first joining it soon gives place to a beautiful Christian feeling of commiseration for those who are unable to see things through one's own spectacles. It is a privilege to have served on a Council in which such peace and harmony prevails. If one looks round the row of portraits of your Excellency's distinguished predecessors that adorn the Council's room it is impossible not to recollect that, if history can be believed, internecine war raged within the walls of the chamber in the days of Warren Hastings, and much later during contemporary history it has leaked out that the Finance Member did not always repose on a bed of roses; but the Council is a sort of pocket millennium.

To return to the "blockade." The operations were under General Sir Charles Egerton (afterwards a Field-Marshal). Besides regular troops, the Waziristan Militia had been employed—I should explain that the institution of local militias was entirely a child of Lord Curzon's, and an admirable conception they were.

Now, it was customary in all frontier operations for a political officer to accompany the military commander, and these militias were under his order.

The Viceroy in this case had allowed a young officer from his staff to be attached to the Waziristan Militia, and when the "blockade" was concluded and no mention was made of him in the general's dispatches, the Viceroy, in his own handwriting, demanded of Military Head-quarters, since he had heard the officer had done well, why his name had been omitted. I replied that, as he had not been under the general, I was not in a position to answer the conundrum, and suggested a reference to the political officer. The file was returned, minuted on by H.E. himself, saying he could not accept my suggestion, and that steps were to be taken instantly to have the officer mentioned. I again took up my pen, and in humble language repeated my previous suggestion, and in order to enable H.E. to appreciate that there was no lack of good intention on Sir Charles's part, I quoted the last paragraph of his dispatch to the following effect:

> Although it is not in my province to bring to notice the services performed by an auxiliary force, I cannot conclude without expressing an earnest hope that, when the time comes for honours and rewards, the excellent work performed by the Waziristan Militia will not be forgotten.

Having sent this off, my mind was at rest, and my astonishment can be imagined when, a day or two subsequently, back came the file again with a minute in the clear handwriting I had got to know so well, saying my views could not be accepted, but that H.E. insisted on steps being taken to have the officer mentioned, concluding with an unjustifiable remark of a disparaging nature about British generals as a class. I, highly indignant, took it straight to my chief; but the latter, always calm and imperturbable, thought it best to leave the matter alone, for he remarked that he was weary of scathing and disagreeable comments from the Viceroy, and that, as he was only officiating commander-in-chief and would soon be relieved by Lord Kitchener, he desired peace for the remainder of the time he was in office.

It was entirely out of sympathy for my chief that I did not resign then and there; I did not do so until a later date, when a proposal of mine of the utmost importance for the efficiency of the army was rejected. This was in connection with the education of officers. I had come to the conclusion that the standard of military knowledge amongst British officers of the Indian army was considerably below that of their brethren in the British army, who had to pass far higher tests of efficiency before they were regarded as qualified for promotion. I accordingly elaborated a scheme which would rectify this, and the scheme was approved by the commander-in-chief, but opposed by the Military Department.

It was decided that the commander-in-chief and his staff should meet the Military Department and discuss the whole question. We met—a somewhat stormy discussion resulted, and I was defeated. This was the last straw, and next day I explained to my chief that nothing would induce me to remain in such a false position a moment longer than was absolutely necessary. Sir Power implored me not to desert him, especially as the new commander-in-chief would be out in two months' time.

I, thereupon, agreed to hold over my written resignation, if he would allow me to go to England by the next mail, and explain the whole situation to Lord Kitchener, who had just arrived in England From the Cape. This he agreed to, and taking a budget of *précis* of all the vexed cases which had occurred in my time, including the two I have quoted vetoing the commander-in-chief's requests (1) to increase the number of camels in cavalry regiments, and (2) to institute the principle of promotion examinations, I reached London in August and sought out Lord Kitchener. I shall never forget that masterful man's face as I read and explained to him case after case. He fairly gasped out, "Is this the sort of thing I have got to compete with?"

I have dealt pretty fully with this subject, as Lord Kitchener has been accused of having gone to India with the firm intention of smashing the Military Department without possessing any real knowledge of their methods. I leave it to my readers to decide whether the fact of the senior staff officer in India asking to resign his appointment because of the difficulties imposed on him by the Indian Military Department system, and having himself given chapter and verse for the same, supported by telling illustrations, was not sufficient to convince any man that radical reforms were necessary. Lord Kitchener was somewhat disturbed by my proposed resignation, and begged me to return to India, if I only remained a month with him, until he had found someone to take my place; and this I agreed to do.

I made the most of the few weeks I was in England by getting married on the 3rd September, and of course had a good deal of official business to get through, but was back at Aden with my wife on the 12th October. I had to spend two days there inspecting the defences in my capacity as a member of the Indian Defence Committee. We were most hospitably entertained by the Resident, General Maitland, though heat and mosquitoes were very trying. We unfortunately got into a cyclone in the Indian Ocean, and had two as miserable days as I ever remember, but were comfortably established in our home, "Balquholly," at Simla on the 23rd October.

Then followed strenuous days of preparation for the army manoeuvres, which were to take place in the neighbourhood of Delhi, and also for the celebration of the Coronation of King Edward VII by a great assemblage and *durbar* at Delhi itself after the manoeuvres. We took up our abode in the Delhi camp on the 22nd November, and next day bade a sad farewell to Sir Power and Lady Palmer, who departed for England to make room for Lord Kitchener, shortly due at Bombay.

I will not attempt to describe the vast extent and magnificent comfort of the great camp, for the splendours of a *durbar* camp have been too often described to need repeating here.

On the 30th I went to Dholepore, where I joined Lord Kitchener and returned with him in his train to Delhi on the 1st December, and three days later the two opposing forces, a

Northern army of 22,000 under Sir Donald McLeod from Um-balla, and a Southern army of 14,000 under Sir Jocelyn Wode-house from Delhi, *i.e.* 120 miles apart, were loosed at each other. I was naturally deeply interested in the success of the manoeu-vres, as Sir Power, knowing he would not be present, and that I should have to assume the role of director and be responsible to the new commander-in-chief, had left the entire planning of the operations to me.

It was, therefore, gratifying to me that when Lord Kitchener arrived he told me to carry on, and was full of praise of the practical nature of the scheme and of the success of the whole operations, and expressed his satisfaction both during their con-tinuance and at the end. They continued almost incessantly un-til the 20th December, when troops moved into camp round Delhi, and prepared to perform their part, and a large one too, in a succession of durbar ceremonies, culminating in the grand review fixed for the 8th January.

A *durbar* assemblage in a setting of such magnificence had never been seen, and was only surpassed by the one held nine years later on the occasion of the visit of Their Imperial Majes-ties, King George V and Queen Mary, to India.

It is only fair to Lord Curzon to say that this latter was based on his conception and plans for the *durbar* I am now describing, and that it was in magnitude rather than in detail that it excelled. For instance, at the *Durbar* of 1902-3 there was only seating ac-commodation for 13,430 persons, whereas on the 12th Decem-ber 1911 the numbers thus provided for were over 70,000.

A committee, presided over by the Foreign Secretary, Sir Hugh Barnes, had assiduously worked out all the details, and except in regard to the army, which was none too well provided for,[1] nothing seemed to have been forgotten.

On the 29th December the state entry of the Viceroy, with their Royal Highnesses the Duke and Duchess of Connaught,

---

1. This lack of consideration for the army was also noticeable in the list of honours bestowed on this occasion. The army fared better in both respects in 1911, under the Viceroyalty of Lord Hardinge of Penshurst.

all mounted on elephants gorgeously caparisoned, followed by the Indian chiefs and high officials along six miles of road and streets lined by troops, was in its splendour a very befitting opening ceremony.

Next day the Arts Exhibition was opened, and on the 1st January the great *Durbar* took place, when the Viceroy, in the centre of an arena, horseshoe in shape, and surrounded by a handsome stand, made a speech in his best oratorical style, and then received the chiefs and their messages of congratulation to His Imperial Majesty the King on his Coronation.

On the succeeding days came the investiture of the Indian Orders, the State Open-air Thanksgiving Service on Sunday the 4th January, the State Ball of 5,000 people, the Review of Retainers of Native Chiefs—by no means the least interesting ceremony—and finally, on the 8th January, the Ceremonial Review of the Army of 30,000 officers and men.

This latter not unnaturally was the day I took most interest in. It certainly was a very fine sight, all in the bright full dress of those days, and everything went like clockwork.

It may be considered by those who appreciate that I was the responsible officer, that I am blowing my own trumpet, but both for this ceremony as well as for the manoeuvres all carefully thought out arrangements which brought success were due to the excellence of the head-quarters staff who worked with me. There was, however, one rather unpleasant incident which somewhat marred the proceedings. There had been considerable feeling shown amongst all the British troops by an occurrence at Sialkot some months before. One regiment was entertaining another, and a somewhat jovial evening resulted. In the course of the festivities a certain Indian cook named Ata died under suspicious circumstances. The local military authorities naturally took steps to trace how this man had met his death, and the general commanding the Punjab, as well as the commander-in-chief, were doing their utmost to trace the cause, and, should it prove a case of murder or culpable manslaughter, to bring someone to justice. A court of inquiry was assembled, and their opinion eagerly awaited.

The Viceroy, who was credited with always being ready to champion a native where British soldiers were concerned, was much excited over the case, and, not content to await the verdict of the court of inquiry, day after day bombarded army headquarters with demands, couched in terms none too pleasantly worded, that the verdict should be hurried up, accompanied with disparaging insinuations on army methods generally. It was most unpleasant for the commander-in-chief, for it was no fault of his that evidence took time to collect, and he was doing all he could to push things on. At last, the final report of the court of inquiry arrived at Simla and was instantly sent to the Viceroy. Unfortunately (1) the court had been unable to fix the responsibility for the death of Ata on anyone, and (2) the summing up by the general who forwarded the proceedings was certainly not in accordance with the evidence taken by the court.

At the time when I read the summing up, which I did before sending the dossier on to the Viceroy, I remarked to my personal assistant, a very capable and charming man (Mr. C. H. West, C.I.E.), "We shall hear no more about the commander-in-chief; General —— has fallen into the jaws of the lion."

Little did I think, though, how headlong he had done so, for next day, or certainly within two days, back came the dossier with a nice little minute covering some sixty to seventy sides of foolscap, in the Viceroy's own handwriting, simply rending the general in question, and tearing him limb from limb. As an example of powerful expression in perfect language, of hard hitting and savage invective, of laborious scrutiny and of biting metaphor, I cannot imagine a more perfect model; but, as the summing up of a ruler who could not be answered back, it did not commend itself to me.

In spite of there being no direct evidence and that circumstantial evidence was only sufficient to point with the hand of suspicion, the Viceroy insisted that one of the regiments concerned should be made to suffer and that their leave should be stopped. It was this decision which rankled in the mind of the army, and when the penalised regiment passed the saluting point with their lances at the carry, looking every inch what they were, namely, one of the crack cavalry regiments of the British army, a murmur of considerable volume arose, and some say it was hissing.

I cannot say I was pleased, for I had hoped the incident had been forgotten, and it seemed hard it should happen during this wonderful Coronation assembly, the beauty, perfect organisation and impressive ceremonies of which were entirely due to the unique powers of organisation and unrivalled brain of the Viceroy.

So far as the lighter side of this *durbar* assemblage was concerned, I did not really see much of the fun myself beyond what there was—and there was quite a lot—to be got out of official ceremonies I had to attend, for it so happened just at this time we had three operations to prepare for: (1) a Somaliland Expedition under General Sir Charles Egerton, (2) an Aden Boundary Commission, and (3) a Seistan Delimitation Commission the head of which was Lieutenant-Colonel A. H. McMahon,[2] a Political Officer who had already made his name on the frontier and who comes into my story again.

Lord Kitchener was always in splendid form, so cheery and happy and such a pleasant chief to serve, and I enjoyed it very much; but I reminded him from time to time that I had only agreed to remain on as adjutant-general until he had found a suitable successor, and about the middle of February he told me he was satisfied he had found the right man in my deputy, Beauchamp Duff, and that if I would remain on another two months I could then take command of a 1st Class District if I liked; and he kept his word.

Had circumstances been such as to necessitate my remaining on the staff, I am sure I should have been perfectly happy with Lord Kitchener, for he was most interesting and instructive, and much less secretive than I had imagined. He discussed every

2. Now Sir Henry McMahon, G.C.M.G., G.C.V.O., High Commissioner in Egypt, 1914-1916.

sort of question openly with me and told me his views, always searching and far-reaching. He had a fascinating habit, when he was considering a question, of speaking his thoughts, arguing with himself all the pros and cons, then summing up and coming to a decision. It was in February that the commander-in-chief paid his first visit to the frontier beyond Peshawar, leaving me behind to "mind the shop."

Festivities in Calcutta were never-ending, and one seldom dined at home. Perhaps the evening I enjoyed most was an old Harrovian dinner given by A. A. Apcar, at which we sat down nineteen.

My new appointment was command of the 4th Division in Baluchistan and at the end of April we were settled at Quetta, a charming spot some 5,700 feet above the sea. The cantonment was in a large plain bounded by snow-capped peaks up to 12,000 feet and distant from the cantonment from six to eighteen miles. A most perfect climate, where everything grew, beautiful fruit and flowers, etc. Hot in summer, though nothing compared with the plains of India, and in winter frost and snow. Occasionally the cold was piercing, and I have vivid recollections of one day when it was blowing hard and the glass stood at ten degrees below zero.

Colonel C. E. Yate—now Sir Charles Yate, Bart.—was installed at the Residency as agent to the governor-general and was succeeded by Mr. A. L. P. Tucker.

From a command point of view, with a frontier of some 800 miles, much of it along the Afghan border, and with sufficient troops to carry out interesting manoeuvres, it was hard to beat.

The tours of inspection of all the outlying stations and frontier posts, which I did about twice a year, were perhaps the most delightful experiences of my five years in Quetta. I will briefly describe my first as a matter of some interest, which I commenced eight days after taking over my new command. First, relays of horses had to be arranged for at the several posts, the first being at the station where I was to leave the railway. I actually averaged just over forty miles a day, the whole tour, lasting twelve days, being spent in inspecting the two large garrisons of Loralai and Fort Sandeman. The country traversed was at a high level, varying from 3,000 to 6,500 feet, and was through a mass of mountainous ranges of the most fantastic and weird shapes, most of them of a rocky and bare description, almost devoid of trees and vegetation beyond rough scrub.

The strata, which was strangely visible, was of a contorted, tilted, and twisted description, and would be of intense interest to a geologist. Patches of cultivation occurred here and there, and larger tracts near the Zhob and other rivers; the crops appeared to be good, especially where water was abundant. The excellent system of irrigation by gravitation, so common in the East, was the one in vogue.

There was very little animal life to be seen, and even birds were conspicuous by their scarcity. The country was sparsely populated, but the inhabitants, Pathans (pronounced Pattarns) were a remarkably fine race of men; tall, of dignified carriage, bearded, with Semitic noses. At each place at which I stopped, especially in the Zhob Valley, I was met by all the big-wigs of the locality, such as the Tehsildar (Government Agent), and the Maliks (big landowners), and at one place by the chief of the whole Zhob Valley, Mahomed Akbar Khan Bahadur, a very handsome man with a long black beard. Magnificent scenery was met day after day, and some of the steep and narrow gorges—forbidding spots, of doubtful reputation, associated with outrages and savage murders—which had to be negotiated, made one glad that the inhabitants were friendly.

The actual road in some places showed very considerable engineering skill. The country was indescribably wild and rough, and the road was often cut out along the face of sheer cliffs with a drop of many hundred feet if one left the track, and built and held up by rough timbers in places to get round awkward corners. The railway itself is a wonderful engineering feat, passing up and down steep gradients, and through tortuous tunnels, over awe-inspiring bridges with torrents raging far below, and along the face of cliffs, round corners and through gorges, the giddy heights and perilous possibilities of which might well alarm the least faint-hearted. I believe the building of this remarkable railway, which has stood the test of time, was due largely to the brain and initiative of a Royal Engineer officer, General Sir James Brown, at one time Administrator of Baluchistan, in which position he made a name which will endure.

The whole trip was a great pleasure to me, and I can never forget the cordiality and hospitality with which I was received by all the units I had to inspect. It was my invariable rule, if I dined with a regiment and was invited to play pool, to accept, as I found that a game round the billiard-table gave me a better opportunity of getting to know the officers personally than any other way. Baluchistan is a monument to the genius of the British race for government, and particularly is the name of Sir Robert Sandeman associated with the peaceful development of this wild and large portion of the globe. They are a difficult people, but understand a friendly attitude in the agent to the governor-general, combined with justice, firmness, and a paternal interest in their affairs.

Although Quetta was nearly 6,000 feet up and never really hot, it boasted of a hill station 2,200 feet higher still, called Ziarat. A really lovely spot in the middle of a juniper forest with a wealth of wild-flowers, outstanding amongst which was the shumshob, a beautiful violet-blue flower which had a growth like lavender, and being in large patches impressed its vivid colour on the landscape generally.

Baluchistan is a fascinating country to wander about in, for it has endless surprises in store for one, such as large trees growing out of bare rocks, and rivers which suddenly disappear into the ground, and others appearing from the heart of a mountain at the bottom of a *tangi*. I will endeavour to describe a *tangi*. It really means a narrow place, and is in fact like an enormously deep crack, or crevice, through a mountain. I have known them just a few feet wide at the bottom and with absolutely perpendicular sides rising several hundred feet—so narrow that, riding along the bottom, one could touch both sides with an ordinary stick. These *tangis* form at times the only track connecting one valley with another.

One of the most interesting surprises I had on one of my long rides, was, on suddenly coming over a low pass, to find below me, within 300 yards, a widish sandy river-bed, with a clear shallow stream running through it; but the water, except here and there where it glistened in the brilliant sunlight, was barely visible owing to an enormous mass of birds drinking. It took me some time to realise that the birds were chikor collected from the hillsides round for their midday drink at one of the few streams in the neighbourhood which had not dried up. It really was a remarkable sight—there must have been many thousands of them.

Dismounting, I watched them through my glasses until they, having drunk their fill, gradually winged themselves away to the hills and valleys—whence they had collected. One feature of this gathering was not unlike a flock of human beings collected for purposes of quenching thirst, and that was the incessant chattering—really a very weird sound. The chikor is the chief game-bird in this part of the world. It is like a red-legged partridge in appearance and markings, and has habits akin to the grouse and the ptarmigan—a combination of the two—and it is remarkable how numbers vary in different seasons.

When I was in Quetta the seasons were especially good, and large bags were obtained. The head of the police of the district, "Beaty," was an adept at circumventing these wary birds. I believe his patent plan was to keep a valley quiet and attract them to it by frequent scatterings of grain, whilst disturbing their rest in neighbouring hills and valleys. At any rate, he accounted for very big bags. One September, with I think four guns, he got about 300 brace in two and a half days, and in 1906, when Lord Minto the Viceroy paid Quetta a visit, he at my request arranged a shoot towards Nushki, and we got over 120 brace in three hours' driving, instead of the usual way of walking them up. These, of course, were exceptionally good years, and since then I hear bags have been much smaller.

One very cold winter, when the whole countryside was many feet under snow, the birds came down into the cantonments, and many of them were knocked on the head.

Quetta was a cheery little station, where there was always plenty to do. We had our race meetings, at which I held my own, especially at one, when I won two steeple-chases and one hurdle-race, riding my own horses, a feat of which, as a lieutenant-general, I was rather proud.

We had, too, an excellent pack of hounds, and quite a good country, and I can see now the Viceroy, Lord Minto, with Lady Minto and their three daughters, at the head of the hunt, in a fast run, one of them having the misfortune to fall into a *kareze* (a watercourse), out of which she came dripping and unconcerned. My wife was always well to the fore in these runs.

I found recreation grounds somewhat limited, especially for the troops; in fact, they were worse than limited, for they were over two miles from barracks and therefore seldom used. Again, there were no amusements for the men, and only a not very attractive native bazaar, with all its attendant ills, for them to spend their spare time in. The cantonment covered a large area, and was built on sloping ground, the upper part, where the barracks were, being bare, unattractive, and devoid of shade.

From them sloped a wide, rugged waste, covered with stones and furrowed by the rains of ages. I conceived the idea of turning this into a park by removing all the surface stones and cutting it into levelled terraces. It was a great work, but before I left was successfully accomplished, giving many grass football and cricket grounds, and well planted with trees. In the midst of it we built a really very fine club for the men, with a dry and wet canteen, supper-rooms, a billiard-room for four tables, a dance-room convertible into a theatre, and some fourteen hot and cold baths.

My difficulty was money, but, so sure was I of its success, that I borrowed money myself and started it. It was run entirely by non-commissioned officers and men under the watchful eye of Captain Basil Ready, my D.A.A.G., and was a great success, and my money was soon repaid. I always held that to develop the characters of men it was essential to give them responsibility and to encourage them to use their initiative, and I carried this out, not only in administration, but also in field training and operations. It certainly took time to eradicate the idea that they could only work if everything was done for them by their officers, and that they could not be trusted.

My motto always was, and still is, "It is only possible to get the best results out of troops if they are made to feel that they are trusted and encouraged to use their own intelligence and initiative, and that such is only possible in the field if the object in a commander's mind and information as to developments are frequently circulated." I remember the committee of the club requesting that a military piquet should always be in attendance in case any men were guilty of rowdyism or breaking club rules—a request I refused, and they very soon learned how to maintain order themselves. I always advocated giving the men more freedom, and I especially carried it out when I took up the Aldershot command, of which I will tell later; and I never had cause to regret it.

I was amused, one day, when my wife told me it was evident I was popular, for one of the bandmasters had told her so, remarking that I was like a real gentleman, and not a bit like a general.

The country round Quetta lent itself to every form of training for war, and we took advantage of it to the full by small manoeuvres and big manoeuvres, small staff rides and large staff rides, artillery practice and musketry on the ranges. But shooting under battle conditions at active service targets was particularly developed, and this was rendered easy, owing to the large stretches of uninhabited country, with natural hill stop-butts to intercept shells and bullets—what may be termed "Glorified Field Firing." One of the most ambitious of these operations happened to take place in 1906, when the then Viceroy, Lord Minto, was present—about which anon.

The large manoeuvre staff rides were carried out by skeleton forces, and, to explain how they were carried out, I had best describe one of them. The one I have chosen was a single staff ride—that is to say, the enemy were not represented—but the double staff rides, when the opposing forces were both represented, were conducted on much the same lines.

The force was a complete division of all arms and a brigade of cavalry. I, as director and G.O.C., had my complete staff, and each brigade similarly had its brigadier and staff; but the units, though only represented by the commanding officer and adjutant, had with them all their signallers, so that a real and complete system of communication could be maintained. The work was carried on exactly as if all the troops had been present. The general idea was as follows: "A hostile force is reported to be moving from Persia, and has reached Nushki (distant ninety-five miles). The Quetta Division will move at once to get into touch with it. The cavalry brigade will make good the roads 'a, b, c, and d,' keeping ten miles ahead of the division, etc., etc."

Three roads about nine miles apart were allotted to the three infantry brigades, and the G.O.C. kept them informed which brigade he was marching with. Thus moving fifteen miles a day the force advanced on a front of twenty miles. The cavalry had sealed envelopes, to be opened at hours stated on them, giving them imaginary information which they were supposed to have obtained, and this was signalled in, and acted on. At times I, as G.O.C., sent imaginary information entailing fresh orders being issued. In this way fresh problems had to be thought out and fresh orders written and issued.

I found the system most valuable, and being original I have thought it worthwhile describing. Each brigade had its conference after the day's work, and I held them myself from time to time, concluding with a long one at the end of the staff ride when everything was thoroughly discussed. Finally, on return to barracks a paper of comments and lessons learnt was printed and circulated. Similar methods were adopted as to conferences at manoeuvres when every officer, British and native, attended. At the autumn manoeuvres, for which all available troops in the command were concentrated, we had over 200 officers present, and everyone was encouraged to raise questions. I have no hesitation in saying that in this way the best possible results were obtained, for all officers, British and native, were drawn into taking great interest and into subsequent discussions amongst themselves, which resulted in a practical understanding of military problems and promotion of initiative.

My chief, Sir Archibald Hunter, an old friend of mine and then commander-in-chief Western command, was most appreciative of my efforts, and his visits to us when making inspections gave very great pleasure. I have happy recollections of his accompanying me twice on long frontier tours. I was very much pleased, one year, to receive a much larger grant of money for training and manoeuvres than any other divisional general in India on the grounds that the chief knew the money would be well spent.

Another matter which pleased me much was a reply to a reference made to Inspector-General of Cavalry Major-General Douglas Haig. He had been staying with us for a few days in March of this year, when inspecting the cavalry of my command, and shortly afterwards I submitted to him my scheme for cavalry training and manoeuvres, which he returned to me, remarking that he could not improve on it. I did not foresee then that in about fourteen years' time it would be due to his genius that our armies were being led to victory in the greatest war that has ever been fought. It was about this time that I received the sad news of the death of my old friend and late Commander-in-Chief Sir Power Palmer.

The event which perhaps made the deepest impression at Quetta in 1903 was the death of the great Lord Salisbury, the profound statesman who had proved such a splendid steward of the Empire, and who for so many years had loomed large in the Councils of Europe.

February of the next year certainly had events of interest, Firstly, my eldest son was born on the fourth anniversary of my promotion to the rank of major-general. Secondly, the Russo-Japanese War broke out. Thirdly, Quetta was visited by a certain

Lieutenant-Colonel Korniloff, who then had the reputation of being one of Russia's most rising soldiers, and who was to prove himself no mean general in the Great War. His visit was somewhat embarrassing, for he had come with the intention of proceeding to Russia *via* Nushki, Seistan, and Persia, whilst I had received instructions from the Government of India that I was to prevent his doing so.

Further, I was told I was not to show him any of our troops, barracks, or defensive arrangements. The reasons for these instructions were, as regards the former, that as we were a neutral country no assistance should be given to either Russians or Japanese, and, as regards the latter, that the paw of the Russian Bear was thought to be ever ready to strike at India, and the less known to them of our military preparations the better. There was nothing left to me, in order to gloss over the official discountenance I was to show him, except a warm and friendly social greeting. Colonel Korniloff accepted the situation in the best possible spirit, and during his three days' stay made himself most agreeable at the dinners, luncheons, and garden-parties given in his honour, and then departed *via* Bombay.

There was a fourth event, however, which I have left until last, for it was by far the most important and gave rise at the time to much controversy, heart-burnings, and sweeping criticisms. I refer to the operations of a special committee, which had been set up with full powers to alter the system of Army Control at the Head-quarters of the British army. The triumvirate forming this omnipotent committee consisted of Lord Esher, Admiral Sir John (afterwards Lord) Fisher, and Colonel Sir George Sydenham Clarke (now Lord Sydenham), and one fine morning all the high officials of the War Office, on reaching their respective offices, were, to say the least of it, surprised to find a notice on their tables saying their appointments had ceased to exist, as in future the affairs of the army would be controlled by an Army Council.

In this curt manner many high officials at the War Office received their *congé*. Whether such drastic upheaval was really necessary to bring about the excellent reforms, including the development of a general staff, which have come in since, or whether the recommendation of the committee could not have produced equally good results under a commander-in-chief, I shall not attempt to discuss, but I think most people will agree that such inconsiderate methods (for which the triumvirate may or may not have been responsible) of clearing the road for the introduction of the Army Council appear to have been unnecessary, and to form an example of how not to do a thing.

At first chaos was the result, and this was well described by a War Office official in a letter to me as follows: "It is just as if the authorities had taken a motor-car and smashed it up and then called in people entirely ignorant of motorcars to repair the damages."

It was in March this year that the eloquent Bishop of Lahore, of whom I have already spoken, paid us a visit, and was good enough to christen my first-born.

The Russo-Japanese War by now was in full swing, and provided plenty of food for discussion. I see from my letters that I had an animated discussion with my dear old mother, who followed every move, and at first was all in favour of victory falling to the Christian adversary. She disliked the idea of a heathen country getting the upper hand, to which I replied that I felt sure the Almighty would prefer honest heathens to a country posing as civilised Christians and whose diplomats no one could believe. General Oku's victory at Wafanchan in June was particularly interesting to me, as I had got to know him when he visited Calcutta some eighteen months previously.

We had, too, a small campaign of our own in progress nearer home, for the expedition into the heart of Tibet under the guidance of Lieutenant-Colonel Younghusband (now Sir Francis Younghusband) was taking place.

This year, 1904, was full of interest, for in it I obtained the services of a most efficient officer as *aide-de-camp*—Lieutenant R. A. Cassels of the 32nd Indian Lancers, who distinguished himself much as a cavalry leader in the Great War, and is now a major-general and Technical Adviser on Cavalry to the commander-in-chief in India.

During it, too, the institution of a Staff College in India was decided on, and Quetta was selected for its location, the site and plan of which were assigned by Lord Kitchener to me to deal with. Again the disagreements between the Viceroy and commander-in-chief were becoming acute, though they did not reach their climax until the following year, and numerous rumours of their intensity found their way to Quetta.

I am bound to admit, although my sympathies were largely with Lord Kitchener in view of my own experiences and my strong opinion that some drastic clipping of the wings of the Military Department had become an absolute necessity, that I felt that he was going too far and was creating a system which, by tying the commander-in-chief to the head-quarters of the Government, would seriously curtail the time available for personal tours and inspections of the army by the commander-in-chief.

Now these tours, by which the commander-in-chief became personally known to the soldiers of India, were, I have no doubt, of the utmost importance, and had a very real influence on the loyalty of the army to the Crown. Therefore any increase in the duties of the commander-in-chief which might curtail them struck me as a reform in the wrong direction, and I can well understand Lord Curzon's objecting. It was argued at the time that, could a commander-in-chief of the calibre of Lord Kitchener be always counted on, there was no danger in the reforms, but there I was not in accord, for I felt then, and still feel, that from the time of their introduction the personal inspection of troops by the commander-in-chief diminished and his magnetic influence grew small by degrees and dangerously less.

Later on, when it was a question of Sir Beauchamp Duff or myself going out to India as commander-in-chief to succeed Sir O'Moore Creagh, I made it clear that I would only go if a general officer was appointed to take charge under me, of all administrative services, thus leaving me free for getting into personal touch with the troops, so as to regain, in the minds of the Indian Army, the prestige of the *Jungi Lad Sahib* (the Indian soldier's name for the commander-in-chief). As I write these *Memoirs* (April 1924) it is distinctly pleasing to me that the present commander-in-chief in India has found such an appointment necessary, for it has actually been made.

Duff was chosen and I was left, and it was lucky for me I was, or I should have missed the, to a soldier, much more valuable appointment, namely, command of troops at the front in the Great War. In November I was summoned to meet the commander-in-chief at Hyderabad Sind, when Lord Kitchener gave me details of his new arrangement of command. This increased my command, which was limited to Baluchistan, by the addition of Sind, thus giving me a territory larger than England and Wales combined.

After leaving Hyderabad I paid my first visit of inspection to my newly acquired port of Karachi, where Mr. A. D. Younghusband, C.S.I., the commissioner of Sind, was in residence. On the railway between Karachi and Quetta there is a place called Larkena, famous during the month of November, when a certain canal overflows its banks and floods the surrounding country, for wild-fowl which rest there on their annual flight southwards into India.

Mr. Younghusband had just received news that the birds were in, and finding that neither the Viceroy, the commander-in-chief, nor himself could spare the time to indulge in a duck shoot, and knowing that the birds would not remain there many days, offered the shoot to me on my return journey to Quetta. Eagerly accepting and arriving at Larkena early one morning, I was met by the local collector, who told me, if a morning shoot was decided on, after a few shots the duck would disappear, but that if I would wait until 2 p.m. he could promise a large bag.

My party was only three: a very great friend of mine, at that time employed as a remount officer, Major Patterson of the 5th Bengal Cavalry, my *aide-de-camp* (and nephew), Eddy Dorrien-Smith, and myself; but the collector said he could produce seven local guns.

Well, we shot from 2 p.m. to 4.30, when it got dark, a bare two and a half hours, and the total bag was over 700 duck, of which my party of three accounted for 450. I mention this incident as an example of the standard of sport India can produce.

Shortly after arriving back at Quetta I started off on my next inspection of Loralai and Fort Sandeman, and my wife accompanied me. It was hard work for a lady, for we did some forty miles a day, almost entirely on horseback, and the rest-places we spent our nights in were hardly luxurious. There was one in particular at which, though she said nothing at the time, she admitted, years after, she had spent a jumpy night—for on reaching it she had been told by the native in charge that the room she was to sleep in had been the one into which some months before Pathans had broken one night and murdered Colonel Gaisford—a dastardly crime of which we had heard much talk since our arrival in Baluchistan.

Just before starting on this trip we had been fired with news from home to the effect that a Russian fleet under Admiral Rozhdestvensky, on its way to reinforce their Fleet in Japanese waters, had sunk two or three British trawlers near the Dogger Bank. The question arose, "Was it a case of nerves, or was it an act of deliberate aggression?" For, if the latter, war with Russia, a very important matter to us at Quetta, could not be avoided. It was ruled to be a case of nerves, and the fleet continued on its way—to meet its fate at the hands of the Japanese Admiral Togo the following May. The newspapers at the time were much excited, and the name of the Admiral provided the wags with much copy. One of them, after Robert Southey's poem *Moscow 1912*, wrote:

And after all this an Admiral came,
A terrible man with a terrible name,
A name which we all of us know very well,
But no one can speak and no one can spell.

Early in 1905 my wife and son went home, and I devoted my

time to carrying out what were styled "The Kitchener Tests."

One of Lord Kitchener's methods of squeezing as much as possible out of subordinates was to encourage emulation. It came to his mind that, in order to raise the standard of military training, it would be an excellent idea to give two cups for the best-trained infantry battalion in the British and Indian Services respectively. He, therefore, had a very exhaustive programme drawn up, embodying exercises in every form of military training and operation.

Every general commanding a district or division had to form a board, with himself as president, to carry out these tests and decide which was his best battalion in each service. Then each command carried out the test between the best battalions of each division. There were four commands, so at the end of these tests four British and four native battalions were left in. Finally an Army Head-quarters Board tested these eight battalions, and the best British and best native battalion in India were selected.

It was undoubtedly a great conception, and raised the standard of military efficiency to a far higher plane; but it took up an immense amount of time, for it required the best part of a week to test each battalion, though it was possible in some exercises to test more than one battalion at a time. Then for the successful battalions, especially those in the final, it was really very hard and time-absorbing work.

So it was not continued, especially as the chief considered that it had achieved its object.

I think the soldier who most impressed me when I was at Quetta was Lieutenant-Colonel Jacob, commanding the 106th Hazara—a thoroughly sound man, with a personality which commanded the respect and affection of all associated with him. He commanded an army corps in the Great War, and is now General Sir Claud Jacob, K.C.B., K.C.M.G., lately chief of the general staff in India.

On the 11th July I received the very gratifying news that I had been made full colonel of my own old regiment, the Sherwood Foresters, and on the 22nd I went on leave to England.

The only incident worth recording during my leave was my attendance at the Kaiser manoeuvres in Germany, when I was immensely, and adversely, impressed by their lack of grasp of modern conditions, especially by the close order in which they moved to attack and the rapidity with which they moved against each other, regardless of fire. My note in my diary regarding one action where two divisions were opposing each other is: "A hammer-and-tongs battle with impossible situations, over in one hour after infantry came into contact."

On the 6th January I was invited to a most interesting lunch at the Carlton Hotel given by an old Staff College friend, Colonel Repington, so well known as a writer on military subjects. I met there Mr. John Morley, who had just become Secretary of State for India (afterwards Viscount Morley), Mr. Buckle, then editor of *The Times,* Sir Ian Hamilton, Lord Esher, and Sir George Sydenham Clarke (now Lord Sydenham), the last two being very much in the public eye then as having recently formed with Admiral Sir John Fisher (Lord Fisher) the *triumvirate* which introduced the Army Council. Discussions on the burning problems of the day by men "in the know" were worth listening to. I sat next to Mr. Morley, a very delightful neighbour, and hearing I was a general in India, he invited me to call on him at the India Office. This I did a few days later, and was surprised to find that he apparently had no knowledge of the people or the country. He was most open about it though, and made me take a map and give him a little lecture on the subject, and as his time was limited then, he insisted on my going again.

This I did a day or two before I sailed for India, and his final remark raised doubts in my mind as to whether I had proved an efficient instructor in geography, for he gave me a message to deliver to someone in Calcutta as I passed through that city on my way to Quetta. I had often heard of ministers being selected to guide departments of which they could have had no previous knowledge, but this was my first personal experience, and I went out from his presence marvelling more than ever how our ship of State ever kept afloat, when it was so often steered by square men in round holes. Only those people who approve of Morley's Indian Reforms, which paved the way for the disastrous Montagu policy, will regard him as a success at the India Office. I would compare him with another Minister who at the same time had become Secretary of State for War, with, I believe, as little knowledge of the Army as Morley had of India, but who was an undoubted success; I refer to Mr. (now Viscount) Haldane. I know by stating this that I run the risk of being dubbed by a friend of mine "a military Simple Simon"—*vide* comments on Lord Haldane in *The National Review* of March 1924—but the army and nation owe it to Lord Haldane that, when the Great War broke out, we had an efficient mobilisation scheme, providing six divisions ready for war, a territorial force behind it of fourteen divisions, and an officers' training corps as a reserve of officers.

Just after returning with my wife to Quetta, that place was honoured by the visit of the Prince and Princess of Wales, the present king and queen. Their suite consisted of, amongst others, Lord and Lady Shaftesbury, Sir Walter Lawrence, Sir Arthur Bigge (now Lord Stamfordham), Sir Charles Cust, Derek Keppel, Clive Wigram, etc. They spent altogether nine days in my command, and won the hearts of everyone. Their Royal Highnesses went everywhere, and saw everything, and were so informal and genial that my wife and I always regard their visit as one of the most agreeable incidents in our lives. Perhaps one of the most enjoyable days was one spent in a visit to the high ground some thirty miles away overlooking Afghanistan. We went in the Royal train about fifteen miles and then rode, except Her Royal Highness, who went in our carriage to the foot of Wolseley Ridge. The latter was 2,000 feet above us, and very steep, and the Princess was carried up it in a sedan-chair.

On the previous evening I had been showing our stud to Sir Arthur Bigge, and had pointed out my wife's favourite hunter, Muskerry, as the most reliable horse for the prince to ride next day, when it gave two or three light-hearted bucks, causing Sir Arthur to place a veto on its being allotted to H.R.H. I said the only alternative was a prodigy of a mule, who had never been known to forget himself, and the mule was decided on.

What was our horror, directly the prince mounted, to see this usually docile creature put its head between its forelegs and indulge in bucks and kicks to which Muskerry's had been child's-play. Luckily H.R.H. was quite unconcerned by this ebullition of good spirits, and as the mule's activities made no impression on his seat, the prince merely waited until our prodigy had finished enjoying himself, and then rode him quietly up the hill. From the top a magnificent view of Afghanistan was obtained, and I had to give a little lecture, pointing out the nature of our defences and the possible lines of advance of the Russians, who were thought to be the most likely enemy to attack us. I was much amused by the prince's chaffingly telling Clive Wigram (at that time assistant to Sir Walter Lawrence) to listen most carefully, as it might help him in his examination for the Staff College, which he was shortly to undergo.

It was all so cheery and pleasant. One night, I remember, when Their Royal Highnesses honoured us at dinner, I asked the princess if I should propose His Majesty the King's health, and she said, "Yes, certainly; but don't drink us." After dinner I mentioned "Bridge," and H.R.H. eagerly said he would like a game, as he rarely got an opportunity.

We were very sorry when, on the 17th March, we saw H.M.S. *Renown* sail with our royal visitors from Karachi. Just before the ship sailed my wife presented Her Royal Highness with a bunch of shamrock, just to show that Ireland is not the only place where St. Patrick's Day is remembered.

Lord Kitchener had by this time started on a long frontier inspection, and I had to fly off from Karachi to meet him where he entered my command at the wild and beautiful Dhana Pass, on the Waziristan frontier, fifty-nine miles beyond Fort Sandeman, the extreme north-east corner of my kingdom. It was a somewhat severe journey, for Cassels, my A.D.C., and I, besides a three-hour train journey, had 225 miles to ride, and we did it in five days.

We found the chief, accompanied by his military secretary, Birdwood (now General Sir William Birdwood and a possible future commander-in-chief), and two *aide-de-camps*, Brooke and Wylly, in the very happiest of moods.

It took us seven days, part of which the chief drove, to get back to Quetta, where he in his best form spent three nights with us, and then returned to Simla.

Just after his departure we had a very interesting guest in the well-known explorer, Dr. Sven Hedin, on his way back to civilisation from "the roof of the world," the Pamirs.

In June I was summoned to Simla, where I spent four days, staying with the chief. My immediate chief, Sir Archibald Hunter, was also there. Lord Kitchener had a charming house, Wildflower Hall, at Mashobra, some ten miles beyond Simla, and over 8,000 feet above the lovely spot.

Hunter and I stayed there one night with the chief, and were much interested in a guest who came to lunch. It was the Chinese commissioner, who arrived with his interpreter—a very agreeable person, with whom we imagined the chief wished to discuss affairs of state, but it appeared that the true reason for his being invited was because he was an expert on oriental china—and after lunch Lord Kitchener put some pieces in front of him, saying that he was meditating giving £150 for them. The Chinaman took them up, just glanced at them, and through his interpreter told Lord Kitchener that they were not worth two *rupees*. The chief was glad he had asked him to lunch.

Lord Minto was then Viceroy, and it was on this occasion I first had the pleasure of meeting him and his delightful family.

I shall never forget my journey to and from Quetta. June, being just before the rains break, is the hottest month in the year, and the Sind Desert through which the railway runs is the hottest part of India, the shade thermometer going up to 126° at Jacobadad and in the valley of the Indus about Sukkur.

The dust is appalling, and, with the ill-fitting windows and doors which existed in those days, nothing could keep it out, and it stood inches deep over everything. One simply sat and dripped, and the dust became mud on one's face and limbs. The joy of reaching the Bolan Pass and rising to the Quetta plain, after forty-eight hours of indescribable discomfort, still looms large in my memories of the past.

In July the news of a very sad event reached us. The beautiful and charming Lady Curzon, who had been so kind to my wife and myself, had died, and our hearts went out in sympathy with Lord Curzon.

The next event worth recording was the autumn manoeuvres—which this year were on a big scale—all the troops in my command being assembled in an area north-east of Quetta. Part of the squadron, battery, and company field training this summer had been the preparation of a great entrenched position on the lines of the Russo-Japanese War.

The idea was that an army had dug itself in on a position of great length with unturnable flanks, and that 2,000 yards in the centre of the position should be actually prepared in every particular, and eventually be available for an attack by the whole of my command troops as a wind-up to the manoeuvres.

The position was laid out on the most up-to-date lines during the spring and summer; first line trenches, second line trenches, third line trenches—the latter complete with dug-outs for orderly-rooms, kitchens, latrines, sleeping-places for troops, and magazines, all of them labelled, and the whole connected up by communication trenches. Behind were hidden emplacements for the bulk of the guns, whilst there were several in the advanced trenches.

Deep holes where men could be perfectly safe were dug behind the gun emplacements from which, in order to simulate guns firing, they could let off bombs so as to make it as realistic as possible. On some of the trenches a certain number of *chatties* (earthenware pots) about the size of a man's head were placed, and, about a mile to the front and a little to one side of this 2,000-yard front, a small position was dug to represent a cavalry outpost to be attacked by the cavalry on the first day.

The manoeuvres, in which each commander had an especially free hand, lasted for about ten days—and then both forces were united some three or four miles from the position, and a regular systematic attack carried out with shot and shell, with hand-grenades and trench-mortars. These latter had been prepared by a very skilful Royal Engineer officer, lately Lieutenant-Colonel Pridham, C.R.E. at Gibraltar.

The whole scheme was explained to every man, and the first day the covering troops established themselves under artillery fire about 1,700 yards from the position at sundown, and dug in during the night. Next night they were reinforced and moved forward about 800 yards, and again dug in before daylight. The third night a further advance of 400 or 500 yards was made, and fresh trenches dug. Not a man was allowed to show himself by daylight, and dead silence was *de rigueur.* All food, ammunition, blankets, etc., were carried up during each night. On the fourth night it was decided to rush the position at dawn, covered by the bomb-throwers, after an overwhelming fire from guns, rifles, and trench-mortars. These latter had been established in a trench within 300 yards of the position.

It was a very impressive operation. The fire and noise were terrific, and the bombs, representing the guns in position, made it very realistic.

Directly it was over, and before the troops were allowed to fall out, each squadron, battery, and company was led by its commander round the whole defensive position, so that every point might be explained to them.

Looking back on it now, it was quite a good forecast of the trench warfare in the Great War.

I should mention that behind the position rose a great hill, which acted as a perfect stop-butt for bullets and shell. To prevent the operations becoming too irksome to the troops there was a six-hours' armistice on each day of this attack, when they were allowed out of the trenches.

Fortunately the Viceroy had selected this time for his visit to Quetta. He was present during the last three days of the manoeuvres, also for a time on each of the days preceding the assault on the position, and finally with Lady Minto and their three daughters at the assault on the morning of the last day.

After all was over we held a conference at which all officers, British and native, were present, and the lessons of the operation were fully discussed—a discussion in which both the Viceroy and Sir Archibald Hunter took part.

The Viceroy spent altogether eight days in Quetta, and it was during this visit that the hunt and chikor shoot, already mentioned, took place.

Lord Minto was my *beau-ideal* of an English "*Sahib*" and sportsman, and it was to those assets I believe his success as a ruler was so largely due. As a sportsman he won many important steeplechases and rode in the Grand National at Liverpool four times, as "Mr. Rolly," which alone gives him a special niche in the Temple of Fame.

Early in January of 1907 a very great event occurred in my life, for I was selected to succeed Sir John French at the end of the year as commander-in-chief at Aldershot, the plum of the British army, largely owing to recommendations made by Sir John and Lord Kitchener to the Secretary of State, Mr. Haldane.

I, having to attend the Poona manoeuvres in the middle of the month, started off with my wife on a most enjoyable trip. We first stayed with Sir Archibald Hunter, who had collected a large party at Poona to see the manoeuvres, and most hospitably he entertained us. Commander-in-Chief Lord Kitchener, and staff were amongst his guests. The manoeuvres, which were full of interest, were directed by one of the best of good fellows and sportsmen, General Sir George Richardson, an Irishman, so well known later as commander-in-chief of the Ulster Army.

From there we went on to visit the Mintos and Lord Kitchener at Calcutta. It was the height of the season there—the *pièce de résistance* being Lady Minto's Fête—quite one of the best entertainments I have seen outside Earl's Court. It had taken months to prepare: every form of amusement was to be found there, and side-shows of great variety were provided, and all thought out by the capable brain of the lady it was called after. The proceeds were to go to a child of her own which still thrives, "The Lady Minto Nursing Fund."

But what made our visit to Calcutta at this time so deeply interesting was the presence of that remarkable personality, Habibullah, the *Amir* of Afghanistan. He had been met on his own frontier by Sir Henry McMahon, who was to be his guide, philosopher, and friend deputed by the Government. Sir Henry, on meeting him, presented him with a cordial letter from King Edward, greeting him as a fellow Sovereign. This recognition of him as a king was very pleasing to him, and he realised at once that he would be called His Majesty and soon showed that he intended to be treated as such.

No ruler of that wild country across our borders had ever visited Calcutta, and it took all the diplomacy and tact of Sir Henry to persuade him to venture out of his own kingdom. He had never entered a civilised country where such modern inventions as railways, telegraphs, motorcars, etc., were part of everyday life, and was nervous and suspicious. Sir Henry told me himself that, having at last got the *Amir* as far as the Jamrud railway station, and showed him a train into which he was expected to get, he jibbed badly, became overcome with suspicion, and actually wanted to return to Kabul. Once, however, arguments overcame his reluctance, and the train started, he became a joyous boy, asked every sort of question about the (to him) strange things he saw, and thoroughly entered into the spirit of his novel experiences.

He was accompanied by a large suite of *Sirdars*, generals, etc., and was met by the Viceroy at Agra. There a large *durbar* had been arranged, and at it the *Amir* was to be invested with the Grand Cross of the Star of India. It was explained to His Majesty that, as soon as he was invested, he should take a seat on a dais one step below the Viceroy, and that the other recipients of honours would take seats below him. This he absolutely refused to do, saying he was a king, and would sit below no one. He argued that if King Edward himself had been present his place would have been alongside him, and that he was certainly not going to sit below his representative. As the *Amir* was obdurate on this point a difficult problem had to be solved, and this was done by arranging that directly he had received his honour he should go straight away.

His Majesty was much impressed by the magnificent display of troops at the big review given in his honour, and, when he saw the size of it, was most indignant with his followers, who had told him our army was an insignificant affair, not to be compared with the Afghan army. He threatened to send some of his *Sirdars* straight back to Kabul —rumour had it, to be blown from the muzzles of guns, for having hood-winked him. Gradually, when he became better acquainted with the British, he took such a fancy to them, and became so bored with his own people, that he sent almost all his suite back, and thoroughly enjoyed himself going about almost alone with his hosts.

The promoters of the "Minto Fête" at Calcutta had every reason to congratulate themselves on the *Amir's* visit coinciding with their show, for, on hearing from Lady Minto the charitable objects and purpose of the fête, the *Amir* at once threw himself into the spirit of it.

Many and memorable were his visits there. On one occasion, on visiting Lady Minto's own stall, at which jewellery was for sale, he declined to purchase anything, saying that the prices asked were beneath his royal dignity to accept. Returning the next evening, and finding articles priced in thousands of *rupees*, he purchased largely.

On another occasion, seeing that Lady G——'s doll stall was but poorly patronised, he gave that lady an agreeable surprise, by purchasing, at one vast sum, the whole contents of the stall, by no means a small one, and by making his dignified *Sirdars* carry off the dolls in baskets to distribute among all the children they could find at the fête.

The stories one heard about this interesting personage, and his methods of governing, would fill a book. It must be remembered that he had a very unruly population to deal with, and that rough-and-ready justice, much of it almost savouring of savagery, was the common custom of the country as, and in the minds of its rulers, necessary to maintain any form of law and decency. The following two stories will illustrate.

The state of society having in the opinion of the *Amir* sunk, owing to immorality, even below its normal level, he instituted a terrible punishment. Anyone guilty of an immoral act was sentenced to be taken to a prominent spot where passers-by could see him, and tied to a stake, and there left with a trickle of water perpetually falling on to his head until he died. Frosty weather was preferred, as the water froze, and the wretched man became a human pillar of ice.

The other story was one concerning a girl, who had seen her father brutally murdered by a person of position, whose riches enabled him by judicious bribery to protect himself against the law. This girl threw herself in the path of Habibullah and craved justice. The *Amir* had the man seized and bound, and giving the girl a sword, told her to do unto him as he had done unto her father.

Whenever he saw anything that took his fancy, he wanted to buy it by the dozen, or rather by the baker's dozen, the magic number of thirteen—such things as motor-cars, billiard-tables, pianos, etc., and I believe he actually had these orders carried out in many cases. The shops in Calcutta simply thrilled His Majesty, especially jewellers, in which he spent a heap of money, and fortunate was the lady he happened to meet after making some of his purchases, for he insisted on presenting her with anything from a pearl necklace to a silver pencil-case.

I met him several times at dinners and other entertainments. Clay pigeon shooting especially took his fancy, and one day he challenged the Viceroy to a match, so the *Amir*, His Excellency, Sir Henry McMahon and myself motored off to Tollygunge, where there was a clay pigeon range. I remember that both he and the Viceroy shot extraordinarily well, but I am not sure, in the enjoyment of the shooting, that the fact of its being a match was not lost sight of. Lord Kitchener and he became great friends, and the chief, a keen Freemason himself, readily fell in with the *Amir's* wish to become a mason. So one night, when my wife and I were staying with him, he invited His Majesty to a very private dinner, at which the only other people present were Sir Henry McMahon, Birdwood, the military secretary, three *aide-de-camps*—Livingstone-Learmonth, Wylly, and (I think) Brooke and myself—my wife having to dine out.

I had no idea what the object of the dinner was, but noticed there was mystery in the air, and immediately after dinner our host and principal guest disappeared, and only returned at 2 a.m., when it was whispered that the *Amir* had been initiated into the rites of freemasonry.

The energies and keen interests of the *Amir* were unlimited, not to say embarrassing. He was up at dawn thirsting for novelties anew, and was almost impossible to get to bed, especially if he could get a game of billiards. That night, for instance, when he got back to Lord Kitchener's house, and every one, not unreasonably, wanted to go to bed, the *Amir* insisted on playing billiards, and it was long past 3 a.m. before he could be persuaded to go to roost.

On the 2nd February we went off to Bombay, where we stayed two days with Lord Lamington (the Governor) and Lady Lamington, and then returned to Karachi to await the arrival of the *Amir* in my command, and on the 27th February he appeared in the Indian transport *Dufferin,* his first experience of the sea. I, for my sins, was invited to lunch with His Majesty on Afghan food, and I can't say I enjoyed the food, though it was lightened by European drinks and excellent cigars.

As an instance of how rapidly His Majesty had taken to civilisation, and how quick-witted he was, I will recite a little story about the cigars. They were very large, and of particularly fine quality, and I remarked on them to the *Amir*. He told me they were a present to him from his friend the Duke of Manchester, then, turning round, called up a servant and said, "Order six boxes of these cigars to be sent to the General *Sahib* from Treacher's." Now Treacher's was a very fine shop in Bombay, which could produce most things, but I felt sure they did not stock this particular brand of cigar, and I turned to him triumphantly, and told him so.

Whereupon, as quick as lightning, he said, "The name must be on the box, bring it here," and it was interpreted to him that the name was Lewis, of London, when he said, "Very well, write there." I protested, but he would not listen, and changed the conversation, and the incident passed out of my mind until two months later, when the cigars appeared. Then I was not sorry he had turned the deaf ear, for the cigars were excellent.

After lunch His Majesty accompanied me in a launch down the harbour, and his excited interest in the ships, wharves, fortifications, etc., was delightful, though his strings of questions as to the how, the why, and the wherefore were many of them very difficult to answer. At that time the mouth of the harbour was defended by submarine mines to be exploded from the forts as a hostile ship passed over them. As the *piece de resistance* it was arranged when we were opposite the fort for a tug to tow a barge loaded with earth over one of the mines. It came off exactly right, the explosion was a big one—earth and bits of wood flying everywhere. The *Amir's* face of astonishment and delight was worth seeing.

Shortly after I did a very foolish thing. His Majesty took out his watch to look at the time. It was one of those very thin watches in a hunter case of gold, and I admired it. Instantly he detached it from the chain, and handing it to me said, "It is yours."

When I wouldn't take it, he put it back in his pocket and said, "Very well, I will send it to my friend Treacher, and have it engraved." Sure enough, a month later the watch appeared, and I have it now.

Towards evening the *Amir* got into his train, and as he said goodbye to me he gave me an enamelled pencil-case for my wife. He was indeed a generous man and loved "giving." I don't think he liked in the least returning to his native state, but he went there then, straight from Karachi, to fall some years later at the hand of an assassin. Poor fellow, there was a great deal to admire in his nature. He was undoubtedly a strong character, with a great capacity for enjoying life and an unfathomable store of generosity. I did not see Sir Henry McMahon again until a month later, when he arrived at Quetta to assume the post of Agent to the governor-general in Baluchistan to succeed Mr. Tucker. Wherever he went or whatever post he occupied he increased his reputation; and his tact, firmness, and pleasing personality soon raised him to the plane of successful administrators of this extensive country, inhabited by a fine and proud race by no means easy to govern.

The time was now approaching when I was to bid my beloved Quetta farewell. I spent the next eight months in tours and inspections. On the 20th September my second son, Peter, was born, and on the 26th October I sailed with my family from Bombay in the P. & O. *Persia* to take up the Aldershot command.

CHAPTER 22

Aldershot, 1907—1911

Lord Morley had recently increased his Council by a Mohammedan and a Hindu representative. There was an interesting
and most agreeable person on board who was on his way to
take up the position of Mohammedan Member of the Council
of the Secretary of State for India in London—Said Bilgrami by
name. I think he had been Prime Minister to the Nizam of the
Deccan. When we left India considerable troubles had been taking place in the Punjab and the ringleader, Ajit Singh, as well as
other rebels had been arrested.

In course of conversation I asked Said Bilgrami what advice
he was going to give Lord Morley on the subject, and his reply
was that to stop the outbreak at once there was only one way
which Indians would understand, and that was to blow them
from the muzzle of a gun. Knowing Lord Morley, but agree-
ing with my new friend, who was a highly educated and most
polished gentleman, I smiled in my sleeve, and told him he must
impress this on the Secretary of State with all his power.

Shortly after arriving in England I, in fulfilment of a promise,
went to see Lord Morley at the India Office. In the course of
conversation I mentioned I had made friends with the Mohammedan Member of his Council, and that he had a real solution
for the Punjab unrest. Lord Morley used all his persuasive powers to induce me to tell him what the solution was, but I told
him to wait and see, but to be sure to act on the advice when
given him. About a month later I again called on his Lordship,

and shall never forget the interview.

As I approached the table he put his hands before his face, saying, "Horrible, horrible—fancy me, a Liberal Minister, endeavouring to carry out measures for improving the lot of the people of India and encouraging them to take a hand in the government of the country, being asked to use barbaric methods only fit for the Middle Ages."

I laughed and said, "But surely, sir, since you appointed Indians to advise you, you are going to follow that advice, for they know what measures suit their own people."

Lord Morley, however, ridiculed the idea, and said he should only follow advice which was convenient to him. On this, as on many other occasions, when I had the great pleasure of a talk with him, he impressed me by his strong views, and the autocratic mind which governed his actions. I had expected more give and take in an advanced Liberal.

In taking over my new duties I was helped cordially by Sir John French, and relieved him on the 1st December. My successor at Quetta was Major-General Clements, an old friend, and fine soldier, whom I had first met when he marched in with his company of the 24th Regiment (now the South Wales Borderers) to reinforce the fort at Helpmakaar, the day after the disaster at Isandhlwana, already described in my account of the Zulu War.

Taking up a command was financially a serious matter in those days—for one was provided with a bare house devoid even of fenders and curtain-poles. It cost me some £3,000 to fit up Government House at Aldershot, buy horses, etc. Since then all has been changed, I am glad to say, and a paternal Government provides. I was greatly honoured on reaching England, first, by lunching at the Marlborough Club with the Prince of Wales, the present king, and a few days later by being invested with the K.C.B. by King Edward VII.

I assumed the Aldershot command with considerable diffidence, as, excepting the two years I was a student at the Staff College, I had been nearly twenty-seven years without doing a day's duty in the United Kingdom.

Throughout the period of my command at Aldershot, although events of local and temporary interest were jostling one another and one's life was as full as it could hold, there was not much of general interest, and, therefore, I shall endeavour to be as brief as possible in my account of my four and a half years there.

I found a very efficient and agreeable staff, and as many of them rose to fame subsequently, I will record the names of those holding the most important posts: Lawson in charge of Administration, now Lieutenant-General Sir Henry Lawson; Robertson, chief of general staff, now Field-Marshal Sir W. Robertson; Major-General Sir Thomas Gallwey, P.M.O.; Brigadier-General P. Buston, C.E.; Major-General Sir James Grierson (who died in France 1914), commanding the 1st Division; Major-General Stephenson, the 2nd Division; Colonel Home, now General Lord Home, was my Artillery Adviser; Rawlinson, now General Lord Rawlinson, commanded a brigade.

The man who was my first Whip when I was Master of the Staff College hounds, Brigadier-General C. McGrigor, was D.A.Q.M.G., to be succeeded later by Walter Campbell, now Lieutenant-General Sir Walter Campbell and Quartermaster-General of the Army. All were imbued with the same ardent spirit in preparing the army for war.

In February 1910 Lawson assumed command of the 2nd Division, and in August of the same year Robertson left me to become commandant of the Staff College; but my luck did not desert me, for in their respective places I got F. S. Robb and F. J. Davies, both of whom afterwards became lieutenant-generals, and were knighted.

It was a compact command, the two divisions being, one might almost say, in a ring-fence, the only really distant spots one had to visit being artillery practice camps on Salisbury Plain, Okehampton in Devonshire and Trawsfynydd in Wales. Although the work was arduous, with the incessant watch one had to keep on every form of training and the frequent calls to London on duties connected with the Selection Board, War Office Committees, and duties at Court as *aide-de-camp* general to the king, I am inclined to think that I had more time for shooting and hunting than I had in my previous command in India or my subsequent one at Salisbury, both of which involved incessant travelling over a large extent of country.

I found Government House itself quite unworthy of the name—being very limited in accommodation, and with great difficulty I persuaded the authorities to help me with material to build a squash racket-court and to add at government expense what they were pleased to call a bull-room; but as they cut off five feet both from the length and breadth of the design I submitted, they spoilt the ship for a ha'porth of tar.

Aldershot had one very great advantage, and that was its patronage by Royalty. Each year it was visited by members of the Royal Family. My first two years Their Royal Highnesses the Prince and Princess of Wales honoured us by staying in the house some four or five days, whilst the king came each of those two years for a one-day Inspection. Then, when King George acceded to the throne, Their Majesties went into residence each year at the Royal Pavilion, when King George spent several days inspecting the troops and barracks. Those first two years, too, the Prince and Princess of Wales visited Aldershot for the final of the Army Football Cup, and gave away the prizes.

H.R.H. Field-Marshal the Duke of Connaught was also a frequent visitor when any operation of particular interest was being carried out.

It was a little difficult to arrange a Field Day for H.M. King Edward, as he rode very little those days, and preferred a motor as a means of getting about. His Majesty was accompanied each year by the Inspector-General, Sir John French, and I gathered from him that we had succeeded in producing Field Days likely to convey to the king the maxims of modern training developments in the shortest space of time.

On the first occasion only did H.M. Queen Alexandra accompany him. They were both most gracious and charming, and before departure insisted on seeing our two small boys. When one of them, quite unabashed, asked which was the King, for there were several people in the room, the Queen, patting him on the back, said, "That stout old gentleman over there."

Naturally we had to entertain a great number of distinguished foreigners. Perhaps the most interesting were amongst the following: the French General Coupillaud, accompanied by Colonel Huguet, the French Military Attaché in London, whom everyone loved; General Desforges, then commanding the 39th Division at Toul; General Yermaloff, the Russian Military Attaché; Generals Garlington and Wotherspan, and Colonel Slocum, of the United States army, the last named being Military Attaché in London; the Prime Minister of Nepal, Sir Chandra Jung Bahadur; General Kamamura, who had commanded the fifth Japanese Army against the Russians, also General Hashimoto and the Princes Nashimoto and Kuni, the latter being the father of the future Empress of Japan, and Colonel Higashi, the Japanese Military Attaché in London, whom we had known in India in a similar capacity.

But perhaps our two visitors of world-wide reputation were Ghazi Mukhtar Pasha, the famous Turkish General, and General Nogi, the conqueror of Port Arthur.

The former was accompanied by Generals Sir John Slade and Sir Ian Hamilton—Slade was known to fame as the man who at the Maiwand disaster in Afghanistan in 1879 had kept his head, saved the guns, and earned a V.C. which he never got. General Nogi was taken care of by the only Japanese-speaking officer then at Aldershot, Woodroffe (now brigadier-general). General Nogi was tall for a Japanese, and much interested in our war training.

It will be remembered that this gallant man and his wife, on the death of the last Mikado, committed Harikari, which was the highest tribute of loyalty payable to their departed sovereign. Inspiring as this example of loyalty is, it would be distinctly inconvenient if many people habitually followed it, for the rapid depopulation of the world would result.

[J. M. Chew : Aldershot.

H.M. KING EDWARD AT ALDERSHOT, 15TH MAY 1909.

Back row standing : Major-General H. M. Lawson ; Brig.-General C. T. McM. Kavanagh ; Brig.-General C. J. Mackenzie ; Brig.-General David Henderson ; Lieut.-Colonel G. L. Holford ; Major-General Sir Thomas Galway ; Brig.-General Sir Charles Fawkesson, Bt. ; Colonel Sir Arthur Davidson ; Brig.-General F. T. Bingoa ; Brig.-General F. Hammersley ; Brig.-General Sir Henry Rawlinson, Bt. ; Brig.-General The Hon. A. Henniker ; Capt. R. G. V. Way ; Capt. Olive Wigram ; Lieut. the Hon. M. V. B. Broit.
Front row sitting : Major-General F. K. Stephenson ; Major-General J. M. Grierson ; Mrs. Robertson ; Lieut.-General Sir Horace Smith-Dorrien ; Mrs. Stephenson ; H.M. The King ; Lady Smith-Dorrien ; General Sir John French ; Lady Gallway ; Brig.-General W. R. Robertson.

I also made the acquaintance of the *Maréchal* Foch, then the commandant of the French Staff College, and had the pleasure of showing him our artillery practice and methods on Salisbury Plain, little thinking I should be brought into close personal touch with him later in the war which we, even then, felt sure would be forced on us by the Germans, and to be ready for which we were devoting every moment. He was accompanied by Colonel Huguet and also by his friend "H. H. Wilson," commandant of our Staff College. What an important factor that friendship was to the successful issue of the Great War is too well known to need discussion. Both became field-marshals, one of them is still the mainspring of military policy in his own country, and alas! the other would have been the same in ours had he not fallen by the hand of a despicable assassin.

In February 1908 the tragic murder of King Carlos and of the Crown Prince of Portugal took place, and I was much interested, on visiting their palace (*Castello de Peno*) at Cintra in 1921, in being shown the rooms the Royal Family were inhabiting at the time. Not a thing had been touched: the newspapers of the day, books they had been reading open, writing-tables, and everything were just as they were left on that fatal day.

It was in February of this year, too, that our first Old Comrades Association Sherwood Forester dinner was inaugurated at Nottingham. I, as colonel of the regiment, attended, and we sat down twenty-two officers and 150 other ranks. Since then, except during the war, this dinner has taken place annually alternately at Nottingham and Derby. The Association has now assumed very large dimensions, and does an infinity of good for old soldiers of the regiment. The dinners, too, have increased in size; last year (1923) we sat down over 300, and this year (1924) about the same number. I mention this as an instance of how far-reaching for good the encouragement of *esprit de corps* may be. A very large number of needy old soldiers are assisted by the Association, and our funds amount to some £5,000. On my getting back from the same dinner on the 29th October 1911, I found a surprise for me, for my youngest son David had appeared in the world that morning.

GENERAL NOGI, LIEUTENANT-GENERAL SMITH-DORRIEN AND CAPTAIN WOODROFFE AT ALDERSHOT

I was very fortunate in my personal staff, my assistant military secretary being Captain Clive Wigram, of the Indian army, and my *aide-de-camp*, Captain Way, of my own regiment. I had had a great struggle to get Wigram, for it was against all precedent that an officer in the Indian army should be employed at home. I fought hard, and with a fair amount of success, to get the principle of employing Indian officers on the staff at home, arguing that it was most important they should learn our ways. It was all the more right as a very large number of English army officers were employed on the staff in India. I went further than this, for I tried to get the same policy carried out with our Dominions, and on the refusal of a brigade by Colonel Otter (now Major-General Sir William, K.C.B.) of the Canadian Forces it was offered to and accepted by Colonel R. H. Davies, C.B., of the New Zealand Forces, and he later commanded a British division Major-General in the Great War.

Again I tried to get units brought over for training, and the 48th Canadian Highlanders came over one year, and were attached to their affiliated battalion at Aldershot, the Gordon Highlanders. The following year, shepherded by Colonel (now major-general) Sir Henry Pellatt of Toronto, the Queen's Own Rifles of Canada came and spent quite a long time training and on manoeuvres.

Apart from the value of the training, such fraternising goes a long way towards cementing the Dominions to the Mother Country, and I should like to see it re-instituted.

To return to Wigram. He was only with me for about two years, for in June 1910 the King was so impressed by his usefulness that he appropriated him, and His Majesty's gain was my loss. However, Way stepped into his shoes, and worthily did he fill them, George Boscawen (alas! killed in France) replacing him as *aide-de-camp*.

I am not clogging these pages with any details of the Annual Army Manoeuvres, for, though I could tell some amusing anecdotes, they might hurt someone's feelings. The only ones in which I was a commander were in 1909 in the Valley of the

Thames, about Lechlade and Faringdon, when I fought Arthur Paget. The scheme was a poor one, for the two forces were actually in contact when the operations started, leaving no scope for manoeuvre. The proof of this was that within twenty-four hours the only battle possible had been fought, and, as many politicians had collected to see the fun, a new scheme to produce a spectacular Field Day had to be improvised.

Colonel C. C. Monro, now General Sir Charles Monro, Bart., G.C.B., etc., who commanded an army in France, ordered the withdrawal from the Dardanelles in 1915, became commander-in-chief in India, and succeeded me as Governor of Gibraltar, was chief umpire with my force at these manoeuvres. The succeeding army manoeuvres at this period, were much more practical and worth the money.

An immense amount of instruction went on incessantly throughout the year, and a series of lectures and debates at the Prince Consort's library were most valuable. Robertson's (the field-marshal) lectures on European situations, strategical values, armies, etc., and on the Canadian frontier were a marked feature.

It was a great comfort to have a man of such wide grasp, so set on war efficiency, and so helpful as Secretary of State for War as Mr. Haldane. He constantly came down to see a unit mobilised for war, or to discuss necessary equipment and organisation, or to attend a conference, commonly called a "*Pow-wow*," after an operation. In this way he got a real practical grasp of what an army meant. For instance, I remember his surprise to find that it took twenty-five minutes for a brigade of artillery mobilised for war to pass him on a road in column of route, and his deduction that to move armies about was no light matter.

Then, at a *Pow-wow* (conference) after inter-divisional manoeuvres one year he expressed his pleasure at the high standard of debating powers shown by officers. On this occasion there were 400 officers seated on the ground, and a raised platform made of wagons was occupied by myself as chief debater, whilst the commanders of the two opposing forces were facing each other a little distance off on each side of the assembled officers. Every lesson of the manoeuvres was discussed—the *Pow-wow* lasting two hours. Mr. Haldane remarked afterwards that it was worthy of the House of Commons. He used to ask me to lunch with him in London, and to discuss matters over long cigars. He was always sympathetic, but I never could persuade him that the only way to be sure that his fourteen divisions of the Territorial Force would be "in being" and trained for war would be by introducing Compulsory Service for Home Defence. He was certainly open to the needs of the country, for on the 31st October 1911 he told me that at last they were sure the Germans meant mischief and that a decision to increase the navy had been arrived at.

Besides those I have mentioned there were two men of whom we were to hear with pride later, the one Lord Cavan, then a lieutenant-colonel commanding a battalion of the grenadiers—who so distinguished himself in the Great War, and is now chief of the general staff, and incidentally is or has been Master of the Hertfordshire Hounds, with which under him I have had more than one gallop; the other, Major C. Harington, Brigade Major of the 6th Brigade who came to the fore as Lord Plumer's chief of the staff in France, and recently showed in the difficult problems to be solved by the commander-in-chief of our Army of Occupation in Turkey, that he was not only a remarkable leader, but a born diplomat.

I pass over accounts of our social life, such as incessant entertaining *chez nous,* meetings with many agreeable and well-known people, royal dinners and functions at Buckingham Palace, Marlborough House, and Windsor, generally to meet some foreign Royalties or persons of distinction; a visit to Their Majesties' beautiful home in the Highlands, Balmoral; public and official dinners in London; frequent calls to the War Office, and delightful visits to country houses, hunting, shooting, etc., for they would form a work in themselves, and would not be of much general interest. My wife and I, however, managed quite a lot of hunting; but what we enjoyed most in that line was the illegitimate use of fox-hounds, such as the Staff College and Aldershot drags.

Field-Marshal Sir Evelyn Wood, V.C., was one of our most regular visitors, and always a welcome one and full of cheerfulness. As an instance of his quick wit, during one of his visits there were a certain distinguished general and his wife also at Government House. One morning the field-marshal, on opening the bath-room door, saw the head of the lady in question above the bath, and without the slightest hesitation said, "I beg your pardon, 'General' ———" and went out.

The lady told us the story herself at breakfast.

A most interesting personality whom we used to see was the Empress Eugénie, who lived at Farnborough Place.

She was well over eighty, though she had a most alert mind, which she retained to the end of her life. Of this my wife and I have first-hand evidence, for on the 22nd April 1920 she sent a radiogram to me at Government House, Gibraltar, saying she was arriving that day by sea, and would we meet her. This of course we did, and found this wonderful old lady of ninety-four full of the *joie de vivre* and simply sparkling with wit, largely at the expense of what Her Majesty called "the undressed modern young woman," her mind having been stirred by the sight of many of her young Spanish relations, who had come on board to see her, with low necks, short sleeves, and shorter skirts.

In the middle of her scathing criticisms it suddenly dawned on her that she had not noticed my wife's clothes, and that she might be wearing offending garments, and she stopped and, scrutinising her closely through her glasses, explained what had struck her, remarking that she need have had no qualms. My wife enjoyed a two hours' talk with her, and then H.M. disembarked with her nephew, the Duke of Alba. She died a few months later after a long life in the highest possible of positions, crowded with tragic incidents and yet cheerful to the last. Truly she must have had a great heart.

To return to Aldershot, the chief bond of union between us was that I had been a friend of her son, the Prince Imperial, and was able to give her particulars of his life in the Zulu War, before his untimely death, already described.

The Empress took interest in everything, and pleased Mr. Cody enormously, one of the first pioneers in the air, by accompanying me to inspect a new aeroplane designed by him, and from which he met his death a few weeks later. Not long afterwards the Empress was being shown the airships in their sheds on Farnborough Common, and someone rashly suggested she might like a trip in one. She was enthused, and her personal attendants proportionately depressed, for she was a very determined old lady, and they knew that when she had set her heart on anything it was almost impossible to turn her. However, they gave my wife a hint, and she told me, and between us we invented insuperable difficulties, and the project was given up.

For some years the Royal Army Temperance Association had been doing a great work for the army, but I considered in March 1909, when I presided at the Annual Meeting at Aldershot, that by over-encouragement of Teetotalism they had created in the minds of those adopting it a Pharisaical impression that they were better than their fellows, resulting in their holding themselves aloof and creating cliques detrimental to the true spirit of comradeship which should exist in every unit. My wife was present at the meeting, and much to her horror, for the prime mover, an old Staff College friend of mine, was staying with us, I told them that in my opinion temperance, and not teetotalism, should be aimed at, though the latter was doubtless valuable to the weak-minded, who lacked self-control.

Perhaps it might be of interest to describe some of the most important of my reforms whilst at Aldershot. I was very much struck, on arriving there, to find every night the roads and streets being patrolled by innumerable small piquets of a non-commissioned officer and four to six men, and on looking at the duty states I saw that over 700 men were employed weekly on this irksome duty. From a long experience of the rank and file, who always play up if trusted, I abolished the piquets forthwith—at the same time publishing an order saying that I did so as I trusted the men to behave, but that if events proved I had formed too high an appreciation of the characteristics of the British soldier I should cancel the order. The provost-marshal, a first-rate officer, was much upset and protested he could not, without piquets, be responsible for discipline, which amused me much, and a little later he again protested, because I was abolishing another order. This latter was to the effect that when troops were moving about the country, doing military training, all public-houses were placed out of bounds. My train of thought, which I explained to my provost-marshal, was that, even if out of bounds, a thirsty man would enter a public-house, and knowing he could not do so often, for fear of the Military Police, would drink as much as he could in a short space of time, and probably get roaring drunk, whereas if there were no restrictions, and he could get his glass of beer whenever he liked, no evil effects would result. I regarded both the piquets and the public-house prohibition order as productive of military offences.

There was a lengthy wrangle in the papers at the time about both matters, but the facts that, after my experiment, piquets gradually disappeared in all commands, and that the Municipal Council of Aldershot, at the end of my command, addressed to me a much-valued letter on the subject, are pretty telling evidence that my action was justified. In this letter they thanked me for the marked improvement in the behaviour of the men in the streets of Aldershot during my command, adding that, since the abolition of piquets, unseemly disturbances had become a thing of the past, and inhabitants could move about without fear of being shocked.

With regard to the order giving the *entrée* to public houses: immediately after the order announcing the fact was issued, we had roughly 30,000 troops moving about in the Winchester neighbourhood for three weeks, and there was only one case of drunkenness, and that in a battalion canteen in camp.

Another theory of mine which I had already proved in India was, "Make barracks more comfortable and attractive, and increase the facilities for recreation, and less crime and happier men will result." I was helped largely in putting this theory into practice by two people, who in the end became as enthusiastic as myself. I refer to my Chief of Administration General Lawson, spoken of affectionately as "Wise Bob," and General Scott-Moncrieff, my chief engineer. Every spot of ground large enough for cricket, football, or hockey was taken up, levelled, and grassed—some prodigious work was done, and in two cases the tops of hillocks were cut off and pitched into the adjacent depressions and a level site obtained.

In this way the grounds were increased by 150 *per cent*, before I left. At first we found it difficult to get the work supervised, but General Lawson placed at my disposal the services of his *aide-de-camp*, Captain R. J. Kentish, an enthusiast, now a retired brigadier-general, but devoting himself to developing play-grounds all over England for the benefit of the youth of the country, and a representative of the Empire in organising the Olympic Games.

The improvements in barracks took the form of larger and more comfortable regimental Institutes, better lighting, dining-halls instead of dining in the sleeping-rooms; more baths, and especially the introduction of shower-baths in any hitherto unused corner. The latter were a speciality of Scott-Moncrieff's. I am bound to say the War Office were most helpful, and improved on our proposals. The messing of the men was also very largely improved, though General Burnett, who was once quartermaster-general, was the real enthusiast, who had set the ball going.

The messing was good, or indifferent, according to the interest taken by the officers—one battalion of the Guards produced most attractive food, fit for a club sideboard, and at no greater cost.

I had not been at Aldershot for many years, and did not expect to find it so overgrown with trees as seriously to restrict the ground available for military training; but there they were, the country between Government House and Norris Bridge was a forest—and on the steeple-chase course only a few jumps could be seen for trees. They had to be got rid of. My chief engineer told me it would take years for the R.E. to cut them down, and that the fir-wood was hardly worth the while of a contractor to buy standing. So I ordered out the two divisions to carry out an operation designed to necessitate taking up a position on the edge of the wood and the clearing of such a field of fire as would cause the disappearance of the obnoxious trees. All went according to plan, and in six hours the trees were down. Those on the race-course went later, as did many more in our training areas, and especially near Bordon. This was how Aldershot became possessed of the flying-ground between Farnborough Common and Norris Bridge.

I naturally made myself acquainted with the Mobilisation Scheme in so far as it concerned the troops at Aldershot. That scheme, of course, involved the calling out of the Reserves; but, on asking whether there was not a lesser scheme for rapidly parading the existing troops, should a sudden emergency arise, such as a sudden invasion, was told there was none. I therefore had a scheme drawn up, and on the 14th June 1909, without a word of warning, at 6 a.m. issued the order for all troops to turn out immediately, fully equipped for active service.

This disclosed many weaknesses which we were able to rectify, and as a sequel to it I issued a scheme for a staff tour, the idea being that the emergency mobilisation had been ordered in consequence of a threatened invasion on the East Coast between Yarmouth and Harwich. We carried this out. It was extremely interesting, and enabled us to mature plans to meet such an invasion should occasion arise. A very detailed report went to the War Office, which, whilst producing a friendly pat on the back, also produced a cynical note from our pen-loving chief of the Imperial General Staff, Field-Marshal Lord Nicholson.

He, by the by, was not fond of inspecting troops, and except once, when ordered down to be in attendance on the King, never came near Aldershot the whole time I was there. The truth was he disliked a horse, and, on that one occasion referred to, telegrams were flying for days to unearth the most docile animal in the army. The Royal Military College produced the favoured quadruped, but I gathered it was not approved of, as the C.I.G.S. only came out with H.M. one morning, looked thoroughly unhappy, and pleading urgent business went back to his office the same afternoon.

General Sir Charles Monro (then Major-General C. C. M.) had, as commandant of the School of Musketry at Hythe, made great advances in the methods for increasing efficiency with the rifle, and the army owe him a debt of gratitude. He had just left Hythe when I went to Aldershot, and I profited by his developments, which I firmly believed in. It had for a long time been evident to many soldiers that, both in the mounted and dismounted services, rapid and accurate fire, such as Sir Charles introduced, might prove a decisive factor in war, and that the days of charges of cavalry in large formations were numbered, and that in a big action their horses would be chiefly valuable to get them to a position quickly, where they could dismount and fire. This had been admirably illustrated by the Japanese in pressing back the Russian Army on Mukden in 1904.

I was, therefore, not at all pleased to find that the cavalry brigade at Aldershot were low down in the annual musketry courses, and further, on field days and manoeuvres, hardly ever dismounted, but delivered perfectly carried out, though impossible, knee to knee charges against infantry in action. So on the 21st August 1909, ordering all cavalry officers to meet me at the 16th Lancers' Mess, I gave them my views pretty clearly, with the result that dismounted work was taken up seriously and the improvement in musketry was so marked that the cavalry went nearly to the head of the lists in the Annual Musketry. I submit that my action was justified by what happened in the Great War, but at the time I am aware that my attitude was resented.

In order to introduce active service conditions into our musketry course, I had a tract of country laid out with every sort of appearing and disappearing target, such as infantry digging a trench, a gun galloping into action, cavalry charging towards the attackers, and so on, all mechanically worked. This was made possible by the laying of a system of small-gauge railway-lines, and the erection of mounds behind which the operators were safe, and from behind which the targets, mostly moved by motors, were started off. A scheme was devised each year which gave wide latitude to the commander of the attacking force, and the several targets were made use of according to the ground he selected to attack over. We made it into a competition, and every squadron and company had to compete as part of the annual course. The prize was a challenge-cup which I gave, and which is still competed for, though the conditions are altered to suit the latest war developments.

Judging from the immense keenness shown and the practice it gave in meeting unexpected counter-attacks and in rapidly aiming at an active service target instead of at a fixed range target, I believe the competition was an unqualified success.

Although on the whole favourably impressed by the system of training I found in England, I think in some ways it was behind India. For instance, I found tents being carried on brigade and divisional operations, an impossibility in real war, and stopped the practice. Then there was no such thing as a light entrenching tool, and it took many months of bombarding the War Office before money was provided. The actual committee which eventually tested and selected the tool did its work at Aldershot under my presidency.

Most of us soldiers felt sure that war could not long be postponed, and our one aim and object was not to be caught napping. My chief general staff officer, Robertson, was very wide awake on the subject, and, thinking a little knowledge of the country through which we firmly believed the Germans would strike would be good for me, in 1909 took me off with Rawlinson (then commanding a brigade, now Lord Rawlinson, commander-in-chief in India) to Belgium. In six days we motored all along the Meuse, through Charleroi, Namur, Liége, looking from the frontier at Maestricht and Eupen. Then through Spa, the place now of doubtfully happy memory to the Kaiser, to Arlon, and the borders of Luxemburg. We then turned north and went through the Ardennes to Dinant, and so back to Brussels—not a bad forecast of the country through which the Germans were expected to come.

Robertson and I had a comic experience on getting back to London on the morning of the 22nd June. It was about 6 a.m., and only a few ramshackle and out-of-date cabs were to be had. We got into an old hansom, and, driving up the steep slope into the old Waterloo Station, both shafts broke and the cab fell over backwards and was merely supported by the driver's seat. The driver, it seemed, rolled down the hill, but we were practically sitting on our shoulders with our legs sticking straight into the air, and so tightly wedged that we were unable to move. Luckily the horse was only too glad to stand still. At last an old man came along and was surprised to find us both laughing. We were extricated without damage. Rawlinson made an amusing sketch of our mishap, which I possess.

We were always having to do showmen to all sorts of people: Dominion magnates, foreigners, etc.; and perhaps one of the most enjoyable parties during my command was the one which arrived on the 12th June 1909. This consisted of 350 people, mostly pressmen, but with a sprinkling of foreign officers, under the guiding hand of Mr. Harry Brittain (now Sir H. Brittain, K.B.E., M.P.). We began with operations on the Fox Hills, and then proceeded to show every conceivable thing which might appeal to them in the way of equipment and our improvements in barracks, etc. Mr. —— (a Cabinet Minister) was a frequent visitor.

He used to appear on foot from nowhere, having walked miles and miles. On one occasion he had walked from Woking. He was very fond of talking to the men, and used to march along with them. He was one of the few politicians I was always glad to see, for I found him interesting. As a rule I avoided gentlemen of that cloth. It was a standing joke amongst my staff, when out at operations, that if they heard me suddenly shout for the horses to be brought up I had spotted a politician in the offing. One day he honoured me at lunch, and I used the occasion to impress on him, as a member of the Government, that it was most important we should be armed with the new Vickers Maxim Machine-gun, which was half the weight of the gun we then had, and much more efficient, and I urged that £100,000 would re-equip the six divisions of the Expeditionary Force. Mr. —— jeered at me, saying I was afraid of the Germans, that he habitually attended the German army at training, and was quite certain that if they ever went to war "the most monumental examples of crass cowardice the world had ever heard of would be witnessed." I think those were his exact words, and recite the incident as a sample of how one of our Cabinet Ministers in 1909 ridiculed the idea of a German aggression. We were only four at lunch—the other two being my personal staff, Wigram and Way.

I now come to a very sad day in my life, the 28th July. In the morning we had a very fine parade of a division at war strength—some 19,000 men. H.R.H. Field-Marshal the Duke of Connaught with the Duchess and Princess Patricia, as well as many of the senior generals in the army, had assembled for the occasion. As soon as the inspection was finished the division moved off to Frensham Common to carry out an operation to end with a dawn attack on the morrow.

When they had marched off Their Royal Highnesses and the generals lunched with us at Government House. Just as lunch was finished a telegram came calling me to my mother's death-bed. With the permission of the Duke I jumped into a motor, and at the end of a forty-mile drive arrived just in time to see her.

As I could do no good remaining, and my duty was with my troops, especially as H.R.H. was to be present at the night operations, I motored back, got to Aldershot at 1 a.m., changed into uniform, and went on to Frensham in time to see the dawn attack and to hold the Conference at the end of the operations. I have already in these pages described my mother as a remarkable woman; she was so closely in touch with the affairs of the world that conversation with her was not only a pleasure but instructive, and her loss created a real void in my life.

The Public School Boys' Training Camps which took place every summer were always a great pleasure, and this year, at their final march past on the 30th July, I was accompanied by my eldest son, aged five. I mention this as it will be of interest to him in the future to be able to state that he started his military career as a mounted man at an early date.

When at Biarritz with my family in March 1910 H.M. King Edward was staying at the Hôtel du Palais as the Duke of Lancaster. He was very ill and suffering much from his throat, but yet as genial and charming as ever. On the 23rd March my wife and I had the honour of dining with him—a party of only twelve. His Majesty sat at the head of the table with a bell in front of him, Lady Sybil Grant on one side and my wife on the other. After each course the servants went out until His Majesty himself rang for them. The king was so gentle and thoughtful, looking after the wants of the guests himself, and yet evidently suffering. It struck me as so extraordinarily self-sacrificing to invite guests under such circumstances.

I saw His Majesty several times, and he was always most cordial and gracious. The king used to take my arm and walk about. He was terribly upset by the political outlook at home and by the efforts of the Government to force the Parliament Bill through. One day His Majesty, on meeting me, asked in his deep voice if I had heard that a certain captain in the army was leaving it to become an M.P., and added: "Fancy a man leaving the army to become a politician; a nice profession that nowadays."

Only five weeks later, when I was undergoing a refresher course of musketry at Hythe, the sad end came. It was on the 6th May that I heard how critical the king's state was. The news was brought to me by a fellow-student, H.S.H. the Duke of Teck, just before dinner, and at 11.45 p.m. His Majesty passed away, and on the 20th May I had the sad honour of riding in the funeral procession to Paddington.

Another sad event for me took place this year, for I lost a favourite sister, Mrs. Tyrwhitt-Drake of Shardeloes, on the 20th October.

BRIG-GEN W. ROBERTSON, H.R.H. DUKE OF CONNAUGHT, LORD STAMFORDHAM, H.M. KING GEORGE, LORD ANNALY AND LIEUT-GEN SIR H. SMITH-DORRIEN AT ALDERSHOT, MAY, 1911

On the 3rd March 1911, I had the honour of dining with His Majesty King George at Buckingham Palace, and was immensely gratified at being told that His Majesty had selected me as his *aide-de-camp* general for his Indian tour, which was to take place in November.

On the 14th March I was invited by Lord Rosebery to meet His Majesty. I merely record this, as the party, though small, comprised somewhat varied schools of thought. There were only twelve altogether, the other nine being the Rt. Hon. A. Birrell (Chief Secretary for Ireland), the Rt. Hon. Sir John Simon, K.C., the Rt. Hon. Sir George Murray (for years Permanent Secretary to the Treasury), Mr. H. T. Baker (later Financial Secretary to the War Office), Councillor Myers, Mr. W. L. Courtney of *The Daily Telegraph* staff, Mr. H. A. Fisher (President Board of Education, 1916), Mr. St. Loe Strachey of *The Spectator,* and Captain Godfrey Faussett, R.N., in attendance on His Majesty.

I had a very pleasing experience before leaving Aldershot, and that was to present the Army Football Cup to a team of my old regiment the Sherwood Foresters, an experience I was to repeat the following year, for the regiment was then in the Southern command, to which I had moved when they again won the cup—a great feather in their caps, and I was naturally proud. They were in the semi-finals the following year, and, had they won, would have kept the cup.

On the 22nd June I commanded half the troops in the streets of London at the Coronation of Their Majesties King George and Queen Mary, and again the following day at the procession through the streets.

During this month too I was offered the succession to Lord Methuen in the South African command, but was allowed to decline it.

In October I saw a pet project of mine mature, and that was a soldiers' club at Bordon on the same lines as the one I had instituted at Quetta, already described.

The autumn of the year was marked by the Agadir incident and the close approach to war between France and Germany over the Morocco disagreement. Strikes in London, too, were very serious, and 15,000 troops had to be sent up from Aldershot.

In spite of my declining the South African command I was, to my surprise, offered the Southern command, to be taken up on my return from India with Their Majesties in the spring. Naturally I accepted it.

Before leaving the subject of my command at Aldershot, there are three matters I should like to record. The first is that it was during my reign that the cross-country running competition by battalions was introduced. It is true I had a good deal to do with it, but the idea was not mine. The idea came from the brain of my old friend, now alas! departed, Major-General the Hon. Arthur Henniker, who was always devoted to all forms of physical exercise. The second was the institution of the employment of searchlights instead of torches for spectacular tattoo parades, which have greatly increased their beauty.

The third was the most valuable pooling of the Aldershot Military Charities. When I went to Aldershot there were at least a dozen of such charities. Units were expected to subscribe to each one of them, the amount being left to the discretion of their commanding officers; the result was some charities got very little, others too much; some units paid too much, others too little. The matter was one in which my wife took the greatest interest, so I handed the matter over to her capable and organising brain. She estimated the total amount required to keep all the charities going and then worked out a scale based on the number and strength of units. She held several committee meetings, where units were represented, and the scheme was eagerly accepted and worked with the greatest success and with the minimum of trouble to commanding officers.

Later on in the Salisbury command she induced the troops at Tidworth to adopt the same system.

CHAPTER 23

India and Salisbury, 1911–1914

It was on 11th November 1911 that, as *aide-de-camp* general to the king, I started with Their Imperial Majesties for India. We left Portsmouth after lunch in the new P. & O. *Medina*. It was a fine sight, the shores black with people, guns saluting, the escort of four cruisers steaming into their positions behind us, and at 5 p.m. we passed between the lines of the Home Fleet of ten battleships under Admiral Bridgeman. I will draw a veil over our experiences of the Bay, which was at its worst—otherwise we had a delightful voyage, touching at Gibraltar, at Port Said (where the Khedive paid a state visit and Lord Kitchener came on board), and at Aden, reaching Bombay at 10 a.m. on the 2nd December. There the Viceroy, Lord Hardinge of Penshurst, and the Governor of Bombay, Sir George Clarke (now Lord Sydenham), met Their Imperial Majesties.

The staff were a little anxious as to the safety of Their Majesties in India, and Bombay in particular, as only recently some malcontents had been very troublesome there, and had had to be suppressed by troops. However, the enthusiasm and loyalty shown, not only there, but throughout the five weeks Their Majesties were in India, soon allayed our fears. The people regarded the king and queen as a god and a goddess, and wherever they went showed them not only the most profound respect, but adoration. Kings and queens to them are of divine origin, and throughout the night following the landing of Their Imperial Majesties at Bombay crowds were praying round Queen Victoria's statue in that city. The one dominant idea in their minds appeared to be a wish to see Their Majesties, whether in the train or in a motor or at a function; there they were, in the most orderly manner, trying to catch a glimpse and bowing low to the ground. At night every station and every level-crossing was crowded, and as the train passed along there was a continuous cry, or it might be more aptly described as a wail, of "*Badshah Ki Jai,*" "*Badshah Ki Jai*"—meaning "Victory to the King."

I am not attempting to describe all the wonderful sights, the ceremonies with their perfect settings, or the less serious side of the Imperial visit, such as the Maharajah of Nepal's unrivalled hospitality when His Imperial Majesty visited him and took part in what I imagine was the most wonderfully organised big-game shoot the world has ever seen, for, although I have a copious diary to refer to, far more able pens than mine have already given full details to the public. My intention is to be as brief as possible, only saying just enough to satisfy the requirements of a *Memoir*, for I was very proud to be selected, and enjoyed every moment of the tour.

On the 9th January 1912, after the most impressive farewells, Their Imperial Majesties re-embarked on the *Medina,* and sailed for England, and to my mind the good done by the visit cannot be exaggerated.

On the 17th January the ship stopped at Port Sudan in the Red Sea to see the Fuzzy Wuzzies, or Hadendowas, who had fought so bravely against us in 1883 to 1885. Their greetings with shields and spears were somewhat less pretentious than those given in India, but none the less warm and honest. A large measure of civilisation was evident since twenty-nine years previously Valentine Baker's gallant attempt against them with a half-trained and wholly insufficient force was defeated, followed by our successful fights against them of El Teb and Tamai. Now we found wharves for big ships, warehouses, and European buildings, a stand with 3,000 people on it, and, most important of all, a railway going straight to Berber and Khartoum. Lord Kitchener and the *Sirdar* of the Egyptian army, General Sir Reginald Wingate (whose best man I had been twenty-three years previously), met Their Imperial Majesties, and after ceremonies at the Port away we steamed seventy miles to the hill station of Sinkat, 3,000 ft. above the sea. There a very picturesque review was held, and by evening we were again in the *Medina* heading for home; and after calling at Malta and Gibraltar, where General Sir Leslie Rundle and General Sir Archibald Hunter were respectively Governors, the *Medina* dropped anchor oft Spithead at 10 a.m. on the 4th February; being Sunday, it was decided that Their Majesties would not make their official landing until next day. It was intensely cold, a bitter wind, and under such circumstances a ship is not a pleasant place to be in.

In spite of the intense cold H.M. Queen Alexandra was on the quay at Portsmouth at 10 a.m. next morning to receive Their Majesties and accompanied them to London. Then followed a procession *via* Victoria Street, Whitehall, and The Mall to Buckingham Palace, and next day, the 6th February, the thanksgiving service at St. Paul's, to which I rode behind Their Majesties' carriage.

On the 9th February a farewell dinner was given at the Officers' Club, Aldershot, to my wife and myself, in view of my early move to Salisbury. Lieutenant-General Sir Henry Lawson presided, and some sixty senior officers were present—a very pleasing and touching evening.

The Southern command was territorially a large one, for it covered twelve counties, with head-quarters at Salisbury. It only had one regular division, the 3rd, but included the depôts and Territorial troops of the twelve counties. In addition the commander-in-chief was responsible for a great extent of coast defence, including the large ports of Portsmouth and Plymouth. The coast-line for which he was responsible commenced east of Portsmouth where Sussex joins Hampshire, and, including the Isle of Wight, extended round the Land's End up to the Severn.

The great training area of Salisbury Plain was also part of the command. It may be inferred from this description that a wide tract of country had to be covered, and therefore it is not

408

surprising that I found myself even more occupied there than at Aldershot.

The great advantage I gained was getting into touch with Territorial troops. Hitherto, excepting my five years at Aldershot, when I practically had nothing but regular troops to deal with, I had, since I came to years of discretion— in other words, since I became a senior officer—served entirely abroad, and I really knew nothing personally of Territorials.

In the Southern command, however, I soon got to know and to appreciate them. Their keen study of soldiering, their earnestness, thoroughness, and, considering the short time they were embodied each year, their remarkable standard of efficiency, impressed me very soon. The more I saw of them the higher the opinion I formed of them, and the greater did my confidence become that in them we really had a most valuable asset should the nation be in trouble. Yeomanry, Artillery, Infantry, Engineer, A.S. Corps and Medical units were all heart and soul in their work and showed great *esprit de corps.*

It was on account of this high opinion formed between the time I took up the command and the outbreak of the Great War in 1914, about two and a quarter years, that, as will be seen later, I urged Lord Kitchener in August 1914 to use them as the basis for expanding the army.

There was a novelty and a charm about the commander-in-chief's house at Salisbury, far away from the everlasting bugles, all the formalities of military barracks and guards, and close to the beautiful cathedral and the agreeable people who inhabited the Close. It was so peaceful and quiet, and more like a home than an official residence. I remember so well remarking to a delightful canon of the cathedral, whilst he was showing me round his old-world garden, on the atmosphere of peace, adding that I feared the place might be rather enervating. He looked at me and said, "Surely you wouldn't have it otherwise. I have lived here nineteen years, and enjoy being enervated."

Soon after taking up our residence at Harnham Cliff, by which name the house was called, our family was increased by two honorary daughters, the two children of my chief in India, Sir Power Palmer, my wife's step-uncle. As they had become orphans and homeless, my wife and I adopted them.

I was, as at Aldershot, very fortunate in my staff. Major-General E. A. Altham (who made a name for himself in the Great War and became Lieutenant-General Sir Edward) was in charge of Administration. I shall not say more about him, except that his writing was not very easy to read, for he might see these *Memoirs*, and, being a modest man, I do not wish to make him blush by describing at length his remarkable abilities and personality.

If he had had a shade of luck he would have gone bang to the top of the tree. He was assisted by Colonel W. H. Rycroft as A.Q.M.G. and it was to him I was to be deeply indebted in 1914, as will be seen in my account of the Great War. Brigadier-General R. A. K. Montgomery (now Major-General Sir Robert), who had been on my staff at Aldershot, was head of the general staff, and a first-rate one too. He had, as his right-hand man, Major W. H. Anderson, afterwards commandant of the Staff College and distinguished in the war as Major-General Sir Hastings A.

The 3rd Division was commanded by Major-General Sir Henry Rawlinson (Lord Rawlinson) and, shortly before the division embarked in 1914, by Major-General Hubert Hamilton. Brigadier-General H. de B. de Lisle (now Lieutenant-General Sir Beauvoir) commanded the 2nd Cavalry Brigade at Tidworth. The Infantry Brigades of the 3rd Division were commanded as follows: the 7th at Tidworth, Laurence Drummond, to be succeeded shortly by McCracken; the 8th at Plymouth, Beauchamp Doran; the 9th at Portsmouth, H. H. Burney, to be succeeded by F. C. Shaw just before the war.

McCracken became Lieutenant-General Sir Frederick and Shaw Lieutenant-General the Right Hon. Sir Frederick, both great fighting Generals. I have gone thus fully into particulars of the senior officers I had to work with, as I wish to emphasise that I was fortunate in having so many who rose to distinction.

I found two expert gunners at Portsmouth and Plymouth. At

the former was Major-General W. E. Blewitt, an old Harrovian who had made a great name for himself as Director of Artillery at the War Office, and at the latter Major-General F. A. Bowles, lately Inspector-General of Artillery in India, who was shortly to be succeeded by Major-General A. P. Penton.

The Territorial Divisions were commanded, the Wessex by Major-General C. G. Donald, and the South Midland by Major-General J. L. Keir (now Lieutenant-General Sir John K.). I should add the names of two other distinguished officers each for some months C.R.A. of the 3rd Division—Brigadier-General J. P. Du Cane (now Lieutenant-General Sir John Du Cane) and Brigadier-General F. Wing.

The latter, alas! was killed in 1914, having just been promoted Major-General for distinguished service and appointed to command a division.

The programme here, so far as I was concerned, was much the same as at Aldershot, as regards training, staff tours, annual manoeuvres, and frequent inspections; but the scattered nature of the command and the units necessitated very heavy travelling.

There are few salient events to record, except that Salisbury Plain had acquired increased importance by the establishment of the centre of training in the Air Service at Upavon, an interest which was considerably marred by the frequency of fatal accidents, almost to be expected from the experimental stage the art of flying was then in.

I see I have noted in my diary that on the 10th August 1912 I became a full general, and on the king's birthday the following year a G.C.B.

On the 22nd May 1913 there was an incident worth mentioning, for that day the Flying Corps made their first appearance on record at a ceremonial parade and flew by the saluting point.

On the 8th September I attended the funeral of the hero of Maiwand, General Sir John Slade, an old and much regretted friend.

LIEUTENANT-GENERAL SIR H. SMITH-DORRIEN K.C.B. IN 1911,
FROM A CARTOON BY "SPY" IN *THE WORLD*

In March 1914 the attempt to enforce Home Rule created a very serious crisis in Ulster, and the Government were much concerned with the attitude of officers who made it pretty clear that they were not prepared to use force against Ulster; it was a mercy that the situation, which became more and more critical, was eventually saved by the outbreak of the Great War. When the tragic murder of the heir to the Austrian Throne, which eventually set the whole of Europe in a blaze, took place, on the 28th June 1914, I was at Le Touquet with my family, and little did I think that three months later I should, after six weeks' desperate fighting, be passing within forty miles of that place at the head of an army corps, as part of a great flank march from the Aisne to join in the saving of the left flank of the Allied armies.

On the 8th July, as chairman of the Harrow Association, I took the chair at the Savoy at a dinner of some three hundred old Harrovians. In the speech I made, after referring to matters connected with the school, I asked permission to assume a somewhat serious tone, when I urged that, as there was a war-cloud hanging over Europe, which might burst at any moment, it behoved every old Harrovian not only to befit himself for the coming struggle, but to encourage his relations to do the same. After dinner I was good-naturedly chaffed by my particular friends and asked what had made me so gloomy that evening.

I mention this as evidence that even then there were few people in England who realised the gravity of the situation. We soldiers had had so many first-hand examples of how Germany was preparing and had failed to convince those in high places that I was almost in despair. One instance especially comes to my mind. When I was commander-in-chief at Aldershot I had planned a staff tour which involved taking a lot of rooms for some days at a certain hotel at a large southern seaport town. My staff applied to the hotel manager for the rooms, but were told that all were engaged during the week we required them by German officers who were also carrying out a staff tour. Can anyone imagine a body of English officers being allowed to carry out a staff tour in Germany without interruption?

I had intended that my *Memoirs*, so far as publication during my lifetime, should end here, but I have been urged over and over again that I owe it to the gallant 2nd Corps, which I had the honour to command, to give the world my personal account of their glorious deeds in the opening weeks of the Great War—and this I have at last decided to do. I have, too, thought it wise to touch briefly on my experiences in command of the 2nd Army, so as to throw some light on my reasons for leaving France.

It will give the public a fair idea of the magnitude of the task these armies had to perform, if I commence by quoting an interesting note to page 83 of the official *History of the War* to the effect that the strength of the two divisions of the 2nd Corps was just under 36,000, whereas Wellington had only 31,585 British troops at the battle of Waterloo. To enable a more complete comparison to be made I will add that at Quatre Bras and Waterloo on the 16th and 18th June 1815 the British losses were about 9,000, and that at the battle of Mons and Le Cateau 23rd, 24th, and 26th August 1914 the losses of the 2nd Corps amounted to 7,645, whilst the hours of fighting, arduous conditions, and the distances marched were infinitely greater in 1914.

I confess I find the task a difficult one. First of all, the account must be a true one, and this is not easy unless actions, not only of those above me but also of those below me, are placed in such strong light as to hurt feelings or injure reputations, and both of these undesirable results it will be my endeavour to avoid. I have in all matters of fact, such as dates, hours, positions, movements and casualties, verified from official documents before recording them herein. The political events which led up to the war are too well known and beyond the province of personal memoirs, so I shall commence with the first event which affected myself.

CHAPTER 24

The Retreat From Mons; le Cateau

On the 27th July 1914 a wire from the War Office directed me to guard all vulnerable points in the Southern command, as Austria was attacking Servia and there were distinct possibilities of Britain being involved in a European War.

Two days later further orders came to the effect that the precautionary period was to be recognised. This was a period provided for under the Mobilisation for War Scheme which involved reinforcing certain stations throughout the command.

On the 3rd August all training was stopped and troops in camp ordered to their peace stations. Next day I was told that mobilisation, to commence from the morrow, had been decided on, and on the 5th war against Germany was declared.

That day too I was directed to hand over my command to Lieutenant-General Sir William Pitcairn Campbell, a proved leader in the Boer War, and to take command of a Home Defence army under Sir Ian Hamilton.

The next few days were taken up in seeing the units of the 3rd Division under Major-General Hubert Hamilton entrain for their ports of embarkation, and in visits to London and the War Office in connection with my new army, and it was not until the 13th August that I actually handed over the Southern command to Pitcairn Campbell.

During my visits to the War Office I had several discussions with Lord Kitchener, who had become Secretary of State for War—especially on the subject of the expansion of the army. I was very insistent that, rather than use all available material for creating entirely new divisions, it were preferable to build up on the existing Territorial Army, splitting each unit so as to provide many more cadres, and filling up the cadres thus created by recruits and the many trained ex-officers and men who offered themselves from civil life.

I argued that this system of expansion would provide efficient units in the shortest time, and would leave available for training purposes a very large number of excellent instructors who would otherwise be merged into the fighting ranks. Lord Kitchener was sympathetic, as he always was, and asked me to draft a scheme. This I did, but it was not accepted.

On the 17th August came the sad news of the death of the commander of our 2nd Corps—poor Jimmy Grierson, the man who was heart and soul a soldier, who, once a *persona grata* with the Kaiser, and a welcome guest in the German army, had of late years seen through their wily machinations, and devoted himself to preparing the army and himself for the day when the Germans should unmask. *Der Tag* had arrived, and Grierson landed in France, bursting with enthusiasm and thirsting for the fray, when the cruel blow fell and the nation lost an unrivalled leader in the very hour of her need.

Little did I think, on receiving the news, how his death would affect me; but the following morning, much to my surprise, I received a telegram appointing me to succeed him, and directing me to go and see the Secretary of State at once.

Lord Kitchener's first words to me, when I entered his room at the War Office that afternoon, expressed grave doubt as to whether he was wise in selecting me to succeed Grierson, since the commander-in-chief in France had asked that General Sir Herbert Plumer should be selected to fill the appointment. However, after thinking the matter over, he adhered to his decision to send me.

I think I justified that decision, for the first six months at any rate, and especially after the battle of Le Cateau, for the commander-in-chief was so genuinely grateful to me for having, as he described it in his generous dispatch,[1] of 7th September 1914, saved his left wing, that he did not stint his praise of the corps during that period.

Perhaps the strongest evidence of his confidence in me was his selecting me at the end of the year for command of one of the two armies, which larger organisations had become necessary by the increase in the size of the British forces in France.

But to return to the 18th August. After my interview I was commanded to Buckingham Palace, and there most graciously received by Their Majesties.

I then returned to Salisbury to say farewell to my family, and on the 20th,. accompanied by my personal staff (Major Hope Johnstone, A.M.S., Captain W. A. T. Bowly, *aide-de-camp,* and Colonel W. Rycroft, who had been appointed as A.Q.M.G. to the 2nd Corps in succession to Colonel Edye (injured in a motor accident), I reached Boulogne in the evening of the 20th, and was much impressed by the lack of excitement, the general cheerfulness and efficient arrangements at that busy port.

On arriving at Amiens at 8 a.m., I was met by the Inspector-General Lines of Communication, Lieutenant-General Sir F. Robb, who gave me my orders, which were to join the headquarters of my army corps at Bavai at once.

The train took me as far as Landrecies, where I was met by Lieutenant-Colonel the Hon. A.V. F. Russell, Grenadier Guards, who was Military Attaché at Berlin and had just had the unpleasant experience of leaving that place, and the less unpleasant one of joining the staff of the 2nd Corps. He took me the fifteen miles to Bavai by motor. After an interview with my new staff and being placed *au courant* with all they could tell me of the situation, I motored back to see the commander-in-chief at Le Cateau, some eighteen miles.

He received me pleasantly, and explained the general situation as far as he could, for the fog of war was peculiarly dense at that time. I gleaned, however, that we were to move on the morrow to the general line of the Mons-Condé Canal, the 1st Corps on

---

1. Dispatch quoted later in chapter.

the right, my corps on the left, the latter's position to be along the line of the canal from Mons westward, but that it was only to be a preliminary step to a further move forward which would take the form of **a** slight right-wheel into Belgium, the British army forming the outer flank, pivoting on the French 5th Army. Shortly after leaving G.H.Q. on my return journey to Bavai I found the road blocked, bullets flying, and the sound of firing.

Fairly puzzled as to how the enemy could have got there, I got out of my motor to find a battery in considerable confusion held up by sharpshooters across the road.

It turned out to be a case of mistaken identity. The battery had been challenged by some French Territorials on outpost duty, and not understanding what was required of it had tried to push on, with the result that fire was opened on it and one of our gunners killed and two wounded. This was a bad beginning, but a brief parley arranged matters and I got to my headquarters at 11 p.m., approved of the orders for the move next morning, and turned in.

The staff of the 2nd Corps differed from that of the 1st Corps, which was the regular Aldershot staff accustomed to work together, in that it had been improvised, and had yet to learn each other's peculiarities; but I had nothing to complain of, for I found an exceptionally capable and highly trained body of officers, who inspired me with confidence at once and fully justified it.

Brigadier-General G. T. Forestier-Walker (now Major-General Sir George) was my able chief of the general staff, assisted by Colonel R. S. Oxley, Lieutenant-Colonel T. H. Shoubridge, Lieutenant-Colonel the Hon. J. H. Gathorne-Hardy, and Captain B. Walcot, whilst the Adjutant and Quartermaster-General's Staff had Colonel W. B. Hickie (now Major-General Sir William) at its head with Colonel W. Rycroft (now Major-General Sir William) and Major J. B. Wroughton as assistants.

The corps was composed as follows:

3rd Division. Major-General Hubert Hamilton.
7th Infantry Brigade. Brigadier-General F. W. N. McCracken.

II Corps positions at Mons, on the Aisne, and in the La Bassée Area.

Line of retreat from Mons to Tournan, and thence the advance across the Marne to the Aisne.

Flank move from the Aisne to help close the GAP between the French left near La Bassée & the sea at Nieuport.

Remainder of Allied Troops (B.E.F., French and Belgians) connecting the Aisne with the sea, showing the GAP as closed.

THE THEATRE OF WAR IN WHICH THE 2ND CORPS OPERATED IN 1914

3rd Worcestershire.

2nd South Lancashire.

1st Wiltshire.

2nd Royal Irish Rifles.

8th Infantry Brigade. Brigadier-General B. J. C. Doran.

2nd Royal Scots.

4th Middlesex.

2nd Royal Irish.

1st Gordon Highlanders.

9th Infantry Brigade. Brigadier-General F. C. Shaw.

1st Northumberland Fusiliers.

1st Lincolnshire.

4th Royal Fusiliers.

1st Royal Scots Fusiliers.

Divisional Troops

C Squadron 15th Hussars.

3rd Cyclist Company.

23rd Brigade R.F.A. 107th, 108th, and 109th Batteries and Ammunition Column.

40th Brigade R.F.A. 6th, 23rd, and 49th Batteries and Ammunition Column.

42nd Brigade R.F.A. 29th, 41st, and 45th Batteries and Ammunition Column.

30th Howitzer Brigade R.F.A. 128th, 129th, and 130th Batteries and Ammunition Column.

48th Heavy Battery R.G.A. and Ammunition Column.

3rd Divisional Ammunition Column.

Royal Engineers. 56th and 57th Companies.

3rd Signal Company, 3rd Divisional Train, and 7th, 8th, and 9th Field Ambulances.

5th Division. Major-General Sir C. Fergusson, Bt.

13th Infantry Brigade. Brigadier-General G. J. Cuthbert.

2nd King's Own Scottish Borderers.

2nd Duke of Wellington's West Riding.

1st Queen's Own Royal West Kent.
2nd King's Own Yorkshire Light Infantry.

14th Infantry Brigade. Brigadier-General S. P. Rolt.
2nd Suffolk.
1st East Surrey.
1st D.C. Light Infantry.
2nd Manchester.

15th Infantry Brigade. Brigadier-General Count Gleichen.
1st Norfolk.
1st Bedfordshire.
1st Cheshire.
1st Dorsetshire.

Divisional Troops
A Squadron 19th Hussars.
5th Cyclist Company.
15th Brigade R.F.A. 11th, 52nd, and 80th Batteries and Ammunition Column.
27th Brigade R.F.A. 119th, 120th, and 121st Batteries and Ammunition Column.
28th Brigade R.F.A. 122nd, 123rd, and 124th Batteries and Ammunition Column.
8th Howitzer Brigade R.F.A. 37th, 61st, and 65th Batteries and Ammunition Column.
108th Heavy Battery R.G.A. and Ammunition Column.
Royal Engineers. 17th and 59th Field Companies.
5th Signal Company, 5th Divisional Train, and 13th, 14th, and 15th Field Ambulances.

Unfortunately our concentration was not completed, but the French were so insistent on our moving forward to cover their left flank that, although short of guns, field hospitals, and engineer units, the commander-in-chief decided to go without them, as the news of the enemy was that they had left Brussels and were advancing west and south of that town.

The morning of the 22nd saw us moving, and some twelve

to fifteen miles took us to the line of the canal, where in accordance with orders we took up a line of outposts extending from Pommerœul (five miles east of Condé) round the north side of Mons to Nimy and thence to Givry, twenty-one miles in all.

The 3rd Division went into billets round Mons in the area of Nimy-Ghlin-Frameries-Spiennes, and were there by 1 p.m., whilst the 5th Division rather later occupied the canal on their left from Jemappes to Pommerœul. Sir Douglas Haig's 1st Corps, which had moved on our right, took up a position facing north-east, prolonging our line by some seven miles, *i.e.* about a quarter of the B.E.F. front. As we were facing north except on the east of Mons, where we faced north-east, it will be appreciated that the British line formed a considerable salient with the town of Mons at the apex.

During this day we saw nothing of the enemy, but the cavalry division and 5th Cavalry Brigade had some smartish work towards Binche.

Our news of the enemy was very vague, but the general opinion was that considerable German forces were moving towards us and that contact on the morrow was almost a certainty.

The delight of the inhabitants, their hospitality, their enthusiastic greetings and hearty cheering as we moved along, were very inspiring, and I own to a feeling of shame when a few days later we were hurrying to the rear leaving these poor people at the mercy of a none too merciful enemy.

My own head-quarters were at Sars-la-Bruyère, south-west of Mons and Frameries, some six miles from the former and three from the latter. That afternoon I motored round the outposts and reconnoitred the positions as far as I had time, for the distances were great and my presence at my head-quarters, with so much to arrange, was necessary for a considerable part of the daylight available.

In my hasty survey I had come to the conclusion that, from a fighting point of view, our position was a very difficult one. The ground on the enemy's side of the canal commanded it from comparatively short ranges, and was densely wooded, giving them the advantage of a covered approach. Any idea of fighting a serious action on the outpost line was therefore out of the question, although such a thing in any case would have been impossible in view of the enormous extension of the corps, covering as it did twenty-one miles with only two divisions.

I came to the conclusion that our only hope, if attacked in force, would be to hold a less extended position in rear on which the outposts could fall back.

This, however, was not very encouraging, as although the ground rose considerably on a general line some two to three miles south of the canal it was so broken up by the pitheads and wired enclosures, and so thickly covered with houses, that any organised effective defence must involve great risks.

To obtain an accurate idea of the unsuitability of the ground, I recommend a careful study of the graphic description given in the *Official History,* written by Brigadier-General J. E. Edmonds, C.B., C.M.G., R.E., from which I quote the following (page 63):

> The space occupied by the 2nd Corps in particular, within the quadrangle Mons-Frameries-Dour-Boussu, is practically one huge unsightly village, traversed by a vast number of devious cobbled roads which lead from no particular starting-point to no particular destination, and broken by pit-heads and colossal slag-heaps, often over a hundred feet high. It is, in fact, a close and blind country, such as no army had yet been called upon to fight in against a civilised enemy in a great campaign.

Then on our right was the salient town of Mons, open to fire from north, east, and west, and quite indefensible, situated as we were.

However, that night I was happy in my mind, for official news of the enemy given me indicated no great strength, and I fully expected that the chief's expressed intention of moving forward again next day would be carried out. I had been given no information of the somewhat serious happenings in the French army on our right, which I learned years later, namely, that it had been forced back,[2] and was already some nine miles south of Mons with a gap of at least nine miles between the right of our 1st Corps and the left of the 18th French Corps, thus leaving us in a very vulnerable, indefensible, and salient position. Had I known of this serious situation I doubt much if my night's rest would have been as enjoyable as it proved to be—for I should have been racking my brain as to what the object of our remaining so isolated was and why we did not retire.

Mercifully, I was in blissful ignorance—nor was I disillusioned next morning when about 6 a.m. the chief appeared at my head-quarters, and, addressing his corps and cavalry division commanders assembled there, told us (*vide* his dispatch of 7th September 1914) that little more than one, or at most two, enemy corps, with perhaps a cavalry division, were facing the B.E.F. So it was evident that he too was in blissful ignorance of the real situation.

Sir John was in excellent form, and told us to be prepared to move forward, or to fight where we were, but to get ready for the latter by strengthening our outposts and preparing the bridges over the canal for demolition. I took the opportunity of emphasising the weakness of my general line and the danger of holding on to the Mons salient, remarking that I was issuing orders for the preparation of a retired position south-west and clear of the town of Mons to cover, should a retirement become necessary, the advanced troops at Nimy and Obourg who would have to fall back behind Mons, as soon as things got so hot as to risk their being cut off.

The chief expressed himself in agreement, and approved my action. He then went off to Valenciennes to order the 19th Brigade, who were detraining there, to prolong the outpost line from my left to Condé. The dispositions of the 2nd Corps were roughly as follows: 3rd Division (Hubert Hamilton). The 8th

---

2. *Vide* Sketch-map from the *Official History*, giving positions of the French 5th Army at 4 p.m. on 22nd August, showing how isolated the B.E.F. was when it fought at Mons on the 23rd August.

Infantry Brigade (Doran) on the right in touch with the 1st Corps, the 2nd Royal Irish holding the hill, Bois la Haut, just south-east of Mons. The 1st Gordons and 2nd Royal Scots about Harmignies. The 4th Middlesex in the outpost line from Bois la Haut to Obourg, north-east of Mons. The 9th Infantry Brigade (Shaw) on the left of the 8th, three battalions, the 4th Royal Fusiliers, 1st Royal Scots Fusiliers, and lst/5th Fusiliers holding the outpost line on the canal from the left of the 4th Middlesex to the bridge of Mariette, some six miles, with the 1st Lincolns in reserve at Cuesme, one mile south-west of Mons.

The 7th Brigade (McCracken) in Divisional reserve about Ciply, two miles south of Mons. The 5th Division (Sir Charles Fergusson) continued the line along the canal westwards from Mariette.

The 13th Brigade (Cuthbert) took the next three miles to Les Herbières. First came the 1st Royal West Kents with the 2nd Scottish Borderers on their left, the other two battalions, the 2nd Duke of Wellingtons and 2nd Yorkshire Light Infantry being in reserve in St. Ghislain. Lastly came the 14th Brigade (Rolt) from Les Herbières, two and a half miles to the extreme left of the corps at Pommerœul bridge, the 1st East Surrey on the right with the 1st Cornwall Light Infantry on the left, and the 2nd Suffolk and 2nd Manchester in reserve.

The 15th Brigade (Gleichen), consisting of 1st Norfolk, 1st Bedford, 1st Cheshire, and 1st Dorset, were preparing a position in rear and in reserve about Dour.

I am not attempting to describe the positions of the artillery, for, owing to the broken nature of the ground, the batteries and even guns had to be very much scattered, and to take up positions where they could. Even if I had personal knowledge of their several positions it would take much space to describe them, and as it is I could only do so by copying from the official account, which is at everyone's disposal; but I can briefly say that the handling, initiative, and courageous action throughout this day and the next was something even for that distinguished corps to be proud of; though even that standard was excelled by their deeds of heroism

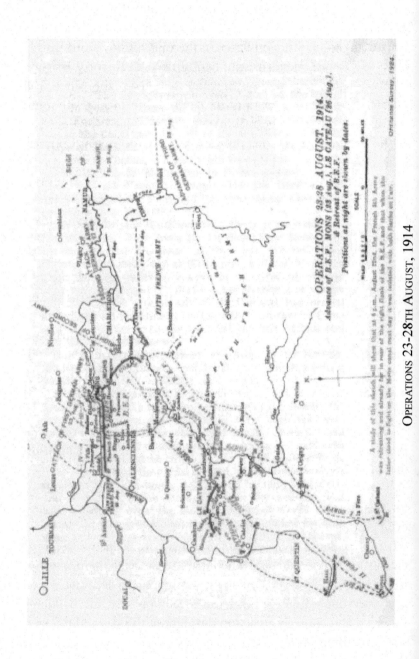

OPERATIONS 23–28TH AUGUST, 1914

and self-sacrifice at the battle of Le Cateau.

Again, I shall not attempt a full description of the fighting, but shall confine myself largely to my personal experiences.

We were not left long in doubt as to the chances of an action, for even whilst the commander-in-chief was talking to us at 6 a.m., though we did not know it at the time, our cavalry was in contact and the 4th Middlesex on outpost about Obourg were exchanging shots with the enemy. It was a Sunday morning, thick and wet at first, but clearing later became a lovely day. The church bells were sounding, and there were streams of people in every village in their black Sunday clothes going to church as if nothing unusual was happening.

At, as far as I recollect, about 9 a.m. I motored to the left of my outpost line at Pommerœul, and leaving the car crossed the bridge and saw an interesting scrap between the Cornwalls and German scouts. I then passed along east on the south side of the canal when about 10 a.m. the first German shell I had seen fired burst on the road just in front of my car close to Jemappes. The German guns, however, had been busy opposite Mons some time earlier, and this was natural from the nature of the enemy advance, which was more or less in the form of a left wheel, their outer or right flank coming on to the canal last; in fact, some of our troops remained north of the canal until 6 p.m.

It was a day of desperate and heavy fighting, especially on our right about Mons. In that salient and on the hill to the south-east of it, Bois la Haut, the 8th and 9th Brigades were tried to the utmost, the 4th Middlesex losing half their strength; but they more than held their own and eventually fell back, evacuating the salient with the greatest skill, and at nightfall, although some-what retired, our line was still unpenetrated. There was, however, a moment when the danger of penetration was very serious.

At about 7 p.m. a report came in saying that the enemy had penetrated the line near Frameries and were swarming through that village. I had no troops left, and all I could do was to request the 5th Division to push out to their right, which they did by sending the 1st Bedfords to Pâturages. Knowing the gap was appreciable owing to the left flank of the 3rd Division in retiring having failed to join up with the right flank of the 5th Division, and that if the Germans realised it there was nothing to prevent their pushing through in large numbers and rendering our position untenable, I sent the following message to G.H.Q.:

> To G.H.Q., G 271, August 23rd. Third Division report at 6.47 p.m. the Germans are in front of his main position and are not attacking at present, they are, however, working round 3rd Division on left flank. If it should appear that there is a danger of my centre being pierced I can see no course but to order a general retirement on Bavai position. Have I your permission to adopt this course if it appears necessary? From 2nd Corps, 7.15 p.m. (Signed Oxley, Colonel.)

I then jumped into a motor and went to General Haig's headquarters at Bonnet, some four miles away, and asked if he would allow Haking's 5th Infantry Brigade, which was on the road about two and a half miles from Frameries, to push on to cover the gap. I found Hubert Hamilton's G.S.O.2, Lieutenant-Colonel F. B. Maurice, there on the same quest. Haig readily gave his consent, and Maurice dashed off to tell Haking. The situation had, however, been almost restored by the 9th Brigade, and the Germans driven back before the 5th Brigade reached Frameries; but I would remark that although I had contracted my front to about twelve miles, it was still far too large for the troops I had and every man was practically in the front line, so that a break through, with no reserves to meet it, must have entailed retreat. Haking's borrowed Brigade remained to hold the gap.

By way of comparison I would mention that at Le Cateau, where the position was infinitely superior for a defensive action, the extreme front was only nine miles, and there I had ten brigades available, whereas in my front of twelve miles on the 23rd and 24th I only had six brigades.

The fighting was over for the time and our troops, though weary, and in spite of their heavy losses, were in tremendous

428

heart and full of confidence in their superiority to the enemy; and in this they were justified, for, although numerically vastly superior, the Germans had succumbed absolutely before the steady discipline and accurate rifle-fire of the British soldier. It was this rifle-fire, and the fog of war so thick on both sides, which were the outstanding features of the day.

The rapid and accurate rifle-fire to which our men had been trained was an eye-opener to the enemy, and they believed at the time that they were opposed by an enormous number of machine-guns. Their losses were very heavy, for they came on in dense formations, offering the most perfect targets, and it was not until they had been mown down in thousands that they adopted more open formations. For some years the British army had toiled to perfect itself in this rapid rifle-fire; it had given an immense amount of hard work and it was satisfactory to find that the toil and trouble had been more than justified.

As to the fog of war, we certainly had no idea that such large forces were against us—the German account gives three and a half divisions against our 3rd Division and two and a half against our 5th—whereas the Germans had no idea of our whereabouts or our strength. In his orders for the 23rd, so our *Official History* tells us, all the German Commander, General Von Kluck, could tell his troops was that he knew of a British squadron of cavalry near Mons, and that a British aeroplane had been shot down. The Germans do not appear to have known where we had landed, or that we were actually in the line of battle.

There is no doubt that the 2nd Corps felt very proud of themselves that night, and justly so; but their losses had been heavy—1,571 killed and wounded, whereas those of the 1st Corps had only been forty.

The day, too, had given me great confidence not only in the troops and their leaders but in my own staff. It had been a great day for testing the latter, as reports, some of them none too rosy, had been coming in in a continuous stream, and Forestier-Walker was never for a moment at a loss as to how to deal with them and as to what instructions to issue to remedy a difficult situation.

It was during this afternoon too that Allenby's Cavalry Division was moved along our rear from east to west to take up a position in the neighbourhood of Thulin, a difficult operation, necessitating keeping roads, thronged with battle impedimenta, clear, and this was admirably carried out by the 2nd Corps Staff. The 8th Brigade (Doran's) had heavy work with the enemy, and it was not until 3 a.m. on the 24th that they were back at Nouvelles, three miles south of Mons and the same distance east of Frameries.

The 2nd Corps then stood generally on the line from right to left Nouvelles-Ciply-Frameries-Pâturages-Wasmes-Hornu-Boussu, confidently awaiting renewal of the battle at dawn; for the commander-in-chief had issued orders that this was to be done.

Nothing could be more flattering to their grand fighting spirit than the German accounts, which show that the enemy were completely stopped all along the line with, to use their own words, bloody losses.

At about 11 p.m. a message from G.H.Q. summoned my chief staff officer to army head-quarters at Le Cateau, about thirty miles away, and it was past 3 a.m. on the 24th when Forestier-Walker returned to my head-quarters to say that the commander-in-chief had, in view of fresh information, decided that instead of standing to fight, the whole B.E.F. was to retire. I naturally asked him for the plan of retirement, and was told that G.H.Q. were issuing none, though he had gathered that the idea was for the 1st Corps to cover the retirement of the 2nd, but that I was to see Haig and arrange a plan with him.

There must have been some very good reason why four or five hours of valuable time had been lost by sending for staff officers instead of sending the order and plan for retirement directly the chief had decided on it. It must be remembered that we had prepared for continuing the fight and our fighting impedimenta, such as ammunition columns, were close behind the troops and blocking the roads, and before a retirement could commence, these would have to be cleared away; also that it would take a long time to get the change of orders to the troops, and lastly that I had to find out what Haig was going to do. All this could have been done and the retirement actually begun before dawn had we known in time. As it was, daylight was already breaking when the order reached me and some hours must elapse before the retirement could commence, by which time we should be in deadly grips with the enemy and would have to carry out one of the most difficult operations in war, namely, breaking off a fight and retiring with the enemy close on the top of us. Such were the thoughts which flashed through my mind. However, my staff were quite unruffled; Forestier-Walker quickly got his retirement orders out, and the invaluable A.Q.M.G., Rycroft, got the roads clear by sending the impedimenta off.

It must have been approaching noon when I found time to seek out Haig near Bonnet and discuss the retirement in accordance with G.H.Q. "plan of action," which was roughly that the 1st Corps should cover the retirement of the 2nd, but that Haig and I were to meet and settle details. By the time I met him the 1st Corps' retirement, ably planned, was in full swing, for Johnny Gough, B.G.G.S.,[3] of the 1st Corps, directly the chief gave his orders to retire, wired from Le Cateau to Haig, so that the latter was able to issue his instructions at 2 a.m. and get his troops started off with such promptness that the main bodies of his divisions reached their destinations at Feignies, La Longueville, and Bavai about 10 a.m., specially detailed rear-guards remaining in positions to help us.

My G.H.Q. at Sars-la-Bruyère not being in telegraphic communication with Le Cateau, Forestier-Walker had had to bring the order to me by motor, and daylight was approaching, as I have already said, when he reached me.

This happened almost simultaneously with the opening of the offensive, for the Germans opened a heavy fire against the right of the 2nd Corps before dawn and by 5.15 a.m. were

---

3. Brigadier-General John Gough, V.C., one of our most promising soldiers, killed on the 22nd February 1915.

attacking along the whole line. The orders issued by Forestier-Walker were clear and to the point. He told the 5th and 3rd Divisions that the 1st Corps was retiring first to certain positions in order to cover the retirement of the 3rd Division; this latter would head for Sars-la-Bruyère and when it did the 5th Division should aim at the line Blaugies and Montignies-sur-Roc. At 6 a.m. the 8th Brigade of the 3rd Division commenced falling back from Nouvelles and were not seriously troubled by the enemy. The 7th Brigade from Ciply and 9th Brigade from Frameries, however, were hard pressed, and drove off several determined attacks in which the Germans, according to their own accounts, lost very heavily, before they could retire. It was 9 a.m. before the 9th Brigade could leave Frameries towards Sars-la-Bruyère, and later still when the 7th Brigade moved off on Genly. The fighting was very heavy in the streets of Frameries, and the Lincolns and South Lanes as rear-guards of the 7th Brigade about Ciply had desperate fighting, the latter losing nearly 300 men before they could move off. These rear-guards by their devoted bravery had done their work, for the German dead lay thick on the ground, giving their *Kameraden* such a salutary lesson that the retirement of the 3rd Division was no longer interfered with.

I would call attention here to the fact that General Joffre had directed that the B.E.F. in its retirement should keep west of the fortress of Maubeuge, and a glance at the map will show that this necessitated a crab-like movement, the 1st Corps crowding in on the 3rd Division and that division on the 5th Division, and unless the last could edge off more to the west the time would come when some troops would be squeezed out. I mention this as the situation actually arose later on and, having been foreseen, was provided for.

I will now briefly describe the movements of the 5th Division. They were holding a line from Pâturages through Wasmes, Hornu, and Boussu—with reserves at Dour. They were subjected to heavy artillery fire before dawn, which continued for four hours, and appears to have made very little impression. Curiously enough, the event which first enabled the Germans to break their line was due to an accident, but as it gives a lesson of military importance I shall recite it. It will be remembered that on the previous evening Haig had lent me the 5th Infantry Brigade of his corps to fill a gap between the 3rd and 5th Divisions, and well they did it. At 9 a.m. on the 24th, however, in accordance with orders from their own division, that brigade began retiring. At the time, although the fire was heavy, not a German was visible. Almost at once the flank of the 5th Division, exposed by the withdrawal of the borrowed brigade, was in trouble, and the Bedfords and Dorsets had to fight hard to save a break through. I impute blame to no one, for in a retirement it was a very possible thing to happen; but the incident is a good illustration of the dangers of a divided command.

A lot of very brisk and complicated fighting took place, and this is best read in the official account, for it is too detailed to find a place in this *Memoir*. The troops behaved magnificently, and many gallant deeds were performed. It was not until 11 a.m., when some of his advanced troops had already fallen back, that I was able to tell Sir Charles Fergusson that he was free to carry out a general retirement. This he proceeded to do, but not without some very severe fighting. One battery and the 2nd Battalion Duke of Wellington's had a desperate fight, inflicting very heavy losses and driving back six battalions of the enemy before they could retire themselves.

This they did successfully but with a loss to the Duke's of close on 400. The cavalry division, with the 19th Brigade, which was attached to it, were retiring on the west flank of the army, and, moving rather faster than the 5th Division, had exposed the latter's left flank. Then took place the action at Élouges so graphically described in the *Official History*, when Colonel C. R. Ballard (now brigadier-general, C.B., C.M.G.), with the Norfolks and Cheshires of the 15th Brigade and the cavalry and guns, covered themselves with glory and held off an overwhelming force of Germans which had been sent by Von Kluck to envelop our left or west flank.

About 2.30 p.m. Colonel Ballard was able to retire, but the day was not over yet, for serious fighting continued all the afternoon. I regret to say that the Cheshires, who fought most gallantly, did not receive the order to retire, and were isolated and surrounded at Audregnies, when they fought until they were almost all killed and wounded and were forced to surrender— only two officers and 200 men out of a thousand of this Battalion were in bivouac with their Brigade that evening.

My head-quarters had moved back in the course of the morning from Sars-la-Bruyère to Hon, and whilst at that place Prince Henri d'Orléans reported himself to me with instructions from the chief that he was to be attached to my staff.

I referred a short way back to the congestion which was likely to occur unless the 5th Division could work off to the west, and to prepare to meet it, should it arise, Forestier-Walker had sent a staff officer (I am almost sure it was Major Kincaid Smith) to report on the nature of the country behind the west flank of that division. When therefore at about 3 p.m. pressure on the flank and the fact that it was fighting a desperate action, put out of the question any edging of the 5th Division to the west, I directed the 3rd Division, then free of the enemy, to move across its rear.

This resulted in the 7th Brigade, which was in reserve, going to Wargnies, six and a half miles west of Bavai, with the 8th supporting it, and the 9th, which had been on rearguard, in reserve nearer Bavai.

This move worked admirably, for it secured the west flank, gave the harried 5th Division an area to fall back into where both its flanks could be secure, and gave more shoulder-room to the 1st Corps, which was getting a bit compressed between Maubeuge and Bavai, chiefly owing to the fact that the direction of retirement rendered it necessary that some of the troops of the two corps should use the same road for a time.

Though this manoeuvre involved an interchange of positions of the two divisions in subsequent movements no complications resulted. Again we had suffered heavy losses, 2,200 in the 2nd

Corps, 250 in the cavalry, 100 in the 1st Corps, and forty in the 19th Brigade. The 2nd Corps' losses thus amounted to 3,784 in the two days, or about seventeen *per cent*, of its infantry war strength.

In a day of such brilliant fighting it would seem almost invidious to mention any troops in particular, but I think I can emphasise the glorious work of the 15th Brigade in the flank-guard fight near Élouges, when they lost over 1,100, one-third of their fighting strength, but saved our exposed flank.

At 6 p.m., hearing the chief had come up from Le Cateau to his advanced head-quarters at Bavai, I sought him out and found him in the Mairie, and, describing the action of the 2nd Corps and its positions, asked for instructions as to our further retirement. The chief replied that I could do as I liked, but that Haig intended to start at 5 a.m. I remonstrated, saying that unless we moved early we should have a repetition of that day (the 24th) when orders had been issued too late to avoid the enemy coming to close grips.

He asked me what I proposed. I replied that I wished to start off my impedimenta, which had already been in bivouac several hours, soon after midnight, followed by the troops at such times as would ensure my rear-guards being south of the Valenciennes-Jenlain-Bavai road by 5 a.m. Sir John concurred, remarking that Haig could still do as he intended.

I then crossed the room to the table where Sir Archibald Murray, the chief of the staff, was working, and asked him to induce the chief to issue an order for the whole force to move early and simultaneously. Murray said he would see what he could do later on, and he was evidently successful, for an order (See below) was issued, timed 8.25 p.m., ordering the B.E.F. to move to the Le Cateau position and to be clear of the Jenlain-Bavai-Maubeuge road by 5.30 a.m.

Operation Order No. 7 by Field-Marshal Sir John French, G.C.B., etc.,
Commander-in-Chief, British Expeditionary Force
Bavai,

24th August 1914.

1. The army will move tomorrow, 25th instant, to a position in the neighbourhood of Le Cateau, exact positions will be pointed out on the ground tomorrow.

2. Corps will march so that their rear-guards are clear of the Maubeuge-Bavai-Eth road by 5.30 a.m.

3. Roads available:

1st Corps, with 5th Cavalry Brigade attached. All roads east of, but excluding, Bavai-Montay road.

2nd Corps. Bavai-Montay road inclusive, up to but excluding the road Wargnies-Villers-Pol-Ruesnes-Capelle-sur-Ecaillon-Vertain-Romerie-Solesmes.

Cavalry Division, with 19th Infantry Brigade attached. The last-named road inclusive and all roads to the westward.

4. Two brigades of the Cavalry Division with Divisional Cavalry of the 2nd Corps, under command of a Brigadier to be named by the G.O.C. Cavalry Division, will cover the movement of the 2nd Corps.

The remainder of the Cavalry Division, with the 19th Infantry Brigade, under command of the G.O.C. Cavalry Division, will cover the west flank.

5. Reports to head-quarters, Bavai, up to 5 a.m., then to head-quarters Le Cateau.

6. A staff officer from Corps and Cavalry Division will report to General Head-quarters, Le Cateau, at 5 a.m. to receive orders as to positions.

(Signed) A. J. Murray, Lieutenant-General, Chief of the general staff, for F.-M. C.-in-C.

Issued at 8.25 p.m.

Soon after midnight the transport, reserve ammunition columns, etc., were on the move, and by 5.30 a.m., in accordance with G.H.Q. orders, my rear-guards were endeavouring to leave the Jenlain-Bavai-Maubeuge road, but the whole corps was delayed somewhat by the passage of General Sordet's Cavalry Corps, which, ordered to the west of the Le Cateau position,

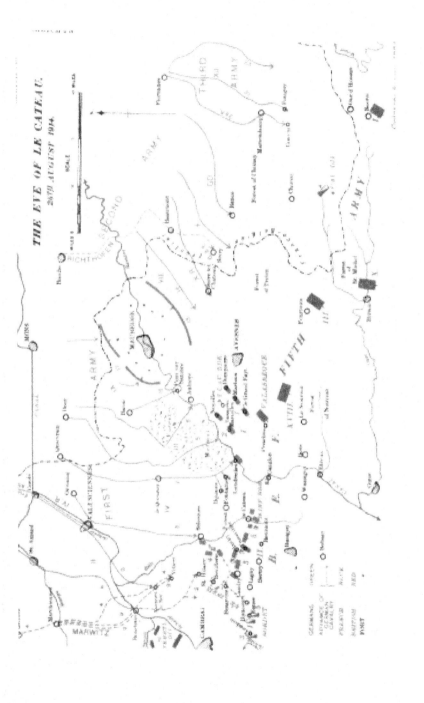

THE EVE OF LE CATEAU.
26th AUGUST 1914.

was moving from east to west.

It will be seen from the order that the boundary, east of which I could not go, which separated the 1st and 2nd Corps in this day's march, was the very straight road from Bavai to Montay, which latter place is one mile short of the town of Le Cateau. On the 1st Corps side of this road is the forest of Mormal, devoid of practicable roads leading in the direction in which the B.E.F. was moving; consequently the 1st Corps had to march on the east side of this forest and to maintain communication with the 2nd Corps through it—a matter of supreme difficulty. As a matter of fact, I heard nothing of the 1st Corps throughout the day. No information was sent me by G.H.Q. concerning it, and I imagined that all was going well and we should join upon the Le Cateau position in the evening according to orders.

The nearest part of the Le Cateau position was some two miles beyond the town, and as the 2nd would occupy the western half and the 1st Corps the eastern half, the distances we had to march were about the same. In any case it was a very long march with troops worn out with incessant fighting and by lack of sleep, for by the shortest road over twenty miles had to be covered and as much as twenty-five by the longest.

I heard, some time afterwards, that the 1st Corps had had considerable difficulties to deal with, for although but little interfered with by the enemy, they had had to cross and recross the Sambre and to share roads with French troops retiring in the same direction, and further that they had been some hours late in starting that morning, with the result that they had only reached the line Landrecies-Maroilles-Marbaix when night overtook them and they had gone into billets, thus leaving a dangerous gap of eight miles between the two corps. These delays were quite unknown to me at the time, and, as I record later, it will be seen that I counted on the 1st Corps coming into line with us on the Le Cateau position in accordance with G.H.Q. operation order, and that I sent back weary troops to the east side of the town of Le Cateau to look out for them and to guard the flank until they appeared.

Whatever the cause, the delay was of very serious moment to the 2nd Corps, and indeed to the whole B.E.F. Had it not occurred the actions at Landrecies and Maroilles would not have taken place, and, instead of being out of touch with each other for the next six days, the two corps would have had a united front on the night of 25th August under the hand of the commander-in-chief and the decision to fight at Le Cateau would not have rested with me. As things were, however, as will be seen later, the news that the 1st Corps was heavily engaged and the fear that their safety might be endangered unless the 2nd Corps made a stand, though not the deciding factor, carried weight with me in coming to the decision I took in the small hours of the morning of the 26th.

It is evident that the G.O.C. 1st Corps considered his situation serious, for I see in the *Official History* that at 1.35 a.m. on the 26th he reported it as critical to General Head-quarters, at 3.30 a.m. he asked that troops near Le Cateau should advance straight on Landrecies to assist him, and further that he issued an order to his troops to dump supplies so that wagons might be freed to carry men's packs. These facts, given in the *Official History,* lead me to believe that the battle of Le Cateau must have prevented the situation in the 1st Corps from becoming even more critical. But to return to my account of the day's proceedings.

The rear-guard of the 5th Division, which was marching along the Bavai-Le Cateau road alongside the forest of Mormal, had a smart scrap with some Germans north-west of Bavai as they were moving off, but otherwise the Division, beyond a desperately hot march on a foot-wearying *pavé* road, were unmolested and began to arrive at Le Cateau town at 3 p.m., though their tail was not there until after 8 p.m., and a few units much later, as will be seen. As the nearest part of the position allotted to them was some two miles south of the town, it was considerably later when they reached it.

The 3rd Division, marching to the west of them, and the Cavalry Division and 19th Infantry Brigade, on roads still farther west, had quite a lot of rear-guard work, and eventually at Solesmes some very heavy fighting. The brigade of the 2nd Corps on rear-guard was McCracken's, the 7th, and so well were they handled and so brilliantly did the two battalions engaged (the South Lancashires and the Wiltshires) conduct themselves, that in consequence of a recommendation of General Allenby's, endorsed by the commander-in-chief, their brigadier was promoted major-general. This recommendation came in the form of a letter from General Allenby to me as corps commander, and was forwarded by me to the chief. It so clearly describes what happened that I give it in *extenso:*

Head-quarters, Cavalry Corps,
1st November 1914.
My dear Sir Horace,
On the 25th August I had the task of covering the rear of the army in its western flank during the retirement on Le Cateau. Towards nightfall a fierce attack was made on the Cavalry Division under my command and a gap was opened between the rear and flank guards. The rear of the 2nd Army Corps was then passing through the town of Solesmes, a defile, and the situation became precarious. I had, at the time, only one Regiment of Cavalry to fill the gap. Riding to the rear of the column, I met Brigadier-General McCracken, and gave him the situation. Brigadier-General McCracken at once rose to the occasion. He collected what troops were near to hand and led them to a position whence they could cover the column entering the defile. At the same time he stopped and brought into action a brigade of R.F.A. and a Howitzer battery. This ready initiative checked the enemy, but they brought several batteries into action under whose cover their infantry resumed the attack. Until after dark Brigadier-General McCracken maintained his stand under severe gun and rifle fire, and did not retire until the rear of the column was in safety. He then withdrew skilfully and with comparatively few casualties. I consider that his ready and daring

440

handling of the rear-guard averted a mishap which might have been a disaster. I am glad to be able to bring his action to your notice, as I think it deserves recognition.

Yours sincerely,

E. H. H. Allenby.

I learned in the course of the morning that the 4th Division (General Snow, now Lieutenant-General Sir Thomas D'Oyly Snow) had reached Le Cateau from England, and was delighted to hear that the chief had immediately pushed it out to Solesmes, about seven miles north-west of Le Cateau, to cover the retirement of the cavalry and 3rd Division. He could not have chosen a better place, for most roads from the north converge on it and it was sure to be an objective of pursuing Germans. It was a very congested spot, and throughout the afternoon reports came in telling of the apparently hopeless mass of transport trying to pass through it on the way south.

There were the wagons of the 3rd Division, the 19th Brigade, and the cavalry division, but there would have been little difficulty about them had it not been for French Territorial troops' *impedimenta* from Valenciennes, and especially masses of country carts and hand-carts laden with household goods and surrounded by countless numbers of civilian refugees, flying before the German advance.

The position of the 4th Division round the southern end of the town was just suited to give the time necessary for this congestion to melt away. This, however, did not happen in a minute, for, in a subsequent account which he sent to me, Snow says:

The movement of the rear-guard of the 4th Division was delayed until after midnight; the result was that the three brigades did not get on to the position[5] till about daylight, that is between 3.30 and 5.30 a.m. on the 26th.

I had confined my own movements almost entirely to the eastern road, and when abreast of the old fortress town of Le

_____

5. He refers to the position allotted to him on the left of the 2nd Corps by General Head-quarters.

Quesnoy witnessed the first fight in the air I had ever seen, and had the satisfaction of seeing the German aeroplane crash to the ground. I reached the town of Le Cateau[6] at 3.30 p.m., and at once went to report myself to the commander-in-chief. He was not there, but I found the chief of staff, who had little fresh information to give me and no news of the 1st Corps. The forest of Mormal, which kept the 1st Corps some four or five miles from us and General Head-quarters, which had also moved west of the forest, for some ten miles of our march, had proved an impenetrable wall.

General Head-quarters was in process of moving to St. Quentin, twenty-six miles to the south, and it was thought probable that the commander-in-chief had gone there. This was unfortunate, as there were several matters I wished to ask him about. From Le Cateau I went south to the position selected by General Head-quarters, on which we were to meet the enemy next day. It was quite a good one —on rising ground with a fine field of fire and with several villages capable of defence along it. The right, or east, flank was certainly turnable, but that did not matter, as the 1st Corps were to go there.

Then, with Forestier-Walker, I allotted the ground for the two divisions to occupy. We were constantly looking out for the arrival of the 1st Corps, and late in the afternoon, when they did not appear, I requested the Commander of the 5th Division to hold the ground on the north-east of Le Cateau until they arrived. This he did by sending back one and a half battalions of the 14th Brigade to entrench themselves there.

Naturally the men were dead tired; they had had two days' desperate fighting, and now had done a march of over twenty miles in a burning sun, and, as sixty *per cent*, of them were reservists, were not in marching condition, and suffered terribly from sore feet. Some of the 5th Division were still out, the 28th Brigade R.F.A. only reaching Reumont, Sir Charles Fergusson's Head-quarters, at 11.30 p.m., and the divisional ammunition column did not arrive until the morning of the 26th. The ardu-

6. *Vide* Map of Le Cateau

442

ous work of the day was much enhanced by a heavy thunder-storm in the evening drenching the troops to the skin.

My staff established our head-quarters at the village of Bertry, where I joined them at dark and awaited news of the arrival of my scattered troops. In the course of the afternoon, as far as I recollect about 6 p.m., I received a note from the sub-chief of the general staff, Henry Wilson, saying the chief had told him to warn me that orders would shortly be issued for continuing the retreat instead of standing at Le Cateau. The actual General Head-quarters' order reached me at 9 p.m., and my order to the 2nd Corps to continue the retirement next day was issued at 10.15 p.m.

It will be difficult for any reader to realise the fog of war which surrounded us that night. Communication was most difficult, and although the corps signallers, under that most resourceful of men, Major A. B. R. Hildebrand, R.E. (now Brigadier-General, C.B., C.M.G., D.S.O.), performed miracles with their wires and cables, it was impossible to find out the 'positions of units until hours after they reached them.

Then it was not as if I only had the 2nd Corps to deal with, for mixed up with them, fighting and retiring together, were the Cavalry Division, the 19th Infantry Brigade, and the 4th Division, none of which were under me, but were reporting their movements to and getting their orders from General Head-quarters, twenty-six miles to the rear. It is true that General Head-quarters issued an order timed 1 p.m. 25th August, placing the 19th Brigade under the 2nd Corps, but it was then with the cavalry division, miles away, and Heaven knows when it got the order.

I only succeeded in collecting them next morning, when they were starting south from the town of Le Cateau. It appears that they had reached that place at 10 p.m. the night before, and, thoroughly exhausted, had dumped down in the marketplace and were resuming their retirement at 6 a.m. when my order caught them. This latter ear-marked them as my own reserves for the day, and most valuable they proved: a busy time of it they had, now supporting one part of the line, now another, and finally forming a rear-guard which, with that of the 15th Brigade, stubbornly covered the retreat of the 5th Division. The Brigade consisted of 2nd Royal Welch Fusiliers, 1st Scottish Rifles, 1st Middlesex, and 2nd Argyll and Sutherland Highlanders, and were then commanded temporarily by Lieutenant-Colonel Ward of the Middlesex in the absence of the Brigadier, Major-General L. G. Drummond.

At last, about 8 p.m., I got news of the 3rd Division; the main bodies of the 8th and 9th Brigades had reached the vicinity of their allotted positions about Audencourt and Inchy respectively about 6.30 p.m.; but there was still no news of the 7th Brigade, nor did I get any until the small hours of the 26th, and then to the effect that it had reached its destination at Caudry about midnight, but with the loss of the 2nd Royal Irish Rifles, part of the South Lancashires, and the 41st Battery R.F.A.

Next day I heard that these units had reached Reumont and bivouacked there at 2 a.m., and had only rejoined their brigade at 9 a.m. when the battle was pretty lively. Of the cavalry division and 4th Division I had no news, for they were not under me, though I had been given permission to call on the latter division for help should I require it. Rumours were afloat during the evening that the 1st Corps were heavily engaged, and reports came in that heavy firing was heard in the direction of Landrecies. This was serious as, if they were not nearer than that, it meant a gap of eight miles between the right of my corps and the left of the 1st Corps.

Thus it will be gathered that, with the exception of a few units of the 5th Division, no fighting units were on the position before dark, that a great many of those of the 2nd Corps were on the move until after midnight, and that the 4th Division only reached the position at daylight next day. I specify "fighting units," as all transport and impedimenta accompanied by baggage guards, cooks, clerks, sick, etc., had moved off from our line positions on the night of the 24th about midnight and had therefore mostly reached their new positions in the course of the next morning, so a large number of men were to be seen cooking, washing, and waiting for the arrival of their corps. I mention this as a good deal has been written on the subject as evidence that troops were in camp early, for I feel sure these detachments I have mentioned were mistaken for the actual fighting troops—Map 9 of the *Official History* illustrates clearly the scattered situations of the troops on the night of 25th-26th August.

However, some of the fog was cleared away by the arrival of General Allenby, accompanied by his G.S.O.I, Colonel J.Vaughan (now Major-General, C.B., C.M.G., D.S.O.) at my head-quarters at 2 a.m. Allenby told me his troops were much scattered, two and a half brigades being about Catillon, five miles east, and the other one and a half brigades at Viesly, six miles north-west of Le Cateau,[7] that his men and horses were pretty well played out, and that he could not get into touch with General Head-quarters. He wanted to know what I was going to do, saying that unless I could move at once and get away in the dark, the enemy were so close that I should be forced to fight at daylight.

I then sent for Major-General Hubert Hamilton, the commander of the 3rd Division, whose head-quarters were close by, and asked him whether his troops could move off at once or at any rate before daylight, and his reply was very definite that the 3rd Division could not move before 9 a.m. The 5th Division were if possible in a worse plight, being more scattered, whilst of the 4th Division, which, though not under me, I could not possibly leave in the lurch, there was no news, except that they had last been seen after dark still in their positions south of Solesmes, covering the retirement of masses of transport and fugitives jammed up in the roads.

The following arguments passed through my mind:

(a) It must be a long time after daylight before the whole force covered by rear-guards can get on the move.

(b) The enemy are in force close to our billets (for such Al-

---

7. The official account makes them even more scattered—4th Brigade at Viesly, part of 1st near Troisville, part of 2nd south of Le Cateau, the 3rd with parts of 1st and 2nd one mile east of Bazuel.

lenby had impressed on me).

(c) To turn our backs on them in broad daylight with worn-out men suffering from sore feet will leave us a prey to hostile cavalry supported by infantry in motors,

(d) The roads are encumbered with military transport and civilian fugitives and carts, some still on the enemy side of our position, and time to allow them to clear off is essential.

(e) The 1st Corps is reported to be engaged some miles north-east of us and to retire would expose their flank to the full brunt of Von Kluck's troops.

(f) The cavalry division can be of little help in covering our retreat, for this Allenby had told me.

(g) Our infantry have proved their staunchness and astounding accuracy with the rifle, our gunners are a marvel, and if Allenby and Snow will act under me, and Sordet will guard my west flank, we should be successful in giving the enemy a stopping blow, under cover of which we could retire.

Well do I remember the dead silence in the little room at Bertry when I was rapidly considering these points and the sigh of relief when, on my asking Allenby if he would accept orders from me, and he replied in the affirmative, I remarked: "Very well, gentlemen, we will fight, and I will ask General Snow to act under me as well."

The die was cast, and it is lucky it was, for it appeared afterwards that the 4th Division did not commence moving back from opposite Solesmes until long after dark, the rear brigade not until midnight, and only reached the fighting positions allotted to them on the west of the 2nd Corps from Fontaine-au-Pire to Wambaix (a front of three miles) after daylight on the 26th. They were very weary, having journeyed straight from England, detrained at Le Cateau on the 24th, and marched thence at 1 a.m. on the 25th eight or nine miles to Solesmes, been in action there all day, and marched back over ten miles in the dark to their position, which was reached after dawn on the 26th. The unfortunate part about this division was that it lacked the very essentials for a modern battle. It had none of the following: Divisional Cavalry, Divisional Cyclists, Signal Company, Field Ambulances, Field Companies R.E., Train and Divisional Ammunition Column, or Heavy Artillery. Let the reader think what that means—no troops to give warning, neither rapidly moving orderlies nor cables for communication, no means of getting away wounded, no engineers, who are the handy men of an army, no reserve ammunition, and no long-range heavy shell fire—and yet the division was handled and fought magnificently, but at the expense of losses far greater than if they had been fully mobilised.

Having decided to fight, there was a good deal for my staff to do. General Head-quarters had to be informed, a message had to be sent to General Sordet to tell him and ask him to guard my west flank, and Snow had to be asked if he would fight under me, and last, but not least, carefully detailed orders for the battle had to be drawn up and circulated. Forestier-Walker, who was a very clear thinker and rapid worker, soon got all this done. To make certain that General Sordet should get the request, in addition to my message to him, a wire was sent to General Head-quarters asking them too to invoke his assistance.

General Snow received my message about 5 a.m. just as he was issuing orders to retire, and readily consented to remain and fight under my orders.

Snow wrote to me subsequently as follows:

When you sent to me the morning of the 26th to ask if I would stand and fight, I ought to have answered: 'I have no other choice, as my troops are already engaged in a battle of encounter, and it must be some hours before I can extricate them.'

The message informing General Head-quarters is referred to in the *Official History*, p. 136, as follows:

A lengthy message was dispatched by 2nd Corps at 3.30 a.m. to General Head-quarters St. Quentin by motorcar, which was received there about 5 a.m., informing Sir John French in detail of the decision taken.

It was acknowledged by a reply, sent off from General Head-quarters at 5 a.m., which, after giving the latest information, concluded:

> If you can hold your ground the situation appears likely to improve. Fourth Division must co-operate. French troops are taking offensive on right of 1st Corps. Although you are given a free hand as to method this telegram is not intended to convey the impression that I am not as anxious for you to carry out the retirement, and you must make every endeavour to do so.

This reply cheered me up, for it showed that the chief did not altogether disapprove of the decision I had taken, but on the contrary considered it might improve the situation.

Consciousness that I was acting entirely without G.H.Q. approval would not have lightened my burden, especially as I had another master to consider, namely, Field Service Regulations, which direct (sub-para. 3. of para. 13 of Section 12 of Part 1):

> If a subordinate, in the absence of a superior, neglects to depart from the letter of his order, when such departure is clearly demanded by circumstances, and failure ensues, he will be held responsible for such failure.

The order to stand and fight drawn up by Forestier-Walker was clear and to the point, but the difficulty was to get it to the troops in time. It was fairly easy for corps headquarters, as they had simply to send copies of the order to the four divisional head-quarters and the 19th Brigade, but the difficulties increased in mathematical progression when it came to informing the smaller units, many of whose positions were only very roughly known. Captain Walcot took the order to the 4th Division and I went myself to Fergusson (5th Division) about 4 a.m. to explain matters to him, and to learn all I could about the positions and state of the troops of his division.

Whilst I was talking to him the rearguard of the 3rd Division passed, having been out all night. Fergusson pointed to them as another indication of the impossibility of continuing the retirement at once. He added that the men of his own division were exhausted, and that, although they might continue their rearward march in a fashion, it would be a slow and risky business; he further remarked he was relieved by my decision to stand and fight.

There is no doubt but that there was the greatest difficulty in getting the orders round—in fact some few units never got them, but conformed to the movements of the troops which had. The orders given provided for the immediate retirement of all transport not necessary to the battle so as to leave our roads free for the troops later.

The disposition of troops was as follows: the 5th Division on the right, or east, the 3rd Division in the centre, and 4th Division on the left, each division having approximately three miles of front. The brigades of infantry, of which there were ten, commencing from the right at the town of Le Cateau, fought as follows: 14th, 13th, 15th, 9th, 8th, 7th, 11th, 10th, and 12th, with the 19th Brigade as my reserve—about Reumont at first.

Thus the 14th and 12th were in the most dangerous positions, being on exposed flanks, and both of them had desperate fighting. Allenby had arranged to dispose his cavalry as far as possible to guard the flanks, the 2nd Cavalry Brigade (de Lisle) and the 3rd Cavalry Brigade (Gough) being on the east flank near Bazuel, the 1st Cavalry Brigade (Briggs) being also on that flank but some miles farther south near Escaufour, and the 4th Cavalry Brigade (Bingham) first at Ligny, and later at Selvigny, that is towards the left or west flank, whilst Sordet's Cavalry Corps was in the neighbourhood of Walincourt, some two and a half miles south of Esnes, where the 12th Brigade had placed its outer flank.

A glance at the map will show that the line from east to west ran from the south of Le Cateau through the villages of Troisvilles, Audencourt, Beaumont, Caudry, Fontaine-au-Pire to Esnes. The head-quarters of the divisions were: 5th at Reumont, 3rd at Bertry, close to my own head-quarters, and the 4th at Haucourt.

As in my account of the Battle of Mons I found it impossible to go into great detail, I shall follow the same principle here, and recommend my readers to study the graphic, detailed, and thrilling account given in the *Official History*.

I myself was almost pinned to my head-quarters, though once (about noon) I went up to see Fergusson. The only other time I left it was at about 6.45 a.m., when a cyclist brought me a message from Bertry Station, distant about half a mile, saying Sir John French wished to speak to me on the railway telephone. I motored there immediately and heard the voice of sub-chief of the general staff Sir Henry Wilson, who had a message to give me from the chief to the effect that I should break off the action as soon as possible.

I replied that I would endeavour to do so, but that it would be difficult, and that I had hoped to be able to hold on until evening and slip away in the dark. Henry Wilson then asked me what I thought of our chances, and when I replied that I was feeling confident and hopeful of giving the enemy a smashing blow and slipping away before he could recover, he replied, "Good luck to you; yours is the first cheerful voice I have heard for three days." With these pleasing words in my ear, which I shall never forget, I returned to my head-quarters. I should mention, however, that before I actually left the station Colonel J. Seely, who had lately been Secretary of State for War, arrived by motor with a similar message from the chief.

The battle commenced in the streets of Le Cateau itself, the Germans having got into the houses and opened fire on the Cornwalls and two companies East Surrey, which troops were in the act of vacating the town, causing them to move out to the east and to fight their way back by a circuitous route taking them right to the rear of their brigade. From now on the battle increased all along the line as more and yet more hostile guns came into action and hostile infantry advanced. An early attempt to turn our right flank was made, luckily not in great strength, and by 11 a.m. it had been foiled by the determined attitude of the 14th and 13th Brigades, helped by the cavalry and R.H.A.

Soon after 9.30 a.m. the pressure on that flank had become so serious that I had to send up the Argyll and Sutherlands From my reserve brigade to assist, and later on another battalion of this brigade, the 1st Middlesex, had to reinforce the same area. About 10 a.m., in view of reports from Ligny, I moved the remaining two battalions, the Scottish Rifles and Royal Welch Fusiliers, westward to Montigny.

On the left, or west of our position, the fighting was early very serious where the 11th and 12th Brigades were, and the King's Own lost nearly half their strength. In the centre of the line matters were not so serious, and our troops easily held their own, but there also it was no child's-play: villages were taken and retaken, and gunners and infantry were conspicuous by their heroic conduct.

The features of the fighting were the overwhelming artillery-fire of the enemy (who had the guns of four, and some say five, corps in action against us), the glorious feats performed by our own artillery, and the steadiness and accurate fire of our own infantry which had proved so deadly at Mons. After six hours' fighting we were holding our own everywhere, and every effort of the enemy to come on was defeated; but the strain was beginning to tell on our exposed east flank, and at 1.40 p.m. Colonel Gathorne Hardy, of my staff, who was watching events for me at 5th Divisional Head-quarters at Reumont, brought me a message from Sir Charles Fergusson, saying his troops were beginning to dribble away under their severe punishment, and he feared he would be unable to hold on until dark.

The Germans had already penetrated between his 13th and 14th Brigades, had practically wiped out the Suffolks, had brought up guns to short ranges, and were shelling heavily his own head-quarters at Reumont. The division had stood to the limit of human endurance, and I recognised that the moment had arrived when our retirement should commence, and, requesting Gathorne Hardy to hurry back to Fergusson and tell him to order an organised retirement at once as the best means of saving a disastrous rush to the rear, I put in motion the plans already in possession of divisional commanders. These were to the effect that, when they got the order, they were to commence retiring by divisions along the roads allotted to them My chief staff officer thereupon sent out the necessary instructions, saying the retirement would commence from the right

I now made the last use of my reserve, which consisted of one battery, the Scottish Rifles and Royal Welch Fusiliers of the 19th Brigade, by sending them off to take up a position astride the Roman road leading from Le Cateau to Maretz to cover the retirement of the 5th Division.

This, as I have already said, and refer to again later, they carried out most efficiently, materially helped, however, by the rearguard of the 15th Brigade under the cool leadership of Colonel Ballard, whom I have already mentioned in connection with similar services two days previously. It was now about 2 p.m., and Edmonds (the official historian), who was then General Snow's G.S.O.I, arrived at my head-quarters in Bertry to tell me that General Snow was quite happy as regards his division, and felt sure he could hold his own and that no retirement was necessary. He wrote me subsequently that he was much amused with my attitude, as all I said was: "The order has gone out, and now I am going to try and get some lunch."

Fergusson's order to his division to retire naturally took some time to reach his troops, and it was well after 3 p.m. before the rearward move of the 5th Division commenced. The troops were so hopelessly mixed up, and so many leaders had gone under, that a regular retirement was almost impossible, especially too as the enemy was close up and pressing hard. Thanks, however, to the determined action of Major Yate of the Yorkshire Light Infantry, who sacrificed himself and his men in holding the Germans off, the troops of the 5th Division got back on to the road.

Luckily the 15th Infantry Brigade was intact, and they about Troisvilles, the 19th Brigade about Maurois, and the R.H.A. guns of the cavalry farther to the east and south kept the enemy off and prevented the envelopment of our flank and enabled the troops to get away. When the 3rd Division saw the 5th retiring they took it up, and finally the 4th Division. Both these two last-named divisions, less heavily assailed than the 5th, and with their flanks better guarded, could have remained where they were certainly until after dark, and had little difficulty in retiring, in comparatively good order, the 9th Brigade in perfect order taking all their wounded with them.

If the 4th Division were slightly more mixed up and irregular in their formations, it was due to the fact that they were immensely handicapped by their shortage of the necessities for fighting a battle (already described), largely in consequence of which their losses had been so heavy, amounting to about twenty-five *per cent*, of their war strength. It was after 4 p.m., when my head-quarters were retiring from Bertry, that I rode with my staff to watch the 5th Division pass along the road south of Maurois. I likened it at the time to a crowd coming away from a race meeting, and I see the same simile in the *Official History*. It was a wonderful sight—men smoking their pipes, apparently quite unconcerned, and walking steadily down the road—no formation of any sort, and men of all units mixed together.

The curious thing was that the enemy were making no attempt to follow. They respectfully kept their distance behind the rear-guards, and later allowed the latter to retire without pressing them. The 3rd and 4th Divisions were, as the plan of retirement provided for, considerably later in taking up the movement to the rear. But what undoubtedly decided the Germans not to follow up was the fact that several detachments did not receive the order to retire, but went on fighting, some of them far into the night, and we have to thank them largely for holding off the enemy, thus preventing his being aware that a general retirement had taken place.

These detachments had marvellous and varied experiences which it is not in my province to relate here, for I did not hear of them until after, but I see the *Official History* describes them as less than 1,000 strong all told, a wonderful illustration of how a few resolute men can hold up an army. We had plenty of experience of that in the Boer War, for our enemies there were real experts at rear-guard fighting.

I had no reports from General Sordet during the day, but had heard that French infantry was fighting in Cambrai. These turned out to be General d'Amade's Territorial troops, who finally left Cambrai in a west and south-westerly direction about 2 p.m. That their help to us was very material there can be no doubt, for on the 23rd d'Amade's advanced troops under General de Villaret, straight from Paris, reached Tournai and on the 24th held up the German 2nd Corps directed on Cambrai for several hours, drawing them after them as they fell back that afternoon and the 25th. The delay, and the brave front shown by these Territorials were of vital importance to us, as otherwise it is almost certain we should have had another corps against us on the 26th.

I had a momentary shock about 5 p.m. on getting clear at the village of Maretz, about three miles south of Maurois or the Roman road, for I suddenly heard very heavy artillery fire away to the north-west, which I reckoned was behind the 4th Division outer flank and feared the enemy had got behind Snow; but was much relieved, on galloping to a hill about a mile in that direction, to recognise the short sharp crack of the famous "seventy-fives," and then I knew they were French guns and probably Sordet's, and this they turned out to be. On reaching St. Quentin I took the opportunity of sending a message to General Sordet to thank him, and also of sending a note to the commander-in-chief asking him to express thanks to him through the French commander-in-chief

In an order of the day which I published on the 29th (see further on) I also informed the troops of our indebtedness to General Sordet's Corps.[6]

---

6. It appears, from the history of Sordet's Cavalry Corps, drawn up under his direction by Colonel Boucherie and published in 1923, that the corps rested the night of 25-26th at Walincourt, some two or three miles behind Esnes, where the left of the 4th Division established itself at dawn on the 26th. The French cavalry was well placed, therefore, to support us in the coming battle. They did not remain there, however, but moved farther west to Gonnelieu, (Continued next page)

We had not been long retiring when down came the rain, and the discomforts of the poor weary troops were increased a hundredfold.

In order to sort out the units and get them formed again, staff officers had been sent ahead two miles beyond Estrées, and most efficiently they performed their work. To this point was a long, weary march of sixteen miles from Reumont. How the men did it I still cannot realise—dead tired, hungry, and wet to the skin; but they did it, and went on again at 4 a.m. on the 27th through St. Quentin to Ham, another twenty miles.

The 3rd and 4th Divisions kept on parallel roads to the west of the 5th. On reaching Estrées at 9.30 p.m. I transferred from a horse to a motor and started off to St. Quentin to report matters to the commander-in-chief, taking Bowly (*aide-de-camp*) and Prince Henri d'Orléans with me. I had an excellent motor and Al chauffeur placed at the disposal of the G.O.C. 2nd Corps by the generosity of Lord Derby.

As we motored along in the wet and dark the head-lights disclosed ammunition boxes glistening in the rain on each side of the road for a considerable distance, and I concluded they had been dumped there as a reserve supply for us by General Head-quarters. On reaching St. Quentin I heard that General Head-quarters had left that place in the middle of the day and had gone to Noyon, thirty-five miles farther off. There was nothing to be done but to go on, but before doing so I went to the sta-tion to find the Director of Railways, Colonel MacInnes, R.E., to ask him what trains he could give me for weary and wounded men in the morning. He told me he had orders from General Head-quarters to send all trains away, but agreed to keep them until I returned from Noyon. Outside the station I saw an ex-cited officer, and asked him what he was doing.

---

seven or eight miles from our flank and ten miles south of Cambrai, and it was not until 1.30 p.m. that a decision to take part in the battle was arrived at. The corps then moved north towards the line Cambrai-Haucourt, and, on crossing the Escaut and seeing German columns coming out of Cambrai and in the neighbourhood of Seronvillers, opened on them with the guns. It was evidently this fire that attracted my attention.

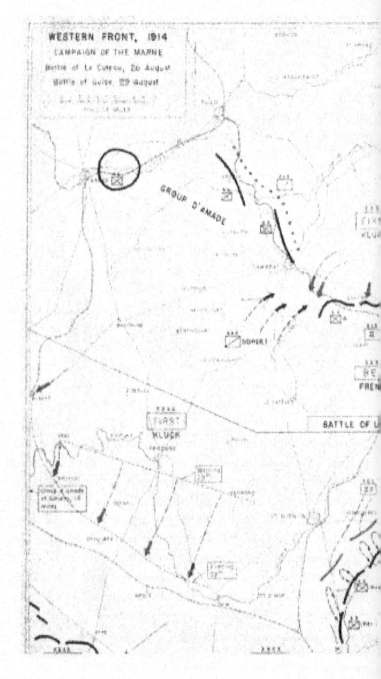

WESTERN FRONT, 1914
CAMPAIGN OF THE MARNE
Battle of Le Cateau, 26 August
Battle of Guise, 29 August

GROUP D'AMADE

FIRST
KLUCK

II

BE
FREN

FIRST
KLUCK

BATTLE OF L

Group d Amade
at Guise, 16
mons

Ba

He said he commanded an ammunition column, and in retreating had heard that German Uhlans were about, in fact he talked of hearing shots. He had, therefore, in order to lighten his wagons, thrown all his ammunition away and galloped into St. Quentin and was just going off again. This accounted for the boxes I had seen in the road. The officer in question proved himself later on both brave and efficient, and I should have omitted the incident had it not given rise to a rumour that German cavalry was closing on St. Quentin, which was perfectly untrue, and unfair to our own cavalry division, which was skilfully covering our east flank and keeping the enemy at a distance.

I reached Noyon at about an hour after midnight on 27th August and had some difficulty in finding the house where G.H.Q. was established. All had retired to rest, but gradually some of the staff appeared and then the chief himself, clad in his *robe de nuit*.

There was a convenient billiard-table in the room with a white cover, and spreading a. map thereon I explained briefly the events of the day. Sir John appeared relieved, though he told me he considered I took much too cheerful a view of the situation, and he again took exception to my optimism two days later. I then, having got permission from Quartermaster-General Sir William Robertson, to use any trains the Director of Railways could spare, hastened back to St. Quentin railway station, getting there as dawn was breaking.

MacInnes placed at my disposal seven trains. I then took up my quarters at the Mairie with my staff, transacted some business and watched all the weary troops march through St. Quentin, turning off those who could march no farther to the railway station. Thus ended the first and principal phase of the retreat. I might be expected to discuss whether the Battle of Le Cateau was worth the candle—with its heavy losses.

The latter were:

Cavalry	15
3rd Division	1,796
5th Division	2,366
4th Division	3,158

Total   7,812[7] and 38 guns.

Of the above 2,600 were taken prisoners, but, whatever the losses, and whatever the results, I think I have shown that, without risking a *débâcle* and jeopardising the safety of the 4th Division and the 1st Corps, I had no alternative but to stand and fight. I claim no credit, but on the contrary realise to the full that fortune was on my side, firstly in having such an efficient force so skilfully and devotedly handled and led, and composed of troops so well disciplined and courageous as to be second to none in the world; and secondly in having an enemy who did not rise to the occasion. It may be inferred from the commander-in-chief's dispatch of the 7th September 1914 that he considered it well worth the candle.

He mentioned me in most generous terms in his dispatches. In that of 7th September 1914, he writes of Le Cateau:

I cannot close this brief account of this glorious stand of the British troops, without putting on record my deep appreciation of the valuable services rendered by General Sir Horace Smith-Dorrien. I say without hesitation that the saving of the left wing of the army under my command on the morning of the 26th August could never have been accomplished unless a commander of rare and unusual coolness, intrepidity, and determination had been present to personally conduct the operation.

And later in the same dispatch:

It is impossible for me to speak too highly of the skill evinced by the two generals commanding army corps.

In his dispatch of the 8th October, on the Battle of the Aisne, he says:

I further wish to bring forward the names of the follow-

---

7. A great number of these casualties were due to orders for retirements not reaching units, and those of the 4th Division to their being short of so many essentials.

ing officers who have rendered valuable services. General Sir Horace Smith-Dorrien and Lieutenant-General Sir Douglas Haig I have already mentioned in the present and former dispatches for particularly marked and distinguished service in critical situations—since the commencement of the campaign, they have carried out all my orders and instructions with the utmost ability.

Again the following from his sub-chief of the staff implies that the battle was of value:

Extract from a *Communique* issued by G.H.Q. a few days after the Battle of Le Cateau

"Information about the enemy's losses.

"In spite of their great superiority in numbers when opposed to the British forces, the enemy has suffered enormous losses.

"The damage inflicted by the 2nd Corps, 4th Division, and 19th Brigade at Cambrai and Le Cateau prevented any serious pursuit during the retreat to St. Quentin, although the enemy's numerical superiority in this fight had been three to one. The losses are mentioned in the diary of a German reservist, killed a few days later, as causing terrible confusion and disorder, which could not be allayed for over an hour. During the fight the general commanding one of the enemy's cavalry divisions sent two wireless messages, which were intercepted, asking for help, adding in a second message that the need was most urgent. These losses have had the effect of making the enemy extremely cautious in his attacks, both with cavalry and infantry, until he has developed his artillery-fire to the utmost.

"The German cavalry refuse to meet either the British or French cavalry in the fight, and whenever they are threatened retire behind the protection of the cyclists, mounted infantry, and guns.

"The shooting of the German infantry and dismounted cavalry is ludicrously bad, and, although the German guns are extremely well served by aeroplane reconnaissance, their lime-fuses are very inferior to those of the British and French artillery.

"H. Wilson.[8]"

The following extract from a letter, which he allows me to publish, from Major-General John Vaughan, dated 24th June 1919, gives the cavalry point of view as to the necessity for lighting and the results of the Battle of Le Cateau:

I remember accompanying General Allenby when we visited your H.Q. at Bertry. I also remember the situation as it appeared at the time to Allenby and me, your setting forth the reasons which determined you to fight, and the fact that Allenby thought you were right in doing so. In fact both Allenby and I were much relieved that you had determined to fight as, *inter alia*, it gave us a chance of getting hold of our scattered brigades again.

I also remember the action of the French cavalry under Sordet, who attacked the German right in the evening.

To my mind this was a very opportune action on Sordet's part, as he had got outside the German flank—and their subsequent advance gave us (British cavalry) no trouble at all. Prior to your action at Le Cateau the German cavalry outflanked us *via* Tournai and Denain, and was a very serious menace.

Feeling, most strongly as I do, that it was your action at Le Cateau, combined with Sordet's outflanking move that made the rest of our retreat possible and easy, I should certainly wish to give any evidence I can in support of this theory.

From the British cavalry point of view I consider that the Huns gave us no trouble at all after Le Cateau, as we were always able to fight delaying actions and retire at our leisure, once the German outflanking movement had

---

8. Afterwards Field-Marshal Sir H. Wilson, Bt., G.C.B., D.S.O.

petered out.

I am quite sure that the above is also Allenby's view.

It is undoubtedly a fact that after Le Cateau we were no more seriously troubled during the ten days' retreat, except by mounted troops and mobile detachments who kept at a respectful distance.

That the enemy received a very serious blow, and losses far heavier than ours, and gained a wholesome respect for the efficiency of British troops are facts beyond dispute, and the failure of their official accounts to expatiate on the battle is ominously suggestive of their being none too proud of the results. Then, again, one has only to study Von Kluck's orders and subsequent movements to appreciate that his army was delayed and misled for a sufficient period to gain valuable time for Paris to prepare.

Those orders of Von Kluck on the evening of the 26th indicate that his army rested that night on the north side of the Le Cateau position, from which it may be deduced that he was unaware of our retirement and had been hit sufficiently hard to prevent his making a further attempt to take the position that evening. Again the hour given in the order for moving on the 27th was not till 5 a.m., which is also significant. The German account of the battle concludes with this statement:

The whole B.E.F., six divisions, a cavalry division and several French Territorial Divisions opposed the First Army.

Which statement alone is flattering to the prowess of the portion of the B.E.F. who stood at Le Cateau. Perhaps Von Kluck's own testimony is as weighty as any which could be produced. I therefore quote from a letter dated 22nd June 1924 from Major-General the Hon. Sir F. Bingham, who, on recently becoming Governor of Jersey, had just resigned the position he had held for years as British Chief of the Military Mission in Germany:

I saw Von Kluck again and asked him if you might quote what he said, and he said: 'Certainly, he may say that I always had the greatest admiration for the British Expeditionary Force. It was the wonderful kernel of a great army. I have already said it in my book. The way the retreat was carried out was remarkable. I tried very hard to outflank them, but I could not do so. If I had succeeded the war would have been won.'

Then, as further proof of the success of our rear-guard battle, I quote the following from the *Official History*:

In fact, the whole of Smith-Dorrien's troops had done what was thought to be impossible. With both flanks in the air, they had turned on an enemy of at least twice their strength, had struck him hard, and had withdrawn, except on the right front of the 5th Division, practically without interference, with neither flank enveloped, having suffered losses certainly severe, but, considering the circumstances, by no means extravagant. The men looked upon themselves as victors, some indeed doubted whether they had been in a serious action, yet they had inflicted upon the enemy casualties which are believed to have been out of all proportion to their own, and they had completely foiled the plan of the German commander.

As a final and overwhelming testimony to the value of the day, General Joffre telegraphed to our commander-in-chief thanking him in the warmest terms for "the powerful effect that battle had had on the security of the left flank of the French army."

There was a short, sharp action on the morning of the 27th. The 11th Brigade of the 4th Division were just to the south-east of Bellincourt (seven miles north of St. Quentin) when at 9.30 a.m. the cavalry reported enemy in the adjacent villages, and German guns opened fire at a thousand yards range.

The Hampshires were ordered to cover the retirement, and Colonel S. C. F. Jackson of that regiment led his men against the guns, and unfortunately was wounded and made a prisoner. His men, however, although they could not recover their C.O., held on until their brigade was safe away, and then withdrew. By that night, the 27th, and early the next morning (August 28th) the whole of the three divisions were south of the Somme Canal, thirty-five miles from Le Cateau, in little over thirty hours. A wonderful performance for troops who were worn out before they left the battle-field; their spirit, too, was splendid, for they were whistling and singing as they came along. The commander-in-chief came up to see them as they marched again south from Ham on the morning of the 28th, and I was very proud of their carriage. The 15th Brigade of Artillery, which had lost all its guns except two and many of its men, went by the chief as though they were in the Long Valley.

Just before the chief came up I had met an officer of the 4th Division whom I had known for years. I had a short talk with him, and, noticing that he was not quite in his usual spirits, asked him if anything was the matter. He replied it was "the order" he had just received from me. He then went on to explain that an order had come to his division a short time before saying the ammunition on wagons not absolutely required and other impedimenta were to be unloaded and officers and men carried to the full capacity of the transport.

He went on to say that the order had had a very damping effect on his troops, for it was clear it would not have been issued unless we were in a very tight place. I told him I had never heard of the order, that the situation was excellent, the enemy only in small parties, and those keeping at a respectful distance, and that I was entirely at a loss to understand why such an order had been issued. Further, that I would at once send to divisional head-quarters to say the order was to be disregarded. My counter-order actually reached the 3rd and 5th Divisions in time, but the 4th Division had already acted on the order, burning officers' kits, etc., to lighten their wagons.

So when I met the chief I told him of this order, being fully convinced someone had issued it by mistake. However, when Sir John told me it was his order and emphasised the necessity for it by refusing to accept, what he called, my optimistic view of the situation, there was nothing more to be said. Later on I ascertained that the order had come from G.H.Q. when I was away, and, being a commander-in-chief's order of an urgent nature, my administrative staff had rightly circulated it at once. It was unfortunate, for had I seen it I should have protested to G.H.Q. before circulating it and I feel sure the chief would have cancelled it on learning the true situation, and thus have saved an increase of suffering to those who by acting on it sacrificed their spare clothes, boots, etc., at a time when they urgently needed them.

This day we marched to Noyon, about twelve to fourteen miles, crossing the Oise at that place. I was able to see most of the troops on the march. They could not understand why we were retiring, for they considered they had given as good as they got every time they had met the Germans, and were anxious to go at them again. I took the opportunity of explaining that we were not falling back because we had been beaten, but to comply with the French strategical scheme. I was particularly struck by the march discipline of the artillery. They made a brave show. How glad we were to get four hours' sleep at last. The whole army wanted it. I reckoned that my staff and I had averaged less than two hours' sleep in the previous six nights.

On the 29th we had a little trouble getting the 3rd and 4th Divisions south of the Oise. Both had been delayed the previous night helping de Lisle's Cavalry Brigade to keep the enemy off. It was on this day that General Pulteney (now Lieutenant-General Sir William Pulteney, K.C.B., K.C.M.G., K.C.V.O., D.S.O.) arrived to form the 3rd Corps and, two days later, took from me the 4th Division and 19th Brigade which General Headquarters had left with me since the 26th. Otherwise, beyond moving my corps five miles, ready for the next day's march, we did little.

I, however, was called to General Head-quarters at Compiègne, some twelve miles south of Noyon, to receive instructions from the commander-in-chief I found with him the chief of staff (Murray), Haig, and Allenby; General Joffre and one or two of his staff were also there. This was very interesting, as it was the first time I had seen the distinguished chief of the Allies. Joffre gave us good news of the progress of an attack by the 18th, 5th, and 10th French Corps towards St. Quentin (known as the battle of Guise) which he had ordered to help us. We heard subsequently that the French right was successful in driving the Germans back, but that their left, as the British did not assist, could make no progress.

The main object of the meeting, however, appeared to be a discussion between our chief and the French chief. The latter wanted us to remain up in the line, but the British chief was insistent that the B.E.F. must continue withdrawing as it was not in a fit state to fight until it had repaired damages, especially in the matter of material. Consequently we resumed our retreat next day, twelve miles to the Aisne. It was on this day that I published the following to the troops:

ORDER OF THE DAY

Headquarters 2nd Army Corps,
29th August 1914.

As it is possible the troops of the 2nd Army Corps do not understand the operations of the last few days, commencing on the 21st instant with the advance to the line of the Mons Canal and ending with a retirement to our present position on the River Oise about Noyon, the commander of the corps desires to let troops know that the object was to delay the advance of a far superior force of the enemy to enable our Allies to conduct operations elsewhere. This object, owing to the skilful handling of the commanders of units and the magnificent fighting spirit shown by all ranks against overwhelming odds, and in spite of very heavy casualties, was achieved, and the French army is now reported to be advancing.

That our difficulties were not greater in the retirement from the Haucourt-Caudry-Beaumont-Le Cateau position on the 26th instant is largely due to the support given by French troops, chiefly General Sordet's Cavalry Corps, operating on the west flank of the British troops, and we may be thankful to our gallant comrades in arms.

General Sir Horace Smith-Dorrien, whilst regretting the terribly heavy casualties and the weary forced marches, in which it has been impossible to distribute the necessary amount of food, begs to thank all ranks and to express his admiration of the grand fighting and determined spirit shown by all ranks, and his pride in being allowed to command such a splendid force.

He is sure that, whenever it is thought necessary to assume the offensive again, the troops will be as pleased as he will himself.[9]

On the 31st we marched fifteen miles to Crépy-en-Valois through some very broken country with a burning sun. It was this day that we again came into touch with the 1st Corps, separated from us since the 25th.

I have really now fulfilled my object, which was to give the public my own account as corps commander of the grand performances of the 2nd Corps at the Battles of Mons and Le Cateau, and in the early days of the retreat, and I shall deal in less detail with my account of the remainder of the time I was in France; for, except in the large strategic movements such as the transference of the army from the Aisne to Flanders, which were in the commander-in-chief's hands, from the time we reached the Aisne, and commenced trench warfare, a corps commander's wings became clipped in so far as manoeuvring was concerned.

As a matter of fact, in the beginning of October, when we first moved into Flanders, there was again a period of open fighting, and there I may have to be a little more discursive.

In trench warfare, excepting when a big push has to be carried out, holding the enemy, attacking him and gaining ground are mainly planned by local commanders, and are largely in the hands of the troops in the trenches, and their splendid deeds are as far as possible recorded in the *Official History*.

However, to take my readers to the Aisne, which includes the

---

9. I only gave credit to General Sordet's Corps in this Order of the Day, as I did not hear till long after of the still more important services performed for us in their retirement on Cambrai by General d'Amade's Territorials, to whom I have given full credit earlier in the chapter.

Battle of the Marne, I will reproduce my diary, written at the time from the 1st to 12th September, as I think it will convey a fair idea of our daily doings.

CHAPTER 25

The Marne, 1914

Diary. *1st September,* Crépy-en-Valois.—A French civilian came in to me about 3 a.m. and said that he had counted forty guns and a large force of cavalry at 1.30 a.m., moving through a village about five miles off, in the direction of the 3rd Army Corps; and this proved to be true, for soon after dawn there were Uhlans busy everywhere, and the 1st Cavalry Brigade found itself in bivouac within 600 yards of this cavalry force. They had a desperate fight, in which a lot of good men and officers were killed, and which resulted in "L" Battery temporarily losing all its guns, but then the Germans retreated, and in so doing lost all their guns, amounting to twelve.

An excellent officer—Colonel Ansell—was killed in this action. When I heard the firing I asked General Fergusson to send a brigade in the direction of Roquemont and Néry, at which latter place the cavalry fight had taken place, to help the 3rd Corps to withdraw. This was successfully accomplished. At the same time the rear-guard north of Crépy of Cuthbert's Brigade was attacked, and had no difficulty in holding the enemy off, getting into their infantry well with artillery-fire, but suffered some forty casualties.

The 3rd Division, which was farther east in the neighbourhood of Vaumoise, had no opposition to speak of. Whilst watching the fight at Levignen, I received a telegram from my wife, evidently sent off that morning, which shows that our communications are good. The heat of the day was again very great. We took up a line that night from Nanteuil to Betz—the 1st Army Corps being in touch with us at the latter place.

2nd September.—Troops were all on the move again by 2 a.m., and I followed at 3 a.m. It was a glorious night, and we halted on the line St. Soupplets-Étrepilly, my head-quarters being at Monthyon, from which place I had a magnificent view looking right across to the forts outside Paris, the nearest of which was only some eleven miles out in the direction of Senlis. The French 7th Corps and Reserve Division were engaged against the German 1st Army. The commander-in-chief was in Lagny, where I was ordered to see him at 2.30 p.m.

It was very sad to see all the roads crowded with refugees flying from the Germans, old and young huddled up in carts with as many household things as they could take away with them. They so blocked the roads as to prove a danger to us in our retirement, and it was only by very strenuous work on the part of staff officers that we were able to get the roads clear and to get these poor people away. The result of our talk with Sir John French was a decision to cross next day to the south bank of the Marne—a difficult operation, as it involved a flank march in the face of the enemy.

We have been, and are still, carrying out one of the most difficult operations in war, and I cannot help being struck by the splendid way all our rearward services are being conducted—Supply Columns, Ammunition Columns, and Mechanical Transport vehicles continue to arrive regularly. We are very short of equipment and of entrenching tools, having lost some eighty *per cent*, of the latter in the Battle of Le Cateau, and, as our base has been changed from Havre to the west coast of France—which means that some 70,000 tons of stores have been sent round there by sea—I see no chance of replenishing these things until our new line of communication is opened.

The general staff work, too, in my own corps is quite excellent; my chief of the general staff, General Forestier-Walker, is quite undefeatable, and I have the greatest confidence in my Divisional Commanders, Fergusson and Hamilton. The troops have quite recovered their spirits, and are getting fitter every day, and all they want is the order to go forward and attack the enemy—but this is not possible with the present rearward move of the French army.

3rd September.—We spent the whole day crossing the Marne to positions on the south bank. Aeroplane reports say that the German corps, instead of following us, are moving off to the east towards Château-Thierry, where the left of the next French army on our right rests. We succeeded in crossing the river without any incident, blowing up all the bridges. I spent the day reconnoitring the position which my corps was ordered to entrench and take up, and which proved to be an absolutely impossible one for defence; but, as the troops did not reach it till dark, there was nothing to be done but to report the matter and make suggestions to General Head-quarters.

4th September.—The news this morning is that the Germans, five corps at least, are on the line of the Marne to the east of us, the nearest being some ten miles from our right flank. What our next move is going to be I am not quite sure, but I imagine, from what the chief said at the conference at Lagny, that with our left flank resting on the Paris forts we shall retire back to the Seine. So long as we keep our left flank safe, I do not think we have anything to fear. The Germans, we hear, are very tired, and have had very heavy losses, and if they attack us I have every confidence in what the result will be.

About midday it became evident that one German corps was crossing the Marne at La Ferté, six miles from my outposts, and as Haig's Corps was already falling back so as to expose my right flank, I had to get Hamilton's Division back a bit. I met Sir John French at Haig's Headquarters at 1.30 p.m., and we discussed the whole plan of campaign. It is very pleasing to me to hear again from the commander-in-chief praise of the way we had extricated our force, and also of the injury we have inflicted on the enemy by deciding to fight the battle at Le Cateau on the 26th August; Sir John also expressed to me over and over again his absolute confidence in me, which was decidedly pleasing to hear.

It was arranged that we are to fall back tonight about twelve miles towards the Seine, to take advantage of the dark to cover our movements, and also to avoid the piercing heat of the sun, so trying to the men and horses. The heat the last few days has really been tremendous, and is telling very much on the horses as well as the men. I am sorry to say my casualty list has not come down as much as I had hoped, and the figures now are 350 officers and 9,200 men— about one-third of my force.

A retirement is always a dangerous operation with regard to discipline, and a good many cases of unnecessary straggling and looting have taken place. Five men are to be tried by court-martial this evening. The losses of officers and non-commissioned officers in certain units makes it very difficult to maintain a proper standard of discipline, especially as the temptations are very great, owing to the hospitality of the country-folk and the desertion of so many houses with valuables in.

5th September.—We completed the night march without incident, having received about 2,000 reinforcements by rail and road during the march, and I took up my abode in the neighbourhood of Presles, at the Château Villepateur. We had one of the most restful days since the war commenced, and were very much cheered up by hearing that the French really are going to take the offensive, and that we ourselves shall move in the right direction tomorrow, namely, north-east instead of south-west.

The chief of the staff, Murray, came and told me that early tomorrow my corps was to get on to the line Houssaye-Villeneuve, that the French 6th Army— consisting of the 7th Corps, the 55th and 56th Reserve Divisions, the Algerian Division, and the Moroccan Brigade—were moving east, north of the Marne, and would be at Lizy-sur-Ourcq at 9 a.m. tomorrow, that the 5th French Army, under Franchet d'Esperey, had its left at Courteçon, and was going to advance north at 5 a.m. tomorrow.

Our army thus forms the apex of the angle of which the two French corps form the sides, and we have enclosed in front of us at least six or seven German corps. I visited the divisions and found the men very elated at the idea of moving forward instead of backwards.

6th September.—We moved at dawn to the position named, my head-quarters going to Château-Combreux, just outside Tournan. The 1st Corps was moving on our right, and was attacked lightly all the morning, evidently rearguards, for the general trend of the German divisions, as given by aeroplanes, was in a northerly and north-easterly direction, indicating that they could get no farther south for some reason or other. Our own advance is very slow, as the commander-in-chief wisely is determined to hold us back until the two French armies have got well engaged with the enemy to hold them to their ground. The news throughout the day was thrilling, as both the 5th and 6th French Armies were heavily engaged and were gaining ground steadily. By evening the 6th French Corps, heading off the 2nd German Corps and the 4th Reserve German Corps, were trying to cross the Marne at Trilport and Changis. In the afternoon we moved forward again to the line Villiers-sur-Morin-Courtry-Les Parichets.

Somehow the 1st Corps hung back, and at night we were far in advance. Hubert Gough, with the 3rd and 5th Cavalry Brigades, was engaging the enemy's machine-guns near Pezarches. Sir John French came to see me, and was most complimentary, repeating what he had said to me before, that our determined action in fighting the battle of Le Cateau had saved the whole situation, and that he was referring to it in such terms in his dispatch. I have an aeroplane squadron now permanently with me, under Salmond (now Air-Marshal Sir John S., K.C.B., C.M.G., C.V.O., D.S.O.), which gets us some splendid information. We got orders to move at 5 a.m. tomorrow, which were subsequently changed to later, as it was found that the French corps had not advanced as much as had been expected.

7th September.—The situation was that the 6th French Army was still fighting north of Meaux, and that the head of the 8th

Division of the IV French Corps which had marched from Paris, had reached Serris and was in touch with Pulteney's Corps, that the French 5th Army extended from Provins-Montreaux-lès-Provins-Esternay, and that the left of the 6th French Army had moved forward to Nanteuil, one division being sent there by rail.

We also heard the situation of the other French armies; immediately to the right of the 6th Army, and in touch with it, was General Foch's army. To the east again, with its left on Sompuis and its right about Vitry-le-François, on the Marne, was the 4th French Army; and to the east again, with its right thrown forward, was the 3rd French Army, stretching from Revigny to Ste. Menehould. Facing these last two armies were the following German corps from east to west—18th, 8th, 19th, and 12th. Facing Foch were the Guard Corps and the 10th Corps. Facing the 5th Army were the 9th, 3rd, and 4th, whilst falling back before us and facing the 6th French Army were the 2nd and 4th Reserve Corps—the whole covered by a great deal of cavalry.

Our advance this day was opposed everywhere by rear-guards, chiefly cavalry and guns. The South Lancashire Regiment, of McCracken's Brigade, had about forty-one casualties last night, and this morning, getting into Coulommiers; young Hadfield, a son of General Hadfield, was severely wounded; I visited them in their improvised hospital.

I took up my abode this night in a *château* at Faremoutiers; the whole village being occupied by Germans last night, it was very dirty. The *château* itself was littered with debris, and the remains of the breakfasts of the officers, which we had to clean up. The inhabitants who had not deserted were distinctly cheered by seeing us back again. I am sorry to say that two of our men had to be shot today, one for plundering, and the other for desertion.

8th September.—Early aeroplane reconnaissances were most interesting, telling us that in our immediate front at La Ferté on the Marne there was a tremendous mass of wagons, guns, and men, trying to get over the river, and that there was very heavy

474

fighting going on in the neighbourhood of Montmirail, in the neighbourhood of the 5th French Army on our right, and to the north of Meaux in the neighbourhood of the 6th French Army. Our orders were for the English Army to advance in the direction of Château-Thierry, and to try to reach the Marne.

It was a day of intricate fighting—the country is very broken in the neighbourhood of the Petit Morin River, and covered with trees, making it very difficult to find out what was opposed to us, and easy for weak rear-guards to hold up large numbers. Both the 1st Corps and the 2nd Corps had a considerable amount of fighting, and also the 3rd and 5th Cavalry Brigades, under Hubert Gough. The brunt of our losses fell on the 8th Brigade in endeavouring to cross the Petit Morin River at Orly. I saw the commander-in-chief at about three o'clock, and he seemed pleased with the way things were going, but disappointed that the Germans were getting away so fast.

After his departure I went out to the front myself and found Fergusson north of St. Cyr at a place called L'Hermitière. His troops looked very fresh and well, and had pushed on fast, capturing 150 Uhlans. Whilst with him bullets and shell, evidently our own, came from the direction of Orly, a place behind the 5th Division, where heavy opposition was holding up the 8th Brigade. In consequence Fergusson withdrew his infantry slightly to avoid loss from our own fire.

By nightfall my corps had gained the south bank of the Marne, where it placed outposts and settled for the night, my head-quarters at Doue. Late in the afternoon the battle appeared to be raging very fiercely, both in front of the 6th and 5th French Armies, especially the latter.

Afterwards I heard that the heavy firing to the east was an attack by one of the Guards Brigades in Haig's Corps, in which they caused a considerable number of Germans to surrender, not, however, without some sad losses in the Guards. My Chief Engineer, Major-General A. E. Sandbach, joined me today.

9th September.—Our orders are to cross the Marne and push straight north, and the advanced guards were over at 6.20 a.m.

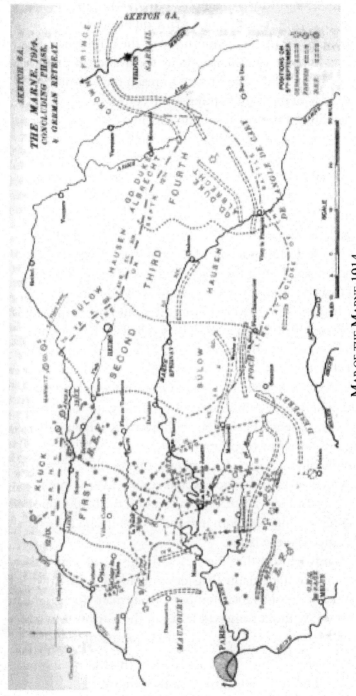

MAP OF THE MARNE 1914

Directly after dawn very heavy firing was heard again in front of the 5th and 6th French Armies. It appears that the Germans are holding the line of the Ourcq from the neighbourhood of Lizy up to Thury-en-Valois, and that they have strongly entrenched the part from Posoy to Thury; further, that the Germans in this neighbourhood have been reinforced. The French extend from Chambry (just north of Meaux) through Marcilly-Puissieux to a wood just south of Betz, and appear to be holding their own, whilst their cavalry, under Sordet, is south of Villers-Cotterets, unable to penetrate the wood there. It seems to me, then, that if we push forward straight north as we are going we shall be in rear of the German position and must force them to retire, possibly to a flank in face of the enemy.

The 8th Brigade had a good many casualties—Gordons, Royal Irish, Royal Scots, and Royal Scots' Fusiliers. I visited our wounded in the village of Saulsoy, two or three miles east of Doue, where I made my head-quarters for the night. The only officer there was poor young Hay of the Royal Scots, badly hit in the stomach. About a hundred casualties altogether, but Captain Hewat of the Royal Scots was killed and about forty other ranks. The weather shows signs of a change. There was a heavy storm threatening in the evening, which ended in a dust storm and a certain amount of rain. A heavy battle has been going all day away to our left, the 5th French Corps' passage of the Ourcq being obstinately resisted by about two and a half German corps—the French 5th Army does not appear to have had much resistance, but on their right General Foch's 9th Army got into a marsh, and were very severely handled, but towards evening made a determined counter-attack and drove the Germans back.

Fergusson and Hamilton pushed north to the Marne at 5 a.m. The former was stopped by guns and infantry, the latter got to the road two miles north of Pezu at 9 a.m. My corps was extremely fortunate in finding the bridges in front of them on the Marne last night intact—whether this indicates that the Germans were too hard pressed to blow them up, or whether they think they may want them again on their return journey, is doubtful. I rather favour the latter view, as their retirement is very orderly. The 3rd Corps, Pulteney's, which had to cross at La Ferté, found the bridges blown up and the far side strongly held by artillery, infantry, and machine-guns.

It was this that exposed the left flank of Fergusson's Division, for the ground between that and La Ferté is high, and gave good positions to the enemy. About eleven I went to Pulteney's head-quarters to see if I could help him in any way by pushing troops in between Fergusson and himself, but he thought he could manage without help. Whilst I was talking to him Sir John French arrived, and expressed himself very pleased with the way my corps was pushing on. He told me that the 1st Corps, which ought to be in line with us, was somewhere behind. The French 5th Army are still having a great battle north of Lizy in their efforts to get across the Ourcq. In one place there are ninety German guns in action. The move of my corps, which is pushing a wedge right in behind their position, is bound to make the Germans withdraw.

The 8th Division of the 4th French Corps, which is just west of the 3rd Corps, is endeavouring to cross the Marne to threaten the left of this great German battery. Aeroplane reports indicate enemy retiring north, opposing us everywhere they can. Two or three divisions are on the line Marigny-Château-Thierry. Our aeroplane officers are real heroes. Not only do they appear to have put the fear of God into the Germans' aeroplanes, for they hunt them wherever they see them, with the result that there have been none in the air for two days; but, in spite of being shot at almost every time they go up, they continue their reconnaissances and bring back quite invaluable, and what always proves to be true, information.

Just now, two of them arrived one after the other; both their machines had been hit several times, and one of the officers had a bullet actually through his clothes, which he produced whilst he was talking to me. The flight attached to me consists of Major Salmond, Captains Jackson, Charlton, Conran, and Cruikshank—Jackson was the man who produced the bullet.

Altogether it was rather a disappointing day, as, with the 1st and 3rd Corps back on our flanks, we were not able to make such progress as we ought to have done, but the effect on the Germans was material; not only did we kill a great many and capture a good many prisoners, but the two and a half corps facing the 5th French Corps thought it wise to retire, as we were uncomfortably near their backs. It seems that in this battle on the Ourcq both the French and Germans have suffered very heavy losses—they say the French 7th Corps alone had nearly 7,000 casualties; but the French have got their tails up well and are fighting splendidly. My casualties today are about 230 wounded, and forty or fifty killed.

Our losses were principally due to an exceedingly well concealed battery in a wooded country, in front of Fergusson, which it was impossible to locate for many hours, but which was eventually knocked completely out by one of our howitzer batteries. Another Q.F. battery gave us a good deal of trouble, but was also silenced, and we captured the whole battery, nearly all the horses and men being killed. At nightfall Montreuil-aux-Lions was still in the possession of the enemy.

In front of that, some very disagreeable wood fighting had taken place. The D.C.L.I, had a good many casualties, but after dark Cuthbert managed to clear the enemy out with his brigade. I took up my head-quarters for the night in Saacy, where I met Hubert Gough, looking extremely well and full of enthusiasm because his men had gained such absolute confidence whenever they came in touch with the enemy. I am not sure how many prisoners we have got today, but something pretty considerable.

10th September.—The 3rd Corps appear to have spent the greater part of the night in getting over the river at La Ferté, and in repairing the bridge, so they are still a long way behind. The 5th and 3rd Divisions started at 5 a.m., covered by Hubert Gough's 3rd and 5th Cavalry Brigades, all going due north. It was a wettish morning's march. Hamilton made great progress, but Fergusson was stopped by the enemy holding Germigny. Enemy's columns were reported by aeroplane trekking away north from Germigny, and Hamilton realised that if he pushed on he would not only get into a better position, but force the people in front of Fergusson to retire. The 1st Corps on the right again was going very hard, and the 2nd Division, the left of Haig's Corps, was even farther forward than Hamilton's Division.

There was a good deal of fighting today, and by midday the 3rd Corps was able to come up into line. Hubert Gough and Chetwode, I hear, were enjoying themselves very much driving back the enemy and collecting stragglers. Quite a lot of Germans were killed. They were very scattered, and dead bodies were alongside the roads wherever I motored, going out to the advanced guard. The number of prisoners captured today by my corps is well over 1,000.

The woods, of which there are a great many, are full of skulkers, and battalions are busy collecting as many as they can. In consequence of the wet, the roads were extremely difficult today, as we were crossing deep valleys, and some of the horses are feeling the fatigue very much, whereas the men seem to improve in spirits and in health every day—in fact, they are in fine fighting fettle.

Today is the first which has made me come to the conclusion that there is real evidence of our enemy being shaken, for the roads are littered and the retreat is hurried; but I still realise that the main bodies of the German corps in front of us may be in perfect order, and that the people we are engaged with are strong rear-guards who are sacrificing themselves to let their main bodies get far enough away for fresh operations against us. Tonight I have taken up my head-quarters in a very fine *château* at Marigny-en-Orxois, and we are all much elated at a letter I received from Wigram dated the 8th, conveying His Majesty's congratulations to the corps.

I am hoping His Majesty realises that all credit is due to those who enabled the troops who fought in Belgium under my command to be extricated. I mean to my staff, both general and administrative—the latter, by their foresight and energy, kept the impedimenta far enough away from the retiring troops to prevent their being hampered, and at the same time not too distant to prevent their getting food and ammunition when required, whilst the general staff foresaw everything, and their chief, General Forestier-Walker, grasped every situation in a moment, and issued the necessary orders without hesitation throughout the six or seven days of hard fighting and anxious situations. To him and his assistants, Colonel Oxley, Colonel Gathorne Hardy, Colonel Shoubridge, and Major Russell, and on the Administrative Staff to General Hickey, Colonel Rycroft, and Major Wroughton, the greatest praise is due. We are a very happy family, and are thoroughly enjoying our campaigning together.

The king's congratulations have pleased us all immensely, as also the rest of the news in Wigram's letter about the several reinforcements which are coming out at once, and the several armies which Lord Kitchener is preparing, and which we suppose will be ready within the next year. We all feel sure now that the king and country are absolutely determined that, even if it goes on many years, the British Empire will remain top dog. This is the most inspiriting news for the troops in the field, and I shall Like good care to let all my corps know about it.

Our Signal Services, under Major Hildebrand and Captain Gandy, have never failed us for an instant. All through the arduous retirement and fighting at Mons and Le Cateau, and throughout the retreat up to the present time, they have always kept us in telephonic or telegraphic communication, both with the troops in the field, and with the commander-in-chief's head-quarters. We have, too, a most undaunted lot of motorcyclists, from universities and public schools, who know no fear and never seem to be tired.

One of them, named Barnett, alas! ran into a German patrol and was killed yesterday. We find the villages and *châteaux* very dirty now we are following the Germans, and strewn with broken champagne-bottles, and the villagers report that they drink very deeply. I am sorry to hear that poor General Findlay, the commander of the artillery of the 1st Division, was killed yesterday by a shell.

General Joffre, the French commander-in-chief, has directed us to move north-west instead of north, and has narrowed our front. This move, with our impedimenta and only two roads between three divisions, is a very difficult one, and a long march is impossible just as it is so necessary to press on and catch up the enemy. Had we been able to make a long march today, we should have caught a lot of the enemy's transport. Our troops were practically unopposed, but lots of stragglers surrendered.

Towards evening, however, Gough's Division, consisting of the 3rd and 5th Cavalry Brigades, joined in with some French troops, and were very busy with their guns against the Germans in the neighbourhood of Soissons, with what result we have not yet heard; but reports say that the town and bridges at Soissons and approaches thereto are thronged with masses of wagons and men and horses.

Unfortunately it has been so thick today, ending in very heavy rain, that it has been impossible for aeroplanes to go up and tell us about the enemy. We have been very lucky up to now in our weather, and, by being kept informed by aeroplanes of the whereabouts of the enemy, have been able to press forward much faster than we should have in the old days: in fact, aeroplanes prevent the enemy from delaying us with their rearguards in the way they used to.

In the afternoon it came on very cold and wet, and I tremble for the health of the troops, many of whom, officers included, have no great-coats, waterproof sheets, nor change of clothing, due to their having lost so much in our retirement from Belgium. This might have been remedied by now, but by being forced from our base at Havre, and having to form a new base at the mouth of the Loire, there has not been time to get our new line of communication working to its full extent, and so we cannot get the necessary things.

Again, when we moved south we destroyed several railway bridges, and now that we are following the enemy find ourselves hoisted with our own petard, for the trains can now only come within thirty miles of us, and in a few days will be farther behind still. Sir John French visited me in Chézy at midday, and was very pleased with our prisoners—over 2,000 of which we captured yesterday, besides an enormous number killed.

Young Lord Stanley, with our spare horses, succeeded in rounding up three German officers and 106 other ranks. I made my head-quarters at Rozet St. Albin in a *château* belonging to the family of Berthier, Napoleon's chief of the staff, my most advanced troops being for the night at the village of Hartennes. We have not done very well in messing up to date, but we are gladdened today by the arrival of a French chef who says he had once been with Lord Rosebery.

There are persistent rumours that a Russian force is being assembled in Scotland to land in Belgium— needless to say, it is not believed. I am glad to say I find that the first reports of my casualties yesterday and today were greatly exaggerated, and I understand now that on the 9th and 10th there were three officers killed, fifteen wounded, and four missing, and of other ranks seventeen killed, sixty-nine missing, and 384 wounded. Unquestionably the fighting has been very hard, and the number of German casualties during those two days enormous, and therefore I do not think our losses are excessive.

I see in *The Times* of the 29th August, which is our latest paper, that all our losses in men and material, including guns, had then been made good. The wish was evidently father to the thought, for, although I have heard of guns being seen on our Lines of Communication, none have reached us, and my corps is still forty-two guns deficient.

The commander-in-chief has adopted the policy of sending on a lot of the divisional artillery with the cavalry, so as to worry the retiring enemy, and this is bound to affect him very seriously, for it is largely the system the Germans carried out in following us from Mons, and I can speak from experience that it tries retiring troops very highly. The pursuit is to be continued vigorously tomorrow, and, as the rain appears to be stopping, we should make good progress and be on the River Aisne in the neighbourhood of Vailly, east of Soissons, by the evening.

Saturday, 12th September.—The operation this day was an advance to the line of the River Aisne, the commander-in-chief's intention being, if possible, to cross it and occupy the high ground on the north side. It was a terribly wet day, with a good deal of wind, and the roads were in an awful state, delaying all wheeled vehicles to a very serious extent. Allenby, with his cavalry division, occupied Braisne in the early morning, but had to call for infantry support to maintain it, and this was given by the 3rd Division.

Later on in the day Gough's Division seized the high ground just north-east of Chassemy, and had an action with some German infantry at Peuplier on the high ground, killing seventy and capturing 150. He was only able, however, to get within 500 yards of the bridge at Vailly, which was held by machine-guns. Throughout the day a tremendous artillery battle was waged by the 3rd Corps and 6th French Army away to our left, the Germans being in position just north of Soissons, and to the east and west of it. The Germans appear to be making a great stand in order to get all their transport away, and one can easily understand that with the roads in their present state they must be more hampered by the weather than we are.

Aeroplanes were only able to do very little, and this made the location of the German guns very difficult. Since the Germans have destroyed all the bridges on the river as far as we can make out, it looks as though the one idea they had in their minds was continued retirement. The 5th Division only got its head as far as Ciry, and found Missy bridge strongly held. In some mysterious way, however, Lieutenant Pennycuick of the Royal Engineers managed to get on the river and to float down within 150 yards of the Missy bridge, enabling him to bring us an excellent report of the state of the bridge, which showed that it was very badly destroyed.

The river is at least sixty yards broad and very deep. Night fell—one of the worst I have ever known: blowing hard and pouring in torrents, finding us unable to establish ourselves on the river. The men, drenched to the skin, were mostly got under cover in some of the villages during the night; but I am afraid they suffered a good deal. We always had the cheering thought that it was worse for our enemies than for ourselves. I located myself in a beautiful *château* at Muret, belonging to the Louvencourts, relations of one of my dispatch riding officers, Lieutenant Chapman. The French are reported to have lost very heavily in the neighbourhood of Soissons.[1]

---

1. Strategically the Battle of the Marne was a great one, but as an actual fight from the soldier's point of view it was not very serious, for the total casualties in the whole B.E.F., that is five cavalry brigades and three infantry corps, only amounted to 1,701 in five days—6th to 10th September.

THE AISNE BATTLEFIELD SEPTEMBER 1914

CHAPTER 26

The Aisne; Flank Move to Béthune

The Battle of the Aisne, for the 2nd Corps, lasted from the 12th September to the 2nd October. It was an extraordinary battle, and our first taste of real trench warfare. Our fighting position was one against all the principles of war, for it was just across the river—and a deep and rapid river too—with our backs to it. Just room there for the front line troops, everything else behind the river. Fighting going on continually with an enemy also in trenches at quite short range.

At first it seemed extraordinary and impossible, but, as the war progressed, we learned that nothing was extraordinary or impossible, and that principles of war applicable to open warfare did not apply here. Day after day and night after night almost perpetual rifle-fire and guns thundering across the valley of the river and aeroplanes, though we hadn't many then, soaring aloft. Supplying, reinforcing, and relieving the trenches were serious difficulties, and had to be done at night, and through much of the time rain increased the hardships of war.

Casualties were heavy most days, and some days very heavy, but our medical arrangements were so good that the wounded were soon got back and looked after, so different to the fate of the poor fellows in our retirement, many of whom had to be left behind. On the 18th September I have noted that Sir John came to see me and told me the total casualties in the B.E.F., since we got on to the Aisne six days previously, amounted to over 10,000.

487

They were strenuous, and at times anxious days, even for a corps commander some way behind the trenches. Reports on the progress in the trenches were continuous day and night and constant fresh provisions had to be made, especially in I he matter of artillery support and devices to strengthen weak parts of the line. Then the trenches had to be visited, troops temporarily in rear inspected and addressed. Personally, I made a point of explaining to the troops, whenever opportunity offered, the general situation in other theatres of war as well as our own, so that they might be able to gain an intelligent idea of the war as a whole and of their own particular share in it. Frequent visits to the wounded also formed part of a corps commander's routine.

On the 19th September Henry Wilson came to discuss digging a second position in case we had to fall back. The difficulty was to find men, but it had to be done, though not very efficiently. Luckily we were never driven to make use of it. The troops were extraordinarily well supplied all this time—waterproof sheets, ample food, rations of rum—in spite of our base having been moved from Havre to St. Nazaire, a move very creditable to the I.G. Lines of Communication, Sir F. Robb. Sir John Cowans at home and Sir William Robertson at the front proved to be wonderful quartermaster-generals, and always seemed equal to the occasion.

On the 19th September fresh 18-pounders and machine-guns to replace our losses began to arrive, and soon after heavy siege howitzers, so necessary to reply to the Black Marias which the enemy hurled at us with great liberality.

In spite of all their hardships, strains, and discomforts, the health of the troops was remarkably good, only two *per cent,* sick, less than the normal percentage in peace.

Casualties were heavy, though—from the 12th to the 25th, 3,211 in the 2nd Corps.

On the 20th September the 2nd Battalion of the Sherwood Foresters—my old regiment—suffered very heavy losses, but made a great name for themselves. Amongst the officers alone there were fourteen casualties, five killed and nine wounded. I was very proud of them, and should like to give the full account, but they were not under me, and thenfore their brave deeds are outside my personal memoirs. The 2nd Corps, too, had heavy losses on the 20th-21st, the 3rd Division losing twenty-five officers and over 500 men these two days.

The light side of nature was by no means absent, and amusing stories used to come back from the trenches. One was of a German who, on being taken prisoner, said all he wanted was to get back to his father in London. Another from the 3rd Division—that on the morning of the 29th September the enemy, with the greatest respect for the accuracy of British fire, put up a dummy figure above one of their trenches, at which our men promptly began to shoot, when out of the trench appeared a spade, indicating against the figure the position of each of the hits—and yet they say the Germans have no sense of humour.

Another day the Germans in a trench amused themselves singing "It's a Long, Long Way to Tipperary." Yet one more, the truth of which I will not vouch for. Our soldiers had been shouting to the Germans opposite to come out, without result, and a subaltern stood up in his trench and shouted, "Waiter," and at once a dozen heads appeared, shouting, "Coming, sir."

On the 2nd October the chief explained to corps commanders that he had at last persuaded General Joffre that unless there was a force in Flanders from La Bassée to the sea our communications with England were in danger, and that, the position was the natural one for the B.E.F. Sir John in went on to tell us that we were gradually to be withdrawn from the trenches and eventually replaced by French troops, so that we could be moved round to the coast.

That day I was glad to be joined by Captain Dermot McCalmont as *aide-de-camp*, for I had lost Major Hope Johnstone, who, owing to the casualties amongst experienced senior officers, had been taken away to command a battery. It was today I heard that Captain Carey, Royal Fusiliers, who had been my *aide-de-camp* at Salisbury, was going round his trenches two nights previously with a serjeant when they were attacked by three Germans, and killed all three. Carey was spoken of as a courageous leader. He, poor fellow, was killed some three weeks later near La Bassée. The men were in great heart all this time, and it was quite usual to see them when out of the trenches kicking a football about, regardless of stray shell. The hostile aeroplanes were rather troublesome, though our few did wonders against them. They, however, had the advantage of efficient air-craft guns, whereas we at this period had none.

In accordance with General Head-quarters' orders the 2nd Corps was silently withdrawn from the trenches this night, and next day was moving away, destination unknown.

I always regard the conception and execution of this great flank move as providing the largest nail in the coffin of the enemy in the whole war.

But for this I am unable to see how the Germans could have been stopped from seizing Calais and Boulogne, and it was only just in time.

Roughly the French armies were in a continuous line from our left on the Aisne about Soissons to La Bassée, some ninety miles, and from La Bassée to the sea near Dunkirk was the dangerous gap of forty miles, only watched by a few French cavalry and Territorial troops. It was to fill this gap that Sir John had persuaded General Joffre to release the B.E.F. from the Aisne.

My troops moved by night and kept hidden by day, some miles behind the French line and right across their lines of communication. Their first objective was the railway at Compiègne, at which place and neighbouring stations they were to entrain.

Extracts from my diary will, I consider, give the clearest account of the following days.

Diary. *Sunday, 4th October* (Château Muret).—Busy day. Great excitement among my staff by arrival of the owner of our beautiful Head-quarters Château, Mile de Louvencourt, accompanied by a Marquis and his wife. She, brave woman, has returned to live on her property. It must have been curious to her to find us in possession. She lunched with us, and appeared to be a very charming and capable woman, and was full of regrets that she had not been here to look after us all the time.

At 6 p.m., having sent off the greater number of my staff and baggage earlier in the day, I motored into General Head-quarters to get my final instructions, and dined with Sir John French, and had the pleasure of sitting next to Prince Arthur of Connaught. The latter appeared to be in the best of spirits, and told me much that was interesting about the German Emperor and Germans in particular, describing how that autocratic monarch was much more agreeable to meet in England than in his own kingdom, where it was quite a chance whether he was genial to his guests or not.

After a very pleasant dinner, General Forestier-Walker, Captains Bowly, Walcot, and McCalmont and myself motored about fifty miles to Verberie. A beautiful moonlight night, and a good deal of the road lay through forest. We passed masses of French motor-lorries, loaded with infantry, as well as a good many of our own columns, and it was not till 3 a.m. that we reached our destination.

Monday, 5th October (Verberie).—Dawn broke with very heavy firing some fifteen miles to the north and north-west of us, and this continued without cessation till long after dark. The French and the Germans have been fighting in the neighbourhood of Roye determinedly for days. Lord Loch brought us information as to how things were going farther west, which was not altogether satisfactory.

In the afternoon our troops started entraining at Pont St. Maxence, and Compiègne and two intermediate stations, and I went and saw them departing. Everything well arranged by the French Staff without any excitement. The troops, with wagons, horses, and guns got off extraordinarily quickly.

On returning from seeing the troops off after dark, my car broke down, and I had to walk back about two miles.

I met a French *Gardien*, who told me he was in charge of a certain section of the road, and was also a gamekeeper of the neighbouring area. He described how he had looked after English wounded on our retirement on the 1st September, and especially an officer of the 5th Dragoon Guards, whose name he did not know. He further said that whenever King Edward had come to Paris he had been the policeman on duty at the Hotel Bristol, and that King Edward always when he went out used to give him a cigar, which he was not allowed to smoke being on duty, but which he used to take for fear of offending His Majesty. He spoke with great enthusiasm of the late King, and further produced out of his pocket a shilling which he said he kept as it had the effigy of Queen Victoria on it. He was very anxious to give me dinner, but this kind invitation I was unable to accept.

Tuesday, 6th October.—Still at Verberie. Little firing today. The commander-in-chief wishes me to postpone my departure to catch up my troops until tomorrow. Alas! it will not be possible to detrain our troops so far forward as St. Omer, and Abbeville has been selected. *N.B.*—It had been intended to get us on to the Ghent-Roulers line and to detrain us as far forward as possible *via* Calais and St. Omer. Some of the trains had already reached Calais and had to be brought back. I went to see the entraining at Compiègne and Le Meux stations.

I was there last on the 29th August, when Sir John French was billeted in Napoleon's old palace, and I saw him and General Joffre. Compiègne is rather a nice town, with a fine statue of Joan of Arc. The big stone bridge over the Oise there was most completely wrecked by our own troops in their retirement five weeks ago.

I then went to Le Meux Station and saw the 9th Field Ambulance (Colonel McLoughlin) entraining. The troops went on entraining all the night. Altogether it will have taken three days—as my corps and its divisional ammunition and two days Reserve Park for Supplies take eighty trains, at the rate of one train per hour.

Wednesday, 7th October.—Quite one of the most beautiful days I have ever seen, after a frosty morning. I motored eighty miles, *via* Beauvais, to Abbeville. An excellent road and fine country. Beauvais Church is very old, and remarkable for its stained-glass windows.

Generals Fergusson and Hamilton had both reached Abbeville before me, and were busy digging their divisions out of their trains into fighting formations. At Abbeville we stayed in a girls' boarding school, the mistresses being present and taking great care of us.

Thursday, 8th October.—Very cold, but beautiful. An amusing incident happened, for it appears it is the first day of the winter term at school, and mothers—not having been apprised of the fact that the town was full of troops, and the school in occupation of my H.Q.—arrived with their children, and had to take them away again.

I spent the day going round the whole of the billets of the corps and saw the six brigadiers, which took me some six hours, for they cover a wide area. Everybody seemed very cheery and happy. Some battalions, *i.e.* W. Ridings and K.O.S.B., so reduced as hardly fit to fight.

On my return to Abbeville, I found Sir John and his Headquarters Staff had arrived, and I went and had a long talk with him and got his instructions for the future. It seems that the Belgians do not intend to fight for Antwerp.

Friday, 9th October.—Another glorious day. During last night my corps marched forward about fourteen miles.

The French are pressing for a hurry forward to cover their flank in the neighbourhood of Aire-Béthune, west of Lille, and have offered us enough motor-buses to carry 8,000 men, and so I am arranging to push forward as much infantry as possible in these vehicles.

It was a complicated operation, and it was not till midnight on the 10th that it was completed. However, it saved the men about a twenty-mile march. Of course, all the wheeled vehicles and mounted troops had to march.

Before leaving Abbeville, I again went and saw Sir John French, and then motored on about twenty miles to Hesdin, a very old town, where there was an old fort famous for a siege in 1632, when Louis XIII made the attacker of the fort a Field-

Marshal of France. The Mairie is a nice old building, and has some quite good prints in it and some very fine tapestry. I was billeted in a house of two old Indies, neither of them under ninety I should think, who were very indignant at anybody being put into their house. This was very old indeed, and the walls of the staircase were covered with beautiful tapestries, otherwise the house showed no signs of wealth.

My staff were fully occupied throughout the night trying to bring the French motor-buses, which had gone astray, to the right places to carry up the infantry.

The weather got distinctly warmer, and, luckily, none the less fine.

Saturday, 10th October.—The commander-in-chief came to see me in the morning. In the afternoon I motored on to my new head-quarters about eleven miles, in the Château Monchy Cayeux, a distinctly nice old house. News, on the whole, appears to be good, although the French troops ten miles east of our columns had been hard pressed all day. We should, however, by pushing forward tomorrow, be able to let this right as it ought to bring us on to the flank of the Germans. The heads of the 3rd and 5th Divisions were at Pernes and Diéval this evening, and I issued orders for a forward move tomorrow.

Just before leaving Hesdin Sir John came to see me again.

Sunday, 11th October.—I think there is no doubt that Antwerp must have fallen, for Rawlinson's 7th Division and Byng's Cavalry Division are between Ghent and Ostend, covering the withdrawal of the Naval Brigade and the Belgian Field Army. The 3rd Corps is detraining at St. Omer, and will not all be out of the train until about the 13th. The 1st Corps, I understand, is still on the River Aisne where we left it. Gough's and Allenby's Cavalry Divisions are being pushed forward in front of us to act on our left flank, the whole forming a corps under Allenby, whose place as commander of the 1st Cavalry Division de Lisle has taken.

An intercepted message from the Germans tells us that some

German attack is to take place from the direction of Lille on Nœux-les-Mines, just south of Béthune, so if that comes off we shall be fighting them before night.

My corps advanced today, the 5th Division to Béthune and the 3rd Division on its left, to the line of the canal north and north-west of Béthune, in the neighbourhood of Hinges and Mt. Bernenchon, posting outposts beyond the canal. There are masses of French cavalry in front of us, but they appear to be falling back before German troops. My Reserve Brigade, the 13th (General Hickie), with the 5th Dragoon Guards, I kept two miles south of Béthune. During the day the Germans attacked the French heavily near La Bassée, five miles east of Béthune, and Fergusson had to send a battalion of the Norfolks to entrench at Annequin.

I, by arrangement, met the commander-in-chief at Camblain-Châtelain at 3 p.m., and afterwards went to see Fergusson at Béthune, and later Hamilton, whom I found in the dark at Le Réveillon. I told both of them my plans for tomorrow, and was glad to hear that a good supply of warm clothing, boots, and blankets was actually arriving in the supply wagons.

Our cavalry, consisting of Gough's and de Lisle's Division, were north-west of us under Allenby. The roads throughout the day were very congested with our own transport, masses of French transport, and French cavalry, and also with crowds of refugees—the latter all men, some of whom were going to join the French Reserve, and others were escaping, having heard that the Germans intended to make prisoners of every able-bodied man, civilian or otherwise, to prevent them fighting against them. It was interesting seeing all the French troops in their gay uniforms, the cavalry being especially brilliant and conspicuous with their cuirasses and plumed helmets. (It was not till a good deal later that their army adopted a less visible fighting dress.)

Late at night I heard that an important bridge at Vieille Chapelle had been evacuated by the French cavalry and occupied by the Germans—this being in my direct line of advance tomorrow, will have to be taken. My head-quarters tonight are in a small *château*, named Lozinghen, belonging to a M. Maquin, a vineyard owner. He says it was built about 1200, but was completely done up after the 1870 war.

Monday, 12th October.—After a very cold, frosty night, the sun got through about 9 a.m., and we had a glorious day. I moved early to Château Hinges[1] to be near my troops during today's fight.[2] The operation consisted in prolonging the line of the French to the left, attacking eastwards from Béthune towards La Bassée on both sides of the canal, the 5th Division on the right, 3rd Division on the left. The country was extraordinarily difficult, being very flat and intersected with canals and dykes and high hedgerows, without any rising ground suitable for artillery positions or rather for places to observe from. I kept one Brigade, the 13th, under Hickie, south of the canal as my reserve, the remainder of the troops all being north. Progress was very slow, as, although the German troops did not appear to be in strength, they disputed every village, stream, and hedgerow.

I met Sir John French in Béthune at 3 p.m. He had sent Allenby's Cavalry Corps north-west to Mont des Cats. The 3rd Corps was getting out of the train at St. Omer and moving to cover Hazebrouck. My corps had an obstinate day's fighting, though nothing serious, and lost about 300 killed and wounded. My plan was to make the 3rd Division wheel to its right and threaten the enemy's rear.

I sent for Hamilton and Fergusson to come and see me at 9.30 p.m., and explained tomorrow's plan. Troops slept where they had fought. In the afternoon the air was thick with aeroplanes. I fear the Cheshires have had a heavy loss, for they got into a farm just west of La Bassée after dark, and were counterattacked, and I am afraid lost their colonel, Vandeleur, who had only just joined them from the Cameronians, and their second-in-command, Young. Poor Major Roper, too, of the Dorsets, was killed—an excellent officer.

---

1. This *château* became my head-quarters throughout the Battle of La Bassée, *i.e.* to the 31st October
2. *Vide* map of Battle of La Bassée.

496

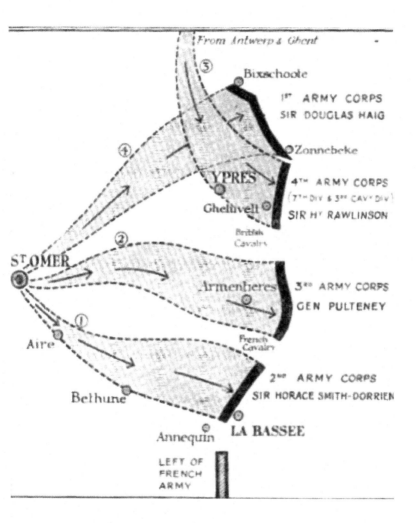

HOW THE BRITISH ADVANCED FROM ST OMER TO
THE YPRES-ARMENTIERES BATTLE LINE

I had had to throw my reserve brigade into the fighting south of the canal early in the day, and so I was left without a reserve and was fighting on a front of about eight miles. I let the 5th Dragoon Guards, which had been lent to me the last two days, return to the cavalry corps.

The streets of Béthune, which is a town of considerable size, were simply crowded with refugees, as were all the roads running in and out of it. Many pathetic scenes were noticeable.

Tuesday, 13th October.—A dull morning, which in the afternoon turned to very heavy rain. I visited Fergusson at 10 a.m., and met Sir John by appointment in Béthune at 11.30. Later in the day I visited both Hamilton at Lacouture and Fergusson at Béthune-Le Quesnoy. The latter had had a very heavy day's fighting. The Dorsets and Bedfords were seriously attacked, and driven back with rather heavy losses. We made very little advance throughout the day along the whole line. At one time, the 5th Division was in rather a critical position—or rather, General Count Gleichen's Brigade of it. Hickie's Brigade, south of the river, maintained its position.

At about 3 p.m. a general attack, combined with the French, took place. It was not very successful. I fear our casualties in the last two days have been something near a thousand. The 7th Division of the French cavalry covered my left flank, and made very little progress.

My head-quarters remain at Hinges.

Further particulars show that the Bedfords were driven out of Givenchy, and thus exposed the flank and rear of the Dorsets, who were south of the village between it and the canal, with a section of guns under George Boscawen, Lord Falmouth's son, the latter on the northern bank of the canal about 1,200 yards east of the Pont Fixe. Thus, the Dorsets were fired into from their rear, and from both flanks, for some of the Germans were south of the canal; but they fought brilliantly, having 130 killed and 270 wounded, and without losing their hold on Pont Fixe. Every man of the artillery detachment was wounded except Boscawen, and the captain, coming up, was killed, and it was not till then that they had to abandon their guns. Boscawen did uncommonly well.

During the night the 15th Infantry Brigade entrenched itself strongly on this new line. Colonel Bols (now Major-General Sir Louis Bols), of the Dorsets, was wounded and captured, and eventually in the dark managed to crawl away back to his own people.

I am sorry to say that Hickie, commanding the 13th Brigade, has had to go on the sick list, and I have had to put Colonel Martyn, commanding the West Kents, temporarily in command of the brigade.

My object now is to right wheel, pivoting on Givenchy, so as to get my left astride the La Bassée-Lille road in the neighbourhood of Fournes and thus threaten the right flank and rear of the enemy's position south of La Bassée.

Wednesday, 14th October.—A very wet morning, and a good deal of artillery-fire—mostly on our side.

This to me is the saddest day of the campaign, for Hubert Hamilton was killed by a chance shell. He was standing with some of his staff and a shrapnel burst near him, and one bullet struck him on the temple and killed him instantaneously. Not only do I lose a very old friend, but a most exceptional commander, and one who inspired all under him with absolute confidence.

I visited General Fergusson in the course of the morning. His troops are well entrenched, but are under considerable shell-fire—though I do not think as heavy as the Germans are under, for we appear to have more guns in action and are not sparing ammunition.

---

3. To show what a loss Hubert Hamilton was to me I quote from a letter I wrote my wife next day:

"An arduous campaign is the most marvellous searcher of persons; some are found to be frauds, others to be giants—Hubert was a giant, believed in by all—I have lost my right arm, for in my army corps he was that to me; however, as you say in your last letter, we must harden our hearts, which in so very true."

The Empire has a great work to perform; those who go to eternity before the task is completed are heroes, and must be thought of as such and not mourned."

At 2 p.m. I met the commander-in-chief by appointment in Béthune, and we discussed the whole situation. He is very pleased with the work of our cavalry corps, and Gough, as usual, appears to have distinguished himself by capturing a most important tactical point at Mont Noir, in a range of hills some seventeen miles north-west of Lille. Pulteney's 3rd Corps, too, has made some progress, but had a good deal of fighting yesterday. There is, however, a wide gap—of eight miles at least—between his corps and mine, and a good many German troops in it.

In the afternoon I went to call on General Maistre, commanding the 21st French Corps—the corps on my right, with whom I am co-operating—but unfortunately he had gone forward to some village, and later in the evening he came to see me. He seems a very agreeable person, and I should think very capable.

Owing to the shell-fire, it was not possible to bury poor Hamilton until after dark. I shall never forget the scene. It took place in the churchyard of the village of Lacouture, about a mile from where he had fallen. The church itself was only about half a mile behind our fighting line. It was a very dark night, and at about 8.30 p.m. as many officers as could be collected from the fighting line, all his staff, and several of mine assembled and marched in procession into the churchyard.

At the time a determined night attack was being made by the Germans all along our line, and just in front of the church was very heavy indeed, so much so that the rattle of machine-guns, musketry, and artillery-fire made it very difficult to hear the chaplain, the Rev. Macpherson, read the service. Quite unmoved by the heavy fire, and the bullets through the trees over our heads, the chaplain read the funeral service beautifully. It was quite the most impressive funeral I have ever seen or am ever likely to see—and quite the most appropriate to the gallant soldier and fine leader we were laying in his last resting-place. I fancy all were much moved by the scene—as I was myself.[3]

Our casualties today were considerable. Brigadier-General McCracken assumed temporary command of the 3rd Division.

Our general line that night was from Givenchy on the right through Richebourg-St. Vaast to Fosse.

Thursday, 15th October.—General Colin Mackenzie (now Major-General Sir Colin, K.C.B.) arrived in the morning to take poor Hamilton's place, and after seeing me, proceeded out to his troops' divisional H.Q.

In the night attack last night we had held our own very well, and there is every reason to believe that the Germans suffered considerably. During the night the 13th Brigade, on the south of the canal, had towards early morning, as soon as the attack died down sufficiently, been relieved by French troops and been withdrawn into reserve north of the canal—very tired after an exhausting night.

Today, the 3rd Division has done extraordinarily well. With their guns dispersed amongst the infantry right up in the firing-line they have managed to drive the enemy out of one entrenched position and loopholed village after another, crossing the dykes with which this country is intersected with planks which they carried along with them, till at last, late in the afternoon, they managed to push the Germans back off the Estaires-La Bassée road. The Northumberland and the Royal Fusiliers, the Royal Scots and 4th Middlesex did extremely well on our left. The Germans must have suffered very heavily, as in our advance large numbers of them were found dead.

The French cavalry operating on our left had shown very considerable dash and push, and co-operated with us most effectively. The French attack on the village of Vermelles, combined with our attack farther north, was of a very desperate nature, having begun yesterday afternoon, going on all through last night, and is still continuing. Truly these Germans are fighting magnificently.

Reports from Pulteney's 3rd Corps show that they are making distinctly good progress, and altogether tonight I shall sleep feeling that our heavy losses of the last four days, which amount to about two thousand, ninety of whom are officers, have not been in vain.

It has taken four days for the left flank of my wheel to get forward three miles, and the fact that so many officers have become casualties is due to the nature of the country, which necessitates officers leading forward small detachments.

We found in the last two days a new use for our anti-aircraft gun, the pom-pom, for it is extremely valuable in clearing out the villages.

Friday, 16th October.—A very thick foggy morning, after a comparatively quiet night, during which my patrols reported all along the line that there were distinct signs of the Germans retiring, and by 9 a.m. I had reports that the whole of the 3rd Division and the left of the 5th Division were getting on well.

Although the enemy had retired they had not gone far, but disputed every hedge, dyke and village, and progress was very slow though successful. As the movement was in the nature of a wheel to the right, my left flank became more and more exposed, and as the French cavalry, who had undertaken to guard it, lost their way and did not appear till 2.30 p.m., the duty devolved on the two divisional cavalry squadrons of 15th Hussars under Captain Courage and 19th Hussars under Major Parsons, both of which were on that flank—too weak a force, but, being well handled and full of dash, did uncommonly well, though naturally they could not exert the same pressure as a larger force. The left flank was brought up at dark by the village of Aubers, which was strongly held.

During the day the 5th Division had made some progress, though they were obstinately held on their extreme right, on the canal bank just west of La Bassée junction. It was a very difficult day's fighting, but as progress was made it became evident that the German losses must have been considerable, and amongst the graves were found several of German officers.

The deep ditches were very favourable for defence and the marksmanship of some of the Germans extremely good—in one spot one man had fired 300 cartridges.

The villagers reported that all vehicles had been commandeered during the last few days to remove German wounded.

The villages which had been loopholed and held had been knocked to pieces by our guns.

I went to see both divisional commanders and some of the troops, and found General Mackenzie pleased with his new command.

The 3rd Corps, to the north of us, appears to have had little opposition, and to be getting on well, and drawing towards us, but there is still a considerable gap. The 1st Corps is still in course of detraining on its arrival from the trenches on the Aisne, and the 4th Corps—General Rawlinson —with General Byng's cavalry, have got into touch with us on the north; so all appears to be shaping out well.

Saturday, 17th October.—A clearer day, but still not clear enough to make any use of aeroplanes. Again were the French cavalry rather late, but they took the village of Fromelles, which was held, and thus guarded my left flank. Until this was done it was impossible to make very much progress.

In the afternoon, the 9th Brigade, handled with great dash by Brigadier-General Shaw, were attacking the village of Herlies, which just at dark was gallantly carried at the point of the bayonet by the Lincolns and the Royal Fusiliers, the Lincolns having a good many casualties. The Royal Irish had been detached to help the French Cavalry in the attack on Fromelles, and captured there fifty prisoners. The 5th Division also made considerable progress, and stood lit dark with its right flank still on the canal bank just west of La Bassée Station, and its left flank curled round the north of La Bassée north-east of Violaines. The Devons on the right, after gaining considerable ground, were wisely withdrawn a little towards their position of last night to avoid a heavy shell-fire.

Our 6-in. Howitzer siege battery arrived during the day, and I hope will be of considerable use in tomorrow's operations.

The 7th Brigade on the right of the 3rd Division failed to get into the village of Illies.

There was considerable movement of German infantry in motors from place to place, evidently to oppose us on the La

Bassée-Lille road. I visited the troops of the 3rd Division in the afternoon, and distributed some of the French decorations which the French Government had bestowed on our troops.

I inspected the temporary hospitals in Béthune with my P.M.O., Colonel R. Porter, and found everything exceedingly well arranged. There were not many in the hospitals at the time, but they had evacuated over five hundred wounded that morning. I was told that a Colonel Lee was inspecting all field hospitals on behalf of Lord Kitchener, and was surprised to find that it was Arthur Lee, M.P.,[4] whom I found in the garb of a staff colonel, and had a conversation with him. I was glad to hear that all his inspections had brought him to the same conclusion which I had formed throughout the war, and that is that the care of the wounded is being extraordinarily well done, and the devotion and skill of the medical officers are remarkable.

Our casualties during today amounted to 199, of whom three officers were killed and five wounded.

Sunday, 18th October.—There was constant firing throughout the past night, which amounted to nothing very particular. My orders were to continue the attack on La Bassée and to the north of it. General Morland arrived to take over command of the 5th Division, as Sir Charles Fergusson, having become a Lieutenant-General, had been called home for an appointment there.

I went to the 5th Division, and presented about a dozen French decorations and found Fergusson sad at leaving his command, while fighting was still on, but outwardly wonderfully cheery. Wishing him goodbye, I went to Count Gleichen's head-quarters at Givenchy. He was trying to push on towards La Bassée, but was receiving considerable opposition. A French battalion had crossed the canal to the north, and took the place of his right battalion to work eastwards along the canal, but it was not till the afternoon that they were able to take a bridge which had been obstinately held by the enemy for two or three days.

I here saw the ground where the Dorsets had suffered so

---

4. Now Lord Lee of Fareham.

heavily on the 13th, and I am convinced that their retirement was most justifiable, for their losses were very heavy indeed. There were actually 113 buried yesterday when we recovered the ground from the Germans, and also a very large number were wounded.

I then went on to the 14th Brigade, and found Brigadier-General S. P. Rolt on the top of a big factory (N.B.—He was shelled out of it just after I left) on the Estaires-La Bassée road, about two miles north of the latter place. His infantry had got to within about 800 or 900 yards of La Bassée, and could make no further progress, as the houses were loopholed and a lot of Germans were firing from them with machine-guns. Our guns were firing very heavily, but not very many German guns replying. I gave French decorations to him, and to Count Gleichen, for their respective brigades, as I was unable to see individuals.

I then went to General Mackenzie's head-quarters, and found that his division was meeting with an obstinate resistance. The village of lilies was very strongly entrenched and loopholed, and he saw no hope of getting it before dark. The French cavalry and cyclists were trying to seize Fournes, but were obstinately opposed and eventually failed to get it.

Just after dark the Germans between Illies and Herlies made a strong counter-attack, but were driven back successfully.

The 9th Brigade took the German trenches on the northern edge of the *château* a mile north-east of lilies at dark, but, as their left flank was entirely exposed, it was considered wise to withdraw them some 700 yards and entrench.

During the afternoon there were distinct signs of an increase in the strength of the Germans. More guns were in action, and after dark a searchlight was shown and star-shells fired. It appears, from prisoners captured and from numbers on uniforms of dead, that the increase has come from the arrival of the 13th Division of the 7th Corps.

Throughout the night heavy firing continued.

I heard later that the Royal Scots Fusiliers had suffered very considerably today, Captain Hurt and Lieutenant Cozens-

Brooke being killed, and I am afraid that Jimmy Boyle, lately my *aide-de-camp* at Salisbury, is wounded and missing. Five officers, too, were wounded, a Lieutenant Longman of the Royal Fusiliers amongst them. The total losses for the day were five officers killed, twelve wounded, and one missing—casualties for the day being a grand total of 303. This brings the losses of my corps in this operation up to 132 officers and 2,724 other ranks.

General Rycroft's horse rolled with him today and broke his collar-bone, mercifully without injuring his brain, which is so valuable to the 2nd Corps. The doctor hopes that if he is kept quiet he may still be able to carry on his work. He is, as usual, most cheerful.

Monday, 19th October.—Again a good deal of firing throughout the night. Quite a nice day as far as weather went. I visited both Divisional Generals, Morland and Mackenzie, and found them both trying to push on, but opposition was very considerable. Machine-guns were entrenched everywhere and houses loopholed, especially all round the outskirts of the town of La Bassée, a factory at Violaines being particularly strongly prepared for defence. We failed to take the village of lilies throughout the day. The French cavalry, which had taken several small positions and established itself close to Fournes last night, had unfortunately fallen back again to Fromelles, thus leaving my left flank open, and the same positions had to be taken again today.

I was sent for to go and see the commander-in-chief at Bailleul, about fifteen miles from my head-quarters, at 2 p.m., and there he, Pulteney, commanding the 3rd Corps, and myself, had a discussion on the situation. On my way, I had to pass through the area where the French cavalry had been fighting for the past week, *viz*. Merville, Neuf Berquin and Vieux Berquin, and many other small places. There were signs of devastation everywhere, houses level with the ground and churches riddled with shells. It was a sad scene, but the most extraordinary part of it was the attitude of the French people themselves—who were all back in their villages, taking things most philosophically, repairing their roofs, and on the whole fairly cheerful.

I hear that yesterday and today there were sundry ladies, with passes from home, visiting our hospitals. I don't know what good they were doing, but they displayed a good deal of idle curiosity, and took up the valuable time of the medical officers, and I trust that we are not going to see many more of them. Ladies working as nurses with the Red Cross are quite a different matter—they are always welcome!

Late in the day, in order to help the French cavalry working towards Fournes, the Royal Irish Regiment under Major Daniell, an AI officer, who had been on my staff in the Boer War, was sent forward to attack the village of Le Pilly. This they did very gallantly, attacking over 800 yards of open country, eventually storming and carrying the village, where they remained and entrenched themselves.

Tuesday, 20th October.—In the early morning there were signs of German activity all along my front. Infantry were seen crossing the La Bassée-Lille road, approaching our positions, and a column of considerable size was moving west through Salome. All corps commanders being ordered to meet the commander-in-chief at Bailleul, at 11 a.m., I went there, and heard from Pulteney that his 3rd Corps, the right of which was at Radinghem, and the left east of Armentières, was being heavily attacked, German troops having been heard coming up by train in the night, and that he feared his right flank might be turned—thus increasing the gap between his corps and mine.

The commander-in-chief placed at his disposal the 19th Brigade, which had been removed to Laventie. Having heard the commander-in-chief's plans, I returned to find that the attacks had increased, resulting in heavy fighting. All attacks, however, were repulsed with heavy loss to the Germans, as our shell-fire was tremendous and our infantry, especially the Cheshires, did a good deal of execution with the rifle. I am afraid, though, that our own casualties are somewhat heavy. I went out and saw both divisional commanders, and agreed with Mackenzie that Le Pilly was dangerously far forward, and that it would be best directly after dark to withdraw the Royal Irish from there, and place them in reserve, making our left at Le Riez, which was to be held by the Gordon Highlanders. He told me he had not had any definite news of the Royal Irish after midday, but believed I hey were under a very heavy shell-fire all day, and were probably pinned to their position, and would possibly be able to fall back after dark. The midday report from Daniell was to say he was strongly entrenched and quite happy in his position.

It was not till after midnight that I got an alarming report that the Germans were in Le Pilly, and that there was no news of the Royal Irish, and later on still another report that a certain number of them had fallen back, but that the bulk of them had been surrounded, and it was feared killed or captured amongst them their gallant C.O. Major Daniell. I also heard that two platoons of the Royal Fusiliers, which had gone forward to keep connection between the villages of Le Pilly and Herlies, had suffered very heavy casualties, and that amongst the killed was Captain Carey, who like Jimmy Boyle, had been my *aide-de-camp* at Salisbury, and whose reputation for courage on the Aisne I have already mentioned.

Wednesday, 21st October.—A very thick morning, followed by a fine day. In the fog the Germans from La Bassée drove the South Lancashires out of their trenches, and kept gaining ground there, but were themselves driven back by a brilliant counter-charge of the Worcesters and one company Royal West Kent at 11 a.m. The 3rd Division held their line without much trouble, although there was fighting going on throughout the day until dark. The 19th Brigade, however, to the east of Fromelles and connecting from there with the right of the 3rd Corps, were heavily attacked all the afternoon, and driven back a mile or two. This necessitated my sending to the French cavalry, three divisions of which are occupying the ground between my left and the right of the 19th Brigade, to tell them that I looked to them to hold their ground strongly.

During the afternoon the 3rd Division prepared a more retired position where there was a better field of fire, with a view to falling back on it before dawn tomorrow morning.

I visited both divisional commanders, and also General Doran at Le Plouich and General Shaw at La Cliqueterie. It was rather a disturbing day, with frequent alarming reports coming in of my own line being penetrated at different places in the 5th Division.

In the evening Colonel J. H. Davidson[5] arrived from the 3rd Corps to say that, in consequence of our cavalry corps north of the River Lys having had to fall back a short distance, the 3rd Corps had been ordered to extend its line north of the Lys, and, therefore, it would be necessary to draw the 19th Brigade nearer towards them—thereby increasing the gap between us and making a bigger task for the French cavalry. Davidson also told me that the 18th Brigade had lost heavily yesterday, and that he feared the Sherwood Foresters heavier than any other regiment; but he could give me no particulars.

Thursday, 22nd October.—After a fairly quiet night, dawn broke with very heavy rifle-fire in front of the 5th Division, and the French to the south of the canal. The French succeeded in repulsing all the attacks and captured a good many Germans, who were forced to surrender. The 5th Division, however, were driven out of the village of Violaines.

It seems that the Cheshires, who were holding it, were hard pressed, and the Dorsets left their trenches and came forward to help them, and both were driven back in a good deal of disorder, losing very heavily. The Germans then occupied Rue du Marais, but were well counter-attacked by the Worcesters and the Manchesters, and driven into the east corner of it, where they remained throughout the day.

No actual attack took place on the right of the 5th Division, and Devons and Norfolks, nor on the 3rd Division; but the French were heavily attacked at Fromelles late in the afternoon, and driven out with considerable loss, thus again exposing my left flank.

---

5. Now Major-General Sir J. H. Davidson, M.P., who has already made his mark in the House of Commons.

CHAPTER 27

Indian Troops: Neuve Chapelle

Diary, 1914

This same day, the 22nd October, under orders from the commander-in-chief, I visited him at Bailleul at noon, and saw Generals Pulteney, Allenby, and Watkis (now Major-General Sir Henry W., K.C.B.) (commanding the Lahore Division of Indian troops). On my way there, I had passed through Indian troops moving up to and into Bailleul. The chief explained the situation, that in yesterday's fighting the Germans had lost very heavily both in front of the 1st and 3rd Corps, and that it was essential that we should, all of us, maintain our present positions to enable other movements of troops elsewhere to take place.

It appears that the Belgians, with their left at Nieuport and right south of Dixmude, have held their own well during the last two days against strong attacks, and that they have been supported by fresh French troops. Further, that our cavalry was heavily pressed yesterday, especially Gough's Brigade, but, on being stiffened with infantry from the left of the 2nd Corps, were able to maintain their position. Also that Rawlinson's 4th Corps had had severe fighting, and driven the enemy back. Altogether, the news appeared to be of a distinctly satisfactory nature, for the Germans, although in considerable force, appear to be of inferior material. Their losses in front of all our corps have been very heavy.

On my way back I called on General Conneau, the commander of the French cavalry corps, responsible for keeping up connection between my corps and Pulteney's, at Estaires; I failed to see him, but had a long talk with his chief of the staff.

I then went on to see my divisional commanders, and it was not until I had a talk with General Morland that I realised that the incidents of the last few days disclosed a worse state of affairs in the 5th Division than I had thought. The men appear to be quite worn out with the incessant digging and fighting of the last ten days. The Germans in front of them are increasing in strength, and it seems doubtful whether the men in their present state, with their heavy losses (for in the last ten days the corps has lost about 5,000), would be able to maintain their position against another determined attack.

It was on my return to my head-quarters, at about 6 p.m., that I heard of the incident I have related at Fromelles, *viz.* the defeat of the French cavalry and the exposure of my left. I decided then that there was nothing left but to retire my whole line during the night about one to two and a half miles to a strong position which I had been entrenching during the last three days.

I wrote to explain the whole situation to the commander-in-chief, sent my letter off to him at St. Omer, twenty-five miles distant, and received his reply about 2 a.m. to the effect that he was sending me all he could spare of the Lahore Indian Division under General Watkis to be at Estaires about eight in the morning, and that I was only to use them in case of urgent necessity, as he really wanted them for work elsewhere.

Friday, 23rd October.—A peaceable night as far as my corps was concerned—in fact, quite the quietest we have had for some time—during which the troops retired to their new position. The French, however, on my immediate right were attacked, but were able to repel the enemy. I am much more comfortable in my mind about the state of affairs. It is a beautiful autumn day, and aeroplanes are able to reconnoitre well, and have already brought me in some reassuring information. It appears, however, that the right of the 3rd Division is being heavily shelled.

In the retirement a small party of the Duke of Cornwall's Light Infantry, under a sergeant, were left in their trench, the order to retire not reaching them, and as daylight broke they realised the situation and began to fall back. They were much pleased because they saw about two hundred Germans charging the empty trenches with fixed bayonets, and they chuckled over their disappointment at finding the trenches empty.

General Watkis came to see me, and I arranged how I wished him to dispose of the Indian troops, namely, north of Pont du Hem with two battalions at Laventie.

The Germans kept advancing today towards our new line, and there was a good deal of shelling and sniping.

I visited Sir John at Estaires at 2.30 p.m., where he held a discussion with Pulteney, Watkis, and myself. General Conneau, commanding the 1st French Cavalry Corps, had drawn up in the Market Square a very fine array of *Spahi* troops to do honour to Sir John. It was an extraordinary sight, and one hardly to be expected in the midst of a great European war. These troops were all mounted on Arabs, arrayed in the very brightest colours, light red and light blue, some of them even with flowing white cloaks, and very smartly turned out.

There was a good deal of saluting and nourishing of trumpets. The scene was more suited to an Eastern pageant than to a town which had been partly destroyed by shell-fire a few days before, and which was still the head-quarters of the French cavalry general, whose guns could be heard at the moment engaged with the enemy not very far distant. After receiving the commander-in-chief's instructions, and giving my own to General Watkis, I called on General Conneau and had a long talk with him on the subject of relieving his troops, who had suffered very heavily yesterday, in holding the gap between my corps and Pulteney's.

I then went to Mackenzie's and Morland's head-quarters, and found them generally in a happier frame of mind, well pleased with the new position.

Most pleasing accounts came in of the doings of the 1st corps. They seem to have achieved a great success and killed a lot of the enemy, and I sent Haig a telegram of congratulations from myself and my corps.

Saturday, 24th October.—Quite a quiet night, followed by an extraordinarily mild and agreeable day. I was informed early that I might expect an attack all along the line. This information proved to be correct, and early in the day firing became general, but mostly artillery-fire. Although the German infantry were seen approaching, they gave us excellent targets, and were prevented from closing.

Having promised to relieve the French cavalry between my corps and the 3rd Corps, I went to see General Carnegy (now Major-General Sir Philip C, K.C.B.), commanding the 8th Indian Infantry Brigade, near Laventie, as I wanted to make quite clear that he understood his instructions. This brigade had been moved there to be in a position to relieve the French cavalry that night, as well as to fill the gap between my left flank at Fauquissart and the 19th Brigade's right at Rouges Bancs. At the time I got there the Indian troops, consisting of the 15th and 47th Sikhs, were being treated to a very heavy shell-fire from what we call the portmanteau guns. The shells are high explosives from a powerful howitzer, and as they land make a tremendous hole and explode, and are considered to be like the arrival of a great portmanteau on the ground.

I afterwards ascertained what it was that made them concentrate on the Indians, for all our British troops have learnt long ago to avoid offering any targets. It appears that the Indians were walking about in the most unconcerned way, with an absolute disregard of shell-fire, in fact rather enjoying it than otherwise, and I have had to point out to their general that, although I have a great admiration for their bravery, I must ask them to remember that concealment of our positions is one of the most important matters to be considered in this war. It is, of course, all very new to them, and no doubt they will soon settle down.

I then went to see Bowes (now Brigadier-General W. H. Bowes, C.B., C.M.G.), who has just taken over the 8th Brigade from Doran (now Major-General B. Doran, C.B.), the latter having said good-bye to me this morning on his way home for a short rest, which all must have after a month or two of the arduous work of a Brigadier in the front line: after that to Mackenzie at Lacouture, Watkis at Locon, and finally to Morland at his original position on the canal. I found the last much concerned with the behaviour of one of his battalions, and agreed with him that it was entirely due to the lack of soldierlike qualities in the commanding officer, whom I would arrange to send home.[1]

Sunday, 25th October.—Very heavy shell-fire all night, and I own to feeling a bit anxious, for although the new position is an excellent one and thoroughly well entrenched, I am afraid some of the troops holding it are in a very shaky state. There was some rain in the night, but it was followed by a most beautiful day.

Reports coming in during the night indicated a good deal of enterprise on the part of the Germans, and that they had penetrated the line in one place, but had been successfully turned out again. They never could have penetrated the line had the troops opposed to them put up even the semblance of a fight.

It is unfair to blame the battalion in question too much—one of the most renowned battalions in the army—for it lost eighty *per cent,* of its numbers, and all its officers except two or three, in August, and has been kept going by drafts, mostly of Special Reserve, and quite young inexperienced officers with one or two exceptions. The battalion has never had a chance of shaking down, for it has been fighting incessantly ever since, and for the last fourteen days has been engaged in most nerve-trying warfare day and night, and they are physically worn out. This, I regret to say, is the condition of many other battalions also, and the marvel to me is how they stick it at all.

During the night, determined attacks were also made on the part of the trenches held by the 15th Sikhs, Royal Irish Rifles, and Royal West Kents, and were successfully repulsed with heavy loss to the enemy. There were twelve battalions of the enemy engaged in the attack.

I was sent for to meet the commander-in-chief at Bailleul at

1. Later reports, however, showed that the C.O. in question was in no way to blame, but that he was a brave and capable leader, and he was reinstated.

11 a.m., to hear his plans and discuss the question of ammunition supply. He was, as usual, full of enthusiasm, and the situation he put before us is that things are as satisfactory as they could be.

I then went to Laventie to find General Carnegy, but found it absolutely deserted, and the place considerably knocked about from a desperate shell-fire which ceased just before I got into it.

From there I went to find General Bowes, commanding 8th Infantry Brigade, and met Captain Belgrave, his staff captain, who told me that the centre of the 3rd Division had been driven in in the neighbourhood of the Royal Irish Rifles, but he believed things had been righted, so I went to Mackenzie's head-quarters, and found that Belgrave's statement was correct. It appears that at dusk the night before a determined attack had been made on the 7th Brigade trenches, which had been repulsed by the Wilts and Royal West Kents, and that at 9 p.m. the 8th Brigade had been similarly attacked and the Gordons driven out of their trenches, which were recovered by a counter-attack of the Middlesex, gallantly led by Colonel Hull (later Major-General Sir Amyas Hull). The shell-fire was very heavy, and Mackenzie was doubtful if the attack came on again very severely whether they would be able to maintain their position. He spoke highly of the handling of the situation by Brigadier-General Bowes.

I then went to Locon, the head-quarters of the Lahore Division, and found General Watkis and disturbing telegrams from the 15th Sikhs demanding more reinforcements, as they had just suffered two hundred casualties.

Thence I went to the head-quarters of the 5th Division, and Morland gave me a grave account of the situation in all his brigades. I then visited the three brigadiers, Generals Maude (later Sir Stanley Maude of Bagdad fame), Count Gleichen, and Colonel Martyn, and they all told me the same story of severe attacks repulsed with difficulty, but also that the enemy had suffered very severely.

Colonel Ballard of the Norfolks was holding the important

position of Givenchy with great determination under great difficulties. The Devons had suffered enormous casualties, especially in officers. The French battalion connecting their right with the canal had been driven out of the trenches, but had reoccupied them. It was then dark, and shell-fire very heavy all along the line, but I received further evidence of the heavy loss inflicted on the enemy.

I returned to General Morland's head-quarters and told him I would give him the only support I had, which was the Manchesters of the Lahore Division, and further that I would try to arrange for more French support.

I went back to my own head-quarters and sent off a staff officer to see General de Maud'huy, commanding the 10th French Army, to explain the situation to him, and, after a mouthful of dinner, motored on to St. Omer to the commander-in-chief's head-quarters, twenty-five miles distant, and explained the whole situation to him, as I thought it was only right that he should know there was a possibility of our being unable to maintain our position. I got back to my own headquarters again at 2 a.m., to find more reassuring reports to the effect that no fresh attacks had taken place.

Altogether it has been a disturbing day, because I realise that the forcing back of my line would be fatal to the commander-in-chief's plans.

After one of the most beautiful days I have ever known, the wind blew and the rain came down in torrents, but by daylight next morning it cleared up and the sun came out.

Monday, 26th October.—Morning reports indicate that the enemy are still active, and at dawn had made attacks on the Manchesters in the neighbourhood of Givenchy, but had been driven back, and, later on, they were again trying to work forward. The French have played up splendidly—General Maistre, commanding the French 21st Corps, having sent two battalions and two batteries of guns. I should add that Sir John French, who had already given me practically every available reserve he had, gave me two more batteries of 4.7 guns.

There is evidently very heavy fighting going on some twenty miles to the north of Armentières, as there is a perpetual roar of guns in that direction. This would be in the neighbourhood of the 1st, 4th, and cavalry corps.

During the morning, along my front, things seemed fairly quiet. Sir John French came over at 11 o'clock, and my Divisional Generals—Colin Mackenzie, Morland, and Watkis—assembled to meet him. He told me that he was sending me further reserves, namely, the 2nd Cavalry Brigade and three more battalions of the Indian army.

Towards midday, very heavy shell-fire developed on the centre of the 3rd Division, followed by an infantry attack. The Royal Irish Rifles, crushed by the shell-fire, had left their trenches, and the Germans, following, occupied the trenches, and got into the village of Neuve Chapelle. I had no real anxiety, for I considered I had quite sufficient troops to deal with the situation; but the Germans had got into the houses and it was impossible to turn them out.

During the night there were sundry attacks, which were all repulsed; but our troops round Neuve Chapelle were unsuccessful in getting rid of the enemy, and this state of affairs remained until far into the next day.

McCracken's 7th Brigade are nearly exhausted from hard fighting, heavy shell-fire, and downright sheer fatigue from want of sleep. However, we are all certain that the Germans are just the same as we are, and that their losses are heavier than ours.

We gather that up in the north, towards Ostend, the German troops are squealing for help.

Tuesday, 27th October.—The 5th Division appear to have had a fairly quiet night, but the 3rd Division, supported by Sikhs, were doing their best to turn the enemy out of Neuve Chapelle. I went off in the morning twenty miles to St. Pol, to call on General de Maud'huy, commanding the French 10th Army. I found him most agreeable and very pleased to see me. I told him how indebted I was to him for the way he had invariably supported my corps with infantry, cavalry, and guns. It was a wettish morning.

The situation round Neuve Chapelle grew graver throughout the day. Our counter-attacks never did much good, owing to the fatigued state of the troops, and to the confusion caused by the mixing up of the different units, and nationalities—47th Sikhs, French Chasseurs, 9th Bhopal Infantry, South Lancashires, Royal Fusiliers, etc., all of which made it difficult to co-ordinate a real attack. However, Colonel McMahon,[2] Royal Fusiliers, managed to clear all the northern part of the village of Neuve Chapelle, when in the early afternoon the Germans made a most determined attack in great force, reinforcing their own people in and on the east side of Neuve Chapelle. The tremendous shelling from their heavy portmanteau guns smashed up the trenches occupied by the Wilts, and those of the Royal Irish Rifles who were still holding the trenches, necessitating their evacuation.

These trenches were immediately occupied by German infantry, and night fell with our line broken, Neuve Chapelle in the hands of the enemy, and our troops in a semicircle round the north, west, and south of the village. The Indian 8th Brigade, to the north again, had been severely attacked the greater part of the day, and had had heavy casualties. Thus, there were two important sections of the defence line requiring reinforcements, which were difficult to provide. There were some grand deeds performed in this struggle. The Royal West Kents especially distinguished themselves: in spite of their being completely outflanked and the fact that both their commanding officer, Major Buckle, and adjutant had been killed, and only two young officers left, Lieutenant White and 2nd Lieutenant Russell, this splendid Battalion refused to retire, and fighting hard every day maintained their position until the 8th November, when they were withdrawn.

General Conneau, who is always most anxious to support us, placed all he had at our disposal. This meant, in addition to 600 Chasseurs already in the fighting line, some 300 cyclists, a battalion of dismounted cavalry, and nine batteries of artillery. He told us also that he could send us some sixteen hundred cavalry.

2. Killed a week or two later near Ypres.

I had, in addition, the 2nd Cavalry Brigade, commanded by Colonel R. L. Mullens (now Major-General R. L. M., C.B.) of the 4th Dragoon Guards, which had arrived in the afternoon from north of Armentières to support my line.

The situation in the 5th Division was better today, so much so that they were able to spare the D.C.L.I., Dorsets, and the Cheshires, three very weak battalions, to move up to the left of their line in case they were required.

At 11 p.m., as reports were by no means satisfactory, although I had had no reason to think there was a great weight of Germans supporting the attack on Neuve Chapelle, I went out to General Mackenzie's head-quarters, and there we discussed the whole situation. Meanwhile, General Wing had gone to see General Conneau at Merville to arrange about the use of his artillery the next day. When he returned, General Mackenzie settled to bombard Neuve Chapelle heavily in the morning, and after that to attack it with the troops he had at his disposal to try and retake it and re-establish his line on the east side. He placed this attack under General McCracken.

I got back to my own head-quarters at about 3 a.m. All reports from the trenches indicate that very large numbers of German dead and wounded are lying about everywhere.

Wednesday, 28th October.—As I lay down for two or three hours' rest at 3 a.m., I heard very heavy gun and rifle fire in the neighbourhood of Givenchy. One has become so accustomed to this that I expect one would hardly sleep well without it. At 7 a.m. Sir James Willcocks arrived to see me. His corps, part of which is already with me, is expected to be in this neighbourhood today. I explained to him the whole situation, and we arrived at a plan for occupying the line in future.

At about 10 a.m. General Conneau came to see me, the chief object of his visit being to express to me that every French soldier he had under his command would die in support of me should they be required. He is a fine fellow, and impresses one very favourably as a soldier.

Morning reports from my divisions indicate that they have

been fairly quiet throughout the night. They have long ceased to take any notice of artillery-fire and rifle-fire, unless it is accompanied by a direct attack of infantry.

It was still too thick to commence the attack to retake Neuve Chapelle until 11 o'clock, when the bombardment by many batteries began.

With Sir James Willcocks I met the commander-in-chief in Merville at noon, when he discussed the arrangements for relieving my corps by the Indian corps. He was very decided that my troops must have a rest, so as to be fresh in a few days to act as a reserve under his orders.

On returning to my own head-quarters, I heard that the attack on Neuve Chapelle was not getting on very well, and later in the day that it had failed. The 47th Sikhs and two companies sappers and miners had attacked in the most spirited way and got half through the village, but exposed their right flank in doing so, and were driven out again. The 9th Bhopal were at once driven back. I fear from what I hear that the casualties in these two battalions were very heavy.

I came to the conclusion that the village was no use to the enemy as they could not stay in it with all our guns turned on to it, and therefore decided to make no further attempts to retake it, but to readjust my line west of the village, and this was satisfactorily accomplished. All the British troops in this attack today did very well, and I was glad to have the help of the 2nd Cavalry Brigade—9th Lancers, 4th Dragoon Guards, and 18th Hussars. There were other attacks on different parts of my line throughout the day, all of them successfully driven off with great loss to the enemy.

General Sir E. Locke Elliot appeared in the afternoon at my corps head-quarters, driven by my old friend Lieutenant-Colonel Colin Campbell, Elliot being adviser to the commander-in-chief on Indian affairs at army head-quarters.

Matters quieted down in the afternoon.

Thursday, 29th October.—There was a good deal of firing throughout the night, especially with artillery. Attacks were made on my extreme left on the Indian Battalions, but were driven off, and the French to my right were evidently very heavily engaged. The morning was cold and frosty, and very thick, not clearing until nearly 10 a.m.

My latest reports of the casualties of the 47th Sikhs, 9th Bhopal Infantry, and the sappers and miners indicate that they were very serious indeed. Alas! my daily casualty list does not decrease, but in spite of this I am glad to say the fighting spirit of the troops improves. The total casualties in this battle bring up the grand total to 358 officers and 8,204 other ranks.

At 11 a.m. Chief of Staff Sir Archibald Murray— Sir James Willcocks and myself had a meeting to discuss details for replacing my corps by the Indian corps, a by no means easy operation with our troops within from fifty to two or three hundred yards of the enemy all along the line, and, of course, impossible in daylight.

There was heavy firing going on most of the day; the 5th Division were especially heavily attacked. It appears that in the early morning, in the fog, the Manchesters had been driven out of their trenches, and as soon as the fog cleared they gallantly retook them, killing seventy of the enemy and capturing many prisoners in doing so. The enemy's infantry showed in great numbers all the morning, attacking the Devons and the Manchesters, and the left of the French—invariably with heavy loss to themselves. Farther north they attacked the native brigade with the same result.

I visited Morland at his head-quarters, and found him working out details for his relief by the Indian troops that night. He was extremely pleased with the splendid way his troops had fought during the last few days—the West Kents, the Devons, and the Manchesters have all distinguished themselves, in spite of very heavy losses amongst their officers.

I then went to the 3rd Division—Major-General Wing had just assumed command of the division, replacing General Mackenzie, who has had to be invalided, never having recovered from an operation for appendicitis which he underwent shortly before he came out. I heard a very good account of the fighting spirit of the troops in the 3rd Division, although the losses in some of the battalions had been stupendous.

The 47th Sikhs and two companies of sappers and miners, in attacking Neuve Chapelle, must have behaved most gallantly.

In the evening a report came in that our patrols had been right through the village of Neuve Chapelle, which had been evacuated by the enemy, but they were still in the trenches captured from us to the east of the village. We hope to recover our wounded from the village during the night. During the evening several units of the 2nd Corps were relieved by the Indian corps.

This exchange of troops in close contact with the enemy is a most difficult and lengthy operation in the dark. Guides have to be provided for every trench, and the men led up, keeping close touch with each other, and quietly exchanged man by man with the men in the trench. It all has to be very quietly done, so that the enemy may not know what is taking place. It is reckoned that it takes two and a half hours to relieve one battalion, and of course it would not be safe to relieve more than alternate battalions at a time, so it is not possible to relieve the whole line in one night.

CHAPTER 28

Messines: the Second Army

On 31st October 1914 I handed over command of my section of the front to Sir James Willcocks, and retired to my new head-quarters at Hazebrouck, but no rest could be given to my unfortunate troops, who were hurried off in motor-buses to help the cavalry, 1st Corps, and 7th Division, hard pressed in the neighbourhood of Messines and Ypres. I was for the next few days practically a general without a corps, for half my troops were helping Allenby about Messines, and the other half helping Willcocks to hold the line I had handed over to him.

There is no doubt this was a very critical period, and I am ashamed to say that I did nothing to help it, but amused myself watching my staff shoot pheasants near Hazebrouck. But I hadn't a man. However, this state of idleness only lasted two days, for I then set to work inspecting any troops I could find disengaged, getting them smartened up and trained, and thanking them for their great services.

The first Battle of Ypres, one of the most glorious in the annals of the British army, in which the 1st Corps took such a leading part, had been won, and the German great attempt to break through defeated by the skill of our generals, and the dogged pluck of the troops; but the effort had exhausted them, and on the 4th November the chief ordered me to prepare to relieve the weary and depleted battalions and batteries of the 1st and 3rd Corps in the neighbourhood of Messines. The 2nd Corps was pretty well depleted, for in the previous three weeks it had had over 11,000 casualties, making a total of 26,505 since the campaign opened some nine weeks before.[1]

In this time, therefore, the corps had lost more than its infantry war strength, which with two divisions is 24,000. Of course battalions had suffered in the same proportion; for instance, the Northumberland Fusiliers had by the end of December lost forty officers and 1,200 other ranks, and all others much the same. I had, however, been fortunate enough to have just received very large reinforcements.

I spent the next few days in visiting all the battalions I could find, with a view to getting the corps together again, ready to take over part of the line when the chief gave the order. It was sad to find how depleted of officers they were, and that fact impressed me more than anything else with wonder at the feats they had performed.

On the 7th November the unwelcome news of the sinking of H.M.S. *Good Hope* and *Monmouth* off Coronel reached us.

All this time the Guards' Brigade under Lord Cavan and the cavalry and troops of the 2nd Corps which had been sent to that area were still having very heavy work round Messines and Ypres, and I expected orders at any moment, but on the 10th November the chief sent for me to St. Omer to lunch with him, and to tell me he wished me to go home to explain certain matters to Lord Kitchener, and to see Lord Stamfordham in case His Majesty wished to question me. Sir John also told me to let as many of my staff as could be spared go home too, for two or three days' rest; and off I went with eight of my staff, all of us elated, like boys going home from school for the holidays.

I was struck by the fact that people in England didn't in the least realise the strenuous nature of the fighting at the front, or

---

1. It will convey some idea of the desperate nature of the fighting, these early days, if I mention that the casualties of the 46th Division, which had some of the heaviest fighting in the war, amounted to 29,569 in three years and ten months; *vide* Major B. E. Priestley's excellent story of the 46th Division, page 122. N.B.—Had the casualties of a division of the 2nd Corps continued at the rate of the first nine weeks their total would have been about 270,000 in three years and ten months, whilst those of the corps would have been 540,000.

that we were a long thin line without reserves which might be broken through at any time. Their minds seemed set on what appeared to me to be a ridiculous fear of an invasion of England. I was graciously received by Their Majesties, had an interview with Lord Kitchener, and was back in France on the 14th November. Whilst dining with the chief that night at St. Omer the sad news came in that the gallant and high-minded bulwark of the Empire, Lord Roberts, had passed away at 8 p.m., in a house close by. It had been very sudden. He had only arrived on the 11th with his daughter, Lady Eileen, and had inspected the Indian troops. The day before he died he had insisted on climbing a steep hill in pouring rain with Allenby to get a view of the fighting, and on going back to St. Omer was taken ill, and remained unconscious until the end came, and the great soldier passed to his rest.

Fighting had been very heavy, whilst I was away, round Ypres, and the fourteen battalions of the 2nd Corps which had gone up to help had covered themselves there with glory. That they proved a great asset to Sir Douglas Haig, and helped him greatly to repel the desperate attempts of the Germans to break through at the glorious first Battle of Ypres, will, I feel sure, be apparent to all when the *Official History* appears. Two brave and promising leaders—Brigadier-General McMahon of the Royal Fusiliers and Brigadier-General Fitzclarence of the Guards—had both been killed, and Brigadier-General Shaw, who had done so consistently well throughout this arduous campaign, had been wounded.

Sir John, as usual, was full of confidence, though sad at his heavy losses. The next few days I was taking over my new front which from Ploegsteert Wood on my right ran south of Messines to opposite Petit Bois, and on the 18th I moved my headquarters to Bailleul. Taking over trenches, as I have already said, is a very trying job for the troops with enemy trenches and our own close to each other. On this occasion the weather increased the difficulties, for it rained every day, and of course all reliefs had to take place at night in silence. The difficulties were further enhanced when parts of the French line had to be taken over, as happened in this case, owing to differences in methods and language. We hadn't enough infantry either, and I had to borrow 1,200 cavalry from Allenby for one section. Who would have foretold, a year previously, that in 1914 cavalry would be fighting chiefly in trenches far from their horses!

The cold, too, became an unpleasant factor, for, when rain stopped, frost and snow succeeded, and the troops suffered very severely from trench-feet. At that time, with our attenuated line, it was impossible to keep the trenches in sufficiently good repair for protection of the troops holding them, and making them comfortable was almost out of the question. It was considerably later that devices for protecting the men and keeping them warm and dry came into use on a sufficiently large scale.

On the 20th November, H.R.H. the Prince of Wales honoured us with a visit, and went with McCalmont to as safe a place as we could find to watch the fighting, but the Prince didn't care about safe places. Two days later H.R.H. was attached to my staff for four days, learning general staff as well as administrative work, with the greatest interest and zeal. H.R.H. gave a touching account of the gallant King and Queen of the Belgians, who were living in a small house at La Panne, on the coast, just behind the left of the allied line. The Honourable Artillery Company Battalion, under Lieutenant-Colonel Treffry, joined me about now, and a most valuable addition they were.

On the 24th November I suffered a real loss, for McCracken, having been promoted major-general, was taken away from the 7th Brigade. The depleted state of some of the battalions was very serious, for some had not been filled up. The Duke of Wellington's, under Major Harrison, had only three officers and 250 men. The Cheshires, too, were much in the same state, commanded by a retired officer, Captain Busfield, with only one officer, named Frost, who had left England with the battalion. Then the Bedfords, under Colonel Griffiths, fifteen days previously a thousand strong, were reduced to six hundred. Were I to give similar particulars of all the battalions, I should fill pages, for these I have described were not exceptions.

But with it all their spirit was remarkable. One battalion I came across one evening moving up to take its place in the trenches as soon as it became dark, and by way of cheering them up I halted them and made them a little speech, telling them the latest news of the war, etc.; but they looked so cheerful and happy that I came to the conclusion they didn't want cheering up—especially as on talking to individuals they assured me they rather enjoyed trench work, as it was great fun sniping the enemy. One young officer of that battalion told me that he thoroughly enjoyed it, as there were lots of pigs and chickens running about between them and the German trench, a hundred yards away, and they used to shoot these by day and crawl out after dark to collect their bag. This was a battalion of the East Surreys under an exceptionally able commanding officer, Lieutenant-Colonel Longley, who shortly after became a brigadier and later a major-general in command of a division and is now Major-General Sir John Longley, K.C.M.G., C.B.

I had, throughout the time I was in France, quite excellent Field Companies of Royal Engineers; not that that was remarkable, for Royal Engineers, in my experience, are always excellent, and the bravest of the brave. What they do for an army would fill a book.

On the 1st December a great event occurred, for His Majesty the King arrived in France to inspect his army, and on the 3rd December honoured my head-quarters by lunching with us. Those of my staff present to meet His Majesty were Generals Sandbach, G. E. Forestier-Walker, R. Porter (P.M.O.), Rycroft and Short, C.R.A., Commandant de Boigne, a most agreeable and helpful French officer attached to my Staff, Colonel Oxley, and Captain Bowly. Besides them there were Lord Stamford-ham, Major Clive Wigram, Colonel Barry, General Lambton (now Major-General the Hon. Sir William L., K.C.B., C.M.G., C.V.O., D.S.O.), and Prince Antoine d'Orléans. His Majesty then motored round and saw all the troops not actually in the trenches, lined up wherever they happened to be. A general parade would have been too dangerous, for, with so many enemy aircraft about, gunfire would have been attracted to it.

His Majesty presented decorations, and it was tragic how many of those awarded had become casualties since the award. For instance, out of ten V.C.s, seven had become casualties, four having been killed. The only special outward show was rather a fine archway erected by the Royal Engineers of the 5th Division, giving entrance to a field where some troops were drawn up, headed "A Welcome to the King." Luckily it was a clear day, and His Majesty was able to see quite a lot of the battle front from the Scherpenberg.

I am saying little about the fighting, but it was going on everyday incessantly, and the casualty list kept mounting up. I have a note under the 4th December that by then the casualties amongst officers in my corps had amounted to 1,000.

Amongst the territorial units which were arriving I inspected on the 11th December a Cheshire Battalion under Lieutenant-Colonel Heywood. I was much struck by a splendid old quartermaster-sergeant with them, sixty-two years old, who had fought at Kandahar in the Afghan War 1879—I think he said in the 63rd (Manchester) Regiment. He had long since retired into civil life, but told me he couldn't sit at home when the country was in danger. It was this sort of spirit which won us the war. Two months later, whilst inspecting Princess Patricia's Canadian Light Infantry of the 80th Brigade of the 27th Division—a very fine body of men, nearly all with two or three medals—I asked one very smart man, who had five or six medals, how old he was, as I noticed he was wearing the ribbon of the 1882 Khedive's Star, and he assured me, with a merry little twinkle in his eye, that his age was forty. Further questioning would have been tactless, so I smiled and moved on.

It was the 11th December when the thrilling news reached us of Admiral Sturdee's brilliant action off the Falkland Islands, in which the German ships *Gneisenau, Scharnhorst,* and *Leipsig* found a watery grave.

I was uncommonly fortunate in my divisional and brigade

commanders at this time. Haldane (now Lieutenant-General Sir Aylmer Haldane) commanded the 3rd and Morland (now General Sir Thomas Morland) the 5th Division, and amongst my brigadiers were Gleichen, Douglas Smith (now Major-General Sir William Douglas Smith), the gallant Maude, the hero of Bagdad, Shaw, Bowes, and Cooper.

Towards the middle of December the chief decided that we should make an attack with a view to effecting a lodgement on the Wytschaete ridge. The day selected was the 14th December. I had had conversations with General D'Urbal, the commander of the French army on my immediate left, and with General Grossetti commanding the 16th French Corps, the corps actually touching me and on the 12th Grossetti had dined with me, wearing the G.C.M.G., of which he was proud, to discuss details. We concluded dinner by drinking "the King." I was to conduct the operation as far as the British troops were concerned. Besides my own corps I was given extra guns and a reserve of 6,000 dismounted men of Allenby's Division. It was an exceedingly difficult position to attack. The enemy's trenches were mostly on higher ground than ours, and had a fine field of fire, especially at what was known as Hill 75, whilst our troops had to cross an open valley except opposite the Petit Bois.

The state of the ground was awful, knee-deep in mud. My head-quarters were on a prominent hill called the Scherpenberg. It was decided that to cross the open ground would be impossible until we had entered the Petit Bois and got forward in it, and until the French on our left had made headway. I had about 180 guns, and at 7 a.m. on the 14th all of them bombarded, and at 7.45 the Royal Scots and Gordons rushed forward into Petit Bois and towards Madelstadt farm to the south of it. The Royal Scots and left of the Gordons established themselves in the Petit Bois, but the right of the Gordons could not make much headway against the many hostile machine-guns across the open ground in spite of the most devoted efforts; for our bombardment had not been very effective, and later on in the war we should never have attempted such an operation without a much more serious artillery preparation and many more troops. Personally I had never been in favour of the attack, and did not expect it to be successful.

The French made no headway at all. That afternoon another attempt was ordered by the commander-in-chief, and from 3.30 to 4.15 p.m. another intense bombardment took place and apparently our infantry made a successful advance, but after dark I found they had, except in the Petit Bois, to fall back on their own trenches.

I then went to General Grossetti's Head-quarters, to find the French had failed too, with 600 casualties.

Next day the chief decided that another attempt to get forward would be useless unless the French made headway, and, as they made none, our men remained in their trenches and the attempt to get forward was given up. As a matter of fact, the French on our left had come to the conclusion that any further attempt at a direct attack was useless, and had decided to devote themselves to working forward by sapping, an operation which was possible for them, as the ground in their area was better drained and of a more solid nature than in ours.

Getting possession of the Petit Bois had, however, been an important gain—but our casualties in the two days had been nineteen officers and 499 men. I consider we got out of it very lightly in view of the nature of the enterprise.

His Royal Highness the Prince of Wales was on the Scherpenberg watching the operation most of the time, as was also the commander-in-chief It is impossible to convey in a brief account a clear view of all that was happening from day to day. The weather was more than trying, the state of the ground beyond description. In that part of the world there appeared to be no stones or gravel, and rain converted the soil into a sort of liquid mud of the consistency of thick porridge without the valuable sustaining quality of that excellent Scots mixture. To walk off the roads meant sinking in at once, so it can be imagined the state the paths leading to and from the trenches themselves got into. As the men built their parapets up they gradually subsided and the trenches filled with water, so to retain any cover at all meant constant work. Sapping was one of the only certain ways of getting closer to the enemy, but for that solid ground was a necessity, and, as that did not exist, as fast as the saps were made they fell in and got washed away, as did also the communication trenches. Devices to improve matters were being thought out every day.

The famous hill and village of Kemmel were in my area, and a nephew of mine, Major E. P. Dorrien-Smith,[2] was staff captain to the 9th Brigade, holding the line of trenches covering them. He established a carpenter's shop on a large scale in the village, and turned out wooden troughs and tubs cut in two with a board for a seat across them and sent them up to the trenches as fast as they could be turned out. The Royal Engineers, too, were turning these troughs out on a larger scale for the army in the neighbourhood of Bailleul. Braziers were also being collected by our thoughtful quartermaster-general, and sent up into the trenches. These contrivances helped to keep the men dry. Later, when more troops could be spared for the work and more material became available, the trenches were regularly lined with wood, and later on still such improvements were made that they became almost comfortable. Until that came about, however, the discomforts and dangers of trench life beggar description.

It was noticeable how much smaller the percentage of casualties became as the trenches improved. I have made an effort at describing the state of the ground, but not of the sanitary conditions, which it can well be understood were most difficult to compete with. What made them worse, especially where attacks had taken place, was the state of the ground between the hostile trenches, called No Man's Land. There dead bodies were lying often for months just outside the trenches, and neither side could bury them.

---

2. He was very seriously wounded later on, and, though he carried on to the end of the war, had to leave the army. He, with Captain C. Hood of the Buffs, had both been my *aide-de-camps* in the Boer War, and curiously enough were both wounded on the same day.

Owing, too, to the paucity of troops it was difficult to get them trained to use such implements of war as mortars and hand-grenades, etc., as well as to instruct them in "going over the top" when an advance took place.

Kemmel Hill itself was valuable to us in that it used up such a lot of the German ammunition. It was a prominent object, and looked as if it must be held by troops, which it was not, and day after day it was battered by every sort of big shell. There was a conspicuous tower on it, and it was six weeks before they put a shell through it, but it took much longer than that before they began to reduce the size of the hill, which they eventually did. They used, too, what the Americans would call "some shell." There was one particular brand which made enormous craters—I measured one—thirty-six feet in diameter and ten deep.

Another very necessary matter was being taken up by divisions, and that was the establishment of laundries and baths on a large scale for their men. As I look back on it all it seems more than wonderful how difficulties were overcome, but what looms largest in my wonder is the heroism and dogged cheerfulness of the troops under awful conditions in spite of the heavy daily toll. To illustrate the last-named, I will take a normal quiet week when there was no special action; in merely holding the trench line on my front from the 17th to 23rd December 1914, the casualties were twenty-four officers and 755 other ranks. But to return to my story:

On Christmas Day I had the pleasure of lunching with the commander-in-chief; Haig was also there. After lunch the chief told us that the number of troops had increased so as to be unwieldy in two army corps, and that he had decided to form two armies, of which the first would consist of the 1st, 4th, and Indian corps under Haig, and the 2nd, 3rd, and 5th Corps under myself.

A number of territorials had arrived and had been posted as 5th Battalions to brigades. In addition to these the 5th Corps under Sir Herbert Plumer was expected in a few days. We certainly wanted all the troops we could get, for, besides holding the trenches, there was much work to be done in making supporting posts and farther back in digging and straightening a second line, called G.H.Q. Line, in case we should be forced back.

On the 28th December the new High Commissioner for Egypt, Sir Henry McMahon, my old friend of Quetta days, paid me a visit and gave me much interesting news *en route* for Egypt. He had with him another old Quetta friend as his secretary, Colonel Chevenix Trench.

On the 31st December my new army staff began to collect. Three days later Sir Archibald Hunter and his C.G.S., Brigadier-General Shute, came from England to have a look round, and visited my head-quarters. These visits from old friends added much to the amenities of life.

On the 1st January 1915 Sir Charles Fergusson, who had so ably commanded the 5th Division at the opening of the war, and had had to relinquish it on promotion to lieutenant-general, arrived with his C.G.S., Brigadier-General Furse (now Lieutenant-General Sir William Furse, sometime M.G.O.) and took over from me the command of the 2nd Corps.

The 27th Division, too, arrived near St. Omer today, the first instalment of the 5th Corps, under my great ally at the battle of Le Cateau, General Snow, and I accompanied the commander-in-chief on his inspection of it. The brigade commanders were the Hon. Charles Fortescue, D. A. Macfarlane, and Lionel Stopford, late commandant of Sandhurst.

Whilst at the parade we heard that H.M.S. *Formidable* had been sunk. I had known the father of the captain, "Loxley," well in my boyhood.

CHAPTER 29

Return to England; Expedition to East Africa; Gibralter

On 2nd January 1915 I established my army head-quarters at Hazebrouck, and here I propose to break away from anything approaching a consecutive story, for I could only give such by treading on dangerous ground. Added to which, whilst I remained in France commanding an army there were no operations on a large scale, and it will be best to leave the account of the costly trench warfare to the able pen of the official historian.

On the 11th January Haig and myself had the honour of being decorated with the *Grand Croix d'Officier* of the Legion of Honour by the President, Monsieur Poincaré, at the commander-in-chief's head-quarters, and that same day Sir Herbert Plumer arrived in France and assumed command of the 5th Corps. His coming was a great joy to me, as he was an old friend of mine, and would be sure to be a delightful person to deal with; and this proved to be the case.

His corps was completed by the arrival of the 28th Division (General Bulfin, now Lieutenant-General Sir Edward B., K.C.B., C.V.O.) on the 17th January. As a matter of interest Major C. B. Thomson, R.E.—who had done so well for me as a subaltern in the Boer War, was then a liaison officer at General Joffre's Head-quarters, and is now Lord Thomson and was Secretary of State for the Air in the first Labour Government—came to see me about this time and gave me much information concerning the Balkan tribes. He knew them well, having been with the Servians in their last war.

My army, as formed, consisted of my old 2nd Corps (Fergusson), the 3rd Corps (Pulteney), and 5th Corps (Plumer), and a very happy family we were. Within the next two months each corps had been increased to three divisions.

Forestier-Walker, promoted Major-General, remained with me as M.G.G.S., but was soon removed to command a division, being replaced by Major-General George Milne, who, later on, distinguished himself commanding our forces at Salonika, and is now Lieutenant-General Sir George Milne. Until the middle of February 1915, things went smoothly and happily with General Head-quarters; and then something, I have no idea what, happened, which appeared completely to change our relations, and so far as these memoirs are concerned I must leave it at that, for I could not relate the happenings of the next few months without departing from the main principle I laid down for my own guidance when embarking on this chapter of my *memoirs*, namely, to avoid incidents a description of which might be interpreted as imputing blame to others.

All I shall say, therefore, is that, from now on, I and the 2nd Army could do nothing right. Matters went from bad to worse, and I gradually became aware that it was the army commander, rather than the army, who had fallen into disfavour, and that until he went the army would be handicapped and the cause jeopardised.

I, therefore, wrote to the field-marshal on the 1st May 1915 on the subject, concluding by asking for an interview; but, my letter remaining unanswered. I again wrote on the 6th May, and the following is a copy:

My dear Field-Marshal,
I have just received an order for army commanders to meet at your house at 9 a.m. tomorrow. I am still in ignorance of the action you intend to take regarding the papers, so important to me and the army I command, I sent

you on the first instant, and it would make things easier for me, were I to know your views before the meeting.

Whatever may be the reason, there can be no question that your attitude to me for some time past has tended to show that you had, for some reason or other unknown to me, ceased to trust me.

Latterly I have been shorn first of one wing of my army and then of the other, on the latter occasion the announcement being made in such a way and in such terms, as to leave no doubt in the minds of many in the 2nd Army that their commander was no longer believed in by their chief.

My position as army commander has become impossible, and I regard my remaining in command with a cloud hanging over me ready to burst at any moment, as a positive danger to the cause for which we are fighting.

Plenty of complicated situations have arisen in the last few months, and the difficulty of dealing with them has been greatly enhanced by the knowledge that unless I was successful, I and the 2nd Army would be blamed—in fact, I have had more to fear from the rear than from the front.

We have got to win this war, and to do so there must be no weak links in the chain. Your attitude to me constitutes a very seriously weak link, and I feel sure that, trying as that attitude has been to me, you have not wished to carry it quite so far as to appoint someone else to command the 2nd Army in my place.

This step is, however, the only one which to my mind will strengthen up the chain again, and it is to render it more easy for you to take it without further delay that I am writing this letter.

Please do not let any false considerations for me personally stand in the way, for the War Office will doubtless find some place for me where I can still do useful work towards helping our army fighting in France.

Yours sincerely,

H. L. Smith-Dorrien.

I again received no reply from the field-marshal, but at 7.30 p.m. that evening (the 6th May) I received the following official from his adjutant-general:

General Sir H. Smith-Dorrien, G.C.B., commanding 2nd Army,

The Commander-in-Chief directs me to inform you that the Secretary of State for War wishes to see you, and he requests that you will proceed to England tomorrow—7th May. Lieutenant-General Sir H. Plumer has been instructed to assume command of the 2nd Army and informed that you will communicate direct with him as to when you leave for England. Kindly arrange this, together with any information you may consider it necessary to give him. Please acknowledge receipt of this memo.

C. F. N. Macready, A.G.

G.H.Q. 6.6.15.

I dislike immensely including even this letter, and the official reply, but am informed that many outside the army are under the impression that I left France under a cloud, and this idea the letters may to a certain extent dispel. I prefer the dignity of silence, and would even now rather have waited for the appearance of the *Official History* of this period of the war before including these limited references to events of this period in my memoirs, for the former will be beyond dispute and will surely vindicate my actions as they did in the first part of the war; but time is going on, and my sons are growing up, and for their sake I want the truth to be known.

On the 10th May I saw Lord Kitchener, who was surprised to see a robust individual, as he had been informed from France that my health had broken down, and next day I was graciously received by His Majesty at Buckingham Palace.

On the 15th May Lord Kitchener, with full knowledge of the facts which caused me to leave France, wrote me a personal letter, saying he was going to recreate the post of Inspector-General in the United Kingdom with a salary of £4,000 a year, and would I accept it, remarking that Treasury approval, of which he had little doubt, would have to be awaited.

On the 15th June, however, he wrote me in his own handwriting that, for some reason, which he did not state, the Prime Minister would not agree. I heard afterwards that, as it had been decided to have a change in the chief command of the army in France in the near future, there would be no appointment to offer Sir John French if the chief military post in England was filled by me.

On the 18th June, however, Sir F. Robb, who had become military secretary, wrote me a charming letter saying, owing to Sir Frederick Stopford's going to the Dardanelles, the command of the 1st Army for home defence would be vacant, concluding as follows:

> The appointment is not of such importance as Lord Kitchener had hoped to find for you, but he does not like to offer it to anybody else without first ascertaining whether you would like to accept it, pending his being able to find something more suitable to your rank.

Of course I accepted it, and on the 22nd June took over the command with head-quarters in Caius College, Cambridge, with two old friends, Brigadier-General H. H. Burney as head of my administrative staff, and the Honourable C. Fortescue of my general staff. Another old friend, Sir Leslie Rundle, who commanded the armies for Home Defence, was my commander-in-chief The actual front of my army was from the Wash to just short of Harwich.

On the 12th July I was invested with the G.C.M.G. at Buckingham Palace.

The next few months, though busy, were certainly very pleasant and agreeable. Having head-quarters at Cambridge gave me my first experience of university life. There was something peculiarly grand, silent, and peaceful living in such beautiful surroundings, especially after the hideous noises of the past ten months, and nothing could exceed the kindness and cordiality shown to us by Mr. H. K. Anderson, the Master of Caius College, and all the Dons, and also by the venerable Master of Trinity, Dr. Montagu Butler, in whose house I had been when a boy at Harrow.

However, I found Cambridge too far back, and on the 16th October moved my head-quarters to Lyndford Hall, kindly placed at our disposal by Captain F. Montagu.

On the 22nd November I was sent for by the Secretary of State for the Colonies, Mr. Bonar Law, and later on by the Prime Minister, Mr. Asquith, and asked to undertake the expedition against German East Africa. This seemed a great opening for me, but Lord Kitchener, when he returned from Gallipoli, was by no means in favour, for he wanted all the troops he could collect for the main theatre of war, though he yielded at last.

I found it a difficult job, however, to squeeze out of him all the requirements I considered necessary for carrying the campaign through to a speedy termination. Sir Bruce Hamilton was appointed to take over the 1st Home Defence Army from me, and with my new staff I settled in London to work out our plans and organise the expedition. That most capable and delightful person, alas now gone to the Great Beyond, Brigadier-General Simpson-Baikie, was my B.G.G.S., and Captain the Honourable Freddy Guest, himself to be one of my staff, placed his house in Park Lane at our disposal as an office.

But, although the War Lord allowed all this to take place, he would not definitely give his approval to the expedition. I had constant interviews with him in my efforts to get guns, aeroplanes and sufficient troops, but obtaining them was like squeezing blood out of a stone.

At last, our actual passages having been arranged for the 24th December, I went to wish Lord Kitchener goodbye on the 20th, when, to my surprise, he said he was not going to give me certain guns, etc., which I had laid down as essential. I told him that under those circumstances I could not undertake the expedition. Whereupon Lord Kitchener replied that I had better explain matters to the Prime Minister. I therefore informed Mr. Asquith by letter, through his private secretary, exactly what the situation was, and within a few hours received a reply to the effect that he had arranged matters with Lord Kitchener, and I was to get all I had asked for.

I should mention that one of the bones of contention was the route I should travel by. The War Office had selected the one by the Red Sea, going straight to Mombasa—whereas I wished to go *via* Cape Town.

My reason for selecting that route was because a very large proportion of the troops for the expedition was to be provided by the South African Government, and all we knew about them was that they had been promised, and were being recruited; but what we did not know was how far advanced their training was; whether their ranks were actually filled; what reserves they were providing to replace casualties; what was their system for keeping the troops supplied, and many other details essential to the plans of a commander-in-chief I therefore considered it essential to go with my Staff to Cape Town to get into touch with the South African Government.

At the last moment, as a result of my insistence, our route was changed, and perhaps it was as well, for the P. & O. *Persia,* on which our passages had been taken, shortly after leaving Marseilles, where it was to have picked us up, was sent to the bottom of the sea. Very large numbers were drowned, and Lord Montagu of Beaulieu had a wonderful escape. Years afterwards he chaffingly accused me of being the cause of the disaster, for he said it was well known that the commander-in-chief of the East African Expedition and his staff were to travel on the *Persia* and he was sure that was why they torpedoed her. I apologised for the ducking he got, and we are still good friends.

My personal staff were Captain Dermot McCalmont, A.M.S., Captain L. G. Murray (son of Sir Archibald) and Lieutenant Alex. Wernher as *aide-de-camps*, both smart and capable officers; the last-named had been attached to my Staff at Cambridge, a high-minded and attractive young fellow, who later on joined the Welch Guards, and was killed in France.

The War Office had early placed at my disposal all available information as to the troops already there, and likely to be detailed, the nature of the country, and all that was known of the activities of the enemy.

So far the latter had had a considerable measure of success—having repulsed an attempt made by a brigade from India to seize the port of Tanga, as well as having pressed back all our troops out of their territories and established themselves in a strong position in our country under the high Mountain of Kilimanjaro,[1] from which they made frequent raids on our railway connecting the port of Mombasa with the capital, Nairobi.

From this information I drew up an Appreciation of the situation and an outline of my proposed plan of campaign, and on the 1st December I sent it in to the War Office, and it was generally approved and printed as a secret document. I have a copy of it before me as I write. As there is now no necessity for secrecy, and my plan differed materially from that carried out by my successor, I give the outline of it, as it may be of interest to students of military history to compare the two.

What is known as the Taveta position was locally a strong one, but could be turned by a wide movement to the west round Kilimanjaro, *via* Longido, or by landing on the coast behind the enemy's right (or east) flank, or by both combined. Turning the east flank by land was practically debarred from the waterless nature of the country, and the presence of the tsetse fly. The only troops in British East Africa already there were some 15,600, of which 3,000 were white infantry, 3,500 African infantry, and 9,000 Indian infantry—of the last-named, however, it was reported that their moral was not very good, and that the total infantry which, owing to sickness, could be counted on for an advance was only 7,600. Of artillery there were only eight 15-pounders, and two mountain-guns, but two 5-inch howitzers and twenty 13-pounders were about to be sent up from South

---

1. This mountain over 17,000 feet high, rising straight out of the surrounding country not much above sea-level, is a very remarkable feature.

Africa.

Reinforcements, however, were in course of being dispatched:

Two Native Battalions from India	1,500
One White Brigade from South Africa	4,000
One White Brigade from England	4,000
Cape Boys from South Africa	1,000
	10,500
Add the 7,600 mentioned above	7,600
and the total infantry available amounted to	18,100

The mounted force to be sent from South Africa was to be 2,000 Boers.

The enemy forces were reported as 2,200 whites and 20,000 to 25,000 black troops.

The key to the problem, in my estimate, was to hold the enemy in front, until the rains were over and our arrangements complete, then to move against Taveta, whilst moving a mobile force round Kilimanjaro to get behind their west flank, the Belgians from the Congo, the column from Rhodesia, and the Royal Navy expedition on Lake Tanganyika operating at the same time; once the enemy were fairly committed to countering these combinations, a force, already at sea, was, like a bolt from the blue, to sail in suddenly and land on the coast behind their east flank, preferably at the enemy capital at Dar-es-Salaam.

Climatic conditions were going to be the chief obstacle, for at the end of March heavy rains commence and last for two months, during which movement is impossible. I therefore made it clear that before the rains I should only drive the enemy's advanced bodies back on their position at Taveta, which was just inside British territory, and hold them there whilst perfecting arrangements for a real advance in June, when interruption by rains would cease. I argued that if I advanced before the rains I could doubtless take the Taveta position, but then would have to halt for two months in a most unhealthy climate, during which the enemy would recover any loss of moral brought about by their defeat.

Once on the run, it was all important to keep them on the run. Then again, our troops, many of them, were only partly trained, lines of communication were not in order, and, as there was no particular hurry, I urged that to make sure of rapid success when we once started we should, as Lord Kitchener invariably did in his Nile campaigns, get ready to the last button before we commenced, and then go right through with it. I asked, too, that another white brigade might be found me by June, so that I might land it behind the enemy, when they were all absorbed in the Taveta position, *i.e.* either near Tanga or Dar-es-Salaam (then the capital) or both.

I further asked for naval co-operation with the object, firstly, of establishing a close blockade of the coast, and later, when the time came for covering the intended landings already mentioned. Admiral Sir Henry Jackson was First Sea Lord and General Sir Archibald Murray was chief of the Imperial General Staff when I was making my arrangements, and from both I received the most unstinted assistance.

Hearing that the day after I was to start for South Africa Sir William Robertson would take up the reins as C.I.G.S., I thought it advisable to leave him a letter so that he might know from me the terms on which I was proceeding and some of my requirements, and, as it sums up the circumstances in a few words, I will quote from it:

I am extremely sorry that I am departing for East Africa the day before you arrive to take up the duties as chief of the staff, as I should like to have had a few words of personal explanation of the circumstances under which I am going out. You will find that Lord Kitchener is very hostile to the expedition, as it was arranged by the Cabinet, when he was away in the Mediterranean. Whether the expedition is desirable or not is not for a soldier to enter into. I was asked to undertake it and agreed to do so on certain terms, and in an Appreciation of the situation, which I drew up, gave my views on the minimum of troops and accessories which would be necessary, and further, a rough plan of campaign based on such information as I have been able to collect. Shortly, my appreciation is that the country which I am required to subjugate is 700 miles long by 600 wide, and that all our efforts to enter and obtain a footing have so far failed, the enemy, as a matter of fact, having one of their main positions actually over our border, as well as several strong advanced positions.

Owing to the difficulties of transport, due to the shortage of shipping, to Mombasa itself, and thence up-country on a single line of railway, it is impossible to do much except attack the enemy's advanced posts before the rains break about the 1st April; but, with these ports in our possession, I should be able during the rains to make roads and railways up to them, and have everything ready for jumping off for the main offensive as soon as the rains cease about the end of June.

Murray will tell you that I have never advocated the campaign, for my view is entirely that the main theatres of war lie in Europe; but, in view of the unfortunate expeditions there have been in other parts of the world, it would be dreadful if, through lack of a few of the weapons and accessories of modern war, the East African campaign should be added to the list of unsuccessful ones.

I then urged on Robertson the importance of supplying my requirements.

The real gist of my Appreciation may be summed up in the phrase "More haste less speed," for I felt convinced that to start before we were ready and before the rains would, for reasons I have given, end in a protracted campaign, whereas, by waiting two and a half months and seizing the enemy's base behind them, a short, sharp and decisive campaign would be probable. It may be of interest if I quote from the final paragraphs of my

Appreciation.

After urging the necessity for at least four British cruisers with not less than 6-inch guns, two to deal with Tanga and two with Dar-es-Salaam, with detachments ready to land and also with a balloon-ship for observing fire, I conclude my Appreciation by emphasising that, though desirable the main offensive should take place in March, such was out of the question owing to the time it would take to collect the necessary force, and the amount of organisation to be perfected after the reinforcements about to be sent had assembled, and then I gave in detail all material requirements.

Unfortunately for me, directly we sailed in the *Saxon* from Plymouth, I contracted pneumonia of such a violent nature that my life was despaired of, and that I am alive I feel I owe to the care and skill of Dr. Stevens of the *Saxon,* and of A. F. R. Wollaston, a delightful and enterprising naval doctor attached to my staff, and to the devoted attention of young Wernher.

On reaching Cape Town I was better, and able to carry on, through the medium of Simpson-Baikie, arrangements for the campaign. Then I got worse and had to undergo two lung operations at the hands of two very clever doctors at Cape Town, Hugh Smith and Elliot, who were so pleased with my improvement that they believed I might still be able to conduct the campaign. However, that was not to be. Whilst I was ill I was carrying on a telegraphic battle with the Union Government at Pretoria, they urging that, for political reasons, the main operations should commence before the rains, I refusing to listen to them.

I then got worse again, and on the 13th February had reluctantly to embark on the *Balmoral Castle* for England, when General Smuts was appointed in my stead. He did not adopt my plan of campaign, but started the main offensive before the rains, and, though the campaign was successful, it was not over when the Armistice was arranged in November 1918, largely owing to the remarkable genius and courage shown by the German leader, Von Lettow-Vorbeck, and his handful of Europeans. As General

Smuts wished to have his own Chief Staff Officer, Simpson-Baikie and Wernher returned to England with me. Dermot McCalmont joined General Smuts as A.M.S.

Whilst at sea I was again in a critical condition, and my life was saved by an immediate operation performed by a skilful surgeon who happened to be a passenger on board Mr. Riviere, called in by the ship's doctor, G. M. F. Nellen, to both of whom I owe a deep debt of gratitude. I was much touched by the marked sympathy and kindness shown me by the Governor-General, Lord Buxton, the Prime Minister, General Louis Botha, Sir Starr Jameson, and Sir Abe Bailey. General Louis Botha actually came on board my ship at Cape Town before I sailed to wish me Godspeed and Sir Abe Bailey placed his house at Muizenberg at my disposal.

My story of the Great War would not be complete for my sons unless I referred briefly to their mother's activities during that period, and I will begin with explaining the one of most importance to the army, namely, her Hospital Bag Fund.

About January 1915 she received a letter from Miss Scudamore-Smith, an army nursing sister in charge of a casualty clearing station at the front, giving a graphic account of her difficulties in safeguarding the contents of her patients' pockets once their uniform was exchanged for hospital clothing. She drew, in her letter, a pen-picture of the small heaps of miscellaneous articles, letters, papers, watches, knives, cigarette-cases, money, etc., which were deposited under each cot until the occupant was moved on to a more permanent hospital, remarking that nothing but odd pieces of paper were available to wrap up each patient's valued possessions.

It appeared that in many cases the wounded man was too ill to bother about his own belongings, and, as often as not, that no one knew to whom the articles belonged, with the result that many small things precious to their owner were lost.

This story set my wife thinking, as, I imagine, Miss Scudamore-Smith had intended it should, and she immediately dispatched a few hundred small linen bags with strong double draw-strings, and glazed labels, on which the wounded man's name, number, etc., could be written.

Soon after this she requested me to consult the D.D.M.S. of my Army Surgeon-General Porter, as to the value of these bags, with the result that I wired her to send 50,000 out as quickly as possible. The compliance with this demand naturally necessitated an appeal to the ever-ready British public, and within a few days every post brought in bags of all descriptions. She quickly collected a number of friends willing to work, and in this way the bags were acknowledged, sorted, baled, and dispatched to the Second Army.

Long before the 50,000 I had asked for were collected, my wife had a letter from Sir Alfred Keogh, then Director-General of Medical Services at the War Office, asking her if she was willing to supply these bags to the entire British Forces, in every theatre of war, adding that she would receive her orders from the R.A.M.C. officers, and all transport would be provided by the War Office. She, of course, agreed.

Such, in a few words, was the origin of the Hospital Bag Fund, which during those four years supplied our fighting forces with just under 6,000,000 bags. This figure includes many hundreds of thousands supplied to the British Red Cross, who at one time gave a standing order to the fund to supply 50,000 a month.

She was fortunate in having houses generously placed at her disposal first by Brigadier-General and Lady Susan Gilmour, and latterly by Sir Reginald Cox.

The work was heavy, and this will be appreciated Prom the fact that the card-index kept at the office registered some 40,000 contributors; bags were received from every part of the Empire, for the fund supplied the needs of our overseas troops equally with our own, and was supported generously not only by our Dominions, but even by our American cousins.

My wife's other important war activity was on behalf of our four-footed friends. About October 1914 she became President of the Blue Cross Fund. This was the title given by the Dumb

Friends League to their war branch.

The committee had considerable funds at its disposal, and the first decision to be taken was, whether the example of the Royal Society for the Prevention of Cruelty to Animals should be followed, and their services placed unreservedly at the disposal of the Royal Army Veterinary Corps. When, however, the committee realised that this would merely mean handing over supplies to the Royal Army Veterinary Corps, and would not of necessity add to the comfort of sick and wounded horses, it was decided to act independently, by ministering directly to the need of the horses at the Front.

It would have undoubtedly been far better had the R.A.V.C. seen their way to allowing extra comforts for their horses to be supplied them by the Blue Cross Fund, for they were naturally only able to provide actual necessities; but this they were unwilling to do, saying that if the Blue Cross worked with them, they must conform to all their rules as regards the nature of assistance given. To have accepted this condition would have prevented the Fund from carrying out the special object they had in view, and further would have prevented their fulfilling the object for which the British Public had generously given their money to the Blue Cross, namely, the provision of special comforts to alleviate the sufferings of animals in the war.

To put it briefly, the aim of the Blue Cross was to do for animals what the Red Cross did for human beings.

Therefore to the Blue Cross Committee there seemed no alternative but to work independently, and every senior officer in charge of horses was notified that he had only to state his needs to have them supplied forthwith.

In this way some £1,000 was spent monthly throughout the entire war.

The French Veterinary Corps were finding it hard, during those early days of the war, to expand their organisation fast enough to compete successfully with the vast demands made on them, and when this state of things was brought to the notice of the Blue Cross, they determined to offer the French Government their help, which was most enthusiastically accepted.

No time was lost in establishing sick lines for horses behind the French lines, wherever the authorities directed, and for the four years the Blue Cross constantly had charge of some thousands of wounded and sick French horses, the French Government providing forage, and latterly the stable personnel, whilst the generous British public subscribed the wherewithal for medical comforts, extra feeding, etc.

The Blue Cross also had the medical care of the 18,000 *chiens de guerre,* which did most successful work for our Allies, carrying dispatches from detachments back to head-quarters of battalions, rat-catching in the trenches, guarding prisoners, carrying ammunition and provisions across bullet-swept areas, etc.

My wife, during inspections behind the French lines, collected many interesting stories showing the valuable work done by these dogs. I will quote two which strike me as particularly attractive illustrations of a dog's intelligence, and their authenticity is indisputable as the dog's master in each case described the incidents.

A wet night in the front trenches, No Man's Land enveloped in a dense white fog, even a stretched out hand invisible, so thick was the shrouding mist. The dog attached to the company holding the front line showed great distress. Too well trained to bark aloud, he growled ceaselessly, strained at his leash, and showed by every means in his power that danger was threatening at a certain point.

The commanding officer had several times objected in no measured terms to the dog's attitude, always being assured by the animal's master that there must be some very good reason for the dog's restlessness, seeing that never before had he behaved in such a manner. At length, more to satisfy the man than because he was himself convinced of danger, the officer ordered the *mitrailleuse* to be turned on to the spot indicated by the dog.

When the mist lifted some hours later, the bodies of several Germans lay disclosed; they had been creeping up to the trenches under cover of the fog.

The other attractive anecdote was told my wife by the owner of a large *chien de Malines* which she found being treated for mange in one of the Blue Cross kennels, during one of her inspections in France. A French infantry battalion was resting behind the lines in a small village, and when taking over their billets information reached them that it was quite unsafe to discuss any matters of importance in the inn parlour, which was being used as the officers' mess, as there was little doubt that all said between those four walls reached enemy ears.

Besides the officers, only the village dignitaries used that room, the doctor, the *curé*, and Monsieur le Maire, all normally above suspicion. One evening, when all were assembled, the colonel, in order to test the rumour, mentioned casually where the new snipers' posts would be on the morrow, without of course the least intention of their being occupied.

The next day these new posts were specially treated to a hail of bullets, so leakage was unquestionable, and it struck the C.O., who had so far jeered at police dogs, that it might, in this case, be worth while trying them; accordingly he asked that a member of the secret service might be sent up with his dog—a *chien de Malines.*

Each night the dog was put into touch with the clothing of a member of the mess, and followed him home, without discovering anything. In this way the officers, the doctor, and the mayor were followed to no purpose; only the cure remained to be tested. The dog in this case surprised his master by taking up the trail right through the village into No Man's Land, where in a lonely spot, well sheltered by trees, he stopped and began scratching, refusing to be led away, and showing evident signs of distress.

Examination of the ground showed that the soil had been recently disturbed, and a few minutes later the concealed mouthpiece of a field-telephone was disclosed, communicating with the German lines.

Monsieur le Curé was shot at dawn, and our four-footed friend had done well for the cause.

During her tours in France my wife gathered that mange was the most prevalent disease amongst horses, and the most difficult to eradicate, and that only by immersing them in a bath of very strong chemicals could they be successfully cured. The erection of such a bath was a costly affair, but so important did it seem that my wife determined to put the project before the British public. She therefore gave a lecture at the Guildhall, with the result that the £3,000 were subscribed at once. The bath was erected at Meaux on the Marne, and proved an unmitigated success, mainly thanks to a range of heated stables into which the horses were put after the immersion, and thus prevented from catching chills.

Many thousands of horses were thus saved to the French army. That her work was appreciated by the French Government is evident from the fact that she was awarded the gold order of the "*Reconnaissance Française.*"

I may mention that for her Hospital Bag Fund work His Majesty honoured her by creating her a Dame of the Order of the British Empire.

To return to myself, it took me a long time to recover from my South African illness, and I did no soldiering, but worked daily at my wife's Hospital Bag Fund until September 1918, when I went out to Gibraltar as Governor and commander-in-chief. My five years there hardly merit any detailed description in these *memoirs*, already too long.

It was a most agreeable appointment, and, thanks to the guiding hand of two particularly able Colonial Secretaries, Sir Frederick Evans for nine months, and Mr. C. W. J. Orr for the remainder of the time, I believe I did no greater harm in the appointment than other Governors have done.

Perhaps I may claim to having rendered the form of government rather less autocratic by forming an elected City Council for the administration of local affairs, and by introducing an Executive Council to advise the Governor on all matters of a non-military nature connected with the government of the Rock.

There were two other reforms of which I can think with

satisfaction, and they were the closing down of certain houses of ill fame, which were proved by an exhaustive test extending over eighteen months to be directly injuring the efficiency of sailors and soldiers, and the recognition of the customs of the Roman Catholics, as exercised in other countries, but not hitherto permitted in Gibraltar.

To explain a little more fully the last-named, I found a long-standing rule that no games or amusements were allowed on Sunday afternoons. I soon realised that, as a direct result, the youth of the town were driven to far less desirable occupations than clean, wholesome games. I therefore rescinded the order, not, however, without considerable protest from the Church of England authorities. I had no doubt myself that more good than harm would result, but it gave me intense satisfaction to have confirmatory evidence, some six months later, in the form of a vote of thanks from parents for having saved their sons from lapsing into vice, of which the one most feared by them was spending their Sunday afternoons gambling in Spain.

Other telling evidence of the good results was the huge crowds to be seen on Sunday afternoons watching the cricket and football matches with marked enthusiasm.

The sports and amusements obtainable from the Rock are too well known to warrant description here; but I found, as I had in all my previous commands, that recreation for the men and civilians was very limited owing to the limited amount of ground available; and I think it will be admitted, especially by my civilian friends, that when I finished my Governorship there had been a great improvement in this respect. It was remarkable how the young Gibraltarians, as soon as they were given space, threw themselves into football and became extremely expert at the game. Hunting, racing, lawn tennis, squash rackets and bathing were the most popular forms of exercise. Incidentally I may mention that, being an old Harrovian, I have always had a predilection for "Squash"—so on arrival at Government House I at once proceeded to have a court built there, and where I am penning these lines I am also having one built, making the fifth

I have been instrumental in adding to my residences in the last thirteen years. I merely record this to show that I learned at least one good thing at my beloved public school.

There was one sport to be had from the Rock, which I believe is little known, and that is "whaling." A company just after the war established a station close to Algeciras and opposite the Rock. Their success was remarkable—four and five whales a day very often, and that close by in the Straits. The company were good enough to take me out twice, and I can thoroughly recommend it as an exciting sport, especially the being towed about by the whale until he is played out. The skill of the man who fired the harpoon gun was marvellous. He never missed.

An interesting and exciting expedition we made under the guidance of the intrepid Colonel Willoughby Verner, not long before his death, is worth mentioning. Verner was a keen naturalist, and devoted a good deal of his time to exploring the habits of birds of prey.

One day he persuaded my wife and myself to accompany him to a spot some twenty miles from Gibraltar to view an eagle's nest. We three started off, accompanied by two of our sons, and were eventually brought to the foot of a sheer cliff rising 200 feet above us. Verner pointed out a dark hole within about twenty feet of the top as the spot where the eagle's nest was. He was determined to have a look into the nest, and had provided himself with a rope for the purpose, so that he could be lowered down. This involved our climbing by a circuitous route to the top of the cliff.

On arriving there he tied himself up with one end of the rope, and made the other fast to a rock, directing me to hold on and lower him down. I am bound to say I did not like the job, but he promised me if I dropped him he would not call me to account. So over the top he went, and, when almost opposite the hole, out flew the eagle.

Verner then shouted that he could see one egg in the nest, and requested to be hauled up again. All went according to plan, but the worst was yet to come, for first my wife, and then my eldest son, insisted on being lowered down, and I was brave enough to comply; I say nothing of their pluck. I too wished to have a look at the nest, but Verner could not undertake the strain, as I was heavier than he was. So I had to be content with the description of the three rash people who had put their trust in me.

Perhaps the most salient of the pleasures during those five years was the enormous number of old friends and interesting people of all nationalities who touched there, and this can be understood, for Gibraltar is a port of call for so many passenger steamers. Statistics for 1918 show that in that year more steamers touched there than at any other port in the world.

The greatest pleasure to me personally was the close touch I was brought into with senior officers in the Royal Navy. It was a joy to work with them and to meet them. The annual visit of the Atlantic Fleet for two months in the spring was an event as regular as Christmas, and as much looked forward to.

Then, again, there were frequent visits throughout the year, not only from ships of our own navy, but from, I believe, every navy in the world, excepting those of our enemies in the war.

I was honoured, during my Governorship, by official visits by the Prince of Wales on His Royal Highness's outward and homeward voyages to India; by His Imperial Highness the Crown Prince of Japan, who stayed for three and a half days, and from His Royal Highness the Crown Prince of Italy, the Prince of Piedmont, who came twice, each time remaining three days. The Crown Prince of Denmark and his brother also visited Gibraltar twice in 1919 as "middies" on the Danish warship *Valkyrien*.

That enterprising and charming personality, Her Royal Highness the Duchess d'Aosta and her son, the Prince Amédée of Savoie, both inveterate explorers and lovers of dangerous enterprises and big-game shooting, frequently called at the Rock and paid visits to Government House, which we greatly appreciated.

Of our own Royal House, Her Royal Highness Princess Bea-

GENERAL SIR H. SMITH-DORRIEN, MARSHALL JOFFRE AND GENERAL DIAZ AT BATALHA IN PORTUGAL, 10TH APRIL, 1921

trice, Prince George, the Earl of Athlone, and Princess Alice and Lady Patricia Ramsay honoured us with visits. To give a list of other guests, many of them important and distinguished, would fill pages, and I shall therefore not attempt it, though their visits gave my wife and myself much pleasure.

I must mention one distinguished visitor who stayed on the Rock some months, though not altogether of his own choice—I refer to the ex-Prime Minister of Egypt, His Excellency Zaghlul Pasha. I admired his dignified and uncomplaining attitude, and I was honestly glad when, on the 3rd April 1923, I was allowed to let him depart.

It was customary for exalted visitors to Government House to plant trees in the garden, and I found those planted by the hands of Their Majesties King Edward VII and Queen Alexandra. (The trees planted by Their Majesties King George V and Queen Mary are elsewhere on the Rock.) During my governorship three heirs to thrones similarly honoured the garden, T.R.H.s the Prince of Wales and the Crown Princes of Italy and Japan.

It seems that Kaiser William also planted a tree when Sir George White was Governor, and a fascinating anecdote is told of the fate of his effort. The *on dit* is that, later on, a very exalted Lady saw the tree with its inscription, and remarked casually to the gardener that in her royal opinion it would not be a matter of supreme importance if the tree ceased to exist. From that moment it began to wither, and eventually died. History does not relate what the gardener did to the tree!

I have only two other incidents to refer to, and I have done with Gibraltar.

In April 1921 I was deputed to proceed to Lisbon to represent the British army at the interment of the two Unknown Portuguese Warriors in the Great War. Commander Holt, R.N., took me and Captain M. G. E. Walker, R.G.A., D.S.O., my A.M.S., in H.M.S. *Rowena*. We duly went up the Tagus, and were berthed alongside the quays ready to land with black bands on our arms, when Portuguese officers came on board, and insisted on our removing the black bands, saying it was a time of national rejoicing, and this it proved to be.

I have never spent a more strenuous seven days, except in the retreat from Mons. The great pleasure to me was meeting Marshal Joffre, who was representing the French army, and we had some most interesting talks, when he told me of the difficulties he had in the 1914 Retreat. I can't repeat what he told me—I wish I could, for it would clear up many cloudy points. Anyhow, his presence those seven days was a great joy to me.

We were in Lisbon and its vicinity three days, and before leaving that town there was a grand distribution of honours to all except British officers, who do not take decorations under such circumstances. It was an imposing ceremony, spoilt somewhat by the crowding in of the mob. Each representative of a nation was called out in turn to be decorated, and the National Anthem of his country was played as the President of Portugal bestowed it. Both the Minister of War and the Minister for Foreign Affairs had, before the ceremony, come to my hotel and said they must see me at once on a matter of the utmost importance.

At the moment, having just come in from Cintra, I was changing my clothes and had reached the stage when fresh ones were about to be put on, and they were told so; but they wouldn't be denied, so in they burst, and I tried to look dignified with a towel round my waist.

They implored me to accept a decoration, and were so deeply in earnest I was sorry for them; but I at last satisfied them that my Government would not hear of such a thing, and they went off scratching their heads, as to how they could avoid giving the impression that England had been slighted, when everyone else was being decorated.

They got out of it very well, for when my name was called out, and I moved up to the President, he emphatically shook me warmly by the hand, regretting I had such a foolish Government, or words to that effect, whilst "God save the King" was being played.

We then moved on to Oporto. There we were given a wildly

enthusiastic reception. Marshal Joffre, General Diaz, who represented Italy, and I were made freemen of the city of Oporto, Doctors of the University there, and presented with handsome cups by the Chamber of Commerce.

One of the interests arranged for us was a visit to the Port Wine Factories. I was the only one who turned up, as we had only got to bed a few hours before, and the other two had not risen to the occasion. It was a disappointment to Messrs. Graham & Co., the well-known Port Firm, for they had three *tonels*[2] of wine for Joffre, Diaz, and myself to christen. I alone could carry out their wishes, but I did it, and the *tonel* bears my name, and very proud I am. It was not a dry honour, for the generous firm sent me several dozens of most excellent wine then, and two dozen more only a short time ago. Oporto is a beautiful town, on the banks of the Douro, and full of interest.

Our next and last visit was to the ancient and famous University of Coimbra. There we were treated with great ceremony as well as enthusiasm. We were made Doctors of Science—hooded and ringed—a very imposing performance. I have the blue silk hood and cap, and the beautiful sapphire ring now. Thus ended our pleasant week in Portugal.

The last incident is in regard to that great pro-consul, Marshal Lyautey, on the other side of the Straits. In the spring of 1919 he and Madame Lyautey invited my wife and myself to pay them a visit. From the moment of our landing at Casablanca we were impressed by an atmosphere of progress and prosperity, due to the personality and ability of the Ruler.

The details of our wonderful visit, the almost royal hospitality, the journeys along roads of which any country might have been proud, I shall not enter into; but there was no doubt that the rapidly advancing state of civilisation we met with everywhere was due to one person, and that person was Lyautey. It was his hand we saw in everything. Whilst holding almost regal court, he was open to the complaints and requests of the humblest of

2. A blending *tonel* holds as much as 130,000 bottles. Those of special wine, such as the one inflicted with my name, holds 20,000 bottles.

the Moors, and ever ready to help them. The marshal showed me the system on which he was working to pacify the country, and that he has been so successful does not surprise me, judging from the smartness and efficiency of the army I saw there. His policy was by no means a purely military one, for as soon as a tract of country had been brought to heel by the army, it was handed over to civilian control, and agriculture and trade encouraged. My wife and I will never forget the kindness and hospitality extended to us by all we met, both military and civil.

Since my visit most of the Marshal's plans have been successfully completed, and in consequence a large patch of Africa is now enjoying the advantages of peaceful civilisation.

My appointed time in Gibraltar was completed in September 1923, and it was a sad day when I left, for I was genuinely happy there. I was, officially and socially, extremely well treated by the people of Gibraltar. I liked the place and climate, and it was with real regret I said goodbye to many kind friends there. It meant, too, more than that to me. It was the end of my official life, and within six weeks I had retired from the army, after forty-seven and three-quarters years' service, having had far more good luck in it than I deserved, for I was promoted major-general on the 11th February 1900, and, therefore, had spent half my time in the army in generals' appointments.

LEONAUR

ALSO FROM LEONAUR
AVAILABLE IN SOFTCOVER OR HARDCOVER WITH DUST JACKET

WAR BEYOND THE DRAGON PAGODA by *J. J. Snodgrass*—A Personal Narrative of the First Anglo-Burmese War 1824 - 1826.

ALL FOR A SHILLING A DAY by *Donald F. Featherstone*—The story of H.M. 16th, the Queen's Lancers During the first Sikh War 1845-1846.

AT THEM WITH THE BAYONET by *Donald F. Featherstone*—The first Anglo-Sikh War 1845-1846.

A LEONAUR ORIGINAL

THE HERO OF ALIWAL by *James Humphries*—The days when young Harry Smith wore the green jacket of the 95th-Wellington's famous riflemen-campaigning in Spain against Napoleon's French with his beautiful young bride Juana have long gone. Now, Sir Harry Smith is in his fifties approaching the end of a long career. His position in the Cape colony ends with an appointment as Deputy Adjutant-General to the army in India. There he joins the staff of Sir Hugh Gough to experience an Indian battlefield in the Gwalior War of 1843 as the power of the Marathas is finally crushed. Smith has little time for his superior's 'bull at a gate' style of battlefield tactics, but independent command is denied him. Little does he realise that the greatest opportunity of his military life is close at hand.

THE GURKHA WAR by *H. T. Prinsep*—The Anglo-Nepalese Conflict in North East India 1814-1816.

SOUND ADVANCE! by *Joseph Anderson*—Experiences of an officer of HM 50th regiment in Australia, Burma & the Gwalior war.

THE CAMPAIGN OF THE INDUS by *Thomas Holdsworth*—Experiences of a British Officer of the 2nd (Queen's Royal) Regiment in the Campaign to Place Shah Shuja on the Throne of Afghanistan 1838 - 1840.

WITH THE MADRAS EUROPEAN REGIMENT IN BURMA by *John Butler*—The Experiences of an Officer of the Honourable East India Company's Army During the First Anglo-Burmese War 1824 - 1826.

BESIEGED IN LUCKNOW by *Martin Richard Gubbins*—The Experiences of the Defender of 'Gubbins Post' before & during the sige of the residency at Lucknow, Indian Mutiny, 1857.

THE STORY OF THE GUIDES by *G.J. Younghusband*—The Exploits of the famous Indian Army Regiment from the northwest frontier 1847 - 1900.

LEONAUR

ALSO FROM LEONAUR

AVAILABLE IN SOFTCOVER OR HARDCOVER WITH DUST JACKET

SEPOYS, SIEGE & STORM by *Charles John Griffiths*—The Experiences of a young officer of H.M.'s 61st Regiment at Ferozepore, Delhi ridge and at the fall of Delhi during the Indian mutiny 1857.

THE RECOLLECTIONS OF SKINNER OF SKINNER'S HORSE by *James Skinner*—James Skinner and his 'Yellow Boys' Irregular cavalry in the wars of India between the British, Mahratta, Rajput, Mogul, Sikh & Pindarree Forces.

A CAVALRY OFFICER DURING THE SEPOY REVOLT by *A. R. D. Mackenzie*—Experiences with the 3rd Bengal Light Cavalry, the Guides and Sikh Irregular Cavalry from the outbreak to Delhi and Lucknow.

A NORFOLK SOLDIER IN THE FIRST SIKH WAR by *J. W. Baldwin*—Experiences of a private of H.M. 9th Regiment of Foot in the battles for the Punjab, India 1845-6.

TOMMY ATKINS' WAR STORIES Fourteen first hand accounts from the ranks of the British Army during Queen Victoria's Empire Original & True Battle Stories Recollections of the Indian Mutiny With the 49th in the Crimea With the Guards in Egypt The Charge of the Six Hundred With Wolseley in Ashanti Alma, Inkermann and Magdala With the Gunners at Tel-el-Kebir Russian Guns and Indian Rebels Rough Work in the Crimea In the Maori Rising Facing the Zulus From Sebastopol to Lucknow Sent to Save Gordon On the March to Chitral Tommy by Rudyard Kipling.

THE KHAKEE RESSALAH by *Robert Henry Wallace Dunlop*—Service & adventure with the Meerut volunteer horse during the Indian mutiny 1857-1858.

Lightning Source UK Ltd.
Milton Keynes UK
UKOW04f1406290917
310131UK00001B/46/P

9 781846 776793